HANDBOOK OF HEALTHCARE MANAGEMENT

HANDBOOK OF HEALTHCARE MANAGEMENT

Editor

Pansy Minett

Socialy PRESS
AN IMPRINT OF SCITUS ACADEMICS

Handbook of Healthcare Management

Edited by **Pansy Minett**

This Book is Printed on Acid-Free Paper. ♾

ISBN: 978-1-68117-736-6

Library of Congress Control Number: 2017938593

Socialy Press

(An Imprint of Scitus Academics),

616, Corporate Way, Suite 2, 4766,

Valley Cottage, NY 10989

www.scitusacademics.com

Printed in United States of America.

PREFACE

Healthcare management is the profession that provides leadership and direction to organizations that deliver personal health services, and to divisions, departments, units, or services within those organizations. Effective healthcare management involves exercising professional judgment and skills and carrying out the aforementioned managerial functions. Healthcare organizations are complex and dynamic. The nature of organizations requires that managers provide leadership, as well as the supervision and coordination of employees. High performance in hospitals can be the result of governance logics, which, compared to simple board characteristics, are associated with better financial outcomes. Hospitals can influence the emphasis placed on different governance objectives and enhance organizational success by creating boards that are small enough to be effective yet diverse enough to profit from a wide variety of expertise and experience. Moreover, the necessary tasks in producing services in healthcare organizations require the coordination of many highly specialized disciplines that must work together seamlessly. Managers are needed to make certain that organizational tasks are carried out in the best way possible to achieve organizational goals and that appropriate resources, including financial and human resources, are adequate to support the organization.

Handbook of Healthcare Management entails the comprehensive analysis of strategic management practices for global healthcare organizations, focusing that insight into and implementation of these practices is indispensable for accomplishment and viable healthcare services. The Handbook examines the intersection of professionalism and complexity science as a source of new insights for improving the health care industry from both a clinical and business point of view. Viewing health care organizations as professional complex adaptive systems suggests leadership tasks for addressing the circumstances that engulf health care. Managers who adopt this view will be able to create new levers for positive movement in their organizations. This Handbook will be invaluable to students in both master and doctoral healthcare management programs, as well as faculty and health services researchers, practitioners in both private and public sectors, policy-makers, and public administrators. It contains chapters contributed from well-known and eminent academic authors internationally in their particular area.

TABLE OF CONTENTS

1

PRODUCTIVITY AND QUALITY OF DUTCH HOSPITALS DURING SYSTEM REFORM

Siyu Zang[1], Maolin Ye[2]

[1].Institute of Health Policy and ManagementErasmus University RotterdamRotterdamThe Netherlands

[2].The Health Care InspectorateUtrechtThe Netherlands

ABSTRACT

This study addresses the productivity of Dutch hospitals since the start of the health systems reform in 2005. We consider DEA based measures, which include efficiency and quality for the complete set of Dutch hospitals and present cross-sectional and longitudinal analysis. In particular, we consider how hospital efficiency has developed. As the reform created an environment of regulated competition, we pay special attention to relative efficiency. Our results suggest that the differences in efficiency among hospitals have become larger. In the years 2009–2010, the number of hospitals identified as (close to) efficient by DEA analysis decreased.

Keywords: Hospitals, Productivity, Data envelopment analysis, Malmquist index, Quality indicators, Reimbursement

1 INTRODUCTION

At the turn of the millennium, The Netherlands used a closed budgeting system for hospital reimbursement, which was primarily based on hospital wide production parameters. This system was viewed to be supply driven [1] and health insurance companies had little influence on the hospital budget. Under this closed budgeting system, the combination of strict macro budgeting and consistent demand increases caused allocation problems and long waiting lists [2].

The 2005 health system reformed relied on market principles, which created an environment of regulated competition for hospitals [3]. As a result of the reform, health insurers and hospitals freely negotiated prices, volumes and quality for a subset of the health services, which was defined between all stakeholders on a national level. The first year, 2005 can be seen as a transition year in which technological implementation was completed, and public insurance funds disappeared. The freely negotiable services accounted for approximately 10 % of hospital budgets for 2005, 2006 and 2007. This percentage rose to 20 % in 2008 and 33 % in 2009. For most other services the price was set by the National Health Authority (NZa).

The system reform was intended to result in a more demand oriented system in which hospitals delivered higher quality at lower prices [4], i.e., to make hospitals more cost effective [5]. Below we generally refer to the combination of efficiency and quality as performance, and we will define it in detail in the methods section.

The reform not only comprised of a change in reimbursement but also included regulations on public reporting, and supervision of quality by the Health Care Inspectorate IGZ [6]. Some evidence suggests that public reporting is effective as an improvement policy for hospital performance [7]. There is however little evidence regarding the effects of regulated competition in combination with public reporting (or relationship) on hospital performance, or more generally the relationship between these constructs. This holds particularly true for Dutch hospitals, and the recent health reform.

In this study, we explicitly aim to study how the performance of Dutch hospitals has developed since the reform of 2005 which introduced regulated competition and public reporting in The Netherlands. We explore three research questions of which the first addresses overall, average, performance developments, and the remaining two address relative hospital performances:

1. How has the overall performance of Dutch hospitals developed?

2. How have the relative performances developed since 2005?
3. How have less efficient hospitals fared?

The first of this research question addresses the performances of all hospitals and is primarily of a longitudinal nature. The second and third question clearly also have a cross-sectional dimension.

The research can also be viewed to study the health services procurement practices of the insurers. As a result of the reform, the insurers have been given the responsibility to arrange cost reduction and quality improvements for an increasing fraction of the hospital services through their purchasing practices. The study provides insights in the achievements of the insurers. More generally, it is the first DEA study, which presents a longitudinal and cross sectional analysis of hospital performance in The Netherlands in the first 6 years of the reform. The study considers various models to provide robust answers to the research questions formulated above.

2 BACKGROUND

Recent studies for the Netherlands regard various aspects of Dutch hospital performance. Blank et al. [8] explore the productivity of Dutch Hospitals over the period 2003–2009, without explicitly taking the reform into account. They conclude after estimating cost-functions per hospital that productivity has increased by 14,7 % over this 7-year period. They find that scale effects contribute negatively to the productivity growth, and that the relative performance has been stable. They attribute the productivity growth to technological, institutional and societal changes. Ludwig et al. [9] use stochastic frontier analysis on 1998–2002 data – prior to the reform - to study principal agent relationships and efficiency. They conclude that increasing efficiency does not seem to reduce quality, although no relationship was found between the efficiency of departments and the efficiency of the entire hospital. Douven et al. [10] explore the effect of the introduction of managed competition in Dutch inpatient hospital care. Interviewing board members of hospitals, these members suggested the way to raise turnover is to increase production. Bijlsma et al. [11] estimate a bivariate model to consider the relationship between the reform and quality improvement. They find that competition explains differences in performance on process indicators, but not on outcome indicators. Further information regarding health services provided by Dutch hospitals can be found in the yearly reports of The Dutch Healthcare Authorities [12, 13].

Across the Dutch borders, several authors have addressed research questions regarding the relationship between reforms and performance which are akin to the research questions pose above using DEA models. Maniadakis [14] evaluate the first 5 years of the reforms in the UK National Health Service in the early nineties focusing on acute hospitals. Their findings 'indicate that there was a productivity slowdown in the first year after the reforms but productivity progress in the subsequent years' resulting in net productivity gain. This gain was mostly attributed to technological change rather than relative efficiency changes. After the first year, they even report a 'small relative efficiency regress'. Incorporating quality diminished the effects. As is the case for our study, Maniadakis [14] relied on data since the start of the reform.

Other authors have been able to apply a before-after design. Sommersguter-Reichmann [15] evaluates the 1997 Austrian hospital financing reform, using DEA analysis, in particular the Malmquist index. She finds 'a considerably positive shift in technology between 1996 and 1998 whereas the intended enhancement in technical efficiency has not yet taken place.' De Castro Lobo [16] consider performance and productivity changes of Brazilian hospitals in the years 2003–2006, in analysis of the 2004 financing reform. Contrary to Sommersguter-Reichmann [15] they find indications that the financing reform provided improvement in the technical efficiency, although the technological frontier has not presented a positive shift.

Finally, Ozcan & Luke [17] studying a reconfiguration of the network of the hospitals of the Veterans Health Administration in the USA. These authors too rely on DEA and Malmquist indices and find indications that the reconfiguration resulted in 'improvements in overall productivity' but 'didn't produce changes in efficiency'.

3 METHODS

As the reform has been introduced without distinguishing an intervention group (of hospitals) and a control group (see for instance Hibbard et al. [7] and Lindenauer et al. [18]), and systematic reporting of the required indicators was introduced as part of the reform, we can neither apply a case control design nor a before after design. We therefore rely on a research design where we consider the performance developments over the years 2005–2010, particularly paying attention to performance differences between consecutive years.

Following the references in the background section, we select a standard approach for performance analysis called Data Envelopment Analysis (DEA). DEA is commonly applied in health care, as can be concluded from the review of Hollingsworth [19] who considers 317 efficiency studies, among which 99 are DEA based studies on hospital efficiency (see also Ozcan, [20] and O' Neill et al. [21]). Since the seminal work on DEA of Charnes et al. [22], it has been repeatedly applied to address the results of hospitals after reform (see for instances Maniadakis et al. [14], Sommersgutter-Reichman [15], De Castro Lobo et al. [16] and Ozcan & Luke [17]).

DEA enables both cross-sectional as well as longitudinal analysis, as befitting our research questions. The longitudinal researchers often use the Malmquist Index (see e.g., [20]), which considers the relative performance improvement between consecutive periods. The Malmquist index has been widely applied to study hospital performance (see e.g., the literature in the background section).

3.1 Data envelopment analysis

DEA formulates efficiency measurement as a linear programming problem. Informally speaking, it solves the problem of measuring performance of each unit in the benchmark set in terms of outputs per inputs, relative to the other units. It explicitly enforces the weighted sum of the outputs to be less than or equal to one (there cannot be more output than input).

$$\frac{\sum_j \beta_j y_{jk}}{\sum_i \alpha_i x_{ik}} \leq 1 \quad \text{for all } k, \tag{1}$$

$$\alpha_i,\ \beta_j \geq 0 \quad \text{for all } i, j, \tag{2}$$

Where αi,βjαi,βj are the weights of the inputs xik,xik, resp, outputs yjkyjk, of hospital *k*. The efficiency of hospital *o* is now defined by setting the weights such that the fraction of outputs per input of hospital *o* is maximized:

$$\max \frac{\sum_j \beta_j y_{jo}}{\sum_i \alpha_i x_{io}} \tag{3}$$

Thus, the problem of determining the efficiency of a hospital is to select weights which maximize (3), subject to (1) and (2). The set of hospitals for which the objective function attains the maximum value of one define the efficiency frontier which 'envelops' the less efficient organizations, whose inefficiency expresses the distance to the frontier [14]. Hospitals on the frontier are often referred to as 'efficient'.

We now firstly describe the research methods to answer the first research question, and address the methods to answer the other two research questions on this basis.

3.2 Malmquist index

The Malmquist Index (MI) considers the relative performance improvement between consecutive periods as follows. To formally define the Malmquist Index (MI), let x_{ik}^{t} define the values of the inputs in year *t*, and y_{jk}^{t} the values of the outputs in year *t* as before. Let *P(u,v)* be the problem arising when benchmarking the performance of hospital *o* in year *u* against the benchmark set of all hospitals from year *v*. It can formally be defined by taking xuikxiku and yujkyjku in the objective function (3) and formulate constraint (1) using x_{ik}^{u} and y_{jk}^{u}. Then the Malmquist index *MI* is defined as:

$$MI = \sqrt{\frac{P(t+1,t)}{P(t,t)} \frac{P(t+1,t+1)}{P(t,t+1)}}$$

Thus it determines the change in performance of hospital *o* from year *t* to *t + 1* as the geometric means of the benchmark of the year *t* efficiency frontier and the benchmark of the year *t + 1* efficiency frontier. The *MI* is greater than one if and only if the relative performance of hospital *o* has improved from year *t* to year *t + 1*. This Malmquist index serves as our prime measure for the development of hospital performance. As we are interested in the performance development of Dutch hospitals in general, we report for each pair of consecutive years, the Malmquist index averaged over all hospitals.

The MI especially allows providing insight in the development of the efficiency frontier over time, after first rewriting it as follows:

$$MI = \frac{P(t+1,t+1)}{P(t,t)} \sqrt{\frac{P(t+1,t)}{P(t+1,t+1)} \frac{P(t,t)}{P(t,t+1)}}$$

The first term in this equation is simply the efficiency of hospital *o* in year *t + 1*, divided by its efficiency in year *t*. This relative improvement of hospital *o* against the benchmark is commonly referred to as the efficiency change. The second term expresses how the efficiency frontier has developed taking hospital *o* as a reference and is commonly referred to as the technology change [20]. We explore the performance improvement of efficient hospitals over the years by considering the subsequent average technology changes.

3.3 Choice of DEA model

Before addressing the methods to answers research questions 2 and 3, we first address a number of methodological issues regarding the choice DEA model. The first issue is about the orientation of the DEA model. Input oriented models consider the minimization of inputs for a given level of outputs. Output oriented models maximize the level of outputs for a given level of inputs (See for a further discussion for instance [14, 20]). The same hospitals will appear as efficient under both orientations, but the efficiency scores of the inefficient hospitals are different. As the aim of the reform has been to provide the necessary services efficiently, i.e., to deliver the required output with less input, rather than to increase output, the input oriented model best fits the nature of the reform. This choice is in agreement with the preference for input oriented models from the viewpoint of cost control [21]. Hence, the remainder of the analysis is based on the input oriented model.

A more fundamental issue concerns hospital scale. Constant returns to scale (CRS) models assume a constant rate of substitution between inputs and outputs [20]. In this case, the size of the hospitals is assumed to have no effect on performance. In other words, the productivity function is assumed to be a linear function. Variable returns to scale models (VRS) assume that scale effects take place. Of course, it is common to assume that initially positive returns to scale exist, whereas at some point negative returns to scale may apply. In DEA models, this can be modeled using piecewise linear production functions. As the reform doesn't consider scale effects but instead aims to improve prices and quality regardless of scale, we firstly consider a CRS model. To explore the sensitivity of our results with regard to scale effects, we also present results for a VRS model.

DEA assumes perfect substitution between inputs and between outputs. Hence, it assumes that an optimal mix of different inputs or outputs can be attained for instance while freely substituting between capital and labor as inputs [23]. Thus, DEA is less suitable if inputs cannot replace each other. Barnum [24] proposes alternative models, which are called fixed factor models. Regarding hospital performance, we recognize that the substitution of technology for labor is possible and hence takes place. At the same time human resources need buildings and equipment to work by and hence these inputs are correlated rather than perfectly substitutable. Our research doesn't methodologically address the modeling of substitution. However, in order to establish the sensitivity of the results for the choice of model we also present efficiency scores for a fixed proportion ratio model (FPR) [24] and present results on the correlations of the efficiency scores found by the DEA and the FPR models.

3.4 Quality

Historically, DEA has been primarily applied to benchmark efficiency, whereas the health reform not only intended to improve efficiency, but also to increase quality. This quality has been measured in terms of structure, process, and outcome measures [25, 26] by for instance the Dutch Health Inspectorate IGZ. As DEA models disregards the structures and processes by which production takes place, only outcome measures can be included in models, provided that they can be suitably quantified to be incorporated in the outputs. O' Neill et al. [21] provide examples of the limited number of DEA papers, which have included quality measures. The outcome measures, which are defined hospital wide and collected consistently over the period 2005–2010 are taken into account in the analysis presented below.

3.5 Efficiency classes and market exit

The first research question can be answered using the methods presented above and considering the efficiency frontier and average hospital performances from 2005 to 2010. The second and third research question requires a more detailed analysis of individual hospital performances. DEA methods qualify a hospital as efficient if its efficiency score equals 1. For the purpose of presentation (and without claiming any theoretical interpretation), we have chosen to specify efficiency classes per first digit of the efficiency score. The first class includes the efficient hospitals, the second class includes the hospitals with an efficiency score ranging from 0,9 to 1, a third class with hospitals having efficiency scores from 0,8 to 0,9 et cetera. A hospital can change class from year to year.

To answer the third research question we especially pay attention to hospitals in the lower classes. As low efficiency may indicate high costs levels and/or low quality, a low efficiency score may indicate a less favorable position on the market. Hence, we pay special in the analysis to low scores. This brings about a methodological difficulty however, as we only include hospitals for which we have data for each of the years 2005–2010. Hospitals, which have exited the market are therefore not included, potentially resulting in a biased answer.

We have analyzed the efficiency scores of all hospitals, which have exited the market over the years 2005–2010. In all cases, this has led to a merger or acquisition, and we present efficiency scores before and after the merger whenever possible. As the hospitals involved in mergers or acquisition have by definition not consistently reported efficiency and quality over the years 2005–2010, they are excluded from the DEA benchmark set. Their DEA scores are calculated per hospital by adding it to the benchmark set and solving (1)–(3), however without requiring that their efficiency is bounded by one. By consequence, the efficiency frontier is not affected. The efficiency score of merging hospitals can therefore exceed one. These methods present a small methodological innovation.

4 DATA AND VARIABLES

4.1 Data

Study data are obtained from two sources. The first source is ZinData, which has provided financial and production data as available through public reporting. All Dutch hospitals are obliged to report these data in fixed format in their annual reports, which must be approved by accountants. Data are available for the years 2005–2010. The second data source was collected by IGZ and consists of quality measures. The Health Care Inspectorate (IGZ) strives to promote public health through effective enforcement of the quality of health services, prevention measures and medical products. The IGZ advises the responsible ministers and interacts with hospitals by means of advice, encouragement, pressure and coercion. IGZ has the task to ensure that health care providers offer only 'responsible' care and to be impartial. http://www.igz.nl/english/ All Dutch hospitals obligatory report quality data to IGZ, which reports the data to the public. We used data that are available for the years 2005–2010 at the public website www.ziekenhuizentransparant.nl.

4.2 DEA input measures

Frequently used input measures for DEA models can be described by three main categories: *capital investment*, *labor*, and *other operating expenses* [21]. More specifically, the following four input measures are the most frequently used: *number of beds*, *operational expenses*, *FTE (full time equivalent) physicians* and *FTE non-physicians*. The measure "number of beds" of Dutch hospital as it is publicly reported refers to the allowed number of clinical beds that a hospital may operate. As this number may deviate substantially from the actual number of beds, and the deviation varies per hospital, we do not include number of beds in our study. Hence, we use three input parameters: FTE employed by the hospital (except physicians), FTE physicians, and the operational expenses.

In contrast to the parameters FTE and FTE physicians, the operating expenses are influenced by inflation. This particularly will influence the longitudinal analysis, as presented through the Malmquist indices. Therefore, the operating expenses for the period 2006–2010 are netted to the price level of 2005. We discount using the official index figures for material costs (without costs for workforce) of the Dutch Healthcare

Authority [12, 13]. Since the reform has been initiated, the regulations regarding valuation of assets have been repeatedly and significantly adjusted for Dutch hospitals over the period 2005–2010. These adjustments were made to account for changes in the reimbursement system for capital costs, after which capital costs have ceased to be reimbursed separately and the Dutch state is no longer involved in carrying risks of capital costs. By consequence, the mandatory reported balance sheet figures for fixed assets over the years 2005–2010 are inconsistent and therefore unfit to be considered as an input variable in the DEA models. On average, capital costs account for less than 10 % of total costs [27].

4.3 DEA output measures

To be congruent with important parameters in the current Dutch reimbursement system for hospitals and with many other DEA studies (see e.g., [19] we consider as output measures: *number of (inpatient) admissions, number of primary outpatient visits* and *day care treatment.* These numbers have been a primary basis for reimbursement before 2005 and have remained important afterwards.

4.4 Quality measures

Quality measures are adopted relatively recently compared to financial and production-oriented measures. This has implications for the quality of the data supplied to the Dutch Ministry of Health. Moreover, many definitions of quality indicators have been adapted over time and many quality indicators have disappeared or are replaced by others over the years 2005–2010. The latter especially occurred when indicators are no longer discriminating among hospitals. As a result, very few outcome indicators have been consistently collected over the period of analysis 2005–2010.

We have selected quality measures based upon the following criteria:

- Available in all years (2005–2010)
- Indicator is measured correctly and uniformly within hospitals and over the years considered
- The indicator addresses the hospital as a whole (as opposed to a single unit or medical discipline).

Table 1 shows all IGZ quality measures and their appropriateness for inclusion. Given the impact of the system change and the aim to improve quality it is remarkable that only two hospital-wide quality measures have been consistently collected since 2005: Prevalence of decubitus ulcers and cancelled surgical operations (except cancellations by patients). Both these quality indicators are ratios: the percentage of cancelled elective surgeries and the percentage of inpatients having decubitus. Ratios as such cannot function as an input/output parameter in DEA [28]. A feasible alternative for both ratios is to correct the output volumes, by only counting as production the volume of surgeries that have not been cancelled, or the volume of admissions, which have not developed decubitus ulcers. As surgery volume is not an output variable in our model, we cannot correct for surgery cancellation, and thus further disregarded this parameter. Hence, decubitus ulcers prevalence is the only quality measure taken into account in our DEA analysis. When taking it into account, we reduce the inpatient admission by the fraction of patients for which decubitus ulcers have been reported.

Table 1. IGZ quality indicators selected scoring positive on the three mentioned criteria

	Are data available over the period 2005–2010 and have relevant definitions remain consistent?	Is it an outcome measure?	Is it a hospital wide measure?	Inclusion ('yes' in each of the previous columns)
Cancelled surgeries	Yes	Yes	Yes	Yes
Stroke	No	Yes	No	No
Decubitus ulcers	Yes	Yes	Yes	Yes
Hip fracture	Yes	Yes	No	No
Intensive Care	Yes	No	Yes	No
Breast cancer	No	Yes	No	No
Pain after surgery	Yes	Yes	No	No
AMI	Yes	Yes	No	No
Blood transfusion	No	Yes	Yes	No
Cataract	Yes	No	No	No
Cholecystectomy	Yes	Yes	No	No
Complication registration	Yes	No	Yes	No
Diabetes	Yes	Yes	No	No
Heart failure	Yes	Yes	No	No
Pediatric surgery	No	Yes	No	No
Medication safety	No	No	No	No
Malnutrition	No	Yes	Yes	No
Unplanned reoperation	No	Yes	No	No
Post-operative wound Infection	No	No	Yes	No
High risk interventions	No	No	No	No
Hospital infections	No	No	Yes	No
ICT infrastructure	No	No	Yes	No
Pregnancy	No	Yes	No	No
Hospital standardized mortality rate	No	Yes	Yes	No
Unexpected extended length of stay	No	Yes	Yes	No

4.5 Exclusion of hospitals

University hospitals have been excluded from the study as they form joint organizations with the medical faculties and therefore have differences in input variables with the general hospitals. Moreover, their objectives explicitly include research and education and therefore consider different outcome variables as well. Finally, academic hospitals function as tertiary hospitals and have a case-mix with a considerably higher complexity. Specialty hospitals have also been excluded.

Since we aim to study efficiency trends over 6 years, we have excluded hospitals that do not report the mandatory data in all years. Table 2 presents a descriptive overview of all measures for the selected hospitals. As mentioned in the methods section, however, a separate analysis is performed on excluded hospitals that have merged or been acquired.

Table 2. Descriptive statistics for DEA variables for the included Dutch hospitals ($n = 65$) over 2005–2010

Variable	Mean	SD	Minimum	Maximum
Input				
FTE (except physicians)	1520	807	408	4186
FTE Physicians	114	52	33	255
Operating expenses	€43.158.768	€25.705.833	€10.468.000	€131.845.207
Output				
Number of admissions	19.673	8582	6141	47.040
Number of day care treatments	18.844	9178	4702	52.411
First outpatient visits	114.197	47.258	37.574	255.948
Quality (n=59)				
Percentage decubitus	4,3	2,4	0,0	15,1
Percentage decubitus	4,3	2,4	0,0	15,1

5 RESULTS

We present the results following the sequence of analysis by different models which firstly regard productivity. We then include the sole quality parameter meeting the inclusion criteria. We conclude by considering the efficiency of hospitals which have merged or been acquired.

5.1 DEA constant returns to scale

Table 3 shows the DEA results per year for an input-oriented constant return to scale model for the years 2005–2010 in which quality is not taken into account. The average efficiency is consistently at or slightly below 0,9 for 2005–2008, and then declines to 0,87 in 2009 and 0,85 in 2010.

Table 3. DEA results with economic parameters only in an input-oriented CRS model for Dutch hospitals ($n = 65$)

Efficiency level	2005	2006	2007	2008	2009	2010
1,0	15	15	12	12	13	9
≥0,9–<1,0	15	14	17	22	15	15
≥0,8–<0,9	28	24	27	24	21	18
≥0,7–<0,8	5	10	7	6	11	18
≥0,6–<0,7	2	2	2	1	5	5
≥0,5–<0,6	0	0	0	0	0	0
Average efficiency	0,90	0,89	0,89	0,90	0,87	0,85
SD efficiency	0,09	0,09	0,09	0,08	0,10	0,11

In the input oriented CRS DEA model results presented in Table 3, the number of efficient hospitals declines from 15 in 2005 to 9 in 2010. At the same time we notice that the number of hospitals with relative efficiencies below 0,8 increase from 7 in 2005 to 23 in 2010.

Table 4 gives the Malmquist Indices for the year-to-year development of efficiency. It shows small overall improvements, except from 2009 until 2010. Notice that values of greater than one for technological change indicate a small but consistent development of the increased efficiency at the frontier over the years. It is also worth considering the average efficiency changes, which reflect the average distance to the efficiency frontier. Table 4 confirms the finding of Table 3 that the average relative efficiency decreases over the years 2009, 2010. In 2009, this is accompanied by an increased technological change, which is not the case for 2010.

Table 4. Malmquist Index with economic parameters only in an input-oriented CRS model for Dutch hospitals ($n = 65$)

	2005–2006	2006–2007	2007–2008	2008–2009	2009–2010
Malmquist index	1,01	1,02	1,02	1,02	0,99
Efficiency change	0,99	1,00	1,01	0,96	0,97
Technology change	1,03	1,01	1,01	1,05	1,02
Malmquist index standard deviation	0,05	0,05	0,07	0,06	0,07
Malmquist index – minimum value	0,87	0,83	0,75	0,75	0,87
Malmquist index – maximum value	1,13	1,11	1,15	1,08	1,36
Malmquist index – maximum value	1,13	1,11	1,15	1,08	1,36

Regarding research question 3, Table 5 presents results on the reoccurrence of low efficiency scores over the years. It shows that 10 of the 65 hospitals have efficiency score of 0,8 or less in at least 4 of the years 2005–2010, while this is the case for 4 hospitals in each of the reported years. These hospitals account for around three quarters of the efficiency scores less than 0,8 between 2005 and 2009, and form almost half of the 23 hospitals with efficiency less than 0,8 in 2010. The majority of hospitals always had efficiency above 0,8. The recurrence frequency of having a score below 0,8 in subsequent years is 87 %.

5.2 DEA variable returns to scale

Table 6 presents the DEA results when using a VRS model instead of a CRS model. One notices that the result displays the same trend, yet that the average efficiency scores are now about 0,05 higher. In particular, we notice that the number of efficient hospitals has approximately doubled and is now more stable until 2010. The number of hospitals with efficiency scores of at most 0,8 is quite stable over the period 2005–2010. When making this comparison, however, let it be noted that the bounds of 0,9; 0,8 et cetera have not been adjusted for changing the model.

Table 5. Frequencies of low efficiency scores during the period 2005–2010 ($n = 65$)

Frequency of scores below 0.80	Number of hospitals
0	38
1	11
2	6
3	0
4	3
5	3
6	4

Table 6. DEA results with only economical parameters in an input-oriented VRS model for Dutch hospitals ($n = 65$)

Efficiency level	2005	2006	2007	2008	2009	2010
1,0	27	26	29	28	29	21
≥0,9–<1,0	19	23	19	24	21	23
≥0,8–<0,9	17	14	16	11	11	17
≥0,7–<0,8	2	2	1	2	4	4
≥0,6–<0,7	0	0	0	0	0	0
≥0,5–<0,6	0	0	0	0	0	0
Average efficiency	0,94	0,94	0,94	0,95	0,95	0,93
SD efficiency	0,07	0,07	0,07	0,06	0,07	0,07

Figure 1 presents linear regression plots of average efficiency versus average total operating expenses over the years 2005–2010 for VRS and for CRS efficiency scores. It distinguishes the non-academic but 'top clinical' STZ hospitals from the other 'general' hospitals (named SAZ in Fig. 1), as STZ hospitals may have a different case mix. Figure 1 clearly displays a scale effect by showing that larger hospitals are less efficient by the negative correlation between VRS score and scale and by the increasing differences in VRS and CRS scores as a function of scale. Any case mix differences, which may exist between STZ and non STZ hospitals, however, do not translate to differences in efficiency between them.

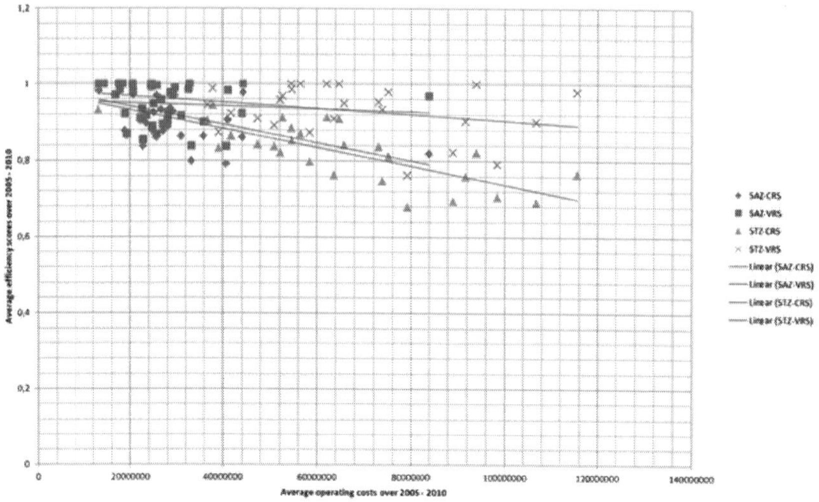

Figure 1.DEA scores versus average total operating expense over the years 2005–2010

5.3 Fixed proportion rate

Table 7 presents the results when using a FPR model. As the model doesn't allow scale effects or substitution between inputs, the average efficiency scores are lower than in the CRS and VRS modeled presented above. We have calculated paired samples statistics of the CRS and the FPR models and found that they are highly (0,896) and significantly correlated. By definition, there is only one efficient hospital in this analysis. Likewise, we notice that the number of hospitals with a score of 0,9 or higher has decreased. Like the VRS model, The FPR model finds that the average relative efficiency decreases and that in 2010 there are more hospitals with low efficiency scores.

5.4 Quality

Table 8 shows the results of incorporating decubitus ulcers as a means of quality adjusted for the patient admissions output parameter in the CRS-DEA model. The paired samples statistics of the CRS with and without the adjustment for decubitus are very close to 1 (0,989) and significant. Notice that the total set of hospitals is not 65 but 59, as not all hospitals have reported the quality data consistently over the years 2005–2010. We observe that the number of efficient hospitals is initially slightly higher yet decreases more than in the corresponding model which doesn't adjust for decubitus. Likewise, the number of hospitals with scores of 0,9 or higher decreases more sharply. The number of hospitals with scores of at most 0.8 now increases from 8 in 2005 to 22 in 2010. The average relative efficiency decreases sharper than in the model with adjustment.

Table 7. Fixed Proportion Ratio results with only economical parameters for Dutch hospitals ($n = 65$)

Efficiency level	2005	2006	2007	2008	2009	2010
1,0	1	1	1	1	1	1
≥0,9–<1,0	13	10	7	13	10	4
≥0,8–<0,9	16	19	18	29	25	20
≥0,7–<0,8	26	22	28	15	18	25
≥0,6–<0,7	5	9	8	5	9	11
≥0,5–<0,6	4	4	3	2	2	4
Average efficiency	0,80	0,79	0,79	0,82	0,81	0,76
SD efficiency	0,10	0,11	0,10	0,10	0,10	0,10

Table 8. DEA results where admissions have been adjusted for decubitus ulcers in an input-oriented CRS model for Dutch hospitals ($n = 59$)

Efficiency level	2005	2006	2007	2008	2009	2010
1,0	16	15	12	10	11	7
≥0,9–<1,0	15	12	18	20	13	12
≥0,8–<0,9	20	23	22	21	19	18
>0,7–<0,8	6	7	5	7	11	18
≥0,6–<0,7	2	2	2	1	5	4
≥0,5–<0,6	0	0	0	0	0	0
Average efficiency	0,90	0,90	0,89	0,90	0,86	0,84
SD efficiency	0,09	0,09	0,09	0,09	0,10	0,10

5.5 Merged hospitals

Finally, we present the results required to the answer the second part of research question 3, by considering the efficiency scores of hospitals which have exited the regulated market during the period of analysis 2005–2010. Recalling that each of these hospitals has merged or was acquired, Table 9 presents analysis for the corresponding pairs of hospitals. Notice that as discussed in the Methods section, efficiency scores exceeding one do indeed occur. Hospital 6 was included in the initial benchmark set. It is presented below because it acquired Hospital-6A, however with very little impact on efficiency.

Table 9. DEA results for excluded hospitals, either merged or acquired, (CRS), excluded hospitals are benchmarked against included

		2005	2006	2007	2008	2009	2010
Merge	Hospital-1 A	0,8333	0,8170	0,8296	0,7794		
	Hospital-1 B	0,7749	0,7697	0,8565	0,9143		
	Hospital-1 A+B					0,7384	0,7090
Merge	Hospital-2 A	na					
	Hospital-2 B	na					
	Hospital-2 A+B		0,8282	0,8220	0,7585	0,6740	0,6258
Merge	Hospital-3 A	1,0299	1,0939	1,1963	1,0670		
	Hospital-3 B	0.8262	0,7231	0,7643	0,7853		
	Hospital-3 A+B					0,5541	0,7682
Merge	Hospital-4 A	1,1084	1,0211	1,0064	na		
	Hospital-4 B	1,0000	0,9484	1,1579	na		
	Hospital-4 A+B				na	1,0312	0,8727
Merge	Hospital-5 A	na					
	Hospital-5 B	na					
	Hospital-5 A+B		na	na	na	0,7512	Na
Acquisition	Hospital-6A	na	na	na			
	Hospital-6	0,6243	0,6359	0,6582	0,6766	0,6828	0,6359

na = not available

We notice that of the hospitals which have merged only hospital 3-B reported an efficiency of less than 0,8 for more than 1 year prior to merger. Unfortunately, data for hospitals 2A, 2B, 5A, 5B, and 6A are missing for the years prior to merger/take-over. We notice that in the 3 cases for which data was available, the efficiency scores after the merger are lower than the unweight average of the efficiency score before the merger., In 2 out of 3 cases, the efficiency score after the merger is less than the minimum score between the two hospitals prior to merger. The efficiency of the other 3 pairs is less than 0.8 after merger.

6 CONCLUSION

Lacking control group data, we cannot attribute any (absence of) development in performance to be an effect of the reform. Although 2005 can be viewed as a baseline, there is no data which is truly from before the reform. Hence, before-after analysis regarding before versus after reform performance differences can neither be made. Our conclusions are simply based on the various efficiency developments as observed after the reform was introduced in 2005.

Regarding the first research question, we observe from Table 3 that, until 2008, the relative average performance has been stable at 0,90 while – as shown in Table 4 - the technological efficiency slightly increased as the technological efficiency shows small improvements of 1 or 2 %. For the year 2009, the Malmquist analysis reveals a higher increase in the technological change to 5 %, which drops back to a more usual 2 % in 2010. 2010 is however the first year where the Malmquist index doesn't show a positive average plus of around 2 % improvement, but a small negative average improvement.

To answer the second research question, the DEA analysis presented in Table 3 shows that the relative average performance decreased in 2009 and 2010 to 0,87 and 0,85 respectively. As this average decrease has been accompanied by an increase in technological change in 2009, the increase in technological improvement by the efficient hospitals explains most of the larger efficiency differences. For 2010, the larger differences are however not explained by increased technological improvement, and can therefore be considered to be caused by decreases in efficiency of non-efficient hospitals. The increased standard deviations of the efficiency scores in 2009 and 2010 confirm these conclusions.

These findings seem partly influenced by the choice of model. The VRS model results display a more stable efficiency development from 2005 to 2010. Average and standard deviation of the efficiency scores remain by and large unchanged, perhaps with a small decline in efficiency in 2010. In combination with the results presented in Fig. 1, the CRS and VRS results suggest that the efficiency gap between smaller and larger hospital has grown larger in 2009 and 2010, and that the VRS parameters compensated for this effect.

The FPR model provides results, which are comparable to the DEA models. The FPR model displays a stable average efficiency of around 0,8 which drops to 0,76 in 2010 while the variance is stable around 0,1 throughout. This might indicate that from a fixed proportion viewpoint, especially the most efficient hospital improved in 2010, while the developments have otherwise been quite stable.

Likewise, inclusion of the sole quality outcome parameter that met the inclusion criteria (it regards decubitus ulcer prevalence) had only a marginal impact on the CRS results. The results don't provide evidence that inclusion of quality measures leads to added insights on performance developments. However, this is mainly due to the definition and stability of the available quality indicators.

With regard to the third research question, we find that there are around 10 hospitals, which have consistently been at least 20 % less efficient than the most efficient ones for the majority of years in a 6 years period. Given the choice of model and input variables this means that they have employed 20 % more physicians and/or staff and/or incurred 20 % higher, other operating costs for the same level of output than efficient counterparts. These 10 hospitals account for around three quarter of such inefficiency until 2009. The conclusions above indicate that several larger hospitals have joined these less efficient performers in the years 2009 and 2010, after the fraction of freely negotiable services increased to 33 % in 2008.

Our analysis provides no evidence that merger (take-over) was related to lack of efficiency before the merger (take-over): the average efficiency scores of the hospitals that have merged have been between 0,89 and 0,96 over the years 2005–2008. Conversely: the average efficiency scores after the merger or acquisition have been between 0,62 and 0,74, placing the resulting hospitals on average among the worst performing hospitals from the benchmark set. The argument of selection bias, which was a prime motivation to consider the merged hospitals thus worked counter to our expectations.

7 DISCUSSION

Before, providing a more general reflection, let us discuss the methodological strengths and weaknesses of the presented analysis and its consequences. As mentioned, the study design inhibits attribution of effects to the reform. Nevertheless, we can observe that the average efficiency of the hospitals has been stable around 0,90 (CRS) or 0,95 (VRS) for the first 3 years after the reform in which the fraction of health services for which prices have been freely negotiable was around 10 %. In 2008, resp. 2009, this fraction increased to 20 %, resp. 33 %, while the CRS average efficiency change dropped from being very close to 1.00 to 0,96 and 0,97 respectively while the technological change increased to 1,05 and 1,02. Our analysis has not revealed a consistent relation between increases in market share of freely negotiable health services and performance change in the same year. Despite the methodological limitations, the 2009 and 2010 technology changes reported in Table 4, in combination with Fig. 1, suggest the following. The reform expanded the fraction for which prices and volumes were freely negotiable. Some of the smaller hospitals managed to achieve efficiency improvements intended by the reform, whereas the efficiency changes reveal that many larger hospitals typically did not.

No model will perfectly capture the efficiency and quality developments of Dutch hospitals since 2005. Therefore, we modeled these developments using a variety of models, and although there is some variation in the results, they confirm rather than contradict each other. Moreover, combining the VRS with the CRS results leads to additional insights. We also notice that the results of the axiomatically different FPR model are highly correlated with the CRS model results. In addition, we observe that the efficiency scores obtained by including quality data are very closely correlated to the initial CRS model efficiency scores.

Considering that the FPR model results displays the same delay in the performance decrease as the VRS model, one may suggest that the scale and substitution effects are interrelated. Have smaller, efficient hospitals started to realize substitutions in 2009, which larger hospitals didn't realize?

As the model which includes quality by and large provides the same results as the CRS model, it supports the viewpoint that quality improvement and economic efficiency go hand in hand (and doesn't conform the viewpoint that more money yields higher quality). Overall, the model triangulation in the research design has strengthened and enriched the findings.

The results are based on using FTEs and operating costs as inputs, while capital is not considered as an input due to inconsistency of capital valuation regulations over the study period. Although capital costs constitute less than 10 % of total costs [27], inclusion of capital as a production factor is worthy of future research. Regarding the quality, it has been somewhat disappointing that only two outcome related quality indicators have been consistently and reliably collected over the years 2005–2010. In particular, since improving quality has been an explicit objective of the reform. This objective therefore appears to be difficult to evaluate for quality at the hospital level.

The set of included hospitals is as nationwide and complete as public reporting allows and considers 6 consecutive years since the reform has been implemented in 2005. Some bias may exist, as not all hospitals are included. Some are excluded because they are academic hospitals or specialty hospitals, others because they have not consistently provided the legally due information. We have explicitly addressed hospitals not selected in the benchmark because of mergers/take-overs.

Although the original closed budgeting system by which at least two third of the average hospital budget was reimbursed over the years 2005–2010 weighs production for different medical specialties differently, case mix is not explicitly accounted for in our study. One may argue that case mix differences exist as some hospitals provide a more extensive service product mix and/or treat more complex patients. The top clinical hospitals (STZ) distinguish themselves from the remaining hospitals by providing a broader product mix and serving more complex patients. Figure 1 however doesn't confirm differences in case mix between STZ hospitals and other hospitals to explain efficiency differences. On the other hand, we cannot rule out a relationship between theses case mix determinants and diminishing scale effects. More generally, we encourage further research explaining the relationship between scale and case mix of Dutch hospitals. This topic is relevant in the ongoing debate regarding the optimal numbers of hospitals and patient volumes in The Netherlands.

The case-mix may not only vary across the hospitals, but also over the years. The population has changed as life expectancy has increased over the years 2005–2010. Moreover, parallel reforms took place in primary care, resulting in a shift in treatment for chronic diseases such as Type 2 Diabetes. Thus, over the study period 2005–2010 a substitution took place from hospital care to primary. Similarly, there have been innovations leading to substitution of care from the tertiary academic hospitals to the general hospitals, and new more effective treatments practices have been adopted by the hospitals otherwise. The performance developments as reported in our study don't include or correct for these contextual changes and technological advancements that the selected hospitals have dealt with over the years 2005–2010.

The average input-oriented CRS DEA scores of around or slightly below 0,9 are slightly higher than the average (CRS and VRS) scores found for EU hospitals of 0,86 by Hollingsworth [19], but slightly below the average of 0,91 reported by O Neill et al. [21]. The average input-oriented VRS DEA score are considerably higher than both these scores, despite the fact that the models use only 3 inputs and 3 outputs. This suggests that the average efficiency of Dutch hospitals (when benchmarked against each other) over the benchmark period is quite high in comparison to other European countries (when benchmarked within their respective countries).

Although the research design inhibits attribution of the efficiency developments to the reform, the reduced average efficiency in the last 2 years are worthy to consider in relation to the reform. On the one hand, one may argue that - counter to the intention of the reform – hospitals which experience less competition, e.g., for geographical reasons, became less efficient when the regulated competition allowed them. An alternative viewpoint is that insurers continued the purchasing practices, which were in place before the reform as even after the reform was introduced prices and volumes were not freely negotiated for the vast majority of services. Likewise hospital management practices may have continued to be primarily aligned with the system by which the majority of services continued to be reimbursed. Therefore, the reform may not have had a substantial impact on hospital efficiency until 2010, but rather initiated purchasing, management and reporting changes as necessary for progression of the reform. Progress is taking place as the fraction of services for which prices and volumes can be freely negotiated has increased to 70 % by 2014 and insurers have implemented more selective purchasing practices in recent years. Research regarding the years 2011 onwards can shed further light on the developments as the reform progresses. Such further research may also address the aforementioned geographical determinants of competition, as well as differences in purchasing and management practices.

This research project was financially supported by the NEVI Research Foundation (NRS).

REFERENCES

1. Enthoven AC, van de Ven WPMM (2007) Going Dutch - managed competition health insurance in the Netherlands. N Engl J Med 357:2421–2423
2. Schut FT, Van de Ven WP (2005) Rationing and competition in the Dutch health-care system. Health Econ 14:S59–S74
3. Schut FT, Van de Ven WP (2011) Effects of purchaser competition in the Dutch health system: is the glass half full or half empty? Health Econ Policy Law 6:109–123
4. Tan SS, van Ineveld BM, Redekop WK, van RL H (2010) Structural reforms and hospital payment in the Netherlands. EuroObserver 12:7–9Google Scholar
5. Oostenbrink JB, Rutten FFH (2006) Cost assessment and price setting of inpatient care in the Netherlands. The DBC case-mix system. Health Care Manag Sci 9:287–294
6. Custers T, Onyebuchi AA, Klazinga NS (2007) Is there a business case for quality in The Netherlands? A critical analysis of the recent reforms of the health care system. Health Policy 82:226–239
7. Hibbard JH, Stockard J, Martin Tusler M (2005) Hospital performance reports: impact on quality, market share, and reputation. Health Aff 24:1150–1160
8. Blank J, Dumaij A, van Hulst B (2011) Ziekenhuismiddelen in verband Een empirisch onderzoek naar productiviteit en doelmatigheid in de Nederlandse ziekenhuizen (with English summary) 2003–2009. IPSE Studies TU Delft
9. Ludwig M, van Merode F, Groot W (2010) Principal agent relationships and the efficiency of hospitals. Eur J Health Econ 11:291–304
10. Meijer S, Douven R, van den Berg B (2010) Recent developments in Dutch hospitals: how does competition impact on inpatient care? CPB Memorandum CPB Netherlands Bureau for Economic Policy Analysis

11. Bijlsma M, Koning P, Shestalova V, Aouragh A (2010) The effect of competition on process and outcome quality of hospital care. An empirical analysis for the Netherlands. CPB Discussion paper CPB Netherlands Bureau for Economic Policy Analysis

12. NZa (The Dutch Healthcare Authority) (2011) Marktscan Medisch specialistische zorg Weergave van de markt 2006–2011. NZa Utrecht

13. NZa (The Dutch Healthcare Authority) (2013) Marktscan Medisch specialistische zorg Weergave van de markt 2008–2012. NZa Utrecht

14. Maniadakis N, Hollingsworth B, Thanassoulis E (1999) The impact of the internal market on hospital efficiency, productivity and service quality. Health Care Manag Sci 2:75–85

15. Sommersguter-Reichmann M (2000) The impact of the Austrian hospital financing reform on hospital productivity: empirical evidence on efficiency and technology changes using a non-parametric input-based Malmquist approach. Health Care Manag Sci 3:309–321

16. Lobo MSC, Ozcan YA, Silva ACM, Lins MPE, Fiszman R (2010) Financing reform and productivity change in brazilian teaching hospitals: malmquist approach. CEJOR 18(2):141–152

17. Ozcan YA, Luke RD (2011) Healthcare delivery restructuring and productivity change: assessing the Veterans Integrated Service Networks (VISNs) using Malmquist approach. Med Care Res Rev 68(1 Suppl):20S–35S

18. Lindenauer PK, Remus D, Roman S, Rothberg MB, Benjamin EM, Ma A, Bratzler DW (2007) Public reporting and pay for performance in hospital quality improvement. N Engl J Med 356(5):486–496

19. Hollingsworth B (2008) The measurement of efficiency and productivity of health care delivery. Health Econ 17:1107–1128

20. Ozcan YA (2014) Health care benchmarking and performance evaluation, 2nd edn. Springer, New YorkGoogle Scholar

21. O'Neill L, Rauner M, Heidenberger K, Kraus M (2008) A cross-national comparison and taxonomy of DEA-based hospital efficiency studies. Socio Econ Plann Sci 42:158–189

22. Charnes A, Cooper WW, Rhodes E (1978) Measuring the efficiency of decision making units. Eur J Oper Res 2:429–444

23. Dyson RG, Allen R, Camanho AS, Podinovski VV, Sarrico CS, Shale EA (2001) Pitfalls and protocols in DEA. Eur J Oper Res 132:245–259

24. Barnum DT, Gleason JM (2011) Measuring efficiency under fixed proportion technologies. J Prod Anal 35:243–262

25. Donabedian A (1988) The quality of care; how can it be assessed? J Am Med Assoc 260(12):1743–1748

26. Jacobs R, Smith PC, Street A (2006) Measuring efficiency in health care. Cambridge University Press, Cambridge

27. BDO-Benchmark Ziekenhuizen 2012 (2012) www.bdo.nl /nl/publicaties/documents

28. Mutter RL, Rosko MD, Greene WH, Wilson PW (2011) Translating frontiers into practice: taking the next steps toward improving hospital efficiency. Med Care Res Rev 68:3–19S

2

FLEXIBLE BED ALLOCATIONS FOR HOSPITAL WARDS

Rene Bekker [1] · Ger Koole[1] · Dennis Roubos[2]

[1] Department of Mathematics, VU University Amsterdam, De Boelelaan 1081a, 1081, HV, Amsterdam, The Netherlands

[2] HOTflo Company, Schoutlaan 26, 6002, EA, Weert

ABSTRACT

Flexibility in the usage of clinical beds is considered to be a key element to efficiently organize critical capacity. However, full flexibility can have some major drawbacks as large systems are more difficult to manage, lack effective care delivery due to absence of focus and require multi-skilled medical teams. In this paper, we identify practical guidelines on how beds should be allocated to provide both flexibility and utilize specialization. Specifically, small scale systems can often benefit from full flexibility. Threshold type of control is then effective to prioritize patient types and to cope with patients having diverse lengths of stay. For large scale systems, we assert that a little flexibility is generally sufficient to take advantage of most of the economies of scale. Bed reservation (earmarking) or, equivalently, organizing a shared ward of overflow, then performs well. The theoretical models and guidelines are illustrated with numerical examples.

Moreover, we address a key question stemming from practice: how to distribute a fixed number of hospital beds over the different units?

Keywords: Clinical capacity, Flexible bed allocation, Bed pooling, Earmarking Queueing model, Optimization

1 INTRODUCTION

Inpatient beds are a critical capacity in the patient care process within a hospital. Traditionally, the clinical organization is according to medical disciplines, resulting in separate nursing units for, e.g., medicine, surgery, cardiology, obstetrics, neurology, gynaelogy. Over the years other classifications have been introduced, such as length of stay (e.g., short and long stay, see for example [29]), level of care (intensive, medium, special or normal care), or urgency (elective, urgent and emergent), each having organizational advantages. A disadvantage of a strict classification of inpatient beds is that this may result in small scale hospital units. Such small scale units suffer severely from the variability of health care processes [7]. More generally, it is well known that the efficiency of service systems often increases as the system becomes larger [32]. This is referred to as 'economies of scale' (abbreviated as EOS). Flexibility in bed usage is thus a key concept for an efficient management of beds, as has been recognized in, e.g., [4, 9, 12, 18], and is of fundamental importance for the increasing pressure to reduce costs.

Table 1. Pros and cons of different bed allocation policies

	Specialization	Flexibility & EOS	Prioritize pat. types	Accommodate diverse LOS	Management & bed guarantees
Separate wards	++	–	+	+	++
Simple merging	–	++	–	–	–
Earmarking	+	+	+	+	+
Threshold	–	++	++	++	–

On the opposite, in manufacturing it has long been recognized that focus on a limited range of tasks improves efficiency. This principle of specialization advocates to divide capacity to patient groups with similar medical conditions, see, e.g., [13, 27, 30] and references therein for some health care related studies. The increasing focus on more complex cases further advocates to organize specialized hospital units, which is evidently necessary to some extent. A further disadvantage of flexibility is that this requires the medical staff, such as nurses, to be able to treat multiple patient types. This may require costly additional training efforts. Moreover, small wards guarantee personalized patient care and may improve work satisfaction and efficiency of nurses.

Apart from medical specializations and the potential improvements from economies of focus, there are some other issues with full flexibility. First, the overall performance may improve, but that may be at the expense of one type of patients. This may be unwanted in case that a particular patient type should be prioritized (e.g., receive specialized care). Related is the example in [9] of cardiac and thoracic surgery, where cardiac patients have priority over thoracic patients. Under their average delay constraints and taking the priority for cardiology into account, it follows that a combined unit would actually need more beds than two separate units. Second, the overall performance may even decrease in case of non-identical average service times (also referred to as average length of stay, abbreviated as ALOS). This observation goes back to [24]. In that case, patients with prolonged hospital stay block access for patients with high turnovers.

In this paper, we propose an intermediate organizational bed assignment that utilizes the efficiency gains of large systems and avoids the drawbacks mentioned above. More specifically, we consider the following bed allocation policies:

- *Separate wards*: Each patient type has dedicated beds.
- *Simple merging*: All patient types share all beds.
- *Earmarking*: Each patient type has dedicated (earmarked) beds, whereas all patient types share a joint ward of overflow with fully flexible beds.
- *Threshold policy*: All beds are fully flexible, but there is a hierarchy in admission of patient types. The most important (e.g., most urgent) patients are always admitted when beds are available, but other patient types are only admitted when the number of available beds exceeds some (prespecified) threshold.

The advantages and disadvantages of the different bed allocation policies are indicated in Table 1. These findings are further supported in the rest of the paper. Specialization refers to all benefits of having small scale units, such as specialized medical teams, single-skilled nurses and efficiency in task performance due to routine operations. Flexibility and EOS refer to all benefits of large systems, such as the ability to handle peaks in demand, flexibility in allocation of beds and flexibility in nurse rostering (see, e.g., Burke et al. [5]). Bed guarantees means that different patient types have allocated beds, making bed management significantly easier. Prioritization and the efficiency in accommodating patients with severely different LOS are further addressed in Section 4.2.

For large scale systems specialization often is a major requirement, leading to the distribution of beds over different medical units. The earmarking policy is then effective (see Section 4.3). At a smaller scale, i.e., within a single unit, further specialization might be unnecessary and the focus is rather on efficient bed usage and accommodation of different patient types (see Section 4.2).

Goals and contribution

The issue of how to allocate partially flexible capacity for clinical wards has not yet been addressed in the literature. Therefore, our contribution is two-fold. First, we identify which structure of the bed allocation policy is appropriate for balancing between flexibility and the issues of large scale systems. For this structure we distinguish two cases that differ in system size, as they require a different approach.*Bed allocation for small scale systems*: at the unit level (like an ICU), the number of beds is shared by different patient groups. For instance, a patient group may represent a medical discipline, patients with a similar diagnosis, or similar level of urgency. As the sizes of the patient groups are small, specialization is inefficient whereas an earmarking policy often is less effective. In this setting, threshold policies are effective when there is a difference in priority for patient types, or patient types have an entirely different ALOS.*Bed distribution for large scale systems*: at the hospital level, the total number of staffed beds should be distributed over the different (often medical) units. To allow for flexible bed usage and avoid large-system size issues at the same time, earmarking is an effective policy. We see that some flexibility is sufficient to accommodate most of the peaks in bed demand. The beds at each ward are dedicated (earmarked) that can be handled by specialized medical teams, whereas the beds at the joint ward are flexible.

In the literature the commonly addressed question is 'how many hospital beds?' [4, 8]. In practice, the overall number of beds is limited due to the building construction and obtained licenses [12]. The typical question for hospital managers therefore is 'how to distribute hospital beds?'. We provide rules of thumb based on square-root staffing for the distribution of the fixed number of total beds across units.The second contribution is that we provide models to support strategic and tactical decision making regarding ward sizes and the level of flexibility. Specifically, using these models, the exact number of beds and its allocation for the corresponding policy can be determined. For large scale systems, the performance of an earmarking policy can easily be calculated due to the product-form solution. To enhance application of threshold policies, the models are suitable for a form of decision support as well. We like to emphasize that well-founded hospital management of bed capacity requires quantitative models to visualize the impact of strategic management decisions and policies.

Queueing literature

We now briefly review some of the basic queueing literature related to pooling. The term bed pooling is also often encountered in the literature when different units fully share their capacity. As mentioned, Smith and Whitt [24] seem to be the first to give counterexamples to show that full flexibility or resource sharing is not always beneficial. Another early paper supporting this from a qualitative perspective is Rothkopf and Rech [23]. In Mandelbaum and Reiman [20], the authors consider queueing networks in which both servers (beds) and queues can be pooled. They quantify the effect of pooling in terms of an efficiency index and show that pooling always helps in light traffic, but that pooling effects can go either way in heavy traffic. We refer to the references in [20] for the application of pooling in different application areas.

In the context of call centers, van Dijk and van der Sluis [25] gave some instructive examples where pooling is not beneficial and they proposed overflow pooling as an alternative. In overflow pooling the servers are dedicated to a queue, but they can serve customers from the other queue in case the server becomes idle. The concept of pooling is also related to skill-based routing in call centers. For instance, Wallace and Whitt [28] showed that "a little flexibility goes a long way", meaning that only a few generalists are required to approach near optimal performance. In Chevalier et al. [6], the authors find that a 80/20 rule works well for a remarkably wide range of parameters. Here, the 80/20 rule means that 20 % of the staffing budget should be spent on flexible (multi-skilled) servers while 80 % should be spent on dedicated (single-skilled) servers. This already hints that flexibility and specialization can go hand in hand in hospital systems.

From a different angle, van Essen et al. [26] consider how departments should be clustered to benefit from scale effects. The authors take into account that not all departments can be clustered and that patients should not be spread over the hospital. Clustering is formulated as an optimization problem where blocking probabilities impose constraints. As the optimization problem is strongly NP-hard, the authors provide two heuristic approaches in addition to the exact formulation.

Organization

The paper is organized as follows. We introduce the general model and assumptions in Section 2. The bed allocation policies and its performance analysis are discussed in Section 3. In Section 4 we show numerical results. The allocation of beds over different patient groups within a unit is studied in Section 4.2. In Section 4.3 we consider the distribution of beds over different units at the hospital level. Section 5 concludes.

2 MODEL

We analyze the patient flow through the clinical wards in the spirit of the Erlang loss model. The aim of this model is to support managerial decision making at the strategic and tactical level. We first introduce the main assumptions in Section 2.1 and then formally define the model in Section 2.2.

2.1 Basic assumptions

The assumptions of the model are based on the data analysis in [4] of 24 hospital wards of the VU medical center in addition to our experience with other Dutch hospitals.

Arrival process

The model assumes that patients arrive according to a Poisson process. This has been widely accepted for urgent patients, see for example [34]. Surprisingly, the number of elective admissions varies significantly as well. This variation can even be larger than the variation in urgent admissions [4, 21]. The Poissonian assumption therefore seems a reasonable approximation for the elective admission process (see also [31]).

Length of stay

The model assumes that the lengths of stay (abbreviated as LOS) are independent and identically distributed for each patient type. This seems an appropriate assumption as long as the patient mix and medical practice do not change. In practice, deviations from this assumption can occur, as the LOS may be affected by the level of congestion and delays in the care chain. In some cases we further assume, for mathematical convenience, exponentially distributed LOS. This often slightly underestimates the amount of variability present, but the impact on the results is typically very small (see Section 4.1).

Beds

The capacity of a unit is based on the number of operational beds. The number of operational beds is important for the distribution of budgets and is generally constant and evaluated on a yearly basis. The actual number of staffed beds may fluctuate slightly, but this rather is at an operational or tactical level.

Bed blocking

The model assumes that patients are blocked and lost from the system in case all appropriate beds are occupied. For urgent patients this means ambulance diversions and reallocation of patients at the Accident & Emergency department (A&E). For elective patients, unavailability of beds implies canceled admissions or surgeries. Such patients are often rescheduled, but this may affect the admissions of patients from the waiting list. As a rough approximation, we consider the rescheduled patients as new admissions.In Dutch hospitals, the waiting time at A&E departments for inpatient beds is usually short, whereas the fraction of transfers to other hospitals due to unavailability of beds is significant (estimated at about 10 %). In addition to our experience with Dutch hospitals, where excessive waiting for beds is uncommon, we chose to incorporate blocking. In the literature, delay models for bed capacity have also been proposed [7, 8]. Note that for the classical models, there is a direct relation between the probability of waiting (delay model) and the blocking probability (loss model). The delay models typically do not take flexible bed allocations into account. We refer to [19] where routing policies from emergency departments to internal wards are addressed in an asymptotic queueing framework.

2.2 Model and notation

We consider the allocation of beds for J types of patients. A patient type typically refers to a medical discipline or to a specific diagnosis group. Patients of type j are assumed to arrive according to a Poisson process with rate λ_j, $j = 1,\ldots, J$. Denote the overall arrival rate by $\lambda=\sum j\lambda j\lambda=\sum j\lambda j$. Let the LOS of type j be denoted by S_j with mean ESjESj, $j = 1,\ldots, J$. The traffic intensities are then $\rho j:=\lambda jESj$. In case the LOS of type j is exponentially distributed, we let $\mu_j$denote the corresponding rate.

The total number of beds available is N. There is no waiting room for patients. This means that when a patient arrives and all beds are occupied, the arriving patient is refused, see Section 2.1. However, patients can also be refused in other situations. For instance, when each ward has its own number of beds ($\text{say } N_j, \text{ with } \sum_j N_j = N$), patients are also refused when the preferred ward is fully occupied.

A major performance measure for clinical wards is the long-run fraction of refused admissions, also called loss or blocking probability. Let b_j denote the fraction of refused admissions (blocked patients) of type j. The weighted total fraction of refused admissions is given by btot $\sum_{j=1}^{J}(\lambda_j/\lambda)b_j$. Let $\alpha_j,\ i = 1,\ldots,J,$, be the relative value for patients of type j. This reflects different levels of priorities for the patient groups that might be caused by, e.g., urgency or strategic focus of the hospital. Let $\mathbf{c} = (c_1, \ldots, c_J)$ be fixed, where c_j is the weight of the loss fraction b_j in the objective function. For instance, in case $c_j = \alpha_j\lambda_j/\lambda$ the objective is to minimize the weighted loss fraction that takes the relative values α_j into account (b_{tot} is then minimized in case $\alpha_j \equiv 1$). Our objective is to minimize a linear combination of the b_j's, i.e.,

$$\min b(\mathbf{c}), \qquad \text{with} \quad b(\mathbf{c}) = \sum_{j=1}^{J} c_j b_j. \tag{1}$$

Another example is the case in which the loss fraction for type j should be bounded by bmaxjbjmax, $j = 1,\ldots,J$. For example, bmaxjbjmax may represent the loss fraction before a reallocation of beds. The optimization problem then reads

$$\begin{aligned} &\min b(\mathbf{c}) \\ &\text{s.t.} b_j \le b_j^{\max}, \qquad j = 1,\ldots,J. \end{aligned}$$

The Lagrange relaxation of this problem is

$$\min b(\mathbf{c}) + \sum_{j=1}^{J} \gamma_j (b_j - b_j^{\max}),$$

which is again a linear combination of b_j's; take $c_j + \gamma_j$, as coefficients in Eq. 1.Our main performance measure is the loss fraction, reflecting the quality of the care process. Due to PASTA[1], the loss fraction is equivalent to the fraction of time during which no bed is available for a certain patient type (bed blocking).

Another important performance measure focusing on efficiency is the occupancy rate. In case of only dedicated beds, by Little's law, the occupancy (in %) for type j is given by

$$\frac{\rho_j(1-b_j)}{N_j} \times 100\%. \tag{2}$$

Since the number of shared beds can differ for different patient types, it is not always clear how the occupancy should be determined (i.e., what the appropriate value for the denominator of Eq. 2 is). However, as the arrival process is assumed to be exogenous, a decrease in the loss fraction directly implies an increase in the average number of occupied beds of the particular type (numerator of Eq. 2). For conciseness and ease of presentation, we only give the loss fraction throughout the paper.

3 BED ALLOCATIONS AND ANALYSIS

In this section, we describe the bed allocation policies (Section 3.1) and consider their performance analysis (Section 3.2). Denote the number of type *j* patients present at an arbitrary arrival epoch by x_j, $j = 1,\ldots,J$, with $x = (x_1,\ldots, x_J)$ the corresponding vector.

3.1 Bed allocations

The bed allocation strategies differ by the rule used for accepting newly arriving patients.

Separate wards

This policy corresponds to the situation in which each patient type has dedicated beds, i.e. has its own ward. Let N_j be the number of beds at ward *j*, with $\sum_{j=1}^{J} N_j = N$. An arriving patient of type *j* is admitted if and only if $x_j<N_j$.

Simple merging

This corresponds to fully join the different wards. An arriving patient (of either type) is now admitted in case $\sum_{j=1}^{J} x_j < N$ and refused otherwise.

Earmarking beds

This policy is useful to guarantee a certain number of beds for each type of patients in addition to a shared ward of overflow. We assume that M_j beds are reserved for patients of type *j*, with $\sum_j M_j \leq N$. In casc all beds for type *j* are occupied there is a ward of overflow that is shared by all patient types. The size of this joint ward is $M_{\text{joint}} = N - \sum_{j=1}^{J} M_j$. In the remainder, the earmarking policy with bed allocation $M_1,\ldots, M_J$ is denoted by $(M_1,\ldots, M_J)$. An arriving patient of type *j* is now admitted in case there is a bed available among the allocated (earmarked) beds of type *j* or at the joint ward, and refused otherwise. For this policy, the earmarked beds should always be used as much as possible. This means that if the ward of overflow is full, it should be checked if it is possible to transfer a patient from the ward of overflow to a dedicated bed (in particular when a new patient arrives). From the above considerations, we can now state that an arriving patient of type j is admitted if and only if

$$x_j < M_j + M_{\text{joint}} - \sum_{i \neq j} (x_i - M_i)^+,$$

where $(x)^+ = \max(x,0)$. Here, $(x_i - M_i)^+$ represents the number of beds of the joint ward occupied by patients of type i.

The earmarking policy may be considered as an intermediate option between separate wards and simple merging. In case ∑jMj=N∑jMj=N the policy of earmarking reduces to the situation of J separate wards, whereas in case $M_j \equiv 0$ this bed allocation policy corresponds to simple merging.

Threshold policies

There can be a hierarchy in the admission of patients. To reserve a number of beds for patients with high priority we employ a threshold policy. For type j there is a threshold value T_j that represents a maximum on the number of occupied beds for which patients of type j are admitted. More specifically, an arriving patient of type j is admitted in case ∑ixi<Tj Note that the patients of highest priority have $T_j = N$. The threshold policy with thresholds $T_1, \ldots, T_J$ is denoted by $(T_1, \ldots, T_J)$.

Optimal policy

The main aim of the optimal policy is to compare the performance of the other proposed policies to best achievable values in case of fully dynamic admission control. Hence, it provides a benchmark for what is ideally possible and allows to evaluate the relative performance of the corresponding policy. Specifically, the optimal admission policy minimizes the objective function $b(\mathbf{c})$. This implies that upon arrival of each type of patient, given the number of patients of each type present x, it is decided whether the patient is admitted or refused. Such a policy might be difficult to implement in a hospital, unless bed occupancy is digitally registered in real time.

3.2 Performance analysis

Roughly speaking, the performance models can be classified in three categories, as addressed below. Some structural properties are discussed in Section 3.3.

Separate wards and simple merging

For the cases of separate wards or simple merging, the performance can be immediately obtained using the Erlang loss model. The blocking probability or loss fraction for separate ward *i* reads

$$b_i = B(\rho_i, N_i) = \frac{\rho_i^{N_i} / N_i!}{\sum_{k=0}^{N_i} \rho_i^k / k!}.$$

The total traffic load for the *J* type of patients equals ρ=∑jρjρ=∑jρj. Using the Erlang loss formula again yields $b_i = B(\rho, N)$ for all $i \in \{1,\dots, J\}$ in case of simple merging.

Earmarking beds

A closed-form result for the number of patients present and the loss fraction can also be derived for the policy of earmarking beds. Let M_i, $i = 1,\dots, J$, and N be fixed, and assume for the moment that the LOS follows an exponential distribution, and let $x(t)$ denote the vector of the number of patients at time t. The stochastic process $\{x(t), t \geq 0\}$ then clearly is a Markov process with state space $\mathcal{S} = \{x \in \mathbb{Z}_+^J : x_j \leq M_j + M_{\text{joint}} - \sum_{i \neq j}(x_i - M_i)^+, j = 1, \dots, J\},$ }, see Remark 3.1 for an alternative representation. The transition rates $q(x, x')$ are given by

$$q(x, x') = \begin{cases} \lambda_i, & x' = x + e_i, \quad x + e_i \in \mathcal{S}, \\ x_i \mu_i, & x' = x - e_i. \end{cases}$$

Let $\pi(x)$ denote the stationary distribution of $x(t)$, which has the following product form:

$$\pi(x) = G^{-1} \prod_{j=1}^{J} \frac{\rho_j^{x_j}}{x_j!},$$

where $G = \sum_{x \in \mathcal{S}} \prod_{j=1}^{J} \rho_j^{x_j} / (x_j!)$ is the normalizing constant. This result can immediately be derived by verifying that $\pi(x)$ satisfies the detailed balance equations

$$\pi(x)\lambda_i = \pi(x + e_i)(x_i + 1)\mu_i, \qquad x, x + e_i \in \mathcal{S}.$$

To obtain the fraction of refused admissions, define the sets $\mathcal{S}_j = \{x \in \mathcal{S} : x_j = M_j + M_{\text{joint}} - \sum_{i \neq j}(x_i - M_i)^+\}$ Using PASTA,we have $b_j = \sum_{x \in \mathcal{S}_j} \pi(x).$

Finally, we note that the product-form result is insensitive to the LOS distribution, see Bonald [2] and references therein. Hence, we only require the average length of stay to determine the performance of the earmarking policy without assuming exponential LOS.

Remark 3.1

Note that the policy of earmarking can also be interpreted as a special case of a loss network, see, e.g., Kelly [15]. Let P(A)P(A) be the power set of *A*. The loss network then consists of *J* routes and 2^J links (the number of elements of P({1,...,J}) A call (patient) on route *r* then uses all links for which r∈P({1,...,J} The number of circuits on link I⊆P({1,...,J}) equals $\sum_{j\in I} M_j + M_{\text{joint}}$. The state space, also giving the capacity constraints, can thus be written as $\sum_{j\in I} x_j \leq \sum_{j\in I} M_j + M_{\text{joint}}, \forall I \subseteq \mathcal{P}(\{1,\ldots,J\})\}$.

Optimal and threshold policies

Contrary to the allocation policies of separate wards, simple merging and earmarking, there are no closed-form results for the performance of the optimal and threshold policies. For the optimal policy, we use dynamic programming to find the policy that minimizes the relative costs $b(\mathbf{c})$. A similar iterative procedure, based on dynamic programming, can be used to determine the performance of threshold policies. For these policies, we require that the LOS follows an exponential distribution.

First, consider the optimal policy. The state space clearly is $S = \{x \in \mathbb{Z}_+^J : \sum_j x_j \leq N\}$. We use uniformization and first rescale time such that $\sum_j \lambda_j + \max_j\{\mu_j\}N = 1$. We associate costs when an arriving patient of type *j* is refused, representing the relative values in loss fractions. More specifically, we associate costs α_j/λ; costs then represent loss fractions in case $\alpha_j$equals 1. We note that the factor $1/\lambda$ in the costs is due to the fact that the average costs in the dynamic programming formulation represent average costs per time unit, whereas we are interested in customer averages instead of time averages.

The dynamic programming value function V_n at the nth epoch can then be determined by

$$V_{n+1}(x) = \sum_{j=1}^{J} \lambda_j \min\{V_n(x+e_j), V_n(x)+\alpha_j/\lambda\}$$
$$+\sum_{j=1}^{J} \mu_j x_j V_n((x-e_j)^+)$$
$$+\left(1-\sum_{j=1}^{J}(\lambda_j+\mu_j x_j)\right) V_n(x),$$

where we use the convention that $V_n(x)$ = ∞ for x∉Sx∉S. Here, the first term represents an arrival, the second a departure, and the third term is due to uniformization. We note that at an arrival there is a decision to make. Either the patient of type j is accepted and the system moves to state $x + e_j$, or the patient is refused and the systems stays in state x and incurs costs α_j/λ. The minimal long-run average costs and the optimal policy can be found using value iteration.

We now turn to the performance analysis of a given policy, e.g., the threshold policy. For convenience, we also apply value iteration to determine the long-run average costs. Let π be a deterministic policy and define $\pi(j, x)$ to be one in case an arriving patient of type j finding x patients present is admitted and let $\pi(j, x)$ be zero otherwise. The value function VπnVnπ at the nth epoch for policy π can then be determined by

$$V_{n+1}^{\pi}(x) = \sum_{j=1}^{J} \lambda_j \left(\pi(j,x)V_n(x+e_j)\right.$$
$$\left.+(1-\pi(j,x))(V_n(x)+\alpha_j/\lambda)\right)$$
$$+\sum_{j=1}^{J} \mu_j x_j V_n((x-e_j)^+)$$
$$+\left(1-\sum_{j=1}^{J}(\lambda_j+\mu_j x_j)\right) V_n(x).$$

We determine the value function and long-run average costs using value iteration again.

3.3 Structural properties

In this part, we discuss a number of structural properties of the bed allocation policies.

(i)The optimal and threshold policies coincide in case the ALOS of the different patient types are identical (and the LOS is exponentially distributed), as can also be observed from the first example in Section 4.1. This is easy to explain by noting that the bed occupancy can then be modeled as a one-dimensional birth-and-death process. Since the ALOS are identical, the decision to accept or refuse an arriving patient now only depends on the available number of beds, and is independent of the type of patients present. This results can already be found in Lippman [17].

(ii)In the setting of call centers, Gurvich et al. [10] and Koçağa and Ward [16] have considered (partly) comparable control problems for Erlang C and Erlang A models, respectively. The authors show that threshold policies are asymptotically optimal, i.e. the limiting control scheme is of a threshold type for a sequence of systems with increasing arrival rates. Although the models are slightly different and the analysis involves an asymptotic framework, this supports the idea that threshold policies should work well in many practical situations.

(iii)In some cases, the patient groups can be indexed according to a priority list based on the values of $\alpha_j\mu_j$. In case of two patient classes and $\mu_1 \geq \mu_2$ and $\alpha_1 \geq \alpha_2$ (and thus $\alpha_1\mu_1 \geq \alpha_2\mu_2$) it holds that if it is optimal to accept patient type 2 in some state, then it is also optimal to accept patient type 1, see Altman et al. [1]. A formal proof of a stronger result seems rather involved (see also [1]), and the structure of the optimal policy may differ, see [22, Example 3].

(iv)The priority list discussed above can be directly used to determine parameter values for threshold and earmarking policies. Again, without loss of generality, let $\alpha_1\mu_1 \geq \cdots \geq \alpha_J\mu_J$. For threshold policies, it can then be argued that $N = T_1 \geq \cdots \geq T_J$, also see [1]. For earmarking, we can directly conclude that $M_J = 0$, as class J needs no protection from other classes.

4 RESULTS ON BED ALLOCATIONS

For determining suitable bed allocation policies, we need to consider two different cases that are related by the size of the system under consideration. Small scale systems tend not to suffer that severely from multi-skilled staffing issues, and are treated in Section 4.2. Multi-skilled staffing is only partly possible in large scale systems, thereby limiting the type of control. Large scale systems and the distribution of beds over the different units is discussed in Section 4.3. To clarify drawbacks related to full flexibility (holding for both small and large scale systems), we start with two instructive examples in Section 4.1.

4.1 Instructive examples

We consider two cases in which differentiating between patient types might be desirable.

Example I: Specialized care

Consider two types of patients in which one type is of specific interest, e.g., it receives specialized care. Assume that the ALOS of both patient types is 4 days, i.e., $\mu_1 = \mu_2 = 0.25$, which roughly equals the ALOS at an Intensive Care (see also [4]). Let $\lambda_1 = 5$ and $\lambda_2 = 2$, yielding $\rho_1 = 20$ and $\rho_2 = 8$.

Now, assume that $N_1 = 20$ and $N_2 = 12$, such that $N = 32$. In that case, the loss fraction for type 1 and 2 patients are 15.9 % and 5.1 %, respectively, with a weighted average loss fraction of $b_{tot} = 12.8$ %. The difference in loss fractions may be a deliberate choice due to, for instance, the specialized care of type 2. Motivated by economies of scale, the bed allocation policy may be changed into simple merging. In that case, the loss fraction for both type of patients becomes 6.6 %. Hence, the average performance improves, but type 2 (specialized care) is negatively affected.

It is possible to prioritize type 2 patients using one of the three alternative bed allocation policies. The relative importance of type 2 is then quantified by c_j (or α_j), $j = 1,2$. In general, it is not directly clear how to value this relative importance, unless the weights are identical. Using different weight combinations, the hospital manager obtains valuable insights to make this trade-off.

The case in which both patient types are equally important ($\alpha_1 = \alpha_2$) is trivial, since the ALOS of both types are also identical and the optimal policy is then simple merging. Consider now the situation that the hospital manager decides that the loss fraction of type 2 should be well below 5.1 % such that type 2 also benefits from the reallocation of beds. In case the value of type 2 patients is twice the value of type 1, i.e. $\alpha_2 = 2\alpha_1$, the optimal values for the three policies can be found in the first part of Table 2, where the parameters of the earmarking and threshold policy are chosen such that $b(\mathbf{c})$ is minimized under the corresponding policy. An earmarking policy (M_1, M_2) denotes that M_i beds are dedicated to class i, $i = 1,2$, whereas the remaining beds, $N - M_1 - M_2$ are fully flexible. Note that b_2 is still above 5.1 % for the optimal earmarking policy. To further decrease the value of b_2 at least 8 or 9 beds should be earmarked for type 2, see the second part of Table 2. The optimal and threshold policies thus outperform earmarking.

Table 2. Loss fractions in % for case I; first part corresponds to optimal values in case $\alpha_2 = 2\alpha_1$, the second part to some earmarking policies

	b_1	b_2	b_{tot}	$b(c)$
Separate wards (20, 12)	15.89	5.14	12.82	14.29
Simple merging	6.65	6.65	6.65	8.55
Earmarking (0, 3)	6.66	6.64	6.65	8.55
Threshold (31, 32)	9.97	1.99	7.69	8.26
Optimal	9.97	1.99	7.69	8.26
Earmarking (0, 8)	8.42	5.12	7.48	8.94
Earmarking (16, 8)	8.40	5.20	7.49	8.97
Earmarking (0, 9)	9.70	4.29	8.15	9.38
Earmarking (16, 9)	9.68	4.37	8.16	9.41

Consider the case that (0,9) is a preferable earmarking allocation (e.g., it is optimal for $\alpha_2 = 4\alpha_1$). In that case, only 9 beds require single-skilled staff and 23 beds require multi-skilled staff. The limited number of multi-skilled staff (one of the main advantages) can then be exploited by choosing a much larger value for M_1 with only a minor loss in performance. For instance, in the second part of Table 2 can be found that the difference in performance of (0, 8) and (16, 8) and (0, 9) and (16, 9) is negligible.

Alternatively, the possible optimal combinations of loss fractions for the three policies can be depicted by the efficiency frontier, see Fig. 1. The values on this line give combinations of b_1 and b_2 that are optimal for the considered policy class. From Fig. 1, it follows that the threshold and optimal policy coincide (see also Section 3.3) and that they (slightly) outperform earmarking especially for highly unbalanced loss fractions. In turn, earmarking outperforms separate wards, in particular for non-extreme blocking probabilities. Note that given the practical disadvantages of the threshold and optimal policy, it may be preferable to apply earmarking in some practical scenario's.

Example II: Patient types with different ALOS

Consider two types of patients with a large difference in ALOS. As an illustration, assume that the ALOS of type 2 patients is 10 times as large as the ALOS of type 1 patients; we take $\mu_1 = 1$ and $\mu_2 = 0.1$. Let $\lambda_1 = 20$ and $\lambda_2 = 2$ such that the traffic loads are identical, i.e., $\rho_1 = \rho_2 = 20$.

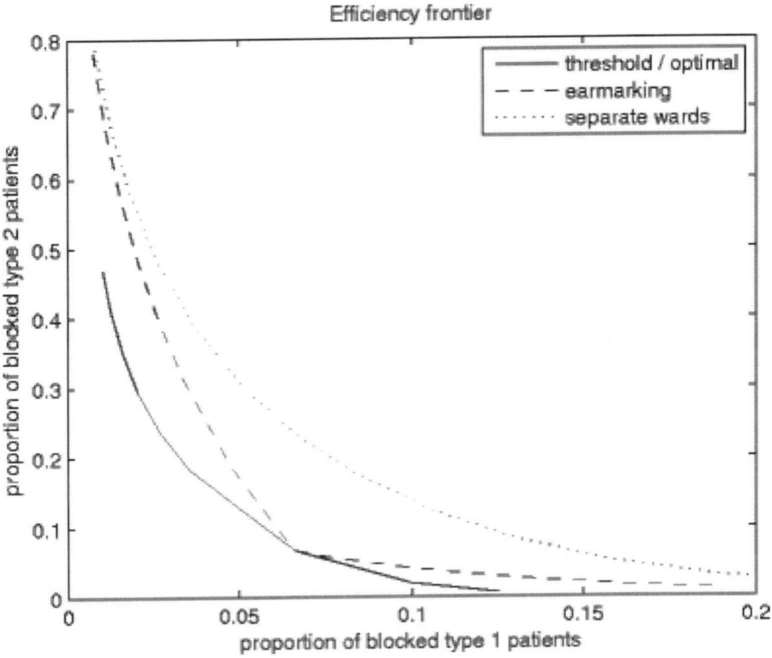

Figure 1. Efficiency frontier in case of specialized care at one ward

The current bed allocation is often determined based on historically acquired privileges. For instance, assume that $N_1 = 27$ and $N_2 = 17$, such that $N = 44$. In that case, the loss fraction for type 1 and 2 patients are 2.7 % and 25.6 %, respectively. This yields an average loss fraction of b_{tot} = 4.8 %. Motivated by economies of scale, the bed allocation policy may be changed into simple merging. However, using the Erlang loss model, the loss fraction then turns out to increase to 6.5 %. Similar results in a different setting can be found in [25], indicating that simple merging does not necessarily work well in case of patient groups with a large difference in ALOS.

Remark 4.1

Since the load is identical for both types of patients it could be suggested to equally divide the number of beds over the two wards, that is $N_1 = N_2 = 22$. In that case, the loss fraction is 10.7 % for both patient types, which is much higher than the average of 4.8 % in case of allocation policy (27, 17). We note that the optimal bed allocation for separate wards in terms of minimal weighted average loss fraction is (30, 14) yielding an average loss fraction of 4.1 %.

For the moment, let us assume that both patient types are of equal importance, i.e., $\alpha_1 = \alpha_2$. The loss fractions (in %) for the different bed allocation policies can be found in Table 3. Note that the loss fraction of type 2 is well above 25 % for all optimal policies (except simple merging). This evidently follows from the large ALOS of type 2 and the fact that type 1 and 2 are of equal relative importance.

Table 3. Loss fractions in % for various policies in case II

	b_1	b_2	b_{tot}
Separate wards (27, 17)	2.68	25.57	4.76
Simple merging	6.46	6.46	6.46
Earmarking (28, 0)	1.10	29.30	3.66
Threshold (44, 38)	1.22	26.67	3.53
Optimal	0.97	27.97	3.43

The impact of changing the relative importance (i.e. $c_j, j = 1,2$) can be seen using the efficiency frontier, see Fig. 2. In this example, both threshold policies and earmarking perform nearly as well as the optimal policy. It can also be observed that both type 1 and 2 may benefit from a different bed allocation compared to separate wards if the blocking probability of type 2 is not too large.

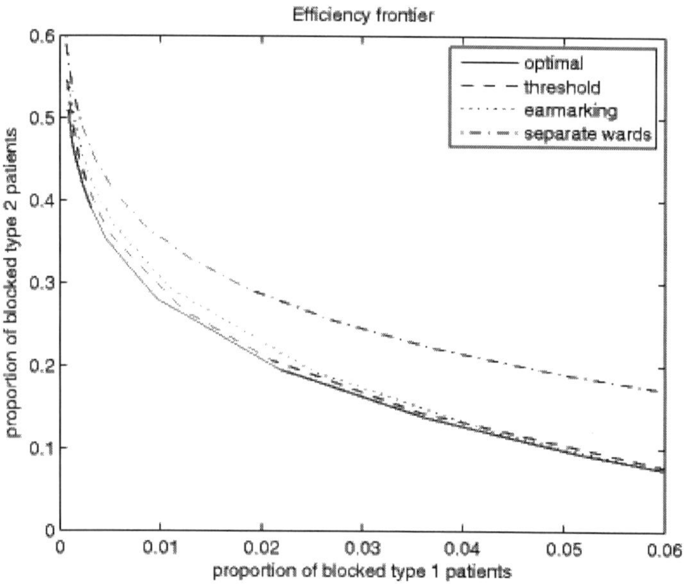

Figure 2. Efficiency frontier for two wards with different ALOS

LOS distribution

For the analysis of the threshold and optimal policy, we assumed that the LOS is exponentially distributed. In practice we sometimes observe that the lognormal distribution gives a better fit for the length of stay. To investigate the sensitivity of our approach to the lognormal LOS distribution we have run several simulation experiments. The average blocking probability for lognormally distributed LOS is obtained using 100M events divided among 25 sub runs so that a confidence interval for the average blocking probability can be obtained using the student's t distribution. The confidence was found to be such that the obtained blocking probabilities are accurate up to two decimal places.

The parameters of the lognormal distribution, denoted by μ and σ^2, are chosen such that the ALOS remains the same, whereas we varied the coefficient of variation. Specifically, the expectation and the variance of a lognormal random variable X are

$$\mathbb{E}(X) = e^{\mu+\frac{1}{2}\sigma^2}, \qquad Var(X) = (e^{\sigma^2} - 1)e^{2\mu+\sigma^2}.$$

Hence, the squared coefficient of variation is $c_X^2 = e^{\sigma^2} -$. Now, we vary σ^2 (or c_X^2) and take $\mu = \ln(\text{ALOS}) - \sigma^2/2$. As mentioned, there is no difference in results between exponentially and lognormally distributed LOS for the policies of separate wards, simple merging and earmarking. The impact only becomes visible for the threshold and optimal policy. We have run experiments for the settings as in Examples I and II. The results are shown in Table 4.

Table 4. Loss fractions of types 1 and 2 in % for the threshold and optimal policy for lognormal LOS

	Example I		Example II	
LOS distr.	threshold (31, 32)	optimal	threshold (44, 38)	optimal
Exp.	(9.97, 1.99)	(9.97, 1.99)	(1.22, 26.67)	(0.97, 27.97)
LogN(μ, 0.05)	(9.96, 1.99)	(9.97, 1.99)	(1.38, 26.85)	(1.09, 28.14)
LogN(μ, 0.1)	(9.98, 1.99)	(9.97, 1.99)	(1.36, 26.81)	(1.07, 28.11)
LogN(μ, 0.2)	(9.97, 1.99)	(9.98, 2.00)	(1.34, 26.79)	(1.06, 28.04)
LogN(μ, 0.4)	(9.99, 2.00)	(9.97, 1.99)	(1.31, 26.73)	(1.03, 28.05)
LogN(μ, ln(2))	(9.97, 1.99)	(9.97, 2.00)	(1.23, 26.66)	(0.99, 28.00)
LogN(μ, 0.8)	(9.98, 1.99)	(9.98, 1.99)	(1.22, 26.61)	(0.97, 27.92)
LogN(μ, 1.0)	(10.00, 1.99)	(9.97, 1.98)	(1.17, 26.57)	(0.94, 27.88)
LogN(μ, 1.2)	(10.00, 1.99)	(9.99, 2.00)	(1.14, 26.54)	(0.92, 27.87)

We conclude from the simulation experiments that there is no significant difference in results between exponential and lognormal LOS for Example I. This can be explained by the structure of the threshold and optimal policy. Both admit arriving patients if beds are available, except for a type 1 patient if there is only 1 bed available, and is therefore similar to an Erlang loss model. Example II shows some difference between the exponential LOS and lognormal LOS. However, the difference is very small and only becomes apparent to some extent for very small or relatively large values of σ^2.

4.2 Small scale systems: bed allocation

At the level of a single unit, the patient population is often diverse. This diversity may be related to medical diagnosis, clinical pathway, urgency, or medical discipline for combined units (such as at an IC that is used by different disciplines). Since diseconomies of scale are large for small unit sizes, organizing dedicated beds for small patient groups should be avoided. Moreover, the medical staff in general can treat all patient types visiting the unit so disadvantages related to multi-skill workers are of minor concern. In terms of our bed allocation policies, a unit usually acts in practice as 'simple merging'.

From the examples in Section 4.1, it follows that such a policy may not always deal well with different patient types in terms of prioritization and ALOS. To determine effective allocation policies, we now study the performance of bed allocations for a set of different problem instances. Since the optimal policy is hard to implement in practice, we compare it with the performance of simple merging, earmarking and the threshold policy. To this end, we generate 50 problem instances at random with the following specifications

- 2 types of patient classes;
- the number of beds N_i is uniformly distributed on [6,36];
- the average length of stay β_i is uniformly distributed on [1,14];
- the importance of a patient class α_i is uniformly distributed on [1,10]; thus, α_i/α_j is the relative importance of class i compared to class j;
- the arrival rate of patients λ_i is such that the relative offered load (i.e., $\lambda_i\beta_i/N_i$) is uniformly distributed on [0.5,1.3].

The performance is measured by comparing the costs of each policy to the optimal policy. Denote by c^* the optimal costs, and let $c^{(s)}$, $c^{(e)}$ and $c^{(t)}$ denote the costs associated with simple merging, earmarking, and the threshold policy, respectively. The performance is then calculated as $(c^{(\cdot)}-c^*)/c^*$. Figure 3 shows boxplots of the 50 problem instances for the three policies. The boxes in the plots are bounded by the

25th and 75th percentiles, while the central mark is the median. The whiskers are the lower and upper adjacent values, respectively, that are within 1.5 times the interquartile range.

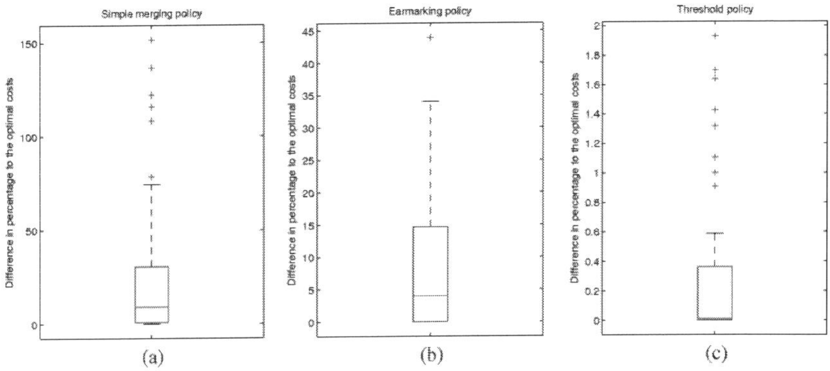

Figure 3. Relative difference in average costs for simple merging (**a**), earmarking policy (**b**) and threshold policy (**c**) compared to the average costs for the optimal policy

The results show that the threshold policy performs almost optimally. The maximum relative difference for the threshold policy is below 3.5 % compared to the optimal policy, and the average relative difference for all 50 problem instances is approximately 0.3 %. Simple merging is the worst among all studied policies with an average relative difference that equals 27 %. A huge benefit is obtained when we switch from simple merging to earmarking, with an average of the relative difference that is approximately 9 %. We note that the difference between simple merging and earmarking becomes larger when the load is larger. For instance, in case we take $\lambda_i$such that the relative offered load is uniformly distributed on [0.8, 1.3] the average relative differences are 0.4 %, 9 %, and 49 % for threshold policies, earmarking, and simple merging, respectively.

It is hard to say something about the situations in which a certain kind of policy performs well. From our numerical results, we have seen that the simple merging policy deviates more from the optimal policy as the difference between ρ_1 and ρ_2 increases. The same holds for the threshold policy. For the earmarking policy it turns out that the higher the difference between α_1 and α_2, the bigger the difference compared with the optimal policy.

Conclusion for practice

Threshold policies turn out to be effective for distinguishing between patient types. Moreover, the rules for admitting patients is relatively simple as it is based only on the number of available beds present at the unit. We therefore advocate to use policies of the threshold type. Our experience in practice is that doctors find it hard to reject patients when beds are still available. An exception might be the distinction between urgency classes, which is supported by medical staff.

4.3 Large scale systems: bed distribution

The distribution of beds among different medical disciplines usually involves tens or hundreds of beds. The scenario of simple merging will then be infeasible in practice, as this would require all medical staff to be trained to treat all patient types. The threshold and optimal policy suffer from the same multi-skill problem. So, on a large scale separate beds for each patient class or earmarking allocations are the only feasible alternatives.

For the earmarking policy, the shared or flexible beds may provide sufficient flexibility to utilize scale effects to a large extent. The lower part of Table 2 already suggested that some flexibility is sufficient for an efficient bed usage. As an illustrative example, consider the case of five symmetrical wards, each having a load of 20. Note that for the performance of any earmarking policy, only the load is required and not the specific arrival rate and ALOS. The total number of beds available for the five wards is 115. In Fig. 4 the blocking probability is displayed against the number of flexible beds (on the horizontal axis). If all beds are dedicated, then each ward gets 23 beds and the blocking probability is 8.49 %. When each ward allows only one bed to be flexible, resulting in 5 flexible beds overall, the blocking probability decreases to 4.89 %. Full flexibility, i.e. letting all 115 beds be flexible, results in 1.36 % blocking probability. As can be seen from Fig. 4, blocking probabilities below 2 % are already attained with 20 flexible beds. This illustration shows that a little flexibility is often sufficient to benefit from economies of scale. In particular, the blocking probability decreases as the number of flexible beds increases, but this happens in a convex way.

The illustration above indicates how many beds should be flexible. Another prime practical question is how to distribute beds across all units. This often is the most relevant issue as the total number of beds in the hospital is fixed, or changes in bed allocation should be such that the total number of beds remain fixed. Such questions can be explored by trying all combinations of bed allocations, but this number increases exponentially fast with the number of units in the hospital. Below, we identify guidelines for how many beds should be allocated to each unit. This allocation generally is a good starting point, but it may be tuned as there often are issues that are specific to local conditions. Examples of such conditions are construction of the building, nurse-to-patient ratios making it effective to be the number of beds being a multiple of some integer, historically obtained rights, policy considerations, etc.

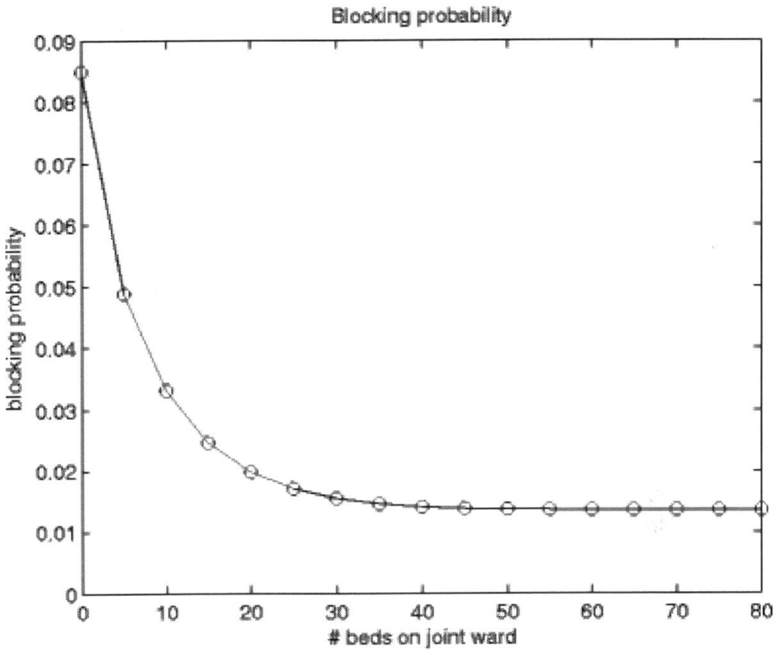

Figure 4. Blocking probability as a function of the number of flexible beds

The principle we propose for the distribution of beds is based on square-root staffing. Recalling that ρ_i is the offered load for unit i, the capacity should roughly be

$$s_i = \rho_i + \beta_i \sqrt{\rho_i}, \tag{3}$$

for some βi∈Rβi∈R. For actual staffing the s_i need to be rounded. The first term ρ_i reflects that each unit should be able to handle the average offered load. The second term $\beta_i \sqrt{\rho_i}$ represents the safety capacity, where β_i is the service level for unit i. Square-root staffing principles originate from heavy-traffic scenarios, but have turned out to be robust for smaller system sizes as well. We refer to, e.g., [3, 10, 11, 14, 32] for a more elaborate discussion. We now distinguish the cases with and without flexible beds; the bed allocation relies on square-root staffing for both cases.

Bed allocation without flexible beds

In the current situation, hospitals generally organize the clinic using separate wards. Admission of patients at other wards do occur, but this is commonly not organized on a structural basis. In Dutch hospitals it is common that admissions at non-preferred wards happen after rather exhaustive personal communications between medical supervisors of different medical units. As such, distribution of beds without organized flexibility is a prominent practical issue at the moment.

Using staffing rule (3), the blocking probability for unit i may be approximated by [14]

$$b_i = B(\rho_i + \beta_i \sqrt{\rho_i}, \rho_i) \approx \frac{\phi(\beta_i)}{\Phi(\beta_i)\sqrt{\rho_i}},$$

where $\phi(\cdot)$ and $\Phi(\cdot)$ are the density and cumulative distribution function of the standard normal distribution. The beds should now be allocated such that the sum of the capacities is N (see Eq. 4) and that the blocking probabilities satisfy the relative priorities (see Eq. 5). This yields the following system of J non-linear equations with as many unknowns β_i, $i = 1,\ldots, J$:

$$\rho + \sum_{j=1}^{J} \beta_j \sqrt{\rho_j} = N \qquad (4)$$

$$\alpha_1 \frac{\phi(\beta_1)}{\Phi(\beta_1)\sqrt{\rho_1}} = \alpha_i \frac{\phi(\beta_i)}{\Phi(\beta_i)\sqrt{\rho_i}}, \qquad i = 2, \ldots, J. \qquad (5)$$

In extreme cases, this system of equations may be infeasible, for instance when blocking probabilities above 1 are required to satisfy relative patient values. In that case, it is recommended to carefully consider the specifications as such situations reflect unusual behavior in hospital operations. Otherwise, we opt to minimize the squared difference between the lhs and rhs of (5) constrained by (4).

As an illustration, we apply the concept above to a specific example. Consider 5 units representing, for instance, the different surgical disciplines. Let the load ρ_i and relative value α_i for each discipline be as given in Table 5. Hence, unit 5 is large, whereas units 2 and 4 have some preference over the other units. We note that blocking probabilities b_i are calculated using the continuous extension of the Erlang loss model, such that non-integral values of s_i can be taken into account.

From Table 5 can be observed that the solution to the system of Eqs. 4 and 5 provides satisfying results and yields a good starting point to determine the final allocation. For the latter, we need at least rounding of s_i.

Table 5. Bed allocation without flexibility

	load (ρ_i)	rel. value (α_i)	β_i	s_i	loss fraction (b_i)
Unit 1	20	1	0.46	22.06	10.5 %
Unit 2	20	2	1.06	24.76	5.4 %
Unit 3	10	1	0.78	12.48	10.2 %
Unit 4	8	5	1.90	13.39	2.5 %
Unit 5	42	1	0.05	42.32	10.9 %

Bed allocation with flexible beds

We assume that the number of flexible beds M_{joint} is given, and is not part of the allocation (otherwise, it could be beneficial to make almost all beds flexible as we did not consider costs for multi-skilled staff explicitly). This seems reasonable, as the decision on M_{joint} is typically influenced by many factors that are difficult to quantify. We note that the example above (Figure 4) provides a good intuition for appropriate choices of M_{joint}.

Since there are now closed-form approximations for the blocking probability, we propose to use the following approximation scheme. Suppose that the flexible capacity is infinite. The number of type *i* patients in the system then has a Poisson distribution with mean ρ_i, which is approximately normally distributed for ρ_i not too small. The probability that an arriving patient needs a flexible bed is then $P(X_i \geq s_i) \approx 1 \; \Phi(\beta_i)$ with X_i the number of type *i* patients at an arbitrary arrival instant. The fraction of time that type *i* needs flexible beds should respect the relative value α_i between the different patient types. This is not precisely the same as the ratio between blocking probabilities, but the relative difference is typically small (unless the blocking probabilities are large).

The reasoning above leads to another set of *J* non-linear equations with as many unknowns β_i, $i = 1,\ldots,J$ (see above in case this system of equations is infeasible). Again, the beds should be allocated such that the sum of the capacities is *N* (see Eq. 6) and that the fraction of time flexible beds are needed satisfy the relative priorities (see Eq. 7):

$$\rho + \sum_{j=1}^{J} \beta_j \sqrt{\rho_j} + M_{\text{joint}} = N \tag{6}$$

$$\alpha_1(1-\Phi(\beta_1)) = \alpha_i(1-\Phi(\beta_i)),\ i=2,\ldots,J. \tag{7}$$

Consider the example above from Table 5, but now assume that it has been decided that 15 beds are flexible. The allocation of beds and the corresponding blocking probabilities b_i can be found in Table 6. Note that the blocking probabilities have decreased significantly compared to the situation without flexible beds. Units 1, 3, and 5 now have slightly less beds than their offered load.

Table 6. Bed allocation with 15 flexible beds

	load (ρ_i)	rel. value (α_i)	β_i	s_i	N_i	loss fraction (b_i)
Unit 1	20	1	–0.37	18.33	18	3.46 %
Unit 2	20	2	0.46	22.06	22	1.84 %
Unit 3	10	1	–0.37	8.82	9	3.14 %
Unit 4	8	5	1.13	11.20	11	0.88 %
Unit 5	42	1	–0.37	39.58	40	3.58 %

Conclusion for practice

Having some flexibility in bed usage is generally sufficient to cope with peaks in demand. As such, earmarking allocations are effective. Moreover, appropriate bed allocations can easily be supported with quantitative models. Our experience is that having fully flexible beds that are shared by all disciplines in hospitals are scarce (except for ICs or acute admission units). The same concept can also be carried out on a slightly smaller scale: related medical disciplines can partly share their beds according to an earmarking allocation. When the scale is large enough, such a cooperation is expected to perform well.

5 CONCLUSION AND DISCUSSION

In this paper we considered different practical alternatives to full flexibility of clinical beds or simple merging. The benefit of full flexibility can be easily explained by the economies of scale. However, full flexibility can be difficult to manage and may suffer from limited options of specialization in addition to issues in training many multi-skilled medical teams.

Our first contribution is that we propose structural and practically achievable bed allocation policies that perform well. For small scale systems, e.g., different patient groups at a medical unit, the benefits of a larger scale outweighs the drawbacks. To accommodate priorities of patient types and differences in lengths of stay, a threshold type of control is effective. In our numerical experiments we have seen that the threshold policy is nearly optimal, and in special cases coincides with the optimal policy.

For large scale systems, e.g., different medical disciplines, full flexibility is usually not desirable. However, a little flexibility is generally sufficient to benefit from most of the scale advantages. This can be implemented using an earmarking policy. Only a few members of the medical team need to be multi-skilled for little flexibility and yet the advantages are significant. In addition, we have addressed a prominent practical question of 'how to distribute a fixed number of beds over different units?'. Using a square-root staffing principle, this can be efficiently determined by solving a set of equations.

The second contribution is that we provide models to support strategic and tactical decision making about the number of hospital beds. The performance analysis for earmarking is being implemented in a decision support system, exploiting the product-form solution, to facilitate hospital management in well-founded decisions about bed management.

From a practical point of view, we envisage that implementation of fair and flexible allocations is involved due to historically obtained privileges. Moreover, some specific characteristics of patient flows may be further explored to improve the accuracy of the model. For instance, in some situations, a delay model could be more appropriate than a loss model. Nonetheless, with the current models we display some key organizational concepts that are valid in a broader setting.

From a scientific standpoint, it is of future interest to find optimal bed allocations when costs are involved for single-skilled and multi-skilled medical teams (although it is not straightforward to quantify this in practice). Asymptotic regimes may give further theoretical support for the different bed allocations. Finally, extending the assumptions of the model could strengthen the conclusion.

FOOTNOTES

1 PASTA is the acronym for Poisson Arrivals See Time Averages, stating that the distribution of the number of customer seen by an arriving customers equals the time average distribution, see [33].

REFERENCES

1. Altman E, Jiminez T, Koole GM (2001) On optimal call admission control in a resource-sharing system. IEEE Trans Commun 49:1659–1668

2. Bonald T (2006) Insensitive Queueing models for communication networks (2006). In: Proceedings of the Valuetools

3. Borst SC, Mandelbaum A, Reiman MI (2004) Dimensioning large call centers. Oper Res 52:17–34

4. de Bruin AM, Bekker R, van Zanten L, Koole GM (2010) Dimensioning clinical wards using the Erlang loss model. Ann Oper Res 178:23–43

5. Burke EK, de Causmaecker P, Berghe GV, van Landeghem H (2004) The state of the art of nurse rostering. J Sched 7:441–499

6. Chevalier P, Shumsky RA, Tabordon N (2004) Routing and Staffing in Large Call Centers with Specialized and Fully Flexible Servers. Working paper, Simon School, University of Rochester, Rochester

7. Green LV, Nguyen V (2001) Strategies for cutting hospital beds: The impact on patient service. Health Service Research 36:421–442

8. Green LV (2002) How many hospital beds? Inquiry 39:400–412

9. Green LV (2005) Capacity planning and management in hospitals. In: Brandeau ML, Sainfort F, Pierskalla WP (eds) Operations research and health care, pp 15–41

10. Gurvich I, Armony M, Mandelbaum A (2008) Service-level differentiation in call centers with fully flexible servers. Manag Sci 54:279–294

11. Gurvich I, Huang J, Mandelbaum A (2013) Excursion-based universal approximations for the Erlang-A queue in steady-state. Math Oper Res 39:325–373

12. Hall R (2012) Bed assignment and bed management. In: Hall R (ed) Handbook of healthcare system scheduling, pp 177–200

13. Huckman RS, Zinner DE (2008) Does focus improve operational performance? Lessons from the management of clinical trials. Strat Manag J 29:173–193

14. Janssen AJEM, van Leeuwaarden JSH, Zwart AP (2008) Gaussian expansions and bounds for the Poisson distribution applied to the Erlang B formula. Adv Appl Probab 40:122–143

15. Kelly FP (1991) Loss networks. Ann Appl Probab 1:319–378

16. Koçağa YL, Ward AR (2010) Admission control for a multi-server queue with abandonment. Queueing Systems 65:275–323

17. Lippman SA (1975) Applying a new device in the optimization of exponential queueing systems. Oper Res 23:687–710

18. Lynck WJ (1995) The creation of economic efficiencies in hospital mergers. J Health Econ 14:507–530

19. Mandelbaum A, Momcilovic P, Tseytlin Y (2012) On fair routing from emergency departments to hospital wards: QED queues with heterogeneous servers. Manag Sci 58:1273–1291

20. Mandelbaum A, Reiman MI (1998) On pooling in queueing networks. Manag Sci 44:971–981

21. McManus ML, Long MC, Copper A, Mandell J, Berwick DM, Pagano M, Litvak E (2003) Variability in surgical caseload and access to Intensive Care services. Anesthesiology 98:1491– 1496

22. Örmeci EL, Burnetas A, van der Wal J (2001) Admission policies for a two class loss system. Stoch Model 17:513–539

23. Rothkopf MH, Rech P (1987) Perspectives on queues: combining queues is not always beneficial. Oper Res 35:906–909

24. Smith DR, Whitt W (1981) Resource sharing for efficiency in traffic systems. Bell System Tech J 60:39–55

25. van Dijk NM, van der Sluis E (2004) To pool or not to pool in call centers. Prod Oper Manag 17:296–305

26. van Essen JT, van Houdenhoven M, Hurink JL (2014) Clustering clinical departments for wards to achieve a prespecified blocking probability. OR Spectrum, appeared online

27. Vanberkel PT, Boucherie RJ, Hans EW, Hurink JL, Litvak N (2012) Efficiency evaluation for pooling resources in health care. OR Spectrum 34:371–390

28. Wallace RB, Whitt W (2005) A staffing algorithm for call centers with skill-based routing. Manufacturing and Service Operations Management 7:276–294

29. Walley P, Silvester K, Steyn R (2006) Managing variation in demand: lessons from the UK National Health Service. J Healthc Manag 51:309–322

30. Wolstenholme E (1999) A patient flow perspective of UK health services: exploring the case for the new "intermediate care" initiatives. Syst Dyn Rev 15:253–271

31. Worthington DJ (1987) Queueing models for hospital waiting lists. J Oper Res Soc 38:413–422

32. Whitt W (1992) Understanding the efficiency of multi-server service systems. Manag Sci 38:708–723

33. Wolff RW (1982) Poisson arrivals see time averages. Oper Res 30:223–231

34. Young JP (1965) Stabilization of inpatient bed occupancy through control of admissions. Journal of the American Hospital Association 39:41–48

3

EARLY WORKPLACE INTERVENTION TO IMPROVE THE WORK ABILITY OF EMPLOYEES WITH MUSCULOSKELETAL DISORDERS IN A GERMAN UNIVERSITY HOSPITAL—RESULTS OF A PILOT STUDY

Monika Schwarze [1], Christoph Egen [1], Christoph Gutenbrunner [1] and Stephanie Schriek [2]

[1]Department for Rehabilitation Medicine, Hannover Medical School, Carl-Neuberg-Str. 1, Hannover 30625, Germany

[2]Company Physician, Hannover Medical School, Carl-Neuberg-Str. 1, Hannover 30625, Germany

ABSTRACT

Health promotion is becoming increasingly important in work life. Healthcare workers seem to be at special risk, experiencing musculoskeletal disorders (MSD); their situation is strongly influenced by demographic changes. The aim of this study is to evaluate the feasibility and outcome of a worksite intervention. In a one-group pretest-posttest design, 118 employees of a hospital were recruited from 2010 to 2011. The raised parameters were satisfaction with the program, work ability (Work Ability Index), and sickness absence (provided by human resource management). Patient-reported questionnaire data was raised at baseline (t1) and after three months (t2). Sickness leave was evaluated in the period six months prior to and six months after the intervention. Means, frequencies, standardized effect sizes (SES), analysis of variance, and regression analysis were carried out. Participants were found to be highly satisfied. Work ability increased with moderate effects (SES = 0.34; $p < 0.001$) and prognosis of gainful employment (SES = −0.19; $p \leq 0.047$) with small effects. Days of MSD-related sickness absence were reduced by 38.5% after six months. The worksite intervention program is transferable to a hospital setting and integration in occupational health management is recommended. The use of a control group is necessary to demonstrate the effectiveness.

Keywords: work ability; musculoskeletal disorders; occupational health; worksite rehabilitation and prevention; sickness absence

1. INTRODUCTION

Health promotion for employees to maintain work ability and participation in work life is becoming increasingly important against the background of demographic changes. Of particular relevance is to keep workers in the healthcare sector healthy and motivated until retirement age. In this sector it is anticipated that a higher number of people will need healthcare due to longer life expectancy, whilst alongside this a shortage of healthcare workers, especially in the nursing sector, is expected to exacerbate the issue [1].

These profound demographic changes are occurring in most industrialized nations, notably including those in Europe. In the context of work life they become apparent in the aging and the shrinkage of the labor force [2]. There are numerous implications associated with these changes in relation to politics, social security systems and companies [2]. In Germany, for example, the retirement age has been raised, thereby prolonging the working lifetime [3]. However, epidemiological studies show with increasing age, the prevalence of chronic disease rises and work ability decreases [4,5]. It is known that approximately one-third of the working population suffers from a chronic disease [6]. This goes along with higher sickness absence and early retirement, owing to an inability to remain at work, due to health problems [7]. Musculoskeletal disorders (MSDs) have a substantial impact on disability among adults of working age. They are also influenced by psychosocial factors in development and onset [8]. With a frequency of 53%, MSDs constitute the highest number of work-related disorders in Europe. They accounted for 49% of all sickness absences lasting two weeks or more and 60% of permanent incapacity cases. Total costs of MSDs were up to 2% of the gross domestic product (GDP) [9]. Compared with workers in other industrial sectors, healthcare workers rank high in incidence in most work-related complaints [10,11].

To encourage labor force participation, different actions have been implemented. The federal government has, for example, initiated a strategy characterized by the slogan "Every age counts", which focuses on healthier, better-qualified employees and a longer work life [12]. In public and private companies, corporate health management and health promotion systems receive additional support and emphasis. As one process in Germany since 2004, Company Integration Management (BEM, Betriebliches Eingliederungs Management) is legally binding. Employers have to offer this tool for all employees who have been unable to work for more than six weeks within a year. The objective of this is to secure participation in employment [13].

In particular, early emphasis on prevention and treatment of MSDs preserves continued participation in gainful work [14,15,16]. A meta-analysis shows moderate evidence of interventions targeting the beginning symptoms of MSDs in the workplace to prevent work disability [17]. Furthermore, preventative and rehabilitative measures have evolved considerably in the direction of vocational orientation to preserve health, the ability to work and gainful employment. Basic components for successfully remaining and returning to work are a combination of early intervention, the cooperation of all stakeholders, multidisciplinary interventions and work-related measures [18,19,20]. It has been shown that stronger work-related rehabilitation has positive effects on vocational participation [21].

In Germany, in the field of medical and vocational rehabilitation carried out by the German pension insurance for legal reasons, the focus lies on participation in gainful working life [22]. Thus, concepts and interventions are largely workplace-orientated. Work-related medical rehabilitation (WMR) has gained importance in clinical practice and research in the last two decades [22,23,24,25,26,27]. Since 2009 the pension insurance has also had the opportunity to provide preventative treatment for policy-holders at high risk of losing earning capacity due to health reasons. Since then, various preventative pilot projects in workplace settings combined with existing structures of the pension insurance have been developed [16].

The concept of work ability used in this study is defined by the Finish Institute of Occupational Health as the balance between human resources and the demands of work [28]. The Work Ability Index (WAI) as an instrument and a tool was developed to identify, maintain and promote work ability. Evidence suggests that investments in active aging and promotion of work ability are worthwhile [28,29,30]. The WAI is also recommended by a German interdisciplinary working group to be used in projects on early interventions to maintain and restore work ability [31].

In our study we introduced a program to preserve the work ability of persons at risk of losing their earning capacity, but without high rehabilitation needs. The out-patient worksite intervention was introduced first in 2009 within the concept of the Job^{Rehab} model [32]. As a result, the health status and working capacity of employees with MSDs improved and a significant reduction of time lost due to sick leave was achieved [33]. Due to the program's promising results in the industrial and service field, in the present study one element of the Job^{Rehab} model (Level I) was implemented for the first time for university employees in the healthcare field [34].

The program includes a three-month combined approach of workplace management, company medical service, and work-related out-patient medical prevention and rehabilitation.

In a pilot study, the feasibility and the outcome of this intervention were the focus. We investigated the employee's satisfaction with the worksite program and examined changes in work ability, prognosis of gainful employment, and amount of sickness leave.

2. MATERIALS AND METHODS

2.1. Study Design

The feasibility study was carried out in a prospective one-group pretest-posttest design. A control group was not established because of ethical reasons. To improve the lack of significance and enhance the meaningfulness of the results, the subjective prognosis of employment (SPE Scale) and regression analysis were added.

The intervention, a three-month work-related program was implemented at a university hospital, and workers were invited to participate. Workers completed questionnaires at baseline (prior to the intervention) and three months later (at the end of the intervention). The hospital's human resources management made available data of the workers absenteeism prior and post to the intervention. The compared periods were six months before and six months after the intervention. The study was approved by the Ethic Commission at the Medical School Hannover, and all subjects signed an informed consent to participate.

2.2. Participants

A total of 645 workers from 11 selected divisions of the hospital were informed and invited. We recruited participants (n = 118) for the interventions from August 2010 to September 2011. Inclusion criteria were used in accordance with the Job^{Rehab} model [32,35]. The criteria included; MSD, work-related functional limitations, anticipated employment period in the company being at least one year and no intention of retirement. Employees with acute pain, incipient paralysis and severe nerve root irritation of the spine were excluded. Depending on the severity of the disease, functional impairments and duration of sick leave 12 months prior to the intervention, as well as different personal and environmental contextual factors, the company physician (CP) recommended the worksite intervention (corresponding to Level I) according to the Job^{Rehab} model [35]. Level I consisted of an intensive, one-week outpatient prevention program with rehabilitative elements. For a detailed description of the selection criteria for the different levels of the Job^{Rehab} concept, see Gutenbrunner and Schwarze 2011 [32].

The assessment was carried out by self-report of the employer and examination of the company physician. The range of MSD went from muscular tension, spine and joint diseases and others.

Further inclusion criteria assessed by the CP were work-related functional limitations, risk of losing earning capacity, anticipated employment period in the company for at least one year, and no reported intention to retire.

Access was voluntary, and participation occurred during paid work time.

2.3. Intervention

Information about the program was spread in the company via superiors, staff meetings, leaflets, and medical services. Enrollment and first registration took place at the company's medical service, followed by an appointment with the CP. The CP checked the inclusion criteria for Level I (worksite intervention), and a short, functional capacity evaluation according to Isernhagen and a workplace description of the employee was conducted [36,37]. Via the use of standardized formats and communication procedures, the CP transferred all information, including recommendations regarding treatment of specific problems in the musculoskeletal system. Qualified employees were then recommended to the rehabilitation physician (RP) [35].

Depending on the job profile information of the CP, the clinical picture, and specific MSD complaints identified, individualized work-related therapy was planned by the RP.

The intervention comprised of a one week (five full days from nine to five) of intensive intervention, training and three months of twice-weekly training (one hour). It consisted of the following preventative and rehabilitative components: diagnostic and assessment, workplace-related medical and physiotherapy, workplace-related occupational therapy, workplace-related medical training therapy, occupational therapy testing at the workplace, if necessary adjustment at the workplace, health and nutrition counseling, and after-care counseling. At the end of the three months, a final consultation with the CP was provided.

During the running of the project it was integrated into the hospital's corporate health management and monitored by a Trust Board consisting of employees' council, personnel development, and representatives of the participants' divisions. In regular meetings, workplace problems, work conditions and current and further project developments and data security were discussed.

2.4. Data Collection and Measurements

Sociodemographic characteristics and information of the work divisions and conditions of the employees were assessed at baseline. The satisfaction of participants with the intervention was recorded with a selection of items of the ZUF-8 questionnaire three months later at the end of the intervention [38]. In addition, self-developed questions by the authors were used.

Satisfaction with the work condition and design, and job motivation were measured with self-design, project-specific questionnaires at t1 and t2. The Work Ability Index (WAI), a seven-part self-assessment was used to measure work ability as a primary outcome. The WAI evaluates: current ability, work ability in relation to physical and mental demands of the job, reported diagnosed diseases, estimated impairment due to health status, sick leave over the last six months, and self-prognosis of work ability in the upcoming two years and mental resources. The four outcome categories are subdivided into "poor" (7–27), "moderate" (28–36) "good" (37–43) or "excellent" (44–49) [39]. Secondary outcomes were prognosis of future employment; this was measured with the SPE-Scale, a short scale assessing the subjective prognosis of gainful employment [40]. Human resource management provided data on days of sick leave. The personal data collected were not documented in the hospital's patient systems but kept in a separate paper file.

2.5. Statistical Analyzes

Descriptive statistics were used to summarize the sample and to describe the main findings. Values were presented as frequencies in percent, as a mean and standard deviation (SD). The same applied to work conditions and satisfaction with the program and work conditions.

The sum scores and categories of the WAI and SPE-Scale were illustrated and described.

To compare means between pre- and post-measurement analysis of variance were carried out and standardized effect sizes (SES) were calculated. When interpreting the effect of the intervention general guidelines analog Cohen were used: small (0.2), medium (0.5) and large (0.8) [41].

Numbers of days of sick leave were compared six months before and the six months post the worksite program.

Regression models, including sociodemographic, and health and work condition related variables, were calculated to identify risk factors affecting the ability to work after intervention.

A p-value < 0.05 was considered to be significant.

We used Statistical Package for Social Science in Version 19.

3. RESULTS

3.1. Sample Description

A total of 118 employees initially enrolled in the program; two dropped out before the intervention started and another 16 participants later dropped out of the program, in most cases because of acute illness. Of the remaining 100 participants, 97 completed the data for the two time points (Figure 1).

Table 1 shows sample characteristics at t1. The average age was 47 with 60.3% women (n = 70) and 39.7% (n = 46) men. In the program, 59.5% of workers had physically stressful work activity (e.g., bed central, laundry, transportation), while 40.5% were office workers (e.g., finance department, patient accounting) of the hospital.

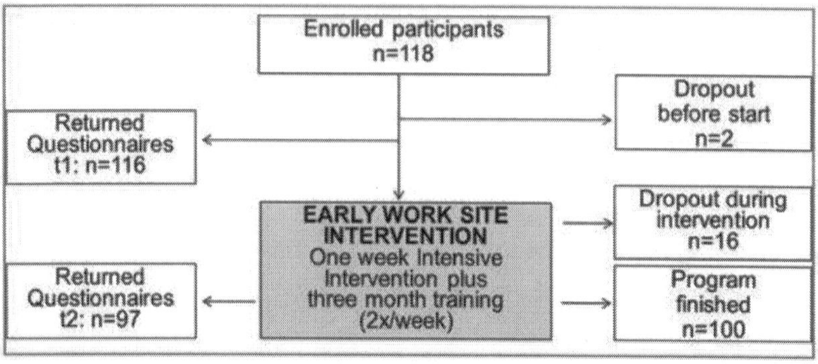

Figure 1. Study group: participation and dropout.

Table 1. Sample characteristics at t1, *n* = 116.

Variables	*n* (%)
Gender	
Female	70 (60.3)
Men	46 (39.7)
Age	
Average (years, SD)	47 8.3
Groups (years)	
<46	46 (39.7)
46–50	25 (29.0)
>50	41 (35.3)
Range (years max–min)	63–20
Occupational groups/divisions	
Blue-collar workers (logistics, transport, kitchen, laundry)	69 (59.5)
White-collar workers (funding, finance, patient-accounting office)	47 (40.5)
Working conditions	
Shift work	26 (22.8)
Display screen work	51 (44.7)
Physically demanding work (high load)	34 (29.8)
Time pressure (high load)	37 (32.5)
Work Ability Index (*n* = 94)	
Excellent (44–49)	8 (8.5)
Good (37–43)	30 (31.9)
Moderate (28–36)	45 (47.9)
Poor (7–27)	11 (11.7)
Prognosis of gainful employment (SPE-scale) (*n* = 97)	
No risk	49 (50.5)
Low risk	26 (26,8)
Strong risk	19 (19.6)
Very strong risk	3 (3.1)
Days of sick leave During six months prior to intervention (days)	13.0

3.2. Participation and Satisfaction with the Worksite Intervention

Of the 116 participants enrolled at t1, 100 workers completed the whole program (i.e., intensive week plus three-month training). Workers rated the program for its help in coping with MSD complaints at the workplace; 52.6% said it was very helpful, 39.2% said it helped some, 7.2% said it did not help, and 1% said it made things more difficult. At the end of the intervention (t2), 95.9% of the participants rated the quality of the program as very good or good, 3.1% rated it as less good and 1% rated the quality as bad. Ninety-eight percent would recommend the program to a colleague.

Participants' WAI scores at t1 were good or moderate for almost 79.8% (Figure 2). Based on these findings, the WAI concept recommended interventions that promote and improve the work ability of those persons. A poor WAI score indicates that high intensive measures such as rehabilitation are necessary. For workers with excellent WAI scores, work ability should be maintained through preventative measures (e.g., recreational sports).

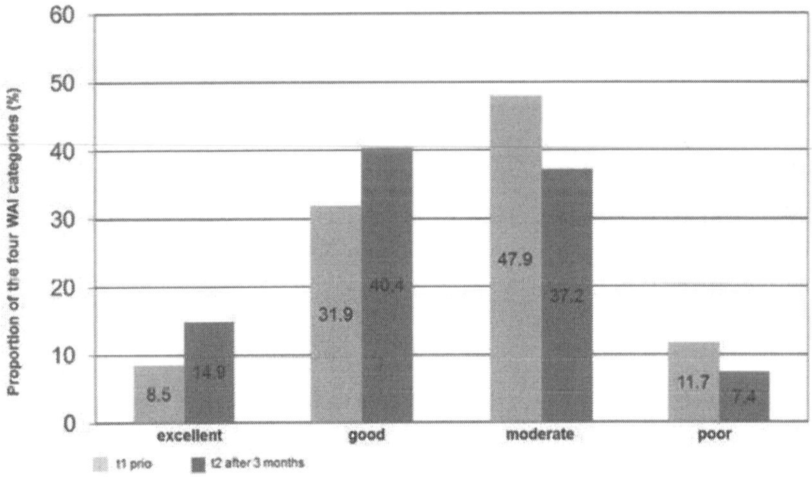

Figure 2. Prevalence of the WAI categories before and after worksite program (n = 94).

By means of the screening with the SPE Scale, 49.5% of the workers reported a low to very high risk of losing earning capacity.

3.3. Workability, Prognosis of Gainful Employment and Sickness Absence

Figure 2 shows the distribution of the four WAI categories from t1 to t2. The percentage of workers in categories with increasing workability rose, and SPE Scale data went in the same direction. The percentage of workers in the group with no risk of losing earning capacity rose from 50.5% to 55.7%. The group with a strong risk of losing earning capacity declined from 19.6% to 14.4%.

During the program, the WAI sum score improved from an average of 35.2 to 37.3 points after three months. This corresponded to an effect size of SES = 0.34, $p < 0.001$. Similarly, participation in the early worksite program had positive effects on earning capacity (SES = −0.19; $p = 0.047$) (Figure 3).

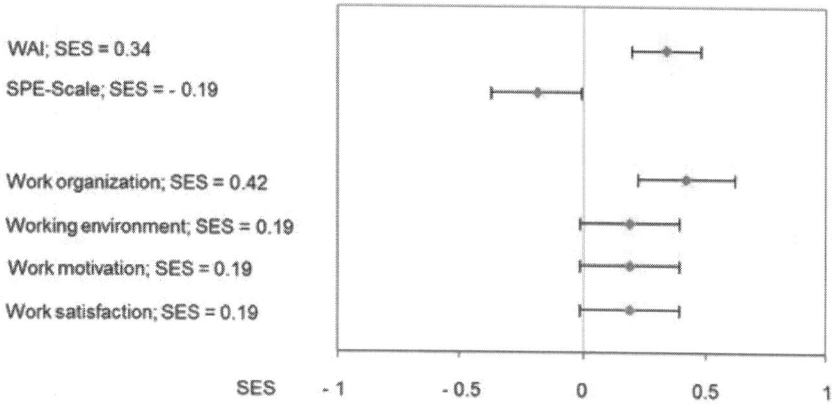

Figure 3. WAI (n = 94), SPE-scale (n = 97) and working conditions (n = 97); Standardized effect sizes (SES).

Regression analysis showed that older participants and men benefited less from participation in the worksite intervention than woman. Shift work, lower work motivation also had negative effects on the ability to work.

After six months, sick leave per participant was reduced by five days (38.5%) compared to the six-month period before the program.

4. DISCUSSION

The aging workforce and increasing numbers of chronic diseases make rehabilitative health management and, specifically, the implementation of early workplace intervention increasingly necessary. Workers in the healthcare sector face special risk factors in their workplace, and musculoskeletal pain and symptoms of MSD are widely reported [9,10,11]. Literature suggests that work health programs (WHP) can increase employees' health and productivity when designed with appropriate components, address the needs of the participants, and evaluate the program effects [42].

4.1. Implementation

The results of this pilot study show that the early worksite program was both practicable and successfully implemented. The program has been widely embraced, and workers were keen to participate. Dropouts, either prior to the start or while the program was being implemented, typically resulted from individuals encountering extraneous or random factors such as illness rather than lack of interest or disapproval. Owing to preparation on an organization level, potential environmental barriers were minimized effectively. A supportive management climate in the company created easy accessibility. Nevertheless, it should be mentioned that although the need of WHP for preventative and rehabilitative measures for workers with MSD in this target group is clear, almost two years of careful planning and preparation prior to the program start were necessary.

A systematic review describes the numerous factors that determine the successful implementation of preventative programs in healthcare settings [43]. This also applies to our study. As a facilitator in our study, cooperation with all involved stakeholders was identified as absolutely essential. Inclusion of members of the employees' council and superiors played a key role, as did coordinating with the decision-makers of human resources management and the hospital board. Persuasion of all parties was needed to clear hesitancy and troubling questions. Positive evaluation results of the Job^{Rehab}program from other industrial sectors that exist were convincing [32,33]. Also, questions relating to the security of data (patient records) seemed a serious barrier, but that problem was resolved satisfactorily.

Financing the program also was a challenge, and was overcome when the management of the company decided to make the necessary investments. Loss of productivity, caused by the fact that the program would be conducted during normal working hours, was considered but deemed acceptable as it was directed to improving the health of the workers. Return of investment and long-term economic benefits were expected. Experience with the Job^{Rehab} concept in the Department of Rehabilitation Medicine initiating the program was highly advantageous. Not least, extra resources in the medical occupational service department had to be provided. The CPs had to be trained in procedures and provided extra services in screening workers. As concluded in a systematic literature research among others as reasons for insufficient reintegration, the unsatisfactory communication and cooperation between rehabilitation and occupational health physicians was seen. CDs in the present study had an objective role as mediators and acted as the connecting piece in relation to the medical interfaces in the rehabilitation process [44].

4.2. Need-Based Approach

Based on the screening by the CPs during the enrollment process, a group of workers most at risk of losing earning capacity due to MSD and job strain could be identified. According to WAI categories, 79.8% of the sample demonstrated the intended inclusion criteria for participation. They were found in need of preventative rehabilitative measures and were able to receive appropriate support to maintain or even to improve their work ability. These findings are somewhat higher than the results found by a working group evaluating a program similar to that described here. They showed that in "Protect Employability", a program in rehabilitation units offered by the German pension insurance, 72.2% of the participants fell in these two WAI categories, and initial WAI scores here were 32.3. Rehabilitants with MSD in orthopedic inpatient rehabilitation units showed a significantly lower work ability (WAI = 29) [45].

A recent methodology study on the prognostic value on sickness absence confirms that the WAI can be used as a suitable instrument to identify workers at risk of prolonged sickness absence. Nevertheless, owing to low sensitivity, the authors recommend using the approach described in combination with others [46].

A critical look should be given to the 8.7% of participants with poor health who need more intensive measures such as rehabilitation as well as to the 11.7% of participants with excellent work ability. For the latter, work ability should be maintained through primary prevention such as physical activity; inclusion of these workers could be rated as an over-under or misuse of the worksite program. However, it cannot be ruled out that participants were included for other meaningful reasons in addition to the WAI screening.

However, focusing on the program's target and intervention group in the first step seems to be more practicable. Introduction of the entire Job^{Rehab} model was not feasible. The essential structures to facilitate and coordinate further steps such as inpatient or outpatient intensive Job^{Rehab} or preventative measures such as physical activity were not yet available. Exclusion of the interested employees from the worksite program was avoided for motivational reasons.

As already recognized and implemented in the previous project, in Job[Rehab] it is essential to provide need-based interventions. However, this has been recognized in the project group and the accompanying trust board and improvements have been tackled. Furthermore, it was obvious that the amount of psychosocial support was too little, so in the future workers should get more and differentiated measures to deal with stress in the workplace.

In a follow-up model, besides the Department of Rehabilitation Medicine, the Institute of Sports Medicine, the Department of Psychiatry, Social Psychiatry and Psychotherapy of the hospital as well as the regional German Pension were included as additional partners. In this way rehabilitation and case management as well as psychosocial measures and physical activity were provided for the workers. In conclusion, employees could use the services of the university hospital for their own health and fitness [47].

4.3. Outcome

Small to moderate effect sizes could be reported in terms of measures of effectiveness of work ability, prognosis of gainful employment, and work situation. Compared with the intervention "Protect employability" in the present study, the risk profiles measured with the WAI and SPE Scale also improved significantly [45]. A review on workplace interventions for preventing work disability concluded that there is moderate evidence that workplace interventions reduce sickness absence among workers with MSD, but where it is not effective is in improving health outcomes [17].

The reduction of sickness absence between 38.5% (six-month period) was found in this study. At Volkswagen Commercial Vehicle, sickness absence declined by 40.5% in the early worksite intervention group (Level I) in a six-month observation period [33]. In further long-term health economics studies, it might be of interest to study if the resources invested for the intervention compared with the cost of production lost due to sickness absence lead to a return on investment.

The results also provide some information about factors determining work ability. Work ability is associated with independent variables such as individual characteristics and workplace conditions [48]. In our study, older participants in particular took less benefit than those that were younger and men took less advantage than woman. Lower work motivation and shift work had negative effects on work ability.

4.4. Strengths and Limitations

Some strengths and limitations have to be considered. A selection bias cannot be excluded because an uncontrolled one-group pretest-posttest design was accomplished and a dropout analysis for responders or non-responders was not carried out. It is unclear whether or not the participants were a representative sample of all workers in the selected 11 work divisions where the program was offered first. Without a control group it is not possible to compare the outcomes with other divisions who did not receive the early worksite intervention and if the effects are due to the intervention. It became clear that instruments and assessment of work conditions, work satisfaction and health status had to be more detailed and differentiated to comprehensively understand employees' health and workplace conditions.

Nevertheless, this study was a pilot study in manageable divisions of the hospital. It can be seen as the most appropriate design to test the feasibility for further use in a future intervention with higher sample sizes in larger divisions, especially for employees in nursing, a significant work field of the university hospital.

A strength of the study is that a multidimensional measurement was used. A synthesis out of self-reported subjective health outcome measures, work ability, indicators of the work situation and objective data was conducted. By means of a pre-/post-design, the outcome of the intervention could be made clear with widespread instruments and parameters. As a successful challenge, the engagement of the stakeholders in all phases of the study can be seen. They were constantly informed and consulted about the implementation of the interventions as well as the study process and findings. Their clinical and organizational expertise was integrated in further study designs.

5. CONCLUSIONS

All these results suggest that the implementation of the original Job^{Rehab} model, especially the early worksite intervention (Level 1) at a university hospital, is feasible. Currently, the worksite program is offered as a routine component in the company health management of the hospital where the authors are employed. It is, meanwhile, a core element in the comprehensive health management system "Fit for Work and Life" (FWL) for employees of the university hospital.

ACKNOWLEDGMENTS

The study was funded by the German Pension Insurance Braunschweig-Hannover. We thank the staff development team of the MHH, Michael Born and Sylvia Degenhardt for their assistance in the implementation of the project. In particular, we thank Peter Burzlaff for providing the sickness absence data. Also our thanks go to the employees' council, represented by Brigitte Stryk and Rüdiger Mechsner, for their suggestions that led to further development of the project. The authors would also like to thank the employees for their participation in this project.

AUTHOR CONTRIBUTIONS

Designed the study: Monika Schwarze, Christoph Egen, Christoph Gutenbrunner, Stephanie Schriek. Analyzed the data: Monika Schwarze, Christoph Egen. Wrote the paper: Monika Schwarze, Stephanie Schriek. Contributed to data collection: Stephanie Schriek, Christoph Gutenbrunner. Contributed to interpretation of analyses: Monika Schwarze, Christoph Egen, Christoph Gutenbrunner, Stephanie Schriek.

CONFLICTS OF INTEREST

The authors declare no conflict of interest.

REFERENCES

1. Schulz, E.; Leidl, R.; König, H. The impact of ageing on hospital care and long-term care—The example of Germany. Health Policy 2004, 67, 57–74.
2. Szinovacz, M.E. Introduction: The aging workforce: Challenges for societies, employers, and older workers. J. Aging Soc. Policy 2011, 23, 95–100.
3. Fehr, H.; Kallweit, M.; Kindermann, F. Pension reform with variable retirement age: A simulation analysis for Germany. J. Pension Econ. Finance 2012, 11, 389–417.
4. Bhattacharya, J.; Choudhry, K.; Lakdawalla, D. Chronic disease and severe disability among working-age populations. Med. Care 2008, 46, 92–100.

5. Müller, A.; Weigl, M.; Heiden, B.; Glaser, J.; Angerer, P. Promoting work ability and well-being in hospital nursing: The interplay of age, job control, and successful ageing strategies. Work 2012, 41, 5137–5144.

6. Scheidt-Nave, C. Chronische Erkrankungen—Epidemiologische Entwicklung und die Bedeutung für die öffentliche Gesundheit. Public Health Forum 2010, 18, 2–4. (In German)

7. Badura, B.; Ducki, A.; Schröder, H.; Klose, J.; Meyer, M. Fehlzeiten-Report 2014: Erfolgreiche Unternehmen von Morgen-Gesunde Zukunft Heute Gestalten; Springer: Berlin, Germany, 2014. (In German)

8. Shaw, W.S.; Hartvigsen, J.; Woiszwillo, M.J.; Linton, S.J.; Reme, S.E. Psychological distress in acute low back pain: A review of measurement scales and levels of distress reported in the first two months after pain onset. Arch. Phys. Med. Rehabil. 2016.

9. Bevan, S. Economic impact of musculoskeletal disorders (MSDs) on work in Europe. Best Pract. Res. Clin. Rheumatol.2015, 29, 356–373.

10. Tullar, J.M.; Brewer, S.; Amick, B.C., III; Irvin, E.; Mahood, Q.; Pompeii, L.A.; Wang, A.; Van Eerd, D.; Gimeno, D.; Evanoff, B. Occupational safety and health interventions to reduce musculoskeletal symptoms in the health care sector. J. Occup. Rehabil. 2010, 20, 199–219.

11. Caruso, C.C.; Waters, T.R. A review of work schedule issues and musculoskeletal disorders with an emphasis on the healthcare sector. Ind. Health 2008, 46, 523–534.

12. Hüther, M.; Naegele, G. Demografiepolitik und Demografiestrategie—Was notwendig ist. In Demografiepolitik; Springer: Berlin, Germany, 2013; pp. 365–378. (In German)

13. Schmidt, C.; Bauer, J.; Schmidt, K.; Bauer, M. Betriebliches Gesundheitsmanagement im Krankenhaus: Strukturen, Prozesse und das Arbeiten im Team gesundheitsfördernd Gestalten; MWV: Berlin, Germany, 2015. (In German)

14. Palmer, K.T.; Harris, E.C.; Linaker, C.; Barker, M.; Lawrence, W.; Cooper, C.; Coggon, D. Effectiveness of community- and workplace-based interventions to manage musculoskeletal-related sickness absence and job loss: A systematic review. Rheumatology (Oxford) 2012, 51, 230–242.

15. Arnetz, B.B.; Sjögren, B.; Rydéhn, B.; Meisel, R. Early workplace intervention for employees with musculoskeletal-related

absenteeism: A prospective controlled intervention study. J. Occup. Environ. Med. 2003, 45, 499–506.

16. Meffert, C.; Mittag, O.; Jackel, W.H. Work place health promotion programmes of the statutory German Pension Insurance. Rehabilitation (Stuttg) 2013, 52, 391–398.

17. Van Oostrom, S.H.; Driessen, M.T.; De Vet, H.; Franche, R.; Schonstein, E.; Loisel, P.; van Mechelen, W.; Anema, J.R. Workplace interventions for preventing work disability. Cochrane Database Syst. Rev. 2009.

18. Schaafsma, F.G.; Whelan, K.; van der Beek, A.J.; van der Es-Lambeek, L.C.; Ojajärvi, A.; Verbeek, J.H. Physical conditioning as part of a return to work strategy to reduce sickness absence for workers with back pain. Cochrane Database Syst. Rev. 2013.

19. Waddell, G.; Burton, A.K.; Kendall, N.A. Vocational Rehabilitation—What Works, for Whom, and When? (Report for the Vocational Rehabilitation Task Group); TSO: London, UK, 2008.

20. Wåhlin, C.; Ekberg, K.; Persson, J.; Bernfort, L.; Öberg, B. Evaluation of self-reported work ability and usefulness of interventions among sick-listed patients. J. Occup. Rehabil. 2013, 23, 32–43.

21. Schonstein, E.; Kenny, D.T.; Keating, J.L.; Koes, B.W. Work conditioning, work hardening and functional restoration for workers with back and neck pain. Cochrane Database Syst. Rev. 2003.

22. Egner, U.; Schliehe, F.; Streibelt, M. Work related medical rehabilitation, MBOR—A process model in medical rehabilitation. Rehabilitation (Stuttg) 2011, 50, 143–144.

23. Bethge, M.; Löffler, S.; Schwarz, B.; Vogel, H.; Schwarze, M.; Neuderth, S. Gelingt die Umsetzung des Anforderungsprofils zur Durchführung der medizinisch-beruflich orientierten Rehabilitation? Rehabilitation 2013, 53, 184–190. (In German)

24. Bethge, M.; Löffler, S.; Schwarz, B.; Vogel, H.; Schwarze, M.; Neuderth, S. Besondere berufliche Problemlagen: Spielen sie eine Rolle beim Zugang in die medizinisch-beruflich orientierte Rehabilitation? Rehabilitation 2014, 53, 49–55. (In German)

25. Buschmann-Steinhage, R.; Brüggemann, S. Veränderungstrends in der medizinischen Rehabilitation der gesetzlichen Rentenversicherung. Bundesgesundheitsblatt Gesundheitsforschung Gesundheitsschutz 2011, 54, 404–410. (In German)

26. Hillert, A.; Müller-Fahrnow, W.; Radoschewski, F. Medizinisch-beruflich orientierte Rehabilitation. In Grundlagen und Klinische

Praxis Köln; Deutscher Ärzte-Verlag: Berlin, Germany, 2009. (In German)

27. Gerdau-Heitmann, C.; Gutenbrunner, C.; Miede, J.; Schwarze, M. Umsetzung des Erwerbsbezugs in der medizinischen Rehabilitation-Analyse von Routinedaten der Deutschen Rentenversicherung Braunschweig-Hannover. Phys. Med. Rehabil. Kurortmed. 2014. (In German)

28. Tuomi, K.; Ilmarinen, J.; Jahkola, A.; Katajarinne, L.; Tulkki, A. Work Ability Index, 2nd ed.; Finnish Institute of Occupational Health: Helsinki, Finland, 1998.

29. Ilmarinen, J. The ageing workforce—Challenges for occupational health. Occup. Med. (Lond.) 2006, 56, 362–364.

30. Ilmarinen, J. Promoting Active Ageing in the Workplace; European Agency for Safety and Health at Work: Bilbao, Spain, 2012.

31. Amler, N.; Felder, S.; Mau, W.; Merkesdal, S.; Schöffski, O. Instrumente zur Messung von Effekten einer Frühintervention auf den Erhalt bzw. die Wiederherstellung der Arbeitsfähigkeit in Deutschland—Stellungnahme einer interdisziplinären Arbeitsgruppe. Das Gesundheitswesen 2015. (In German)

32. Gutenbrunner, C.; Schwarze, M. JobReha-bedarfsgerechte arbeitsplatzbezogene Rehabilitation: Systematische Modellentwicklung. Phys. Med. Rehabil. Kurortmed. 2011, 21, 234–241. (In German)

33. Teumer, F.; Wassmus, A.; Cyganski, L.; Teichler, N.; Gutenbrunner, C.; Schwarze, M. Gesundheitsökonomische Evaluation der JobReha bei Volkswagen Nutzfahrzeuge Hannover. ASUpraxis Arbeitsmed. Sozialmed. Umweltmed.2010, 45, 102–104.

34. Neugebauer, T.; Bethge, M.; Egen, C.; Burzlaff, P.; Schriek, S.; Miede, J.; Gutenbrunner, C.; Schwarze, M. Evaluation einer arbeitsplatzorientierten Maßnahme nach dem Modell der JobReha für MitarbeiterInnen einer Universitätsklinik. DRV Schriften 2013, 101, 318–319. (In German)

35. Schwarze, M.; Spallek, M.; Korallus, C.; Manecke, I.; Teumer, F.; Wrbitzky, R.; Gutenbrunner, C.; Rebe, T. Advantages of the JobReha discharge letter: An instrument for improving the communication interface in occupational rehabilitation. Int. Arch. Occup. Environ. Health 2013, 86, 699–708.

36. Oesch, P.; Meyer, K.; Jansen, B.; Kool, J. Functional Capacity Evaluation: Performance of patients with chronic non-specific low back pain without waddell signs. J. Occup. Rehabil. 2015, 25, 257–266.

37. Isernhagen, S.J. Functional capacity evaluation: Rationale, procedure, utility of the kinesiophysical approach. J. Occup. Rehabil. 1992, 2, 157–168.

38. Schmidt, J.; Lamprecht, F.; Wittmann, W. Zufriedenheit mit der stationären Versorgung. Entwicklung eines Fragebogens und erste Validitätsuntersuchungen. Psychother. Med. Psychol. 1989, 39, 248–255. (In German)

39. Jedryka-Góral, A.; Bugajska, J.; Łastowiecka, E.; Najmiec, A.; Rell-Bakalarska, M.; Bownik, I.; Michalak, J.M.; Kochmański, M. Work ability in ageing workers suffering from chronic diseases. Int. J. Occup. Saf. Ergon. 2006, 12, 17–30.

40. Mittag, O.; Glaser-Moller, N.; Ekkernkamp, M.; Matthis, C.; Heon-Klin, V.; Raspe, A.; Raspe, H. Predictive validity of a brief scale measuring the subjective prognosis of gainful employment (SPE-scale) in a cohort of blue collar workers with low back pain or functional syndroms of Internal Medicine. Soz.-Präventivmed. 2003, 48, 361–369.

41. Cohen, J. Statistical Power Analysis for the Behavioral Sciences, 2nd ed.; Routledge: Hillsdale, NJ, USA, 1988.

42. Goetzel, R.Z.; Ozminkowski, R.J. The health and cost benefits of work site health-promotion programs. Annu. Rev. Public Health 2008, 29, 303–323.

43. Koppelaar, E.; Knibbe, J.J.; Miedema, H.S.; Burdorf, A. Determinants of implementation of primary preventive interventions on patient handling in healthcare: A systematic review. Occup. Environ. Med. 2009, 66, 353–360.

44. Völter-Mahlknecht, S.F.; Rieger, M.A. Patientenversorgung an der Schnittstelle von Rehabilitation und Betriebsärzten. Systematische Literaturübersicht zur Versorgungsgestaltung. Dtsch. Med. Wochenschr. 2014, 139, 1609–1614. (In German)

45. Olbrich, D.; Beblo, A.; Passeik-Hartmann, D. Zur Bedeutung des Work Ability Index (WAI) im GUSI-Präventionsprogramm für Versicherte der Deutschen Rentenversicherung Bund und Westfalen. Available online: http://www.bsafb.de/fileadmin/downloads/pa_21_12_2010/pa21_12_2010_zur_bedeutung_des_WAI_im_GUSI_Praeventionsprogramm_fuer_versicherte_der_DRV_bund_und_westfalen.pdf (accessed on 31 August 2016).

46. Reeuwijk, K.G.; Robroek, S.J.; Niessen, M.A.; Kraaijenhagen, R.A.; Vergouwe, Y.; Burdorf, A. The prognostic value of the work ability index for sickness absence among office workers. PLoS ONE 2015, 10, e0126969.

47. Gutenbrunner, C.; Egen, C.; Kahl, K.; Briest, J.; Tegtbur, U.; Miede, J.; Born, M. Entwicklung und Implementierung eines umfassenden Gesundheitsmanagements (Fit for Work and Life) für Mitarbeiter/innen eines Universitätsklinikums–ein Praxisbericht. Das Gesundheitswesen 2015. (In German)

48. Van den Berg, T.I.; Elders, L.A.; de Zwart, B.C.; Burdorf, A. The effects of work-related and individual factors on the Work Ability Index: A systematic review. Occup. Environ. Med. 2009, 66, 211–220.

4

AN AGENT-BASED SIMULATION MODEL TO STUDY ACCOUNTABLE CARE ORGANIZATIONS

Pai Liu[1,2] & Shinyi Wu[1,3,4,5]

[1].Daniel J. Epstein Department of Industrial and Systems EngineeringUniversity of Southern CaliforniaLos AngelesUSA

[2].Palo Alto Research CenterPalo AltoUSA

[3].School of Social WorkUniversity of Southern CaliforniaLos AngelesUSA

[4].RAND CorporationSanta MonicaUSA

[5].School of Social Work and Daniel J. Epstein Department of Industrial and Systems EngineeringUniversity of Southern CaliforniaLos AngelesUSA

ABSTRACT

Creating accountable care organizations (ACOs) has been widely discussed as a strategy to control rapidly rising healthcare costs and improve quality of care; however, building an effective ACO is a complex process involving multiple stakeholders (payers, providers, patients) with their own interests. Also, implementation of an ACO is costly in terms of time and money. Immature design could cause safety hazards. Therefore, there is a need for analytical model-based decision-support tools that can predict the outcomes of different strategies to facilitate ACO design and implementation. In this study, an agent-based simulation model was developed to study ACOs that considers payers, healthcare providers, and patients as agents under the shared saving payment model of care for congestive heart failure (CHF), one of the most expensive causes of sometimes preventable hospitalizations. The agent-based simulation model has identified the critical determinants for the payment model design that can motivate provider behavior changes to achieve maximum financial and quality outcomes of an ACO. The results show nonlinear provider behavior change patterns corresponding to changes in payment model designs. The outcomes vary by providers with different quality or financial priorities, and are most sensitive to the cost-effectiveness of CHF interventions that an ACO implements. This study demonstrates an increasingly important method to construct a healthcare system analytics model that can help inform health policy and healthcare management decisions. The study also points out that the likely success of an ACO is interdependent with payment model design, provider characteristics, and cost and effectiveness of healthcare interventions.

Keywords: Agent-based model, Health policy simulation, Accountable care organization, Congestive heart failure, Payment model

1 INTRODUCTION

The current health system in the United States lacks mechanisms and incentives for providers to control rapidly rising healthcare costs and improve quality of care [1]. Hence, an idea was proposed in 2007 of an accountable care organization (ACO), a group of providers who accept greater accountability for total costs and quality of care [2, 3]; this has been widely discussed since it was outlined in the Patient Protection and Affordable Care Act [4] in 2010. The Centers for Medicare & Medicaid Services (CMS) have established a Medicare Shared Savings Program to create ACOs implementing shared saving payment models [5]. In addition, many private insurers and healthcare organizations have launched or will launch their ACO demonstrations in the near future [6].

However, an ACO could implement a broad range of delivery and payment models (capitation, bundled payment, shared saving) [7]; it is unclear how ACOs should be structured and implemented [8] to deliver high-quality care and control spending. Meanwhile, an ACO demonstration is costly in terms of time and money and could cause safety hazards because of immature design. Therefore, the design and implementation of ACOs are complex and risky, and there is a need for predictive analytics tools that can predict future outcomes of different ACO models and generate recommendations based on goals set by policymakers.

Industrial and Systems Engineering (ISE) methods have the potential to address this need. However, traditional ISE approaches are facing challenges in modeling some important features of an ACO, which is composed of multiple interacting individual stakeholders from multiple sectors–including payers, providers, and patients–who are working to maximize their own interests. Consequently, the Agency for Healthcare Research & Quality (AHRQ) has called for methodologies that can incorporate different objectives and behaviors of multiple interacting stakeholders from different sectors into the model and make optimal recommendations for the overall system [9]; AHRQ has identified the methodologies as a critical area of ISE research in healthcare.

The main contribution of this article is that an agent-based model was developed to address the needs of predictive analytics for ACOs from a cross-sectoral point of view. By combining different agents' varying goals and behaviors from their vantage points in a system model, the analysis reveals new, integrated insights to help inform health policy and healthcare management decisions. A simulation study that analyzes ACOs aiming to deliver better care for congestive heart failure (CHF) was also developed to demonstrate the use of the agent-based model. CHF was selected in the model because it is the leading cause for hospitalization and high healthcare costs for elders [10]. In addition, multiple meta-analyses of clinical trials have shown that interventions of disease management programs could reduce CHF readmission rates and improve other health outcomes, including survival rates and quality of life [11, 12]. Therefore, payers and ACOs have the potential to create incentives and mechanisms to facilitate the adoption and implementation of this evidence-based care. The goal of the agent-based simulation model is not to substitute an ACO pilot program but to facilitate ACO design and implementation processes by providing analytic supports for decision-makers to make informed decisions.

A shared saving payment model for the ACOs was examined in the agent-based model because it is a popular payment model used in the CMS Shared Savings Program [5] and many other current and planned ACO demonstrations. Furthermore, it serves as an important bridge between the traditional fee-for-service model and more fundamental risk-sharing payment models, such as episode-based payment. Under shared saving payment, if a group of providers can control or reduce the total healthcare costs of a patient population while meeting quality measures, a portion of the saving will be awarded to the providers.

In this paper, Section 2 describes the agent-based model developed and a simulation study to demonstrate the model. Section 3 presents the results of the simulation study. A baseline analysis was conducted to compare the performance of an ACO health network and a controlled health network. In addition, multiple scenario analyses were conducted to examine the impacts of payment model designs and provider characteristics on the outcome measures.

2 METHOD

In this chapter, the agent-based model developed to provide predictive analytics for ACOs is described, followed by the modeling settings of the simulation study for CHF patients. Section 2.1 briefly introduces the methodology of agent-based modeling and its advantages to model ACOs. Section 2.2 describes the framework of the agent-based model and the designs of each type of agent, including agent's objectives, characteristics, behaviors, and how an agent interacts with other agents. Section 2.3 provides a gain and cost analysis from different agents' perspectives in order to model agent decision-making. Section 2.4 discusses the configurations of the simulation run to demonstrate the model.

2.1 Agent-based modeling

Agent-based modeling (ABM) can be viewed as a mindset rather than a specific modeling technique. ABM describes a complex system from the bottom-up perspective and models it as a collection of multiple autonomous agents who have their own objectives, behaviors, and interactions with other agents and the environment. As in the real world, global behaviors and trends emerge from the behavior of and interactions between individual agents [13, 14].

ABM can model individual behaviors of each stakeholder in an ACO and their dynamic interactions. This is a limitation and difficulty of traditional equation-based or discrete event modeling approaches. Because providing coordinated care is an essential part of an ACO, the ability to model agent collaborations and communications is a required function for an ACO model. The structure of ABM makes it easy to define dynamic agent interactions through functions such as message passing and agent networks.

Because ABM does not require predefined aggregate level flow and structure (as in System Dynamics), it is more flexible to expand through adding agent behaviors, interaction rules, and learning capacity. In addition, working as a platform, ABM can incorporate other modeling techniques. For example, it can apply artificial intelligence to model agent behavior changes and can incorporate stochastic process models to simulate agent internal state transitions. Furthermore, because ABM models the system from the individual agent level, it can take advantage of the increasing amount of individual level data.

2.2 Model description

As shown in Fig. 1, the agent-based model includes three types of agents who are the key stakeholders of an ACO demonstration: the patient agent, the provider agent, and the payer agent. Two classes of provider agents were defined because they are the main providers involved in CHF care: the hospital agent and primary care physician (PCP) agent. Under each agent, there are modules, each of which represents a set of related functions for the agent.

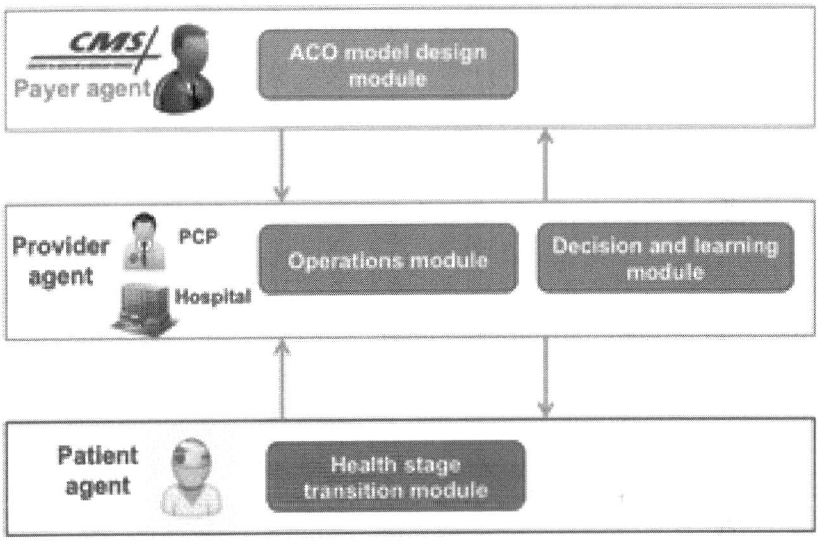

Figure 1. Agent-based model structure

2.2.1 Patient agent

A patient agent denotes a Medicare patient whose age is 65 or older. Each patient agent is characterized by four demographic variables (age, race, gender, and income) and three health condition variables (diabetes, hypertension, and CHF). These variables were the key factors that have impacts on CHF disease progression and healthcare utilization [15–18].

Patient agent characteristics were estimated from the National Health and Nutrition Examination Survey (NHANES) of 1999–2010. Because the variables of a patient agent are correlated, the joint distribution of these variables was estimated on the basis of a conditional probability model:

$$P(\text{CHF and Hypertension and Diabetes and Demographics})$$
$$= P(\text{CHF}|\text{Hypertension and Diabetes and Demographics})$$
$$*P(\text{Hypertension}|\text{Diabetes and Demographics})$$
$$*P(\text{Diabetes}|\text{Demographics})*P(\text{Demographics})$$

The patient agent's CHF disease progression and healthcare resource utilization are modeled in the patient agent state transition module shown in Fig. 2. A patient agent starts in either the CHF free state or CHF onsite state, depending on whether the agent has CHF when he/she was generated. In the CHF free state, a patient agent is exposed to the risk of developing CHF in either the outpatient setting (moving to the CHF onsite state) or the inpatient setting (moving to the CHF-related hospitalization state). A patient agent in the CHF onsite state is at risk of CHF-related hospitalization (moving to the CHF-related hospitalization state). Patient agents in any of the above states also have the possibility of death (moving to the mortality state, in which case the patient agent will be deleted from the simulation).

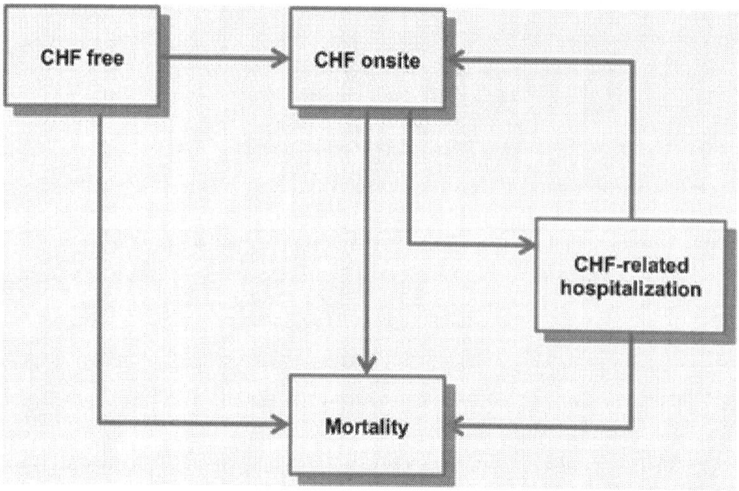

Figure 2. Patient agent transition model

The CHF-related hospitalization was defined as a hospitalization in which CHF is listed in any of its first seven diagnoses. Because this model targets CHF care, non–CHF-related hospitalizations were not included. In addition, patient agents who have not been diagnosed with diabetes or hypertension are exposed to the risks of developing diabetes or hypertension. Because CHF, diabetes, and hypertension are incurable chronic diseases, once a patient agent develops any of these diseases, he/she will have it for the rest of the simulation.

There is a wide range of cycle time in the CHF modeling literature depending on the measurement needs of the studies [19–21]. The cycle time in the patient state transition module was set to half a month (15 days) in order to catch hospital readmissions within 30 days since previous discharge. At each cycle, a patient agent will move to other states or remain at the current state according to state transition probabilities, which are determined by the patient agent's characteristic variables and are adjusted if the patient agent receives the CHF intervention care. The intervention here refers to the comprehensive discharge planning with post-discharge follow-up. More details about it can be found in Phillips et al. [12].

The impacts of these risk factors on the state transition probabilities are derived from the literature and public health surveys and statistics. First, the CHF incidence rate is risk-adjusted by the patient's age group [22], diabetes [23, 24], and hypertension [16, 18, 24]. With regard to the mortality rate of CHF patient agents, Curtis et al. [22] showed there is a significant difference in mortality rate depending on whether the patients were first diagnosed with CHF in an inpatient setting or an outpatient setting. Thus, the diagnosis source was added as a risk factor for mortality, and two separate survival curves were constructed from data reported by Curtis et al. [22] (shown in Table 1) for each diagnosis source.

Table 1. CHF survival curve

Time since onset of CHF	Survival proportions	
	Outpatient diagnosis	Inpatient diagnosis
0	1.00	1.00
30 days	0.98	0.84
1 years	0.87	0.66
5 years	0.49	0.33

For non-CHF patient agents, the mortality rate was estimated from the U.S. life tables of 2006 [25]. The CHF-related hospitalization rate was adjusted by age group based on the estimations from Fang et al. [26] and Chen et al. [27] shown in Table 2. Diabetes incidence rates were developed based on McBean et al. [28], and hypertension incidence rates were calculated from Dannenberg et al. [29] and Dischinger et al. [30] as a function of patient's race.

Table 2. Transition probability from the CHF-diagnosed state to CHF-related hospitalization

Age (years)	Transition probability
65–74 (age group 1–2)	0.01663
75–84 (age group 3–4)	0.02360
>=85 (age group 5)	0.03489

A patient agent generates inpatient care utilization by moving into the CHF-related hospitalization state. For outpatient care utilization, each patient agent's regular outpatient visits were modeled as a Poisson process because it is a common approach to modeling patient arrivals [31–33]. The average number of regular outpatient visits estimated from the literature ranges from eight to ten visits per year [21, 34, 35]. Hence, the parameter of the Poisson process is set to nine visits per year. In addition to regular visits, a follow-up visit after hospital discharge will be scheduled if a patient agent receives the intervention.

2.2.2 Provider agent

The model includes two types of provider agents: the hospital agent and PCP agent; each represents a hospital or a PCP clinic, respectively. The goal of a provider agent is to maximize the utility of the hospital or clinic by deciding whether to conduct the CHF intervention.

The CHF intervention has been demonstrated by a number of clinic trials and meta-analysis studies as able to reduce hospital readmission and mortality rate for CHF patients [11, 12]. The effects of the intervention are modeled by reduction in transition probabilities to the CHF-related hospitalization state and mortality state. The risk reduction was derived from a meta-analysis of CHF interventions [12]. The average risk reduction is 20 % for CHF hospitalization rate and 13 % for CHF mortality rate.

Because most published CHF intervention studies involve collaboration of hospitals and PCPs [11, 12], the full effects of the intervention, it was assumed, could only be achieved when both the hospital where a patient was admitted and the patient's PCP conducted the intervention. If only one party was conducting the intervention without collaboration with the other party, the intervention could only achieve partial effect.

The well-established psychological theory, the Theory of Planned Behavior (TPB) [36], was applied as the framework to model the provider agent decision-making. As shown in Fig. 3, TPB suggests that a person's actual behavior is determined by his/her intention to perform the behavior, and the intention is influenced by three predicting factors: attitude, subjective norm, and perceived behavior control (PBC).

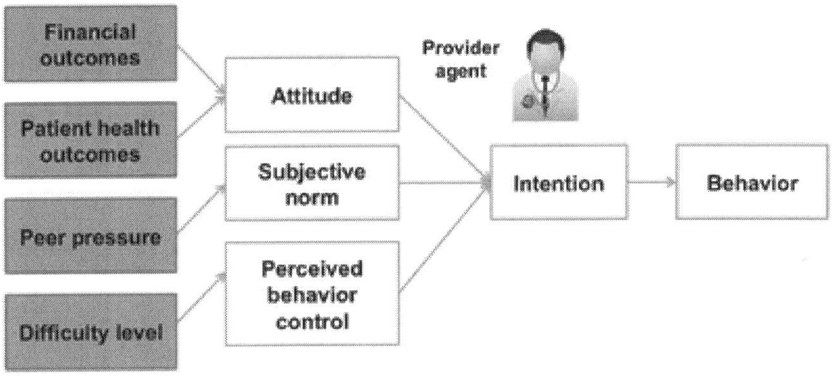

Figure 3. Application of the theory of planned behavior

Attitude in TPB is a person's belief about the consequences of a particular behavior. In the model, the provider agent's attitude toward the intervention is influenced by his/her financial return as well as his/her client's health outcomes measured by the CHF hospitalization rate and mortality rate. Hence, attitude A of a provider agent is formalized as

$$A_{j+1}^{k} = \beta_1 \cdot U_p\left(EP_{j+1}^{k}\right) + \beta_2 \cdot U_q\left(EQ_{j+1}^{k}\right),$$

where $EP_{j+1}{}^{k}$ and $EQ_{j+1}{}^{k}$ are the expected profit and expected quality performance, respectively, if behavior k will be performed in year j + 1. U is a function that transforms the expected profit or the expected quality performance into a utility value from 0 to 1. β is a weight parameter that can be configured by users.

Subjective norm is a person's perception of whether people important to him/her believe he/she should perform a behavior. The provider agent's subjective norm was defined in terms of peer pressure, which is a provider agent's perception of other provider agents' attitudes toward the intervention. The perception of other agents' attitudes is modeled through agent communication. Based on his/her current attitude toward the CHF intervention, a provider agent will send a supportive message either for the behavior of implementing the intervention or for the opposite behavior of not implementing the intervention to a random agent within his/her network. A provider agent can then estimate other provider agents' attitudes based on the number of supportive messages received for each behavior. Hence, the subjective norm is expressed by

$$SN_{j+1}^{k} = U_{sn}\left(nm_{j}^{k}\right),$$

where nm_j^k is the number of supportive messages received for behavior k during year j, and $U_{sn}$is a utility function that transfers the number of messages into a utility value ranging from 0 to 1.

The third predicting factor, PBC, is a person's perceived ease or difficulty of performing a particular behavior. As the CHF intervention is a collaborative behavior between hospitals and PCPs, the effects of the intervention are compromised if only one side of the agents conduct the intervention. Therefore, an agent's perceived ease or difficulty at successfully performing the intervention is influenced by other agents' behaviors. Hence, the PBC of a provider agent is defined as the perception of the percentage of other agents who are actually conducting the intervention. The process was modeled through agent interactions between hospital agents and PCP agents. An interaction happens when a patient agent is discharged and its hospital agent and PCP agent communicate to update the patient agent's information and simultaneously to perceive if the other agent is conducting the intervention.

The PBC for the behavior of conducting the intervention $(k = 1)$ in year $j + 1$ is formalized as

$$PBC_{j+1}^{1} = {}^{ni_j}\Big/{}_{ti_j},$$

where ni_j is the number of interactions in which the other agent is conducting intervention responses and ti_j is the total number of interactions. Because an agent does not need any collaboration from other agents to not conduct the intervention $(k = 0)$, $PBC_{j+1}{}^{0}$ was set to 1.

After the intention is formed, a softmax function can be used to calculate the probability that a provider agent will choose to conduct the intervention:

$$P_{j+1}^{1} = \frac{\exp\left(I_{j+1}^{1}/\tau\right)}{\exp\left(I_{j+1}^{0}/\tau\right) + \exp\left(I_{j+1}^{1}/\tau\right)}.$$

The parameter τ is used to adjust the irrational level of decision-makers. In the demonstrating simulation study, rational decision-making was assumed, so the behavior with higher intention will be performed. The users of the agent-based model can set the parameters to reasonable values for their specific context or learn them empirically.

Last, to examine the impacts of provider characteristics, three hypothetical types of provider agents were defined in the demonstrating simulation study by varying the weights of $\beta = [\beta_1, \beta_2]$. The three types of provider agents are profit-oriented with $\beta = [0.8, 0.2]$, quality-oriented with $\beta = [0.2, 0.8]$, and neutral with $\beta = [0.5, 0.5]$. Scenario analyses with different mixes of these three types of provider agents were conducted and are described in Section 3.

2.2.3 Payer agent

The payer agent hypothetically represents CMS in the model because it is the primary payer for CHF healthcare services. (Note. In the text below, all references to CMS are hypothetical. The study does not reflect the view of the CMS, rather solely the views of the authors.) The CMS will collect cost and quality data, as well as calculate and distribute the shared saving. To calculate the shared saving, two provider agent networks were included: the ACO network and controlled network, each of which serves a patient population with identical patient characteristics. At the end of each year or decision cycle, the total CHF-related healthcare costs per CHF patient will be calculated for each network. The cost difference between these two networks is the saving per CHF patient from the payer's perspective.

One key parameter of the shared saving payment model is shared saving rate (SSR), which defines the percentage of the total saving that will be awarded to providers. The shared saving per CHF patient is calculated by multiplying the saving per CHF patient with SSR, and the total shared saving is determined by multiplying the shared saving per CHF patient with the number of CHF patients that the ACO network serves.

The total shared saving will then be distributed among hospital agents and PCP agents in the ACO network. The distribution of the shared saving is defined by another key parameter: sharing rate to hospital (SRH), which is the percentage of the total shared saving distributed to hospital agents. Within each type of provider agent, the shared saving was assumed to be distributed equally. If the cost per CHF patient of the ACO network is higher than that of the controlled network, there will be no saving.

2.3 Healthcare costs

The cost analysis was conducted from different agents' perspectives. The cost for the payer agent representing CMS is the reimbursement paid to providers for CHF-related services plus the shared saving. For CHF-related hospitalization, the AHRQ's estimation [37] is used for costs of hospital service, and the physician inpatient cost is estimated to be 18 % of the reimbursement for hospital service [21, 38]. The reimbursement for outpatient visits is determined by the CMS Physician Fee Schedule [39].

For a hospital agent, negative margins were reported for hospital services of Medicare patients [40, 41]. A −8.4 margin for CHF inpatient services was estimated based on Medicare's reported reimbursement [42] and hospital operating costs [43, 44]. For CHF intervention cost, a meta-analysis of CHF interventions [12] showed that the pooled intervention cost was $108 per patient per month for a usually 6-month-long intervention. The intervention effects were assumed to last for 1 year, which gives us an average cost of $54 per patient per month.

A PCP agent's operating cost was estimated to be 60 % of its revenue [45]. The intervention cost from a PCP agent's perspective was defined as the opportunity cost of communicating with CHF care managers. If the time used for communication was 15 min per patient per year, it could be otherwise used for a standard outpatient visit reimbursed at $69 [39]. The healthcare costs are summarized in Table 3, and all values are converted into USD (2011) using the U.S. Consumer Price Index (CPI).

Table 3. Healthcare costs

Service	Amount paid by agent, USD (2011)		
	Payer agent	Hospital agent	PCP agent
CHF hospital cost	−14,822	−1,186	
Inpatient physician fee	−2,668		
Outpatient visit	−85		34
Intervention cost per patient per year		−648	−69

2.4 Model implementation

The demonstrating simulation study was implemented using AnyLogic version 6.6 (XJ Technologies, Chicago, IL). In the study, the simulation time was set at 5 simulation years, which is reasonable to test the effects of an ACO demonstration.

The model generates one singlepayer agent hypothetically representing CMS and two networks of provider agents (one ACO network and one controlled network). Both the provider networks are composed of three hospital agents and 15 PCP agents. The ACO network is reimbursed under the shared saving model, and the controlled network is reimbursed under the traditional Medicare fee-for-service (FFS) model. The simulation model generated 10,000 patient agents and randomly assigned them to the ACO networks or the controlled network. For each patient agent, the values of its characteristic variables were assigned on the basis of the joint distribution estimated.

At the end of each simulation year, the payer agent will collect the performance measures for both provider networks, including the payment per CHF patient, the hospital admission rate, and the CHF patient mortality rate. Using those data, the payer agent will calculate and distribute the shared saving to the provider agents in the ACO network. Then, the ACO provider agents will go through the decision-making process to determine if they will conduct the intervention in the next simulation year.

The outputs of each simulation run are the average saving to the payer agent per CHF patient per year, average annual CHF-related admission rate, and CHF patient mortality rate for each provider agent network over 5 simulation years. For each setting of the model input parameters, 500 simulation runs are performed to calculate the mean and 95 % level confidence interval.

3 SIMULATION RESULTS, MODEL VALIDATION, AND SCENARIO ANALYSES

A baseline analysis was conducted to compare the performance of an ACO health network and a controlled health network. Results below show the baseline model (Section 3.1) and its validation (Section 3.2). Section 3.3 describes the multiple scenario analyses conducted to examine the impacts of payment model designs and provider characteristics on the outcome measures. To examine the influence of provider types on the model outputs, three scenarios were created. The setting of the provider agent type in scenario one is the same with that in the baseline model. In scenario two, all the provider agents are profit-oriented, and in scenario three all the provider agents are quality-oriented. In each scenario, two key parameters of the shared saving payment model, i.e., SSR and SRH, were systematically varied to determine an optimal payment model design. The simulation was rerun for each combination of the values of SSR and SRH in each scenario. A sensitivity analysis was conducted to examine how the uncertainty in other key model inputs influenced the model outputs (Section 3.4).

3.1 Baseline model

In the baseline model, the three hospital agents in the ACO network were a profit-oriented agent, a quality-oriented agent, and a neutral agent. A

PCP agent in the ACO network had equal probability of being assigned as one of the three types. The key payment model parameters, SSR and SRH, were set at 0.5 and 0.7, respectively, which means half of the saving was shared with provider agents and 70 % of the shared saving was distributed to hospital agents.

The ACO network performed better in the CHF-related hospitalization rate and annual mortality rate of CHF patients owing to the implementation of evidence-based care. The annual CHF-related hospitalization rate was 63.94 % (95 % CI: 63.74–64.14 %) for the ACO network and 72.46 % (95 % CI: 71.78–73.14 %) for the controlled network. The annual mortality rate of CHF patients was 18.41 % (95 % CI: 18.33–18.49 %) for the ACO network and 19.72 % (95 % CI: 19.64–19.80 %) for the controlled network. From the payer's or the CMS's perspective, the average saving after distribution of the shared saving was $765 (95 % CI: $740–790) per CHF patient per year, or a 5.65 % saving compared with the $13,550 (95 % CI: $13,520–13,580) payment per CHF patient in the controlled network. The saving in the ACO network was mainly caused by the reduction in the hospitalization rate.

3.2 Model validation

Because the controlled network provides usual care and does not conduct intervention, its CHF-related hospitalization rate and mortality rate were used to validate the model with the value reported in literature. The mortality rate for CHF patients reported in clinical trials ranges from 15 to 28 % [46–48]. Note that their sample sizes are usually small, and this could cause larger variation in their estimations. Hence, the mortality rate in the model (19.72 %) is comparable to and within the range of the mortality rates reported in the literature.

Derived from the results of Chen et al. [27] and Fang et al. [26], the CHF-related hospitalization rate was estimated around 68.6 %. In addition, the SOLVD study [49], a large CHF trial whose estimates have been used by many CHF simulation studies, reported an average annual hospitalization rate of 72.9 %. The CHF-related hospitalization rate in the model (72.46 %) is therefore comparable to that reported in the literature.

3.3 Scenarios analyses

To examine the influence of provider types on the model outputs, three scenarios were created. The setting of the provider agent type in scenario one is the same as that in the baseline model. In scenario two, all the provider agents are profit-oriented, and in scenario three, all the provider agents are quality-oriented.

In each scenario, two key parameters of the shared saving payment model were systematically varied to determine an optimal payment (model design: SSR and SRH). The simulation was rerun for each combination of the values of SSR and SRH in each scenario. The results of the multiple runs were analyzed and used to generate Figs. 4, 5, 6, 7, 8, and 9.

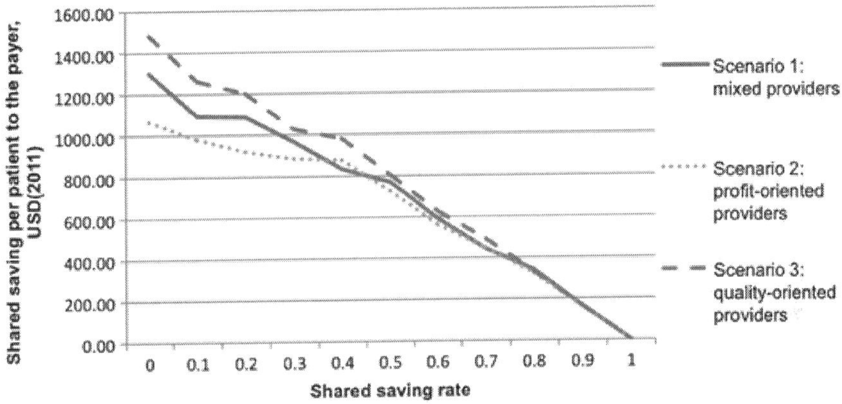

Figure 4. Shared saving to the payer by shared saving rate

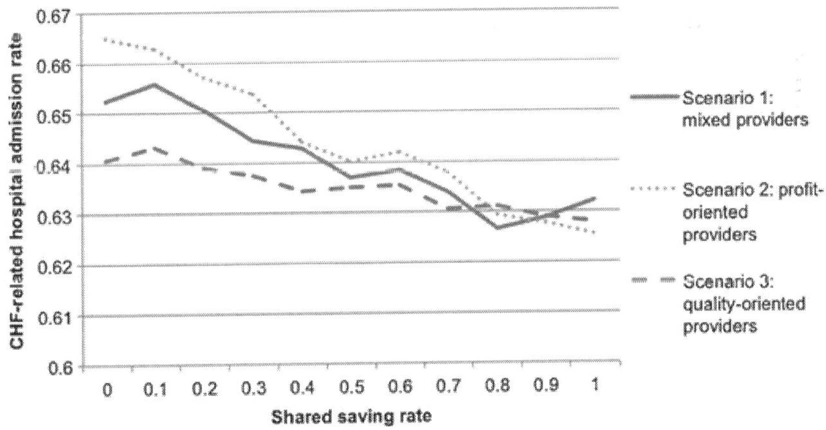

Figure 5. CHF-related hospitalization by shared saving rate

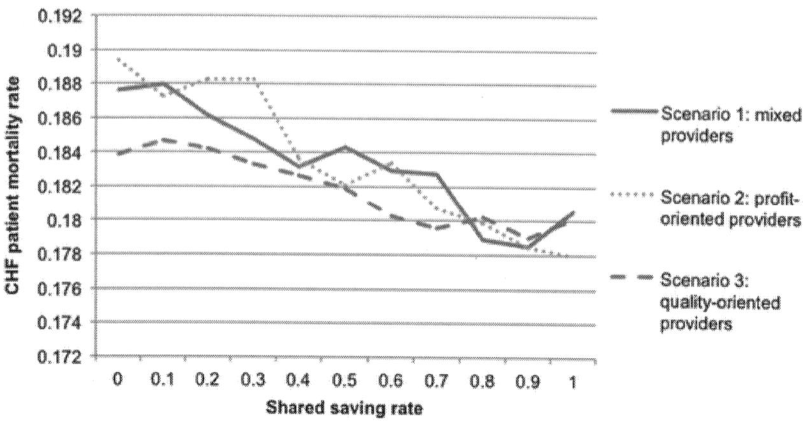

Figure 6. CHF patient mortality rate by shared saving rate

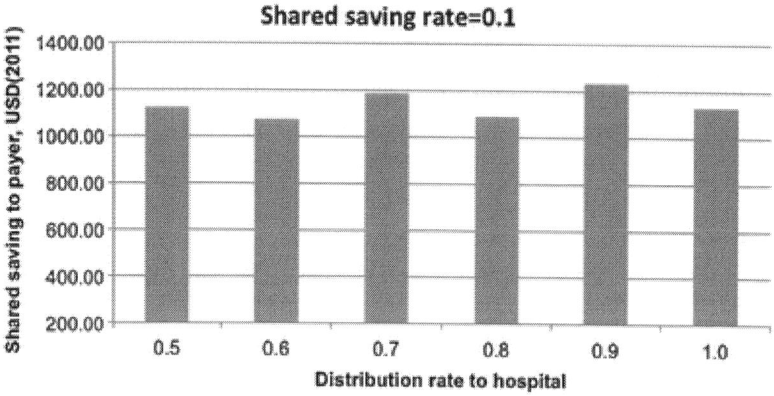

Figure 7. Shared saving to payer by sharing rate to hospital with the shared saving rate = 0.1

Figure 4 shows that the shared saving to payer (SSP) decreases as SSR increases in all three scenarios. When the payer agent increases the SSR, the resulting additional financial incentives motivate more provider agents to conduct the intervention, causing a reduction in annual CHF-related hospital admission rate (shown in Fig. 5) and in annual CHF patient mortality rate (shown in Fig. 6). The reduction in the CHF-related hospital admission rate then generates more total saving in the system; however, the SSP actually decreases because more saving is shared with the provider agents. Therefore, the payer agent is faced with a trade-off between financial return and quality of care when determining the value of SSR.

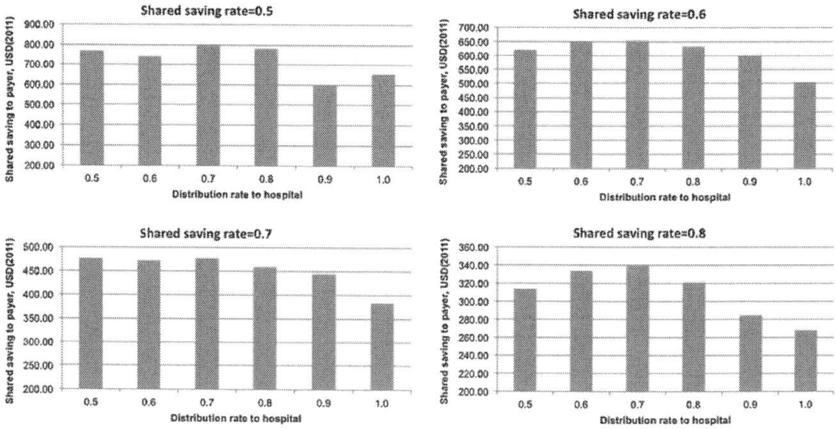

Figure 8 Shared saving to payer by sharing rate to hospital with shared saving rate from 0.5 to 0.8

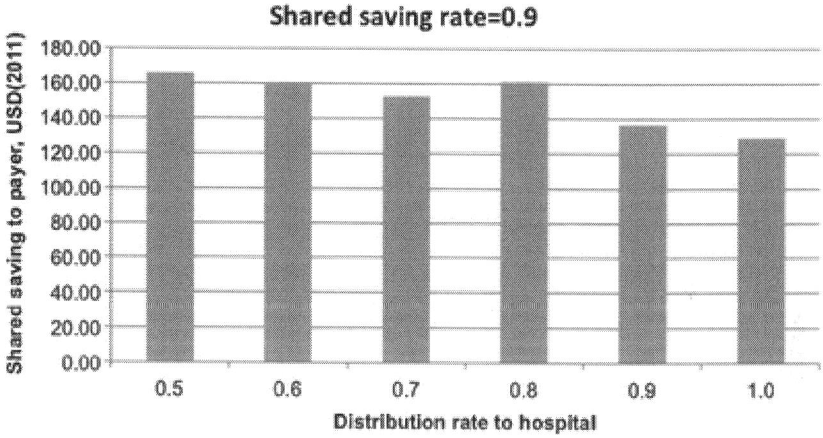

Figure 9. Shared saving to payer by sharing rate to hospital with the shared saving rate = 0.9

This scenario analysis also shows how provider agents in different scenarios respond to changes in SSR. As shown in Fig. 4, given the same SSR, scenario three (all the provider agents are quality-oriented) always yielded higher financial return to the payer agent, followed in order by scenario one and scenario two. The profit-oriented provider agents are most sensitive to the changes in SSR.

The effects of varying SRH given a certain SSR were further examined. Analyzing the payer's financial return (i.e., SSP by SRH in scenario one), different patterns were observed when the SSR was set at different values. When the SSR was low, there was no clear relationship between SSP and SRH (shown in Fig. 7 when the SSR was set at 0.1). Even if all the saving was distributed to hospital agents (when SRH is 1), it was not enough to cover the intervention cost for the hospital agents and motivate their behavior changes.

When SSR was set to 0.5–0.8, a pattern emerged with a concave shape, whereby the maximal financial return is achieved when the SRH is 0.7 (shown in Fig. 8). Because the effects of the intervention can be fully achieved only when both the hospital agents and PCP agents are conducting it, the 0.7 value of SRH seems to be a good balance point that can motivate both the hospital and PCP agents to conduct the intervention and thus achieve a maximal financial return for the payer agent.

When SSR was high (0.9), Fig. 9 shows a relatively flat trend of SSR when SRH was around 0.5–0.7, and when the SRH was greater than 0.7, SSR decreased as SRH increased. Because the hospital agent had enough financial incentives to conduct the intervention, a clear hospital agent behavior switch was not observed as SRH increased from 0.5 to 0.7. Similar patterns have also been observed in the other two scenarios.

3.4 Sensitivity analysis

After the scenario analyses were conducted on the shared saving payment model and provider types, a sensitivity analysis was conducted to examine how the uncertainty in other key model inputs influenced the model outputs (using SSP). In general, for each testing parameter, a higher value (increased by 20 %) and a lower value (decreased by 20 %) were tested.

From the results (shown in Fig. 10), SSP was most sensitive to the effects of the intervention on hospital admission rates. This was expected because the saving was mainly generated by the reduction in hospitalization. Next, the effects of the intervention on CHF patient mortality rate were discussed. This is important because the quality outcomes would also affect provider agents' attitude toward the intervention. Hospital intervention and operating costs, both affecting hospital agents' profit, were the other two sensitive parameters. Because the hospital agent has the financial capability and covered the main cost of the intervention (such as hiring care managers), SSP was not sensitive to the parameters on the PCP agent's side.

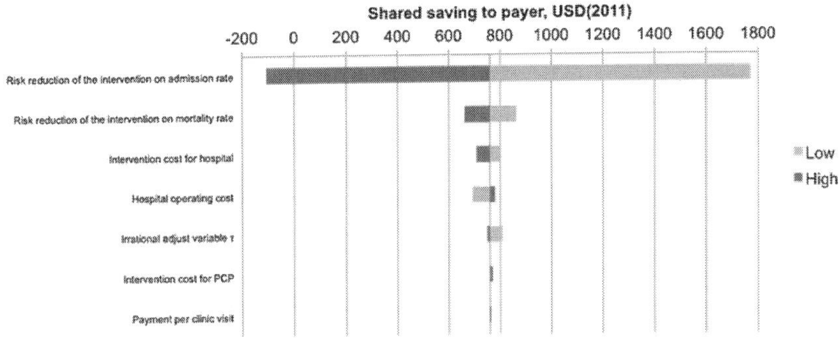

Figure 10. Sensitivity analysis to identify influence of model inputs uncertainty on the shared saving to payer output

4 DISCUSSION

How to provide incentives to improve shared accountability in U.S. healthcare systems is a difficult policy issue with a great deal of uncertainties and trade-offs [50]. The CHF agent-based simulation model demonstrated and quantified how different implementations of the ACO and the shared saving payment model can influence provider behavior regarding the evidence-based intervention and therefore generated different financial and quality outcomes. The model can help decision-makers better understand the complexity and risks of ACO design and facilitate more informed decision-making.

From CMS's perspective, objectives include both controlling the cost and promoting the quality of care. The scenario analysis showed that there was a trade-off between the payer's financial return and the quality outcomes when setting SSR. The model can help decision-makers understand the constraints when determining SSR. In a hypothetical scenario, if CMS wants to achieve a quality target to control the CHF-related hospital admission rate to 64 % when all the providers are profit-oriented, the model results indicate that CMS should set SSR at 51 %, which would generate a $700 saving per CHF patient per year (shown in Fig. 11). The payer therefore would not achieve a financial objective, say $1,000 saving per patient, at the same time. Hence, with the understanding of these constraints, CMS can determine an SSR value that can balance its two objectives.

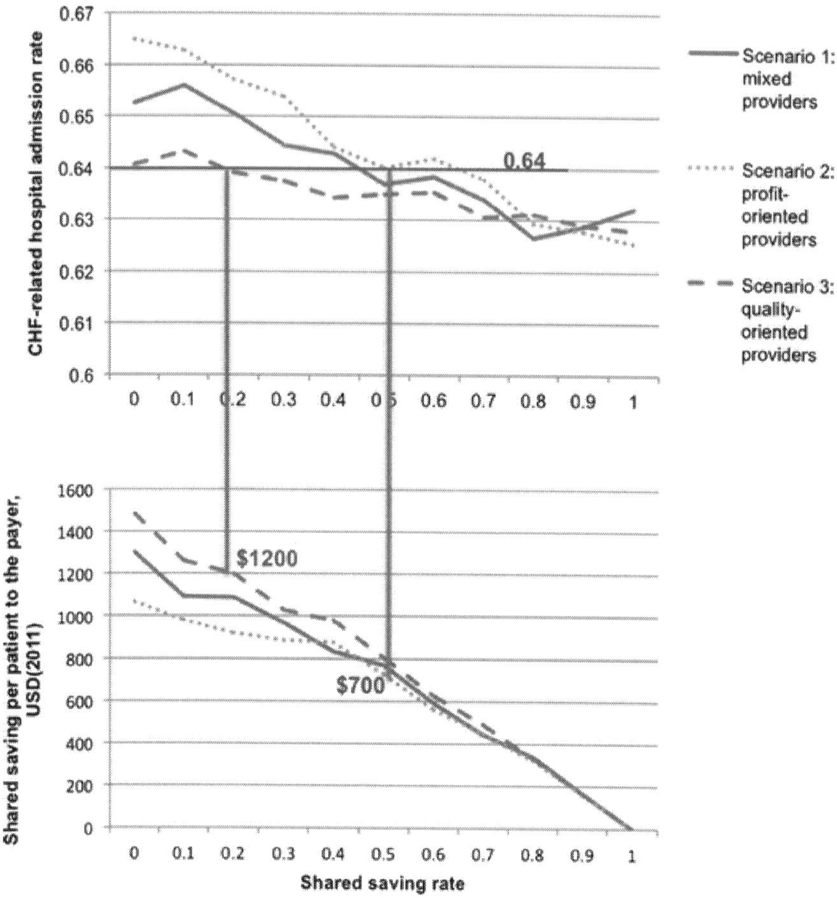

Figure 11. Effects of provider type on shared savings

Once the SSR is decided, the next step is to determine an SRH value that can motivate both the hospital agents and PCP agents to work together on the CHF intervention. Creating a mechanism to promote cooperation between hospitals and physicians is difficult, and an immature payment model may incite tension and competition between hospitals and physicians [51]. The simulation results have identified different patterns of outcomes by SRH, which can help decision-makers choose the optimal SRH value to maximize the outcomes based on the configuration of SSR.

The model can help analyze how provider types and priorities could influence payment model designs. In the same hypothetical scenario shown in Fig. 11, if all the providers are quality-oriented, CMS can set SSR at 18 % to achieve the same goal of controlling the CHF-related hospital admission rate to 64 %. This setting will generate a $1,200 saving per CHF patient per year instead of a saving of $700 when all the providers are profit-oriented.

This result shows that the payer agent needs to provide different levels of incentives for different types of providers to achieve the same level of quality outcomes. This brings up the problem that the more profit-oriented a provider agent is, the more financial reward he/she will receive from the payer. This problem could be addressed by expanding the payer's strategies to develop mixed motives to simulate all types of providers [52], such as aligning the payment with quality requirements, public reporting of quality performance, and initiating education programs to increase awareness of quality of care [53–55].

The sensitivity analysis showed that the outcomes were most sensitive to the effects of the intervention, followed by the intervention cost. Hence, selecting the cost-effective intervention is critical for the success of an ACO. For broader applications beyond CHF, ACO stakeholders need to wisely choose improvement opportunities to pursue based on their capability and current situations.

There are some limitations to the agent-based model for CHF care. First, the model parameters are based on the best information obtainable. The results reflect a national average trend for Medicare patients. Adjustments should be made when referring to some specific patient demographics, provider characteristics, and geographic locations. Second, the weight for each behavior-predicting factor in the provider decision module is not drawn from a survey of physicians. A national physician's behavior survey with information to provide the values of these weights was not identified in a literature search. Hence, the users of the model can configure the provider agent parameters on the basis of the characteristics of the providers with whom they are working.

5 CONCLUSION

The agent-based simulation model provides predictive analytics and recommendations for decision-makers to make informed decisions on how to design an ACO and its corresponding shared saving payment model, given their current provider and patient population environment, to maximize the desired outcomes.

The agent-based simulation model has identified critical determinants of an optimal design for the payment model that can motivate provider behavior changes to achieve maximum financial and quality outcomes. The model has quantified the trade-off between the payer's financial return and the quality outcomes, helping decision-makers configure the shared saving model based on their objectives.

The complexity and risks of the ACO model design generate a need for modeling and simulation tools that are flexible, capable, and user-adjustable to facilitate the design and implementation of an ACO model for different disease conditions, payment models, and provider and patient agent characteristics. For future use of the model, users can, based on their situations and objectives, configure the ACO design parameters, generate corresponding patient and provider agents, and then analyze different scenarios and optimize their ACO models.

This study presents the promising application possibilities of ABM, an increasingly important method to support policy and management decision-making in broad and complex healthcare systems. Different from aggregated-level modeling methods, ABM can incorporate various goals and behaviors of individual stakeholders. It is also capable of modeling agent communication and interactions. These advantages make ABM a closer approximation of the real world. Also, because each agent represents a real entity in the health system (such as a physician or a patient), healthcare practitioners are likely to understand and accept the agent-based model. Therefore, the solutions recommended and insights generated for an ACO model design by the agent-based model increase the chance of improving the real health system.

ACKNOWLEDGMENTS

The authors acknowledge the California HealthCare Foundation for a grant to evaluate the Lean Initiative in four California public hospitals to improve performance of CHF care (Grant identification number 08-1889, Principal Investigator Dr. Shinyi Wu). This evaluation project has helped the development of the CHF simulation model presented in the paper. The authors also acknowledge the support from the USC Roybal Center for Health Policy Simulation (Grant number: P30 AG024968), a National Institute on Aging–funded center for developing better models to assess the impact of aging on health, health spending, and healthcare delivery sponsored by the Leonard D. Schaeffer Center for Health Policy and Economics. The authors are grateful for the insights, constructive criticisms, and support from Dr. Carl Kesselman, Dr. Michael Nichol, Dr. Alex Chen, and Dr. Azad Madni of the University of Southern California for this work.

REFERENCES

1. Newman D (2010) Accountable care organizations and the Medicare Shared Savings Program. Congressional Research Service

2. Fisher ES, Staiger DO, Bynum JP, Gottlieb DJ (2007) Creating accountable care organizations: the extended hospital medical staff. Health Aff (Millwood) 26(1):w44–w57

3. Fisher ES, McClellan MB, Bertko J, Lieberman SM, Lee JJ, Lewis JL, Skinner JS (2009) Fostering accountable health care: moving forward in medicare. Health Aff (Millwood) 28(2):w219–w231

4. U.S. House of Representatives (2010) Compilation of patient protection and affordable care act [as amended through May 1 2010]. Washington, DC

5. Centers for Medicare & Medicaid Services (2011) Medicare shared savings program. https://www.cms.gov/sharedsavingsprogram. Accessed 9 March 2014

6. Delbanco SF, Anderson KM, Catherine Eikel Major, Kiser MB, Toner BW (2011) Promising payment reform: risk-sharing with accountable care organizations. The Commonwealth Fund

7. McClellan M, McKethan AN, Lewis JL, Roski J, Fisher ES (2010) A national strategy to put accountable care into practice. Health Aff (Millwood) 29(5):982–990

8. Shields MC, Patel PH, Manning M, Sacks L (2011) A model for integrating independent physicians into accountable care organizations. Health Aff (Millwood) 30(1):161–172

9. Valdez RS, Ramly E, Brennan PF (2010) Industrial and systems engineering and health care: critical areas of research—final report. Agency for Healthcare Research and Quality, Rockville

10. Philbin EF, DiSalvo TG (1999) Prediction of hospital readmission for heart failure: development of a simple risk score based on administrative data. J Am Coll Cardiol 33(6):1560–1566

11. McAlister FA, Stewart S, Ferrua S, McMurray JJ (2004) Multidisciplinary strategies for the management of heart failure patients at high risk for admission: a systematic review of randomized trials. J Am Coll Cardiol 44(4):810–819

12. Phillips CO, Wright SM, Kern DE, Singa RM, Shepperd S, Rubin HR (2004) Comprehensive discharge planning with postdischarge support for older patients with congestive heart failure: a meta-analysis. JAMA 291(11):1358–1367

13. Macal CM, North MJ (2010) Tutorial on agent-based modelling and simulation. J Simul 4(3):151–162

14. Bonabeau E (2002) Agent-based modeling: methods and techniques for simulating human systems. Proc Natl Acad Sci U S A 99:7280–7287

15. Bahrami H, Kronmal R, Bluemke DA, Olson J, Shea S, Liu K, Burke GL, Lima JA (2008) Differences in the incidence of congestive heart failure by ethnicity: the multi-ethnic study of atherosclerosis. Arch Intern Med 168(19):2138–2145

16. Bertoni AG, Hundley WG, Massing MW, Bonds DE, Burke GL, Goff DC Jr (2004) Heart failure prevalence, incidence, and mortality in the elderly with diabetes. Diabetes Care 27(3):699–703

17. Conen D, Chae CU, Guralnik JM, Glynn RJ (2010) Influence of blood pressure and blood pressure change on the risk of congestive heart failure in the elderly. Swiss Med Wkly 140(13–14):202–208

18. He J, Ogden LG, Bazzano LA, Vupputuri S, Loria C, Whelton PK (2001) Risk factors for congestive heart failure in US men and women: NHANES I epidemiologic follow-up study. Arch Intern Med 161(7):996–1002

19. Chan DC, Heidenreich PA, Weinstein MC, Fonarow GC (2008) Heart failure disease management programs: a cost-effectiveness analysis. Am Heart J 155(2):332–338

20. Nichol G, Kaul P, Huszti E, Bridges JF (2004) Cost-effectiveness of cardiac resynchronization therapy in patients with symptomatic heart failure. Ann Intern Med 141(5):343–351

21. Cowper PA, DeLong ER, Whellan DJ, Allen LaPointe NM, Califf RM (2004) Economic effects of beta-blocker therapy in patients with heart failure. Am J Med 116(2):104–111

22. Curtis LH, Whellan DJ, Hammill BG, Hernandez AF, Anstrom KJ, Shea AM, Schulman KA (2008) Incidence and prevalence of heart failure in elderly persons, 1994–2003. Arch Intern Med 168(4):418–424

23. Grenard JL, Munjas BA, Adams JL, Suttorp M, Maglione M, McGlynn EA, Gellad WF (2011) Depression and medication adherence in the treatment of chronic diseases in the United States: a meta-analysis. J Gen Intern Med 26(10):1175–1182

24. Nichols GA, Gullion CM, Koro CE, Ephross SA, Brown JB (2004) The incidence of congestive heart failure in type 2 diabetes: an update. Diabetes Care 27(8):1879–1884

25. Arias E (2010) United States life tables, 2006. National Vital Stat Rep 58(21):1–40

26. Fang J, Mensah GA, Croft JB, Keenan NL (2008) Heart failure–related hospitalization in the U.S., 1979 to 2004. J Am Coll Cardiol 52(6):428–434

27. Chen J, Normand SL, Wang Y, Krumholz HM (2011) National and regional trends in heart failure hospitalization and mortality rates for Medicare beneficiaries, 1998–2008. JAMA 306(15):1669–1678

28. McBean AM, Li S, Gilbertson DT, Collins AJ (2004) Differences in diabetes prevalence, incidence, and mortality among the elderly of four racial/ethnic groups: whites, blacks, hispanics, and asians. Diabetes Care 27(10):2317–2324

29. Dannenberg AL, Garrison RJ, Kannel WB (1988) Incidence of hypertension in the Framingham study. Am J Public Health 78(6):676–679

30. Dischinger PC, Apostolides AY, Entwisle G, Hebel JR (1981) Hypertension incidence in an inner-city black population. J Chronic Dis 34(8):405–413

31. Kelton WD, Law AM (2000) Simulation modeling and analysis, 3rd edn. McGraw Hill, Boston

32. Duguay C, Chetouane F (2007) Modeling and improving emergency department systems using discrete event simulation. Simulation 83(4):311–320

33. Shechter SM, Bryce CL, Alagoz O, Kreke JE, Stahl JE, Schaefer AJ, Angus DC, Roberts MS (2005) A clinically based discrete-event simulation of end-stage liver disease and the organ allocation process. Med Decis Making 25(2):199–209

34. Chen L, Hay JW (2004) Cost-effectiveness of primary implanted cardioverter defibrillator for sudden death prevention in congestive heart failure. Cardiovasc Drugs Ther 18(2):161–170

35. Bogner HR, Miller SD, de Vries HF, Chhatre S, Jayadevappa R (2010) Assessment of cost and health resource utilization for elderly patients with heart failure and diabetes mellitus. J Card Fail 16(6):454–460

36. Ajzen I (1991) The theory of planned behavior. Organ Behav Hum Decis 50(2):179–211

37. AHRQ (2010) 2010 National Healthcare Quality Report. Agency for healthcare research and quality. http://www.ahrq.gov/research/findings/nhqrdr/nhqr10/nhqr10.pdf. Accessed 9 March 2014

38. Angus DC, Linde-Zwirble WT, Tam SW, Ghali JK, Sabolinski ML, Villagra VG, Winkelmayer WC, Worcel M (2005) Cost-effectiveness of fixed-dose combination of isosorbide dinitrate and hydralazine therapy for blacks with heart failure. Circulation 112(24):3745–3753

39. Centers for Medicare & Medicaid Services (2012) Medicare program: physician fee schedule look-up tool. http://www.cms.gov/Medicare/Medicare-Fee-for-Service-Payment/PFSlookup/index.html. Accessed 10 Nov 2012

40. Titler MG, Jensen GA, Dochterman JM, Xie XJ, Kanak M, Reed D, Shever LL (2008) Cost of hospital care for older adults with heart failure: medical, pharmaceutical, and nursing costs. Health Serv Res 43(2):635–655

41. AHA (2012) Underpayment by Medicare and Medicaid fact sheet, 2012 update

42. Centers for Medicare & Medicaid Services (2011) Medicare program; hospital inpatient prospective payment systems for acute care hospitals and the long-term care hospital prospective payment system and FY 2012 rates; hospitals' FTE resident caps for graduate medical education payment. http://www.gpo.gov/fdsys/pkg/FR-2011-08-18/pdf/2011-19719.pdf. Accessed 20 March 2014

43. Healthcare Financial Management Association (2010) National average costs by department for heart failure and shock. Healthc Financ Manage 64(3):122–123

44. Healthcare Financial Management Association (2011) Medicare claims show remarkable variations by region, hospital ownership, and teaching status. Healthc Financ Manage 65(3):142–144

45. Rickert J (2012) Do Medicare and Medicaid payment rates really threaten physicians with bankruptcy? HealthAffairs Blog. http://healthaffairs.org/blog/2012/10/02/do-medicare-and-medicaid-payment-rates-really-threaten-physicians-with-bankruptcy/. Accessed 9 March 2014

46. Doughty RN, Wright SP, Pearl A, Walsh HJ, Muncaster S, Whalley GA, Gamble G, Sharpe N (2002) Randomized, controlled trial of integrated heart failure management: the Auckland Heart Failure Management Study. Eur Heart J 23(2):139–146

47. Capomolla S, Febo O, Ceresa M, Caporotondi A, Guazzotti G, La Rovere M, Ferrari M, Lenta F, Baldin S, Vaccarini C, Gnemmi M, Pinna G, Maestri R, Abelli P, Verdirosi S, Cobelli F (2002) Cost/utility ratio in chronic heart failure: comparison between heart failure management program delivered by day-hospital and usual care. J Am Coll Cardiol 40(7):1259–1266

48. Cline CM, Israelsson BY, Willenheimer RB, Broms K, Erhardt LR (1998) Cost effective management programme for heart failure reduces hospitalisation. Heart 80(5):442–446

49. The SOLVD Investigators (1991) Effect of enalapril on survival in patients with reduced left ventricular ejection fractions and congestive heart failure. N Engl J Med 325(5):293–302

50. Epstein AM (2009) Revisiting readmissions—changing the incentives for shared accountability. N Engl J Med 360(14):1457–1459

51. Berenson RA, Ginsburg PB, May JH (2007) Hospital-physicians relations: cooperation, competition, or separation? Health Aff (Millwood) 26(1):w31–w43

52. Biller-Andorno N, Lee TH (2013) Ethical physician incentives—from carrots and sticks to shared purpose. N Engl J Med 368(11):980–982

53. Lindenauer PK, Remus D, Roman S, Rothberg MB, Benjamin EM, Ma A, Bratzler DW (2007) Public reporting and pay for performance in hospital quality improvement. N Engl J Med 356(5):486–496

54. Pham HH, Coughlan J, O'Malley AS (2006) The impact of quality-reporting programs on hospital operations. Health Aff (Millwood) 25(5):1412–1422

55. Rosenthal MB, Fernandopulle R, Song HR, Landon B (2004) Paying for quality: providers' incentives for quality improvement. Health Aff (Millwood) 23(2):127

5

CONTINUITY OF CARE IN COMMUNITY MIDWIFERY

John Bowers[1], Helen Cheyne[2], Gillian Mould[3], Miranda Page[4]

[1].Stirling Management SchoolUniversity of StirlingStirlingUK

[2].Nursing, Midwifery and Allied Health Professions' Research UnitUniversity of StirlingStirlingUK

[3].Stirling Management SchoolUniversity of StirlingStirlingUK

[4].Nursing, Midwifery and Allied Health Professions' Research UnitUniversity of StirlingStirlingUK

ABSTRACT

Continuity of care is often critical in delivering high quality health care. However, it is difficult to achieve in community health care where shift patterns and a need to minimise travelling time can reduce the scope for allocating staff to patients. Community midwifery is one example of such a challenge in the National Health Service where postnatal care typically involves a series of home visits. Ideally mothers would receive all of their antenatal and postnatal care from the same midwife. Minimising the number of staff-handovers helps ensure a better relationship between mothers and midwives, and provides more opportunity for staff to identify emerging problems over a series of home visits. This study examines the allocation and routing of midwives in the community using a variant of a multiple travelling salesmen problem algorithm incorporating staff preferences to explore trade-offs between travel time and continuity of care. This algorithm was integrated in a simulation to assess the additional effect of staff availability due to shift patterns and part-time working. The results indicate that continuity of care can be achieved with relatively small increases in travel time. However, shift patterns are problematic: perfect continuity of care is impractical but if there is a degree of flexibility in the visit schedule, reasonable continuity is feasible.

Keywords: Home health care, Staff scheduling, Routing, Simulation

1 BACKGROUND

a. Continuity of care and maternity services

Across many areas of health care, continuity of care is often cited as a major element in patient satisfaction, improving communications and helping to establish greater trust and a willingness to confide in the professional carer. Health professionals also value continuity of care; it can increase their sense of responsibility and tendency to act as an advocate for the patient [1]. Continuity of care can improve both the effectiveness of health care and its efficiency with fewer staff-handovers and more consistency in the care provided. While the benefits of continuity of care are dependent on the particular service, it can have particular value in community-based care. Greater continuity of care can reduce the demand for additional services, reduce hospital admissions and increase patient satisfaction [2, 3]. In maternal health services women receive care at various stages: antenatal, intrapartum and postnatal, both in the community and in hospital. This can lead to a disrupted pattern of care with a mother experiencing many different professional staff [4].

Continuity of care has many interpretations [1]. "Information continuity" emphasises the need to ensure effective communications between health care professionals, while "longitudinal" and "relational" continuity focus on the patient having interactions with as few staff as possible, and sufficient time to develop a useful relationship. This study focuses on longitudinal continuity of care and in particular an objective of minimising the number of staff-handovers. In the United Kingdom's National Health Service (NHS) the delivery of maternity care varies in different areas. However, a mother usually attends community based antenatal clinics, receiving advice and care from a midwife before giving birth in hospital, or midwifery led unit. Most mothers are then discharged between 6 and 48 h after giving birth, followed by four or five postnatal care visits at home. Postnatal visits serve many purposes: specific medical checks of the mother and baby; parenting and feeding advice; identifying the need for additional support due to social conditions or the mother's mental health. Continuity of care helps develop a trusting relationship with the mother and the midwife can monitor the more tacit signs of changing behaviour over a number of visits.

Various models of care have been proposed to maximise continuity of care from pregnancy to 28 days following birth [4]. Team-midwifery provides co-ordinated care from a number of staff; information-continuity can be provided but relational-continuity is impaired. Caseload-midwifery, where women receive individualized care, ideally from a single midwife, offers comprehensive continuity but this model of care is very difficult to deliver in practice.

While antenatal care can be planned around pre-determined stages of pregnancy the unpredictable nature of birth makes complete continuity through all stages of maternity care problematic. It was suggested that longitudinal, relational continuity of care was impractical even for just the antenatal and postnatal stages, given the difficulties of staff availability and the need to avoid excessive travel. The objective of the current study was to develop the understanding of the logistical and resource implications of delivering continuity of care, as part of a larger programme examining the design of postnatal care in the NHS in the United Kingdom. Even if 100 % continuity of care is an unrealistic target, is it feasible to achieve a reasonably high degree of continuity without incurring substantial extra travelling costs? The study examines a typical area in an attempt to determine whether continuity of care is feasible in community midwifery.

b.A home health care problem

The study is an example of the Home Health Care Problem (HHCP) [5, 6], which can be categorised as a variant of the Multiple Travelling Salesman Problem [7]. In most HHCP studies, the focus is to minimise the total staff travelling time while respecting time windows. The current study does not consider time windows: at present the common practice in community care in the NHS is to organise home visits assuming that the patients have no significant time constraints. Instead this study emphasises the desire for continuity of care. Other HHCP studies have considered the allocation and routing of single sets of home care visits; the current study is concerned with providing a series of visits for each patient over a number of days, striving to maximise continuity of care, while minimising the total travel time. Thus a patient's preference for a particular member of staff on a particular visit i is determined by their allocation of staff for visit $i-1$. Other HHCP studies have incorporated patient preferences, either as a constraint [8–10] or as a component of the objective function [11], but the preferences were modelled as being determined externally and part of the problem specification, independent of the allocation and routing solution. In the current study the problem specification for any one day is dependent on allocation decisions of the previous days, increasing the dimensionality of the HHCP. A study [9] of a more traditional vehicle routing problem developed a "record-to-record" algorithm to include a hard constraint that customers should have their orders delivered by the same driver over a series of days. However, in the current problem meeting the patient's preference is treated as a soft constraint, accepting that a need to avoid excessive journey times and to respect staff daily availability will often preclude perfect continuity of care. Patient preferences have been included as soft constraints in other studies, using penalty costs in the objective function. However, the problems examined had substantial hard constraints, notably strict time windows that severely limited the number of permutations, enabling the final routing and sequencing to be determined using enumeration [11].

The scale of the problem was further increased by the need to consider the stochastic nature of demand, over time and geography. The current study considers daily sets of requests, including both newly discharged mothers requiring their first postnatal visit and follow-up visits for other mothers. The daily problems can be classified as static and stochastic [12] and were explored with an allocation and routing algorithm embedded in a Monte-Carlo simulation framework, sampling the new mothers according to specified geographical distributions. In practice there are also some dynamic features to the routing problem [12] with mothers being absent and repeat visits having to be made. This additional complexity was omitted from the present study. An additional requirement for the algorithm was that the resultant simulation should provide a sufficiently rapid response to provide statistically robust results for a variety of experiments exploring various policy options and developing an appreciation of the critical trade-offs between efficiency and the quality of care as measured by the preference satisfaction. A similar challenging requirement is found in designing operational systems. One system, LAPS CARE, which included continuity of care as a key quality objective, adopted a repeated matching algorithm, uses splitting to help avoid local optima [9]. As in other application-focussed HHCP studies [13], the choice of algorithm was strongly influenced by the requirements for speed of response and the flexibility to readily incorporate additional constraints, such as varying staff availability.

Other studies of the Multiple Travelling Salesmen Problem [14], and variants of the HHCP [13] in particular, have used algorithms based on the classic Clarke-Wright heuristics [15] to deliver speed and flexibility with only a small reduction in performance compared to optimal solutions [16]. This study adopted such an approach, developing an algorithm that was then incorporated in a discrete event simulation to explore the trade-offs between travel time and continuity of care. This provided a practical basis for examining policy issues, for example incorporating typical staff availability as dictated by their shift patterns when determining a possible target for continuity of care for community postnatal care. However, further research would be valuable, examining the viability of adapting more sophisticated branch-and-price algorithms [8] or genetic algorithms [17]. Even if such approaches cannot be readily incorporated in a simulation, they would provide a useful basis for comparison when assessing the performance of the modified Clarke-Wright algorithm, and identifying possible better choices.

The study just considers the staff travel time, though this will be strongly correlated to costs: the mileage expenses paid to midwives, their salaries and also the opportunity costs which could be significant in areas where there is a shortage of midwives.

c. Developing the model

The paper first considers a self-contained HHCP, developing a simple allocation and routing algorithm based on a modification of the Clarke-Wright [15] heuristics. This is illustrated in a small example, demonstrating the possible trade-off between travel time and satisfying preferences. The algorithm is embedded in a simulation, incorporating some of the basic characteristics of organising community care. This simulation is then refined to include more of the features of community postnatal care, notably that the preferences are generated by the desire to have the same midwife visiting a mother on every occasion, or at least striving for a high level of continuity of care. Later sections introduce more refinements reflecting the problems of shift patterns and part-time working, and also the value of flexibility in visits rather than having to keep to a strict sequence.

2 THE TRAVELLING NURSES' PROBLEM

a. A variant of the multiple travelling salesmen problem

The trade-offs between continuity of care and travelling time require a reasonably efficient staff allocation and routing algorithm. The problem could be described as a variant of the multiple travelling salesman problems with load balancing [7]. The multiple travelling salesmen problem considers the allocation of patients to staff selected from a team with the objective of minimising total travel time while considering the relative workloads. The current problem is distinguished by a patient's preference for specific staff, notably the staff that provided the care on the previous visit. It may be acceptable to have an anonymous salesman visit a customer but in health services it is important to have the same trusted staff: the travelling nurses' problem introduces additional allocation and routing challenges.

The objective of the current study was to inform the design of postnatal care. A model was required that could be used to explore various policies and undertake sensitivity analyses of key design parameters to develop a better understanding of the implications of continuity of care. The major requirement was for an algorithm that could be readily incorporated in a simulation model. While the algorithm had to provide good solutions to the travelling nurses' problem, speed and ease of use were also necessary. The approach adopted in this study was based on the classic multiple travelling salesmen problem algorithm [15]. The Clarke-Wright algorithm assumes an initial solution with simple journeys directly to and returning from each of the locations to the central depot. The possibility of introducing single new links is considered, identifying the potential savings in travel time. A "greedy" approach is adopted, selecting the new link offering the largest saving, repeating the process until all of the requests have been satisfied. While the Clarke-Wright algorithm does not always provide optimal solutions, it offers good solutions [16], speed and a flexibility that have been exploited in many variants of the capacitated vehicle routing problem [13, 14]. This study modified the Clarke-Wright algorithm, including an additional component in the "saving" to reflect the benefit of the chosen staff matching the preference of the particular patient. This additional "preference saving" (*PS*) reflects the relative priorities for minimising travel time or maximising preference satisfaction. When *PS* = 0 there is no benefit in matching staff to patients, with a small value of *PS*, there is some reallocation of staff to patients, satisfying preferences as long as no major diversions are required. As the value of *PS* is increased, there is greater emphasis on matching staff to patients' preferences. With large values of *PS*, greater than the mean travel time between patients' homes, the large majority of patients' preferences will be satisfied. When *PS* >> mean travel time between patients, the problem degenerates into a set of independent sub-problems minimising the total travel time of each member of staff separately. Although heuristics based on the Clarke-Wright savings usually perform well, it is possible to identify test cases in which the algorithm offers far from optimal solutions. In some applications this failing in specific cases could be critical but is less important in a simulation-based study. However, further study might usefully explore alternative solutions and the ranges of validity of the current simple algorithm. Branch and bound or genetic algorithms may not be practical when analysing multiple sets of visit requests, as required in simulation experiments, but they would provide a valuable comparison to determine the range of validity for the simple algorithm adopted in this study.

b. The travelling nurses' algorithm

Consider a set of requests for patient visits, with each patient j having a preferred member of staff n_j. The travel time from patient j to patient k is c_{jk}, and c_{j0} is the time to travel from patient j to the depot or base station. Extending a member of staff's route, as in the Clarke Wright algorithm, typically involves adding a new, previous unallocated request j, to a request k at the start or end of a chain of links defining a staff member's sequence of visits. Adding a new link to the start of a sequence implies travel from the depot to patient j and then to the patient k, producing the standard Clarke-Wright saving of:

$$s_{jk} = c_{j0} + c_{0k} - c_{jk} \tag{1}$$

Similar savings may be achieved by adding new links to the end, rather than the start of the evolving chain of links, though it cannot always be assumed that the travel times are symmetrical. In the travelling nurses' problem, the saving is dependent on the particular staff v allocated. If the new link involves employing the preferred staff to visit request j, then a greater saving may be achieved:

$$s_{jkv} = c_{j0} + c_{0k} - c_{jk} + PS \quad \text{if } v = n_j \tag{2}$$

When identifying the initial link in the development of a staff member's route, it is possible that both previously unallocated requests j and k have the same preference and the saving is greater with a preference saving associated with both patients:

$$s_{jkv} = c_{j0} + c_{0k} - c_{jk} + 2PS \quad \text{if } v = n_j = n_k \tag{3}$$

Thus when PS is large, compared to the mean travel time between patients, the greatest savings will be associated with patients having identical staff preferences, living close to each other but at a large distance from the base depot: such links will be prioritized when constructing staff routes.

The complete set of potential links is identified, with separate entries for each option corresponding to Eqs 1–3, and then ordered to produce a list S'. Each entry in S', beginning with the one offering the greatest potential savings, is considered in turn, checking whether the new link is feasible, given the state of the evolving allocation and routing solution. Visits are added to each staff's sequence developing routes in parallel until all requests have been allocated, or no more staff-time is available. The algorithm is illustrated in Fig. 1; it involves multiple iterations, reconsidering some potential links since they may only become relevant as the routes evolve. The algorithm constructs routes in parallel for each member of staff; a parallel approach is often recommended for multiple vehicle routing problems [18]. When considering a potential link in *S'* there are two main requirements:

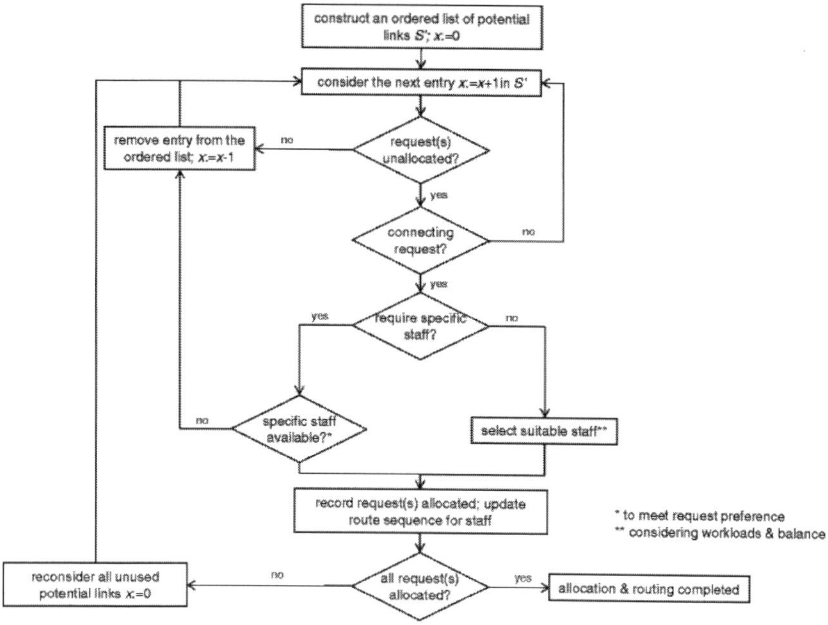

Figure 1 Travelling Nurses' algorithm

- Have the request(s) *j* and *k* already been satisfied; if not is one of them available at the start, or end, of an existing chain of links defining a staff's route?
- If the saving associated with the potential link is dependent on a particular member of staff, are the staff available? This assessment compares the allocated workloads with the specified shift-times and may also include workload balancing to ensure a reasonably even distribution across the staff.

c. Applying the algorithm

The application of the algorithm is illustrated in an analysis of a set of 10 requests, distributed over an area surrounding a central depot, with each request having a preference for one of three staff, as in Fig. 2. A simple workload balancing requirement is incorporated with a constraint that no member of staff should be allocated more than 4 patients. This assumes that all patients require the same staff-time, excluding travel. A more sophisticated algorithm could consider the complete workloads and the likely time commitments associated with each patient-visit, including the time for direct patient contact and indirect administrative tasks.

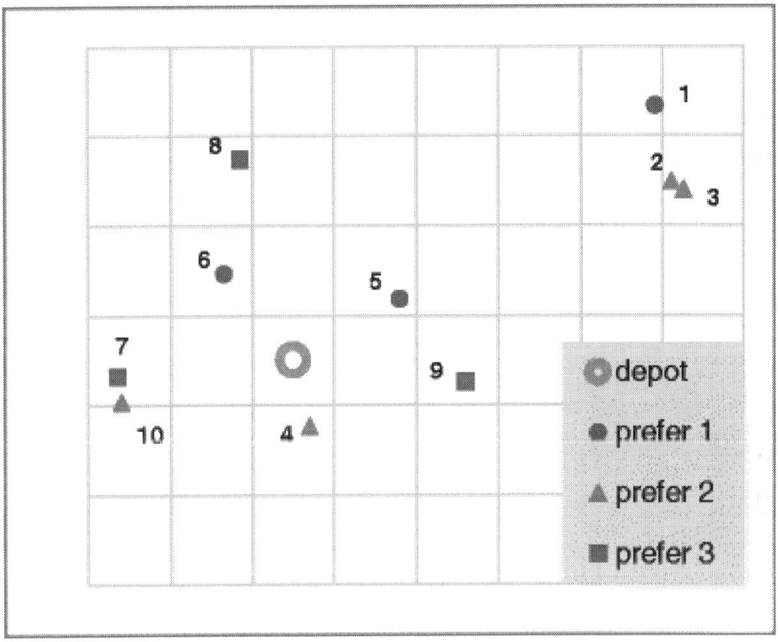

Figure 2. Mapping a set of requests (10 requests; 3 staff)

The algorithm calculates the modified Clarke-Wright savings using Eqs 1–3; assuming a relatively low priority for patients' preferences ($PS = 10$) the first 16 of the ordered possible links and their potential savings, S', are noted in Table 1. In order to avoid unnecessary calculations, S', records just the possible links with distinct savings, noting any specific staff needed to achieve the specified saving; staff = 0 implies that any staff may be used and the saving is just associated with efficient routing rather than satisfying a patient's preference. In the example of Table 1, the most desirable link is that between patient 3 and 2, using staff 2. If this is an initial link for staff 2 with no connecting link required, i.e. as in Eq. (3), a total saving of 139 min is possible, including 2 × 10 = 20 min for satisfying the patients' preferences. Entry 3 relates to the possibility of adding the request from patient 3 to an existing sequence of visits for staff 2, connecting via patient 2. The additional saving, as in Eq. (2), is smaller since just one additional patients' preference is satisfied. If the request from patient 3 is added to an existing sequence of visits for staff other than the one preferred (staff = 0), as specified in entry 7, the saving is lower still, as in Eq. (1). Other entries 1–10 reflect the symmetrical possible links; in some examples the savings may not be identical if the travel times are asymmetric. Entries 7–10 all note the possible savings if preferred staff are not used (staff = 0); such links would only be adopted if the preferred staff were unavailable.

Table 1. Extract of the order list of potential links S'

	Request 1	Request 2	Connecting link	Staff	Savings
1	3	2	0	2	139
2	2	3	0	2	139
3	3	2	2	2	129
4	2	3	3	2	129
5	3	2	0	2	129
6	2	3	0	2	129
7	3	2	2	0	119
8	2	3	3	0	119
9	3	2	0	0	119
10	2	3	0	0	119
11	3	1	1	2	118
12	1	3	3	1	118
13	2	1	1	2	118
14	1	2	2	1	118
15	3	1	0	2	118
16	1	3	0	1	118

d. **The trade-offs between travel time and patient preferences**

Applying the algorithm with no concern for patients' preferences ($PS = 0$) produces an allocation and routing with a travel time of 424 min, as noted in Fig. 3. If patients' preferences are considered, but with just a low priority ($PS = 10$), the same routes are adopted, with the same total travel time of 424 min, but a better allocation of staff such that 50 % of the preferences are satisfied. Placing greater emphasis on the preferences ($PS = 30$) induces a change in the allocation, and routes, such that 60 % are satisfied though travel time increases a little to 434 min. Increasing the emphasis on patients' preferences still further ($PS = 60$) ensures that all are satisfied, though the travel time is now 562 min.

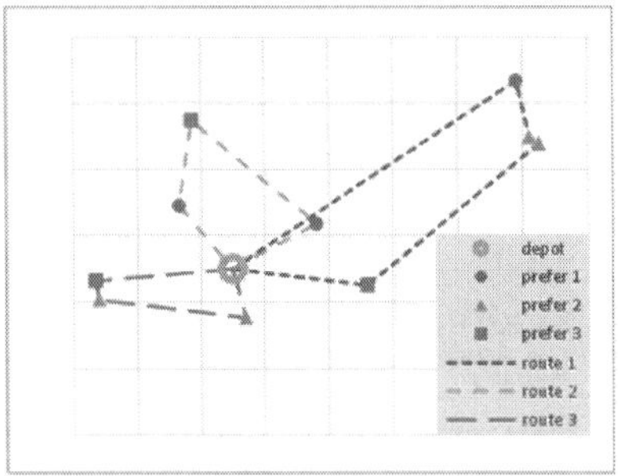

PS=0
PS bonus=0
total travel time=424

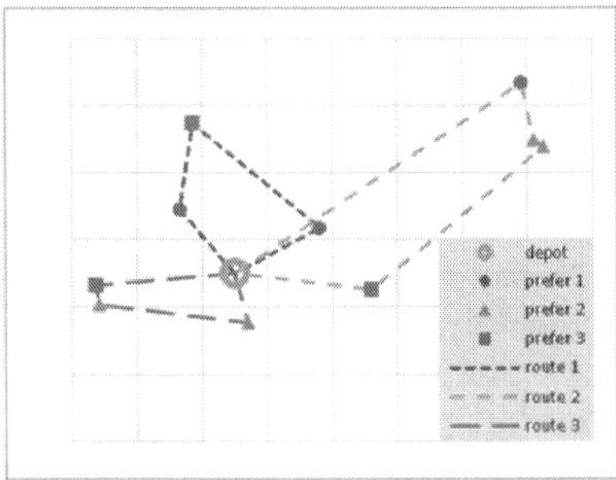

PS=10
PS bonus=50; preferences = 50%
total travel time=424

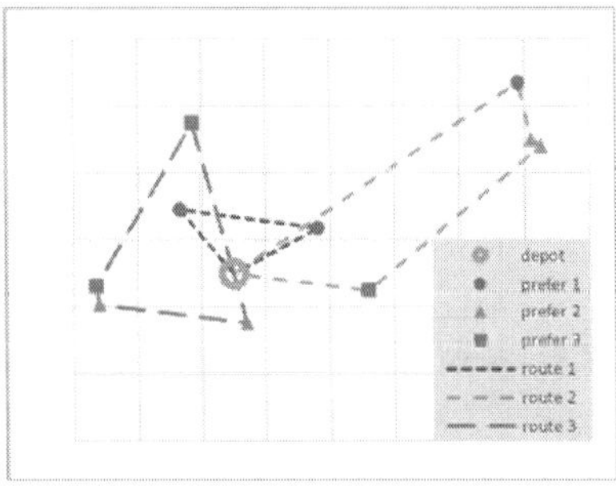

PS=30
PS bonus=180; preferences = 60%
total travel time=434

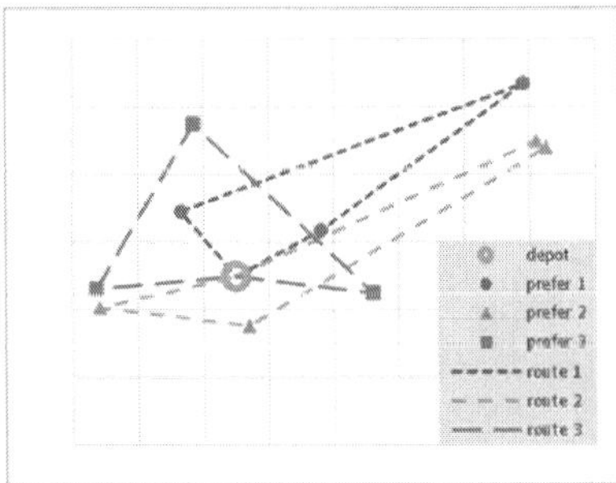

PS=60
PS bonus=600; preferences = 100%
total travel time=562

Figure 3. Shifting the emphasis on patients' preferences (*PS* preference saving associated with satisfying a single patient's preference; *PS* bonus=total saving=no. patients with preferences satisfied×*PS*)

3 SIMULATING POSTNATAL CARE IN THE COMMUNITY

a. Simulating the sequence of postnatal visits

The pattern of maternity care can vary, depending on local practice and the mother and baby's needs, but this paper considers the care provided by a small team of midwives in a typical area. Women attend their local antenatal clinic and begin to build a relationship with a midwife. After the birth in hospital, the mother and baby return home and receive a series of four visits over a period of 10–15 days. A standard pattern of visits might be days 1, 2, 6 and 12 though there may be some flexibility about this schedule, as discussed later. Ideally the first visit will be from the midwife who provided the mother's antenatal clinic, with all subsequent visits from the same midwife, minimising the number of handovers.

The simulation, illustrated in Fig. 4, was constructed in Simul8 to model the pattern of visits, incorporating the travelling nurses' algorithm to allocate mothers to staff and to construct efficient routes while striving to provide continuity of care. The simulation captures the critical stochastic nature of demand, with considerable variability over time and geography. A new set of mothers is generated each day, with a Poisson distribution corresponding to a specified mean demand. Each mother has a home postcode, randomly generated reflecting the geographical distribution of the population. The midwives are associated with GP practices and local health centres where the antenatal clinics are held. Thus the mother's location implies a relationship with a particular midwife which, ideally, will be maintained throughout her postnatal care. Every day in the simulation, the set of mothers requiring visits, both initial and follow-up, is analysed using the travelling nurses' algorithm to allocate a midwife to each mother and identify the sequences of visits.

The results presented in this paper refer to a typical unit serving a specified area, though often units will co-operate when there are particular needs such as staff sickness. There were 6 midwives providing cover over 7 days per week, though given shift patterns and other work or training commitments there were typically just 3–5 midwives available on any 1 day visiting 10–40 mothers.

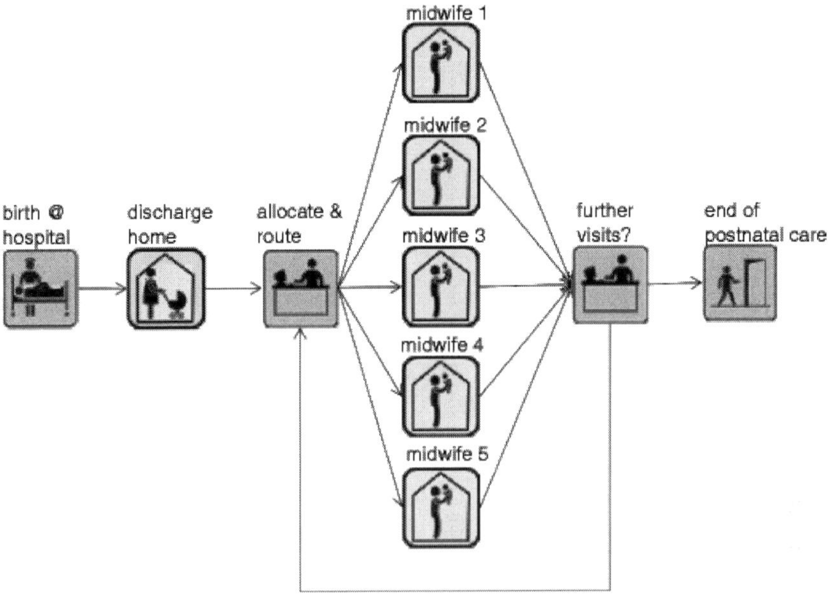

Figure 4. Simulating postnatal care

Simulation experiments

The simulation was used in a series of experiments, as summarized in Table 2, refining the problem specification and introducing additional complexities in a phased series of experiments to help develop understanding. Throughout the paper 95 % confidence intervals are quoted, based on 20 trials each composed of 30 simulated days and a warm-up period of 10 days reflecting the typical time for the completion of a mother's series of postnatal visits.

Table 2. Simulation experiments

Experiment	Problem specification	Objective
Travel & Preferences	Each mother requires a single home visit, with preferences generated randomly.	To understand the basic trade-off between satisfying preferences and total travel time.
Travel & Continuity	Each mother requires four home visits; the initial preference is random but the subsequent preferences are determined by the staff from the previous visit.	To assess the effect on the trade-off when the preferences are dictated by a desire for continuity of care.
Antenatal clinics	The initial preference is dictated by the mother's home location.	To understand how the natural geographical clustering of demand may ease the problem.
Shifts & p/t	Shift patterns are incorporated.	To determine the magnitude of the additional challenge of staff availability to achieving continuity of care.
Flexible visits	The timing of some home visits may be flexible.	To assess whether a small degree of flexibility might be sufficient to help deliver continuity of care.

4 TRAVELLING TIME AND SATISFYING PREFERENCES

The initial simulation experiment assumed that each patient required a single visit, with a randomly generated preference for one of five midwives, each of whom was available every day. The experiment was designed to examine the relationship between travelling time and the satisfaction of preferences for particular staff. Later experiments explored more realistic scenarios involving more complex interrelationships. Three levels of demand were considered (mean daily demand = 16, 20, 24 requests per day) and four degrees of priority for satisfying the preferences (*PS* = 0, 10, 30, 60). When demand is relatively low (mean daily demand = 16) and preferences are ignored (*PS* = 0) the mean travel time per visit is 32.7 ± 0.5 min and 19.6 ± 0.9 % of preferences are satisfied, as noted in Fig. 5. When demand is higher (mean daily demand = 24), the travel time per visit is reduced to 27.0 ± 0.3 min, with 19.9 ± 0.6 % of preferences satisfied. Some of this reduction, 2.6 min, is a consequence of each midwife having more visits per day and hence fewer legs per visit, allowing for the initial and final journeys to the base station. But 3.1 min of the reduction in travel time per visit may be attributed to exploiting the additional allocation and routing options inherent in a higher level of demand.

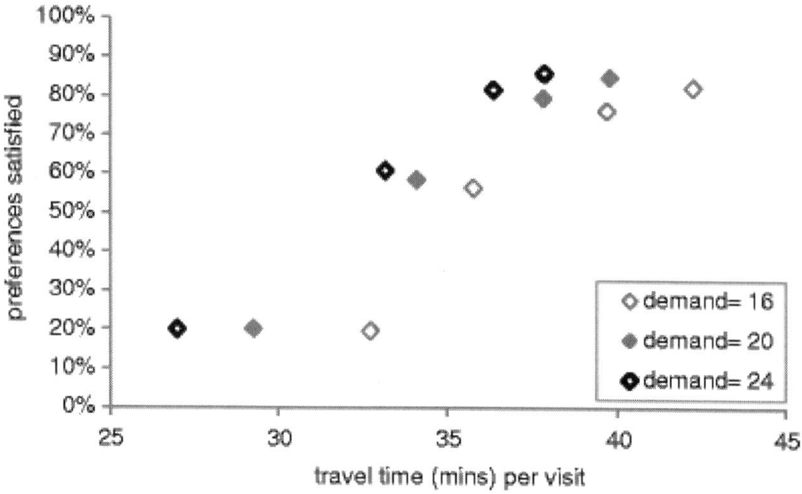

Figure 5. Travel time: preferences trade-off (noting the results of experiment 1 with *PS* = 0,10,30,60 for each specified mean demand)

Even a small consideration of preferences (*PS* = 10) produces a substantial increase in the proportion of satisfied preferences: with low demand (demand = 16) 56.3 ± 1.2 % of preferences are satisfied, though with a small increase in mean travel time to 35.8 ± 0.5 min. As recorded in Fig. 5, further improvements in preference satisfaction might be achieved but at the expense of greater travelling time: 82.3 ± 0.8 % of preferences could be met if a mean travel time of 42.2 ± 0.6 min is accepted. Similar improvements in preference satisfaction are observed in the experiments exploring higher levels of demand, though the mean travel times are always lower when the demand is higher.

5 TRAVELLING TIME AND CONTINUITY OF CARE

In the study of maternity care, the preferences were dictated by a desire to minimise the number of handovers, enhancing longitudinal continuity of care. In experiment 2, each mother received four home-visits: the preference for the first visit was still random but on the three subsequent home-visits, mothers preferred to receive their care from the same midwife as the previous visit. Other preference functions might be explored, possibly modelling small team-working, though this would require a more complex allocation and routing method. The mean daily number of newly discharged mothers was specified as 5, hence the total daily mean demand for home-visits was 20, identical to that of experiment 1. In experiment 2 it was again assumed that all five midwives were available every day of the week; this assumption was explored in later experiments. Different priorities were considered again ($PS = 0$, 10, 30, 60) and the resulting mean travel times and preference satisfactions are illustrated in Fig. 6 as experiment 2 "travel & continuity". Travel times are reduced and the preference satisfactions increased, compared to the results of experiment 1 "travel & preferences" when all of the mothers' preferences were random. In experiment 3 "antenatal clinics", the initial preferences are determined by the mother's home location, assuming that she attended the local clinic and established a relationship with the midwife associated with the area. The three subsequent visits' preferences, reflecting the desire for continuity of care, tend to ensure that the midwife is usually allocated to the same set of locations, though workload balancing considerations may occasionally preclude such an obvious allocation. Hence the objectives of minimising travel time and maximising continuity of care are often complementary: high levels of preference satisfaction, 84.6 % can be achieved with just an increase of 0.8 min per visit ($PS = 10$), compared to the minimum travelling time solution ignoring preferences ($PS = 0$), as illustrated in Fig. 6.

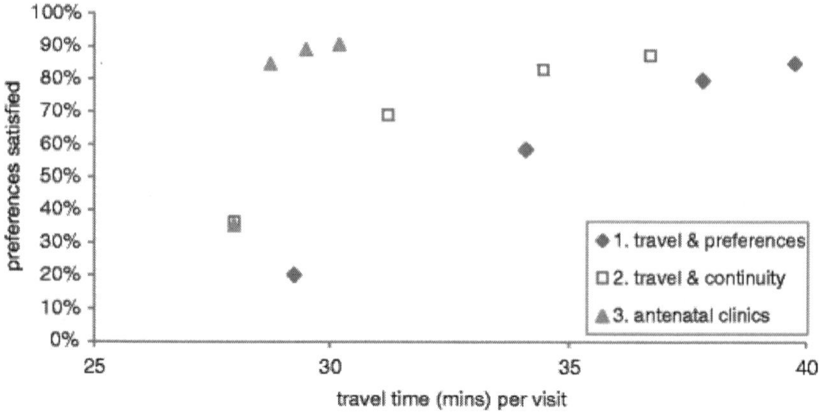

Figure 6. Travel time: continuity of care trade-off (mean daily demand=20; considering *PS* = 0,10,30,60 for each scenario)

6 SHIFT PATTERNS, PART-TIME WORKING AND CONTINUITY OF CARE

In practice, midwives are not available every day of the week and handovers will be generated by the shift patterns: staff work a 5 day week arranged such that the whole team provides 7 day coverage. However, this is further complicated by midwives having commitments to tasks other than postnatal care, and also part-time working. A typical shift pattern for a team of six staff, with two part-time midwives, is illustrated in Table 3. Adopting this shift pattern in the simulation, the results of experiment 4 "shifts & p/t", as illustrated in Fig. 7, suggest that even when continuity of care is prioritized (*PS* = 30), the proportion of visits satisfying the preferences is just 39.2 ± 1.2 % with a mean travel time of 33.0 ± 0.8 min per visit. However, there may be some flexibility in the visit schedule with larger time windows. Although it is essential to visit the mother on the first day at home, even if the preferred midwife is not available, the precise days of the subsequent visits may be adjusted, as noted in Table 4. For example the third visit might occur on 5–7 days after discharge. Assuming such flexibility the handovers can be reduced substantially, as noted in experiment 5 "flexible visits" in Fig. 7, increasing the proportion of satisfied preferences to 68.5 ± 0.9 % with a mean travel time of 34.5 ± 0.8 min per visit (*PS* = 30). Given the sequence of 4 home visits and assuming a binomial distribution, this implies that only 22.0 % of mothers would have the same midwife throughout their postnatal care though 62.5 % should have no more than one change of staff. This degree of continuity is achieved at a relatively low cost of an additional 4.7 min, or 16 %, of travelling per visit compared to the minimum suggested by this analysis (when *PS* = 0, mean travel time = 29.8 min).

Table 3. Typical postnatal care shift pattern (hours available)

	Staff						
	1	2	3	4	5	6	Total
Monday	0	8	8	0	4	0	20
Tuesday	8	4	0	4	4	0	20
Wednesday	8	0	4	0	0	8	20
Thursday	4	8	8	0	0	0	20
Friday	4	8	0	0	8	0	20
Saturday	4	0	0	8	8	0	20
Sunday	0	0	8	2	4	6	20
Total	28	28	28	14	28	14	140

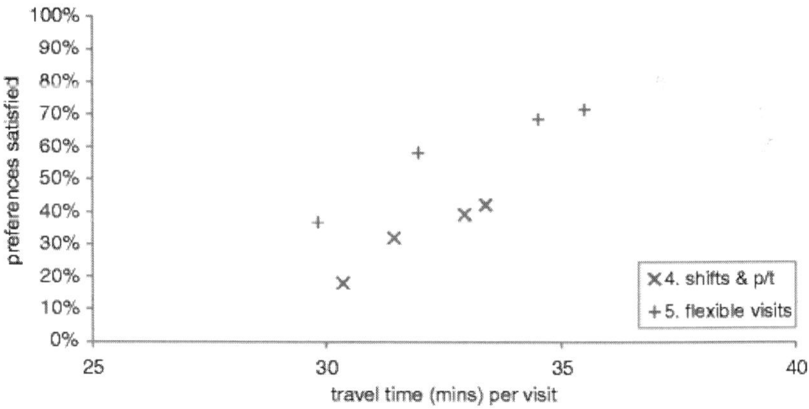

Figure 7. Managing restricted staff availability off (mean daily demand=20; considering *PS* = 0,10,30,60 for each scenario)

Table 4. Visit flexibility

	Days after discharge			
Visit	1	2	3	4
Fixed schedule	1	2	6	12
Early schedule	1	2	5	10
Late schedule	1	3	7	14

7 FURTHER DEVELOPMENTS

The current study has a number of limitations which deserve further work:

- Comparing alternative measures of continuity of care
- The possibility of team working, i.e. second preferences for midwives such that any handovers are restricted to a small, coherent team who can share information about mothers, facilitating information continuity even if longitudinal and relational continuity are impaired
- Effect of changing system parameters to reflect local conditions, e.g. varying the number of home visits received by each mother or the amount of part-time working; this would enable more specific recommendations that might be incorporated in practical allocation and routing guidance
- Exploring variants of the Clarke-Wright algorithm to improve performance of the travelling nurses' algorithm
- Comparisons of the travelling nurses' algorithm with more rigorous approaches; branch and bound or genetic algorithms may not be practical when analysing multiple sets of visit requests as in the simulation experiments but they would provide a valuable comparison to determine the range of validity for the simple algorithm adopted in this study.

8 CONCLUSIONS

The results of the simulation experiments suggest that high degrees of continuity of care can be achieved at a relatively low cost in terms of additional travelling time. However, shift patterns and part-time working disrupt continuity of care considerably. Even then a high degree of longitudinal continuity of care is achievable in postnatal services if there is reasonable flexibility in the schedule of home visits. 100 % continuity is impractical but this study suggests that 70 % of visit preferences might be satisfied, though specific targets for continuity of care should reflect the local conditions.

The study has potential relevance beyond healthcare to other services where travel time is important and the staff should not be viewed as anonymous “service deliverers”. Simulation modelling of flows of activity usually focus on measures such as utilisation, process and waiting times. Quantitative measures of continuity of service provide a mechanism to relate simulation to other aspects of quality which so often depends on the relationships between staff and their patients or clients.

ACKNOWLEDGMENTS

This study was funded by the Royal College of Midwives, Scottish Government Health Department and ESRC.

REFERENCES

1. Parker G, Corden A, Heaton J (2010) Synthesis and conceptual analysis of the SDO’s programme’s research on continuity of care, national institute for health research evaluations. Trials and Studies Coordinating Centre, Southampton
2. Cabana MD, Jee SH (2004) Does continuity of care improve patient outcomes? J Family Pract 52(12):974–980
3. Dreiher J, Comaneshter DS, Rosenbluth Y, Battat E, Bitterman H, Cohen AD (2012) The association between continuity of care in the community and health outcomes: a population-based study, Israel J Health Policy Research 1(21) available at http://www.ijhrp.ord/content/1/1/21 accessed 27.11.13
4. Sandall J, Hatem M, Daven D, Soltani H, Gates S (2009) Discussions of findings from a Cochrane review of midwife-led versus other models of care for childbearing women: continuity, normality and safety. Midwifery 25:8–13

5. Kergosien Y, Lenté C, Billaut J-C (2009) Home health care problem: an extended multiple Traveling Salesman Problem, Multidisciplinary International Conference on Scheduling : Theory and Applications. Dublin, Ireland 85–92.: http://www.schedulingconference.org/previous/publications/displaypub.php?key=2009-085-092-P&filename=mista.bib. Accessed 12 June 2013

6. Steeg J, Schroder M (2008) A hybrid approach to solve the periodic home health care problem, Operations Research Proceedings 2007 http://link.springer.com/content/pdf/10.1007%2F978-3-540-77903-2_46. Accessed 12 June 2013

7. Bektas T (2006) The multiple traveling salesman problems: an overview of formulations and solution procedures. OMEGA 34(3):209–219

8. Rasmussen MS, Justesen T, Dohn A, Larsen J (2012) The home care crew scheduling problem: preference-based visit clustering and temporal dependencies. Eur J Opl Res 219:598–610

9. Eveborn P, Flisberg P, Rönnqvist M (2006) LAPS CARE – an operational system for staff planning of home care. Eur J Opl Res 171:962–976

10. Groër C, Gloden B, Wasil E (2009) The consistent vehicle routing problem. Manuf Serv Oper Manag 11(4):630–643

11. Bertels S, Fahle T (2005) A hybrid setup for a hybrid scenario: combining heuristics for the home health care problem. Comput Oper Res 33(10):2866–2890

12. Pillac V, Gendreau M, Guéret C, Medaglia AL (2013) A review of dynamic vehicle routing problems. Eur J Opl Res 225(1):1–11

13. Begur SV, Miller DM, Weaver JR (1997) An integrated spatial DSS for scheduling and routing home-health-care nurses. Interfaces 27(4):35–48

14. Altınel I, Öncan T (2005) A new enhancement of the Clarke and Wright savings heuristic for the capacitated vehicle routing problem. J Opl Res Soc 56:954–961

15. Clarke G, Wright JW (1964) Scheduling of vehicles from a central depot to a number of delivery points. Oper Res 12(4):568–581

16. Ballou RH, Agarwal YK (1988) A performance comparison of several popular algorithms for vehicle routing and scheduling. J Bus Logist 9(1):51–65

17. Mutingi M, Mbohwa C (2013) Home healthcare worker scheduling: a group genetic algorithm approach, Proceedings of the World

Congress on Engineering 2013 Vol I, WCE 2013, July 3–5, 2013, London, UK

18. Laporte G, Semet F (2001) Classical heuristics for the vehicle routing problem. In: Toth P, Vigo D (eds) The vehicle routing problem. SIAM monographs on discrete mathematics and applications. SIAM Publishing, Philadelphia, pp 109–128

6

TELEMEDICINE, TELEHEALTH AND M-HEALTH: NEW FRONTIERS IN MEDICAL PRACTICE

Elizabeth A. Krupinski [1,*] and Ronald S. Weinstein [2]

[1]Department of Medical Imaging & Arizona Telemedicine Program, University of Arizona, 1609 N Warren Bldg 211, Tucson, AZ 85724, USA

[2]Arizona Telemedicine Program & Southwest Telehealth Resource Center, University of Arizona Health Sciences Center, P.O. Box 245105, Tucson, AZ 85724, USA

Telemedicine is changing the practice of medicine. It is part of the ever-growing use of communications technology in health care being used in prevention, disease management, home health care, long-term (chronic) care, emergency medicine, remote medical imaging, and many other applications. The pace at which telemedicine is being adopted and integrated into the healthcare enterprise is exponential and, for many (even those in the field!), it is often difficult to keep up with all of the changes occurring. Thus, it is useful periodically to stand back and summarize recent advances, to take stock, analyze where we have been, and project where we are headed.

This Special Issue of *Healthcare* features invited papers by experts, on important topics in the fields of telemedicine, telehealth and mHealth (*i.e.*, mobile Health). After a gestation period of a half a century, since the first multi-specialty telemedicine service was created in Boston at the Massachusetts General Hospital in the late 1960s, telemedicine is now reaching its stride as an important and practical way to deliver a broad spectrum of healthcare services to patients. Over 60 subspecialties of medicine and nursing are involved with telemedicine and telehealth. For example, teleradiology has become a standard-of-care for night time coverage in rural and urban hospitals. Telestroke networks may become the next essential "urgent care" service. Telepsychiatry is commonplace in many practice environments. The "smart phone" is being shown to be well suited for use in many mobile telehealth applications. Today, thousands of healthcare apps are being developed, tested and marketed to healthcare providers as well as patients. This Special Issue of *Healthcare* features original papers by leaders in telemedicine whose work is at the leading edge of this rapidly advancing field.

The issue features a paper by Tim Hunter, MD on teleradiology that will prove very useful to those "shopping" for a teleradiology service entitled "University-Based Teleradiology in the United States" [1]. It reviews the long-standing and very successful University of Arizona's teleradiology practice, as well as university-based teleradiology practice in the U.S. in general. It very nicely describes the unique benefits and challenges of engaging a university-based radiology practice for teleradiology services, including a discussion of reimbursement models, consultation models, and what types of questions one should ask when searching for a teleradiology service. Readers will find Table 4 in the article very useful as it succinctly summarizes nine key recommendations for a successful university-based teleradiology practice that both those seeking and those providing services can readily refer to.

Dr. Elizabeth Krupinski also submitted a paper, "Human Factors and Human-Computer Considerations in Teleradiology and Telepathology", that deals with teleradiology, but from a very different perspective that also addresses telepathology [2]. Both of the specialties are in many ways more developed than other clinical specialties, perhaps because both are traditionally image based and for the most part have fewer direct patient encounters. This paper reviews the rather unique digital viewing environments for teleradiology and telepathology, providing a new look at how to optimize case reading environments and address human factors issues. It reviews key components that need to be optimized for effective and efficient practice of teleradiology and telepathology using conventional digital imaging workstations, as well as some of the newer mobile viewing applications.

Although the practice of telemedicine is slowing being integrated into traditional healthcare delivery systems, in many ways it still requires a dedicated workspace or at least special attention to converting an existing workspace into one that is amenable to the tele-encounter. In "Telemedicine Workplace Environments: Designing for Success", Dr. Krupinski further explores the topic of ergonomics in telemedicine by looking at the workspace environment [3]. Although the future practice of telemedicine is likely to be more of a mobile-based practice and centered more in the home than it is now, it is still very important to consider ways to optimize the design of clinic-based telemedicine facilities. This is true on both ends of a consultation—where the patient is and where the consultant is. The paper covers everything from lighting and acoustical considerations to what color the walls should be painted, outlining a variety of easy to take steps to optimize rooms for telemedicine.

Setting up the basic technology and networking infrastructure for telemedicine is one thing, but convincing practitioners to actually use telemedicine is often another challenge unto itself. There are many ways to champion telemedicine and find converts, but giving someone a practice guideline developed by experts engaging telemedicine on a daily basis can often be the most convincing and useful tool you can provide. In "Standards and Guidelines in Telemedicine and Telehealth", Dr. Krupinski provides an overview of the development of guidelines and standards that help insure effective and safe delivery of quality healthcare [4]. The paper reviews critically important, sustained, efforts by the American Telemedicine Association in developing telemedicine practice guidelines, review the role of research in guidelines development, review data regarding their use, and discuss some of the additional areas where guidelines are still needed. There are lots of references to the existing guidelines that readers can download freely and adopt today!

Finally, there is a paper by Chan *et al.*, "Mobile Tele-Mental Health: Increasing Applications and a Move to Hybrid Models of Care" that very nicely describes the vast potential of mobile devices for psychotherapy, psychosocial interventions, and other behavioral health programs [5]. Particular emphasis is placed on novel interventions that integrate sensors to monitor patients and algorithms that provide "interpretations" of these data to help predict when patients require some sort of intervention. As with the first article on teleradiology, the benefits and challenges associated with mobile devices are reviewed and a number of recent key studies in the topic summarized. Some key clinical scenarios in which mobile options are proving to be useful are described, followed by a discussion of what is still needed to make these devices are part of regular care, including more research validating them, more clinical trials, and adoption of existing guidelines.

The final few sentences of the Chan article provide a glimpse of what is certainly going to be healthcare in the very near future—a "hybrid" practice in which mobile and other emerging technologies are used regularly as part of every practice to effectively and efficiently monitor, connect with, educate and care for patients. Each of the articles in this Special Issue will provide readers with insights into the practice of telemedicine that will hopefully inspire them to join the telemedicine community sooner rather than later as it clearly is here to stay!

REFERENCES

1. Hunter, T.B.; Krupinski, E.A. University-based teleradiology in the United States. *Healthcare* **2014**, *2*, 192–206.
2. Krupinski, E. Human factors and human-computer considerations in teleradiology and telepathology. *Healthcare***2014**, *2*, 94–114.
3. Krupinski, E.A. Telemedicine workplace environments: Designing for success. *Healthcare* **2014**, *2*, 115–122.
4. Krupinski, E.A.; Bernard, J. Standards and guidelines in telemedicine and telehealth. *Healthcare* **2014**, *2*, 74–79.
5. Chan, S.R.; Torous, J.; Hinton, L.; Yellowlees, P. Mobile tele-mental health: Increasing applications and a move to hybrid models of care. *Healthcare* **2014**, *2*, 220–233.

7

CHANGES IN HOSPITAL EFFICIENCY AFTER PRIVATIZATION

Oliver Tiemann [1,2] Jonas Schreyögg[1,2]

[1.] Hamburg Center for Health EconomicsUniversity of HamburgHamburgGermany

[2.] Institute of Health Economics and Health Care ManagementHelmholtz Zentrum MünchenNeuherbergGermany

ABSTRACT

We investigated the effects of privatization on hospital efficiency in Germany. To do so, we obtained bootstrapped data envelopment analysis (DEA) efficiency scores in the first stage of our analysis and subsequently employed a difference-in-difference matching approach within a panel regression framework. Our findings show that conversions from public to private for-profit status were associated with an increase in efficiency of between 2.9 and 4.9%. We defined four alternative post-privatization periods and found that the increase in efficiency after a conversion to private for-profit status appeared to be permanent. We also observed an increase in efficiency for the first three years after hospitals were converted to private non-profit status, but our estimations suggest that this effect was rather transitory. Our findings also show that the efficiency gains after a conversion to private for-profit status were achieved through substantial decreases in staffing ratios in all analyzed staff categories with the exception of physicians and administrative staff. It was also striking that the efficiency gains of hospitals converted to for-profit status were significantly lower in the diagnosis-related groups (DRG) era than in the pre-DRG era. Altogether, our results suggest that converting hospitals to private for-profit status may be an effective way to ensure the scarce resources in the hospital sector are used more efficiently.

Keywords: Hospitals, Privatization, Performance measurement, Data envelopment analysis, Propensity score matching, Germany

1 INTRODUCTION

Rising health expenditure and tight public budgets over the past four decades have led decision makers in many Western industrialized countries to seek ways to improve the performance of health care organizations. Hospitals, in particular, are increasingly being held accountable for their efficiency and financial performance. Having identified inefficiencies and financial risks in public hospitals, national and local governments in a wide range of countries have responded by privatizing these institutions. The chief motivation behind the privatizations that have taken place in these countries during the past twenty years has been the expectation that shifting from public to private ownership would lead to gains in organizational performance, especially in terms of efficiency. Considering the importance of this topic, not least in the political debate, the lack of quantitative empirical studies on the effects of hospital privatization is surprising [1, 2].

The present investigation is the first to examine the effects of privatization on technical efficiency in the hospital market. To do so, we examined a large sample of German hospitals that changed from public to either private non-profit or to private for-profit status. Following an extensive wave of privatizations that began in the mid-1990s, the large hospital market in Germany is now fertile ground for investigating these effects. In Germany, three different types of hospital ownership have co-existed for decades: private for-profit, private non-profit, and public. As their classification implies, both types of private hospitals are owned by private entities, whereas public hospitals are owned mainly by public entities, such as local or regional governments. Between 1995 and 2008, a substantial number of local and regional governments in Germany sold their hospitals to private for-profit and private non-profit owners. The total number of private for-profit hospitals increased by 164, or 44%, which represented a rise in market share from 6 to 18% measured in terms of hospital beds. During the same period, the market share of private non-profit hospitals decreased slightly, from 38 to 36%, because some private non-profit hospitals were also converted to private for-profit ownership [3, 4].

In the present study, we focused on technical efficiency to assess changes in hospital performance following privatization. After using a bootstrapped data envelopment analysis technique to estimate efficiency scores for each hospital in our sample [5, 6], we employed propensity score matching to ensure that the two groups of hospitals in our analysis (i.e. privatized and non-privatized) were comparable in terms of organizational characteristics, environmental characteristics, and patient heterogeneity [7–9]. Subsequently, following an approach suggested by Simar and Wilson [10], we estimated a second-step regression model for truncated longitudinal data, with bootstrapped DEA efficiency scores as dependent variable. Finally, while controlling for the impact of hospital organizational and environmental characteristics, we applied a difference-in-difference specification of the regression model to examine whether privatization improved hospital efficiency.

Section 2 of this paper reviews the relevant theoretical and empirical literature on privatization and its impact on hospital performance. Section 3 presents the setting, data, and methodology used to explore this relationship. Section 4 describes and discusses the results of our analysis, and the fifth, and final, section 5 draws conclusions and suggests topics for future research.

2 PREVIOUS LITERATURE ON PRIVATIZATION

Theoretical predictions regarding the performance effects of hospital privatization can be made based on a large body of literature investigating the various effects of different ownership types. There are three fundamental theories that can be drawn upon when comparing public and private hospitals, each of which provides different explanations of a common outcome. According to agency theory and property-rights theory, as well as public choice theory, the rationale for privatization is that the resulting changes in an hospital's objectives, incentives, and control mechanisms lead to improved performance: Public hospitals acquired by a private for-profit organization are expected to maximize profit through a high degree of technical efficiency, producing services in such a way that marginal cost will equal marginal revenue. In turn, public hospitals acquired by a private non-profit organization are expected to improve technical efficiency by suppressing politically motivated resource allocation and expanding their output at least to the point where total cost equals total revenue [11–18].

Generally speaking, there have been—from an empirical point of view—two categories of studies that deal with ownership and privatization. The first, and by far the most numerous, of these have compared the performance of public and private entities in industries in which both types of ownership coexist [19]. In a meta-review of studies of this nature that focused on the hospital market, Shen et al. [20] concluded that there was little evidence supporting the standard assumption that private for-profit hospitals outperform hospitals with other types of ownership. Herr [21] and Tiemann and Schreyögg [22] found that public hospitals outperform hospitals with other types of ownership in the German hospital market. Because none of these studies investigated changes in ownership type during a specified period—and thus did not examine the effects of privatizing public entities—they will not be discussed in any further detail below.

The second category of studies has focused on privatization and its impact on organizational performance, usually employing a longitudinal design. From a methodological perspective, these studies have taken two different approaches. The first was introduced by Megginson et al. [23], who compared the means and medians of the periods before and after privatization according to defined performance criteria. Few of the studies that have taken this approach, however, have included control groups consisting of non-privatized state-owned organizations. The second approach has involved much larger samples of privatized entities and, defining the privatization event as an intervention, has applied methods proposed in the literature on program evaluation [24, 25]. The majority of these studies have used some kind of difference-in-difference method to analyze the effects of privatization on performance compared to the performance of a control group of non-privatized entities, controlling for time-invariant differences between the groups. As part of our literature review, we were able to identify ten studies from different industries that used such a method to evaluate privatization effects, including four studies on hospitals: Picone et al. [26], Shen [27], Shen [28] and Farsi [29], all of whom examined ownership conversion effects in the US hospital market.

Three of these four studies assessed the quality of care after a change in ownership and found that conversions from private non-profit to private for-profit status had a significantly negative impact [26, 27, 29]. One study [29] found that a change from private for-profit to private non-profit status also had a negative effect on the quality of care. Thus, the negative effect of conversions in both directions may suggest that conversion activity by itself may lead to disrupted organizational routines (e.g., in surgeries) or other organizational problems due to the restructuring process that end up in lower quality of care. Based on this negative effect on the quality of care following conversion activity it seems crucial to control for the quality of care when examining efficiency gains after hospital conversion.

Using profit margins, capacity, staffing ratios, salaries, patient mix, and the amount of unprofitable care as measures, Shen [28] and Picone et al. [26] examined the impact of changes in ownership on hospital performance. Both studies found that hospitals converted from public or private non-profit status to private for-profit status increased their profit margins and reduced staffing ratios. In addition, Shen [28] found that these hospitals reduced cost and increased revenue. She also found that a change from public or private for-profit status to private non-profit status resulted in slight reductions in cost and in nursing staff, but did not lead to increased profit margins.

Although all four studies were pioneering in their approach and focus, they have several important weaknesses. First, Shen [28] and Picone et al. [26] used profit margins as a measure of performance. There is evidence, however, that public hospitals are averse to seeking profit maximization [30]. As a result, it seems reasonable to assume that using financial performance criteria, such as profit margins, may lead to bias in pre-post comparisons of privatized entities and control group designs. For this reason, we believe that productivity, in terms of technical efficiency, is a more suitable measure of changes in performance among hospitals that have undergone a conversion in ownership type. Second, none of the four studies specifically examined the phenomenon of privatization, which would have required a focus solely on changes from public status to private non-profit or private for-profit status. Instead, they examined the effects of conversion from any form of ownership to public, private non-profit, or private for-profit status. Third, Shen [27, 28] was the only author to address the problem of causal interference, using a difference-in-difference method combined with a matching approach to investigate the impact of privatization. Finally, all four studies implicitly assumed that changes in performance are attributable primarily to changes in ownership status. There may, however, be other changes to the market environment, such as the introduction of DRGs, that also interact with the privatization event. By focusing on the impact of privatization on technical efficiency and employing a difference-in-difference matching approach, we attempt to address these shortcomings and contribute to the current understanding of the consequences of hospital privatization.

3 ESTIMATION STRATEGY AND DATA

3.1 Data envelopment analysis

In studies on the hospital sector, DEA is the most frequently used approach to measuring efficiency [31, 32]. It is a non-parametric frontier method which uses linear programming to evaluate the relative technical efficiency of an individual hospital based on observed data. Essentially,

DEA compares an individual hospital's observed level of outputs and inputs with the best practice production frontier. This frontier was derived by those hospitals that could maximize output given inputs (output-oriented model) or minimize inputs given output (input-oriented model). DEA applies linear programming to construct a piece-wise linear-segmented efficiency frontier based on observed best practice (for a detailed description of the transformation into a linear programming model, see Charnes et al. [33], Banker et al. [34] and Ozcan [35]).

DEA allows multiple inputs and outputs to be considered simultaneously, which seems particularly well-suited to measuring the efficiency of complex service organizations like hospitals. In contrast to parametric methods such as stochastic frontier analysis (SFA), DEA has the advantage of not requiring that any assumptions be made about the functional form of the production or cost frontier. This reduces the need for a theoretical exposition of the model. SFA is also frequently used to measure efficiency in health care organizations. Because both techniques have their strengths and weaknesses, Coelli et al. [36] propose evaluating their suitability depending on the context of study. As in other investigations that have measured hospital efficiency, our decision to use DEA was driven by data availability [37]: our data set contained a range of input and output variables suitable for DEA, but did not contain input prices, which are an important prerequisite for SFA.

Based on our understanding of the market constraints within the German hospital sector, we assumed variable returns to scale, which may be appropriate when it is impossible to assume that all observed units are operating at an optimal scale [34]. In the health care sector, imperfect competition and budgetary constraints, as well as regulatory constraints on entry, mergers, and exits, can often cause organizations to operate at an inefficient scale size [38]. In light of this theoretical framework, we used the following empirical model in our analysis. In the input-oriented case, we estimated the variable returns to scale model by Banker, Charnes, and Cooper (BCC) as a linear programming model, as follows [34]:

- ϑ_i, $i = 1,\dots,n$ is the hospital's efficiency, where n represents the number of observations (i.e. the number of hospitals).
- $\vartheta i=1/\theta i\vartheta i=1/\theta i$, where θ_i is the inefficiency.

Matrix $X \in Rk\times nX \in Rk\times n$ refers to k observed inputs of n compared hospitals, and matrix $Y \in Rr\times nY \in Rr\times n$refers to r observed outputs of the compared hospitals. Vectors $xi \in Rkxi \in Rk$ and $yi \in Rryi \in Rr$ represent the inputs and outputs of unit i (i.e. the ith columns of matrix $\mathbf{X}$ and $\mathbf{Y}$, respectively). Furthermore, $\mathbf{1}$ refers to a column vector of ones with a suitable dimension. The DEA efficiency score, which is the reciprocal of the inefficiency θ_i, can be obtained by solving the following BCC linear programming model [39]:

$$\begin{aligned} &\theta* = Min\theta, \\ \text{s.t.} \; &Y\lambda - y_0 \geq 0, \\ &-X\lambda + \theta x_0 \geq 0, \\ &1^T\lambda = 1, \lambda \geq 0. \end{aligned} \tag{1}$$

Using DEA efficiency scores for a second-stage regression has been found to result in inconsistent estimates unless these scores are corrected by a bootstrapping procedure. According to Simar and Wilson [5, 6] the statistical properties of the estimated efficiency measures are essential for their interpretations and here a serious problem arises in a two-stage analysis (i.e. DEA followed by some form of regression analysis) from the fact that DEA efficiency estimates are serially correlated. The serial correlation occurs in finite samples due to the fact that perturbations of observations lying on the estimate frontier will in many, and perhaps all, cases cause changes in efficiencies estimated for other observations. In the general multi-output multi-input DEA framework, the bootstrapping procedure seems to offer the only means of inferring the statistical properties of the estimated DEA efficiency scores (i.e. to estimate the bias and variance, and to construct confidence intervals). The basic idea of the bootstrap method is to approximate the sampling distributions of the DEA efficiency estimator by using the empirical distribution of resampled estimates obtained from a resampling simulation. The bootstrapping procedure applied in the present study follows the approach developed by Simar and Wilson [5, 6]. In our case, the bias-corrected scores were derived from 500 bootstrap iterations, which allowed us to improve the statistical efficiency in the second-stage regression (see Section 3.3).

When selecting inputs and outputs for the first stage of our analysis, we followed the example of other studies that have developed DEA frameworks for measuring hospital efficiency [35, 37, 38, 40]. For our purposes, we chose six inputs and two outputs. The first input variable (SUPPLIES) represents the amount spent on supplies per year, including operational expenses, but excluding payroll, capital, and depreciation expenses. Taking into account the relative importance of resource use in terms of labor in the hospital production process, we chose the number of full-time equivalents (FTEs) for the following personnel categories as additional input variables: physicians (PHYS), nursing staff (NURSE), other clinical staff (CLIN), administrative staff (ADMIN), and other nonclinical staff members (NONCLIN).

In our first DEA efficiency model, we used the number of inpatient cases per year in each hospital as the only output variable (INPATIENT). A second model specification served as a sensitivity analysis to test whether the efficiency scores and ranks remained stable when a measure of quality of care was employed as a second output [41]. To do so, we used the average in-hospital mortality rate per year for each hospital to adjust for variations in the quality of care between hospitals. The second output thus represents the number 1 minus the average in-hospital mortality rate per year (1-MORTALITY).

Using output variables like these can be problematic if patient heterogeneity (i.e. case mix) varies systematically across the hospitals in a sample. This is because hospitals with a more complex case mix are likely to receive lower efficiency scores. To address this potential shortcoming, we used patient-level data to condense a comprehensive set of comorbidities to a single numeric score that (a) summarized disease burden and resource use and (b) was sufficiently discriminative for predicting mortality. In order to generate this case-mix index for each hospital, we relied on the comorbidities included in the Elixhauser Comorbidity Index [42]. The Elixhauser Comorbidity Index provides pre-defined weights for each of the comorbidities. We applied these weights to the set of diagnoses of each hospital and determined a case-mix index for each hospital. We rescaled the index to provide values between 0 and 1 used this case-mix index to risk-adjust both of the output variables for the DEA models by multiplying each of the variables INPATIENT and 1-MORTALITY with the case-mix index. Another common approach would have been to use a case-mix index whose weight reflected the relative costliness of DRGs. Carey [43, 44], however, reported that individual-level measures represent a vast improvement over such aggregate case-mix measures when controlling for patient heterogeneity.

A correlation analysis showed that our multiple inputs were positively correlated with our output set. This is an important prerequisite for applying DEA. In the present study, the input variables, in particular, were highly correlated, which suggests that a limited number of inputs might have been sufficient to represent the selected input set in our efficiency assessment. Several authors (e.g., Dyson et al. [45]; Jacobs et al. [38]), however, emphasize that correlation is an aggregate measure of the closeness of two sets of observed data and argue that omitting a highly correlated variable can lead to significant changes in efficiency estimates. As a result, variations in the input levels for individual hospitals may have little impact on the correlation while significantly affecting the measured efficiency. A comprehensive set of inputs and outputs may also increase the chance of identifying the presence of a production technology common to all decision-making units. In addition, Dyson et al. [45] argue that omitting variables to increase discrimination is less effective when using large data samples. Based on these considerations, we chose to use all of our input variables for the DEA model. Table 1 shows the descriptive statistics for in- and outputs of our sample used in the DEA models stratified according to the intervention and control groups.

Table 1. Descriptive statistics of in- and outputs for the matched sample

For-profit										
Number of hospitals	$n=99$		$n=99$		$n=90$		$n=77$		$n=66$	
PHYS	71.46	(73.12)	73.32	(74.91)	71.74	(72.76)	70.47	(75.18)	74.97	(79.41)
NURSE	199.7	(168.4)	188.9	(165.2)	179.3	(153.9)	173.2	(153.8)	177.3	(154.7)
CLIN	127.1	(125.8)	126.7	(126.2)	118.5	(118.9)	114.5	(117.8)	120.5	(121.8)
ADMIN	33.55	(29.81)	33.48	(28.27)	31.85	(26.78)	30.98	(26.50)	30.94	(26.17)
NONCLIN	66.07	(57.01)	56.84	(54.95)	48.97	(47.75)	45.20	(47.25)	43.07	(45.14)
SUPPLIES	14.5	(15.7)	15.1	(15.7)	15.3	(15.3)	14.7	(14.5)	16.1	(15.9)
INPATIENT	13147	(10860)	13386	(11286)	13002	(10649)	12822	(11142)	13537	(11780)
1-MORTALITY	0.974	(0.011)	0.975	(0.010)	0.975	(0.010)	0.976	(0.010)	0.976	(0.009)
Non-profit										
Number of hospitals	$n=33$		$n=33$		$n=24$		$n=23$		$n=22$	
PHYS	40.64	(41.08)	42.82	(44.35)	49.04	(50.40)	52.54	(53.04)	55.56	(54.46)
NURSE	132.1	(119.5)	128.6	(122.4)	14.4	(137.62)	151.7	(134.9)	156.4	(133.7)
CLIN	78.3	(84.92)	78.8	(84.97)	91.4	(97.96)	96.3	(99.66)	100.7	(100.8)
ADMIN	22.98	(21.42)	22.57	(23.74)	27.01	(29.52)	27.37	(29.45)	28.67	(29.85)
NONCLIN	60.05	(62.30)	56.37	(62.85)	64.05	(77.76)	59.64	(75.01)	59.73	(77.96)
SUPPLIES	7.8	(6.7)	8.3	(7.3)	9.0	(8.6)	10.1	(9.2)	10.6	(10.1)
INPATIENT	8232	(6668)	8631	(7358)	9773	(8526)	12093	(8612)	10316	(8607)
1-MORTALITY	0.978	(0.009)	0.978	(0.011)	0.977	(0.009)	0.976	(0.010)	0.977	(0.009)
Control										
Number of hospitals	$n=128$		$n=128$		$n=113$		$n=99$		$n=87$	
PHYS	65.50	(72.50)	69.62	(76.55)	72.73	(79.68)	71.65	(84.07)	69.66	(80.05)
NURSE	189.0	(172.8)	187.2	(168.4)	191.1	(169.9)	183.8	(165.5)	181.3	(166.8)
CLIN	119.4	(141.5)	120.5	(140.7)	124.2	(143.5)	119.7	(139.4)	121.6	(146.9)
ADMIN	32.70	(33.05)	33.08	(33.47)	33.49	(34.57)	31.57	(32.83)	32.11	(34.43)
NONCLIN	73.81	(77.88)	68.42	(71.34)	68.27	(71.91)	66.26	(71.47)	65.35	(71.25)
SUPPLIES	12.0	(13.4)	13.6	(15.5)	14.5	(16.8)	14.3	(17.6)	14.6	(19.6)
INPATIENT	12435	(10516)	12606	(10587)	13049	(10984)	12630	(10736)	12594	(11278)
1-MORTALITY	0.973	(0.013)	0.973	(0.013)	0.974	(0.011)	0.973	(0.013)	0.973	(0.012)

t−1 is defined as the year before privatization occurred, while t+1, t+2, t+3 and t+4 represent the four post-privatization years.

3.2 Propensity score matching

The difference-in-difference estimator has the advantage of eliminating unobserved time-invariant hospital-level effects between privatized and non-privatized hospitals. It does not, however, address the problem of potential baseline imbalance between these two groups, which can be caused when large differences in group characteristics prior to privatization lead to selection bias. For instance, if only smaller hospitals are sold by the state, this may result into smaller hospitals in the intervention group of privatized compared to the control group of non-privatized hospitals. In the case of baseline imbalance, results may be very sensitive to the model specification, and regression analysis may effectively extrapolate outside the support of the data. Methods such as propensity score matching have been shown to avoid unreliable inference in parametric models. For example, if privatized hospitals are systematically smaller than the control group of non-privatized hospitals and we assume that smaller hospitals are generally less efficient than larger hospitals, efficiency gains after privatization will be smaller than they would have been without selection by size, i.e. providing equal hospital sizes in both groups. Whereas the use of matching estimators alone is usually unsatisfactory due to the strong assumption that selection is based only on observables, several authors have proposed that a combination of difference-in-difference and propensity score matching methods significantly increases the quality of non-experimental evaluation results [46, 47].

We thus applied a propensity score matching approach proposed by Rosenbaum [7] and Rubin [8, 9] and extracted a sub-sample of non-privatized hospitals in which the distribution of covariates was similar to that in our sample of privatized hospitals. In the first step, we estimated the conditional probability that any hospital in the two samples had been privatized during the study period given the vector of our defined covariates. The propensity scores were derived by performing a logistic regression. In order to achieve a propensity score model that minimizes the conditional bias, it is important to determine predictors and confounders of the intervention–outcome relationship and to identify predictors of exposure, i.e. we determined variables with significant effect on the probability of being privatized [48]. To determine appropriate predictors of exposure, we tested different variables in the logistic regression models, allowing for interactions between variables (for a detailed description of the variables, see Section 3.3). Subsequently, we calculated the predicted probabilities of belonging to the sample of privatized hospitals. Based on this score, each privatized hospital was matched to one non-privatized hospital in the corresponding baseline year (i.e. one year before the privatization occurred). Because the propensity score was the only pre-intervention measurement, the matching algorithm minimized the absolute differences in propensity score [49]. By using one-to-one matching with replacement i.e. each hospital in the control group could be drawn more than once, the total distance between matched pairs was also minimized; known as optimal matching, this method ensures that conditional bias is reduced to a minimum [7, 9, 50]. The number of pairs in the matched sample was further restricted by using calipers of width equal to 0.2 of the standard deviation. A comparison of different caliper widths found that this width was superior to others at reducing conditional bias in the estimation of intervention effects [51].

We assessed the appropriateness of our propensity score matching by using standardized differences for continuous variables and differences for non-continuous variables as recommended by Austin [48]. Standardized differences represent a good measure of appropriateness for the matching procedure, as they depend neither on the unit of measurement nor on the size of the sample [52]. Furthermore, we applied Hotelling's T-square statistic to test the reliability of our propensity score matching. Whereas standardized differences and differences rely on the cross-sample difference of each variable included in the propensity score matching model, Hotelling's T-square test considers whether these differences can be taken as jointly insignificant. In the present study, we divided the sample by propensity score quartiles and conducted the test for each sub-sample [53].

3.3 Difference-in-difference estimates

In our regression analysis, we applied a generalized linear regression model for truncated longitudinal data with DEA efficiency scores as dependent variable. A difference-in-difference specification of the regression model was used to assess whether privatization led to improvements in efficiency while controlling for patient heterogeneity and the impact of hospital organizational and environmental characteristics. Truncated regression models were chosen owing to the truncated distribution of the DEA-based relative efficiency estimates [10]. All of our difference-in-difference regressions were modeled with fixed effects and random effects because the results of the Breusch–Pagan and Hausman tests suggested that the assumption of the random effects specification was also appropriate. The fixed effects estimator generally provides more consistent estimates and may pick up much of the unobserved heterogeneity in the hospital-specific effect. Because of this, the fixed effects estimator was our preferred model. Therefore we only report the fixed effects regression results. Our model was as follows:

$$\vartheta_{it} = \beta_0 + \beta_1 PRIV_i + \beta_2 POST_{it} + \beta_3 PRIV_i POST_{it} + \beta_4 Z_{it} + u_i + \varepsilon_{it} \quad (2)$$

where ϑ_{it} is the efficiency of the *i*th hospital at year *t*, $t = 1,\ldots,13$; $PRIV_i$ is a dummy variable for privatization, with $PRIV_i$ being assigned a value of 1 if a hospital was privatized at any time between 1997 and 2007 and a value of 0 if not; $POST_t$ is assigned a value of 1 in the years after privatization and 0 before the year during which the hospital changed its status to private for-profit or private non-profit; and Z_{it} are observable factors affecting the efficiency of hospital *i* at year *t* (i.e. hospital characteristics, environmental characteristics, and patient heterogeneity) $u_i$is the fixed effect. The random term ε_{it} is assumed to be gamma distributed.

The variable $PRIV_i$ was included to control for time-invariant differences between privatized hospitals in the intervention group (i.e. hospitals that were converted from public to private for-profit or private non-profit status) and non-privatized hospitals in the control group. The coefficient of interest is the interaction between $PRIV_i$ and $POST_t$, which identifies changes in efficiency after a hospital was privatized relative to efficiency in the comparator group. The difference-in-difference methodology assumes that all other temporal factors affecting hospital efficiency had the same impact on hospitals in the intervention group as they did on hospitals in the control group. We thus assume that any changes over time for which we did not control affected all hospitals in the same way. For sensitivity purposes, and to check the robustness of our estimates, we allowed for four alternative post-privatization periods (i.e. first, second, third, and fourth year). The pre-period was defined as the year before privatization occurred and alternatively year 2 before privatization was used.

An important assumption in our study was that environmental and organizational factors can influence the efficiency of hospitals in addition to a change in ownership status. We assert that considering the impact of such covariates on hospital efficiency provides a better explanation of variation in efficiency and more robust findings on the post-acquisition effects of privatization than the approaches taken in previous studies on this topic, none of which controlled for these effects. The use of control variables is of particular importance when examining the hospital market because there are usually a range of structural and regulatory determinants of efficiency that a hospital itself cannot influence. Table 2 provides a comprehensive outline of our statistical analysis.

Table 2. Outline of the statistical analysis

Steps	Implementation	Sample Size
1. Increasing homogeinity of the sample	To ensure the comparability of the hospitals in the sample we	Randomly selected data from 1,878 German acute care hospitals were obtained between 1996 and 2008
	(1) Excluded hospitals providing only psychiatric care, university hospitals, day clinics, hospitals with fewer than 50 beds and more than 2,000 beds	A total of 1,187 hospitals remained in the sample
	(2) Excluded non-privatized non-profit and private for-profit hospitals during our study period	A total of 548 hospitals remained in the sample
	(3) Eliminated hospitals with measurement errors and hospitals that had observations in less than 7 years between 1996–2008	A total of 493 hospitals remained in the sample
2. Identification of intervention and control groups	Seperation of intervention and control groups	Intervention group: 132 privatized hospitals were found, i.e. 99 public hospitals were acquired by a private for-profit hospital and 33 public hospitals were acquired by private non-profit hospitals Control group: 361 public hospitals
3. Data Envelopment Analysis (DEA)	Application of an input-oriented variable returns to scale model by Banker, Charnes, and Cooper (BCC) for all privatized and non-privatized hospitals. DEA was performed per year.	
4. Bootstrapping	Derive bias-corrected DEA efficiency scores from 500 bootstrap iterations	
5. Proponsity Score Matching (PSM)	(1) Estimate probability for being privatized based on our defined covariates by means of logistic regression	
	(2) Match privatized hospitals to non-privatized public hospitals based on predicted means by using a one-to-one matching with replacement; we used an optimal matching algorithm i.e. we minimized the total distance of matched pairs	Number of hospitals in control group after matching: 128 in first year after matching, 113 in second year after matching, 99 in third year after matching, 86 in fourth year after matching
6. PSM diagnostics	Assessing appropriateness and reliability of the PSM results by using	
	(1) standardized differences and	
	(2) Hotelling's T-square statistic based on quartiles	
7. Regression analysis	Use of a generalized linear regression model for truncated longitudinal data with DEA efficiency scores as dependent variable. Difference-in-difference interaction was used to examine effects of privatization on efficiency compared to control group of non-privatized hospitals controlling for patient heterogeneity and the impact of hospital organizational and environmental characteristics	
8. Sensitivity analysis	(1) Re-estimation of the DEA model by employing 1-MORTALITY as a second output	
	(2) Estimated multiway clustered regression including time and firm fixed effects	
	(3) Allowed pre-privatization period of two years instead of one year	
	(4) Re-estimation of the DEA model without those inputs having a strong correlation	
	(5) Reduction of of the multi-step procedure to a substantially reduced two-step procedure	

In the second stage of our analysis, heterogeneity in hospital characteristics was covered by several variables. The first of these was the number of licensed and staffed beds (BEDS), an approach taken in previous studies to control for hospital size [54–56]. In the context of hospital planning in Germany, the number of beds per hospital can be seen, at least over the medium term, as an exogenous factor that is not under the direct control of hospital management. To account for higher resource consumption due to differences in teaching activities, we included a variable (TEACHING) for the training activities of non-medical staff. These activities are represented by the ratio of trainee positions and the sum of all non-medical personnel. Another important point to consider is that hospitals in Germany are allowed to lease hospital beds to self-employed private-practice physicians, although the vast majority of hospital physicians in Germany are employees. The self-employed physicians use the hospital facilities to provide inpatient care. The DEA efficiency scores calculated in the first stage of our analysis were higher for hospitals that had leased beds because the cases referred to these physicians had been counted as hospital output (i.e. inpatient cases), whereas the corresponding resource use in terms of physicians had not been considered on the input side. To control for this, we defined the proportion of all hospital beds that had been leased (LEASED BEDS) as a variable in our regression models.

The set of explanatory variables representing the different environmental characteristics were as follows: The Hirschman-Herfindahl index (HHI) was applied, which measures competitive pressure in a hospital's market and is a standard economic measure of market concentration. The market area was defined as the county in which a hospital was located, which is a frequently used definition in hospital studies [57–61]. Although there has been some controversy about the most appropriate way to define a hospital's market area, Garnick et al. [62] reported that for the purpose of measuring competitive activity it makes little difference whether a hospital's market is defined as a county or a radius. The HHI is obtained by squaring a hospital's regional market share (reflected by the distribution of treated cases) and subsequently summing the market shares of admissions for all of the hospitals in a given county. The higher the HHI, the more concentrated the regional market. We used HHI to measure the effects from the changes over time in a hospital's competitive environment. This specification allowed us to differentiate between the effects of privatization and the effects of changes in market structure resulting from health care reforms. In recent years, the most significant reform in the German hospital market was the introduction of a new system of reimbursement based on DRGs. The chief motivation behind this fundamental overhaul of the old reimbursement system, which was based on per diem charges, was to create financial incentives that would increase hospital efficiency [63]. We thus defined a dummy variable (DRG), which was assigned a value of 1 in the DRG era (i.e. 2003 through 2007).

These variables for hospital and environmental characteristics were also used in the propensity score model, as were the case-mix index (CMXI) derived from the Elixhauser Comorbidity Index [42] and the pre-privatization efficiency (EFFICIENCY) of privatized and non-privatized hospitals. We used this last variable to minimize potential bias because public entities may prefer to sell hospitals characterized by lower levels of efficiency while keeping those that are performing well. Table 3 shows the descriptive statistics for the variables used in the second stage analysis stratified according to the intervention and control groups.

Table 3. Descriptive statistics of variables used for the second stage analysis for the matched sample

Period	t−1		t+1		t+2		t+3		t+4	
	Mean	SD	Mean	SD	Mean	SD	Mean	SD	Mean	SD
For-profit										
Number of hospitals	*n*=99		*n*=99		*n*=90		*n*=77		*n*=66	
BEDS	344	(268)	344	(273)	332	(261)	327	(262)	342	(272)
LEASED BEDS	0.037	(0.074)	0.032	(0.073)	0.028	(0.050)	0.026	(0.047)	0.024	(0.047)
TEACHING	0.146	(0.154)	0.171	(0.177)	0.162	(0.191)	0.177	(0.202)	0.129	(0.147)
CMXI	0.161	(0.063)	0.155	(0.061)	0.160	(0.056)	0.154	(0.052)	0.147	(0.048)
EFFICIENCY	0.761	(0.122)	0.757	(0.121)	0.772	(0.123)	0.774	(0.114)	0.772	(0.117)
HHI	0.399	(0.294)	0.393	(0.284)	0.413	(0.291)	0.450	(0.288)	0.443	(0.267)
Non-profit										
Number of hospitals	*n*=33		*n*=33		*n*=24		*n*=23		*n*=22	
BEDS	237	(179)	232	(189)	264	(220)	267	(214)	274	(216)
LEASED BEDS	0.060	(0.067)	0.055	(0.064)	0.037	(0.047)	0.039	(0.047)	0.055	(0.097)
TEACHING	0.151	(0.156)	0.165	(0.159)	0.141	(0.151)	0.182	(0.125)	0.099	(0.138)
CMXI	0.141	(0.042)	0.146	(0.044)	0.142	(0.043)	0.128	(0.034)	0.132	(0.037)
EFFICIENCY	0.730	(0.144)	0.757	(0.131)	0.743	(0.129)	0.738	(0.140)	0.716	(0.157)
HHI	0.404	(0.210)	0.439	(0.253)	0.463	(0.274)	0.469	(0.278)	0.475	(0.285)
Control										
Number of hospitals	*n*=128		*n*=128		*n*=113		*n*=99		*n*=87	
BEDS	332	(257)	329	(256)	336	(257)	321	(248)	319	(250)
LEASED BEDS	0.048	(0.078)	0.045	(0.078)	0.047	(0.083)	0.043	(0.078)	0.051	(0.094)
TEACHING	0.148	(0.153)	0.146	(0.158)	0.148	(0.158)	0.142	(0.154)	0.146	(0.160)
CMXI	0.162	(0.072)	0.162	(0.070)	0.160	(0.067)	0.154	(0.050)	0.157	(0.061)
EFFICIENCY	0.765	(0.127)	0.746	(0.121)	0.750	(0.129)	0.747	(0.133)	0.747	(0.119)
HHI	0.390	(0.231)	0.394	(0.241)	0.395	(0.242)	0.390	(0.249)	0.398	(0.247)

t−1 is defined as the year before privatization occurred, while t+1, t+2, t+3 and t+4 represent the four post-privatization years.

3.4 Sample

The data for our study were derived from the annual hospital reports collected and administered by the Research Data Centre of the Statistical Offices of the Länder. This rich dataset covers all public, private for-profit, and private non-profit hospitals in Germany and contains hospital-level information on cost and hospital infrastructure, as well as patient-level information on age, diagnoses, and procedures performed. Our study is based on data from the years 1996 through 2008, and the unit of analysis was the hospital. Due to data privacy issues, we were able to obtain randomly selected data for only two-thirds of German acute care hospitals (n = 1,878). To ensure the comparability of the hospitals in the sample, the following institutions were excluded from further analysis: hospitals providing only psychiatric care; university hospitals; day clinics; hospitals with fewer than 50 beds or more than 2000 beds; and private non-profit and private for-profit hospitals that had been privatized before the study period. In addition, manual plausibility checks were conducted to identify any measurement errors. Ultimately, a total of 548 public hospitals remained in our sample, including 132 that were privatized between 1997 and 2007. Of these 132 hospitals, 99 were acquired by a private for-profit organization and 33 were acquired by a private non-profit organization [64]. Table 4shows the number of hospital privatizations per year.

Table 4. Number of hospital privatizations per year

Period	Number of privatizations		
	Total	Non-profit	For-profit
1997	15	5	10
1998	13	8	5
1999	7	0	7
2000	4	2	2
2001	15	0	15
2002	13	2	11
2003	14	3	11
2004	11	2	9
2005	13	1	12
2006	16	2	14
2007	11	8	3
Total	132	33	99

4 FINDINGS AND DISCUSSION

Table 5 shows the degree of imbalance before and after propensity score matching for our subset of covariates (interactions are not shown).

The differences in covariate means between the unmatched samples indicate that it was especially the size of non-privatized hospitals (in terms of beds) that was likely to be larger than that of privatized hospitals. After propensity score matching, the differences in covariate means between the privatized and non-privatized hospitals were substantially smaller than those seen in the pre-matching distribution. All of the differences between the groups were less than 6% in the post-matching distribution. Table 6 summarizes the results of Hotelling's T-square test. Reassuringly, the balancing conditions were satisfied within each propensity score quartile (i.e. the *P* values for all quartiles were substantially higher than 0.10).

Table 5. Balance in measured covariates before and after matching

Group	Unmatched sample					Matched sample				
	Control (n=361)		Intervention (n=132)		d_i	Control (n=128)		Intervention (n=132)		d_i
	Mean	SD	Mean	SD		Mean	SD	Mean	SD	
Variable name										
BEDS	351	(259)	317	(252)	12.89%	332	(257)	317	(252)	5.68%
LEASED BEDS	0.069	(0.091)	0.043	(0.073)	2.60%	0.048	(0.078)	0.043	(0.073)	0.50%
TEACHING	0.169	(0.172)	0.147	(0.154)	2.20%	0.148	(0.153)	0.147	(0.154)	0.10%
CMXI	0.157	(0.058)	0.156	(0.059)	0.10%	0.162	(0.072)	0.156	(0.059)	0.60%
EFFICIENCY	0.772	(0.111)	0.753	(0.128)	1.90%	0.765	(0.127)	0.753	(0.128)	1.20%
HHI	0.401	(0.242)	0.400	(0.275)	0.10%	0.390	(0.231)	0.400	(0.275)	1.00%

Table 6. Results from Hotelling's T square test by propensity score quartile

Quartile	T squared statistics	*F* test statistics	*P* values
FIRST	3.593	0.551	0.768
SECOND	4.647	0.712	0.641
THIRD	4.066	0.615	0.717
FOURTH	4.933	0.746	0.615

The regression results for our first model, which used DEA efficiency scores as dependent variable in the regressions, are summarized in Table 7 and stratified according to whether public hospitals were converted to private for-profit or private non-profit status. Two sets of regression results are shown for each type of conversion: one based on the unmatched samples and the other based on the samples after propensity score matching. The coefficients shown in Table 7 are those for the difference-in-difference interaction between the variables PRIV and POST and can be interpreted as marginal effects. The interaction terms identify the changes in efficiency after a hospital was privatized relative to changes in efficiency in the comparator group.

Table 7. Regression results for the efficiency model

Post-privatization year	Public->For-profit		Public->Non-profit	
	Unmatched	Matched	Unmatched	Matched
1st year after privatization	0.005 (0.008)	0.021** (0.011)	0.029** (0.012)	0.050** (0.021)
2nd year after privatization	0.019** (0.008)	0.036*** (0.011)	0.017 (0.015)	0.053** (0.024)
3rd year after privatization	0.023*** (0.009)	0.041*** (0.013)	0.020 (0.015)	0.045* (0.024)
4th year after privatization	0.029*** (0.009)	0.049*** (0.013)	0.008 (0.017)	0.037 (0.027)

*$P \le 0.10$; **$P \le 0.05$; ***$P \le 0.01$; SE in parentheses

The regression results for public hospitals that were converted to private for-profit status show that there was a significant increase in efficiency compared to the control group starting the second year after privatization in the unmatched sample and even in the first year after privatization in the matched sample. Throughout all estimations of our efficiency model, the effects of this change in status increased with the number of years after privatization. For instance, four years after their conversion to private for-profit status, the formerly public hospitals experienced an increase in efficiency that was 2.9 to 4.9% greater than that seen among non-privatized hospitals over the same period. In the matched samples, the standard errors were larger than in the pre-matched sample. This can be attributed, in part, to the smaller size of the control group; nevertheless, the general finding remained the same. The estimations also suggest that the increase in efficiency seen in public hospitals that were converted to private for-profit status is permanent and not simply a transitional phenomenon after which hospital operations revert to their pre-privatization state.

In the unmatched sample, the regression results for public hospitals that were converted to private non-profit status show that, at least in the first year after privatization, there was a significant increase in efficiency of 2.9% compared to the control group. For years 2 through 4 after privatization, we observed no significant effects apart from those seen in year 2 and 3 in the matched sample. In the matched sample, public hospitals converted to private non-profit status showed a significant increase in efficiency of 5.3% in the second year after privatization and 4.5% in the third year after privatization compared to the non-privatized hospitals. Throughout most estimations, however, the effects of a conversion to private non-profit status decreased as the number of years after privatization increased. This points to a transitory rather than a permanent effect.

To gain a better understanding of these findings and the restructuring that occurred after hospitals were converted to private for-profit and non-profit status in our sample, we conducted a series of exploratory regressions. Using the same model specification to identify the effect of privatization on the quantity and type of resource use (i.e. employing input variables from the first-stage analysis as dependent variables of the second-stage regression) compared to the non-privatized public hospitals, we found that hospitals that were converted to private for-profit status substantially reduced all of the analyzed labor inputs during the post-privatization period with the exception of physicians and administrative staff (i.e. nursing staff, other clinical staff and other nonclinical staff). This finding can potentially be explained by the two lines of internal authority—medical and managerial—that characterize most hospitals: In contrast to nurses and technical staff, physicians are often part of the top management and make decisions on the allocation of resources. Being clinicians or former clinicians themselves, members of top management may be predisposed to avoiding reductions in the number of physicians. Another explanation may be that avoiding physician lay-offs is a strategy to reduce resistance to change by compensating physicians for coping with the organizational adjustments associated with privatization. For hospitals converted to non-profit status reductions of labor input tend to be smaller compared to conversions to for-profit status. Figure 1 shows the changes in staffing and supplies per case-mix-adjusted inpatient hospital case that can be seen four years after the conversion to private for-profit or non-profit status compared to the control group of non-privatized hospitals. We use the fixed effects specification based on the matched sample for these illustrations.

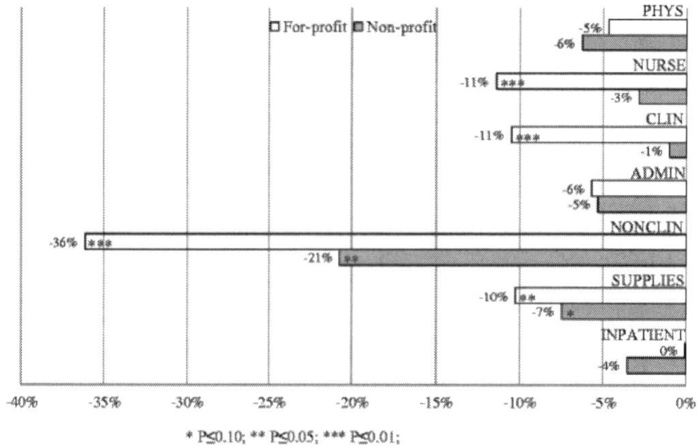

Figure 1. Changes in staffing (FTEs) and expenditure on supplies per case after conversion to for-profit or non-profit status compared to the control group. Note: Changes in staffing and supplies per case-mix-adjusted inpatient hospital case four years after conversion to for-profit or non-profit status compared to the control group of non-privatized hospitals. *FTE* full-time equivalents

To explore our results yet further, we examined the interaction effects between a given privatization (difference-in-difference coefficient) and the competitive environment (HHI) in which this privatization took place. In their summary of the theoretical literature, Sheshinski and López-Calva [65] argue that privatized organizations are likely to have lower efficiency gains in non-competitive markets than they would under the discipline of a competitive market. They assume that organizations in monopolistic or oligopolistic markets restrict output and have higher average costs and lower efficiency than competitive organizations. Rosko [58–60] and Rosko and Chilingerian [61], however, have found that efficiency in the US hospital sector is negatively related to market competition. Using HHI as a proxy for competition in our present study, we were unable to observe any effect of this variable on efficiency after privatization.

We also examined the interaction effects between privatization and the introduction of yardstick competition through DRGs in the year 2004 in Germany. There is reason to believe that efficiency gains are larger for privatizations after the introduction of yardstick competition, especially in the case of hospitals converted to private for-profit status [63, 66–68]. We used a dummy variable to model the pre-DRG and the DRG period. In doing so, we defined each of the years 2001 through 2004 as the cut-off point between pre-DRG and DRG periods because hospitals may have changed their behavior after the introduction of DRGs or beforehand based on their knowledge of the new system and its upcoming implementation. Table 8 summarizes the corresponding regression results based on a fixed effects regression model.

Table 8. Changes in efficiency after privatization in the DRG era compared to the pre-DRG era

Post-privatization period	Matched sample			
	t+1	t+2	t+3	t+4
Public->For-profit				
2001 cut-off point	−0.020 (0.016)	−0.019 (0.018)	−0.031*** (0.020)	0.012 (0.028)
2002 cut-off point	−0.021 (0.014)	−0.012 (0.018)	−0.037** (0.018)	−0.035 (0.022)
2003 cut-off point	−0.018 (0.014)	−0.032** (0.015)	−0.037** (0.018)	−0.039** (0.019)
2004 cut-off point	−0.026* (0.014)	−0.023* (0.015)	−0.047*** (0.016)	−0.042** (0.018)
Public->Non-profit				
2001 cut-off point	−0.015 (0.031)	−0.001 (0.038)	−0.030 (0.031)	−0.035 (0.055)
2002 cut-off point	−0.015 (0.031)	−0.026 (0.037)	−0.030 (0.033)	−0.057* (0.035)
2003 cut-off point	−0.015 (0.031)	−0.026 (0.037)	−0.050 (0.033)	−0.057* (0.035)
2004 cut-off point	−0.003 (0.033)	−0.049 (0.036)	−0.050 (0.033)	−0.076** (0.035)

*$P \leq 0.10$; **$P \leq 0.05$; ***$P \leq 0.01$; SE in parentheses

t−1 is defined as the year before privatization occurred, while t+1, t+2, t+3 and t+4 represent the four post-privatization years.

The regression results for hospitals that were converted to private for-profit status reveal a significant negative association between post-privatization performance and the introduction of DRGs. In particular, the efficiency gains seen in hospitals converted to private for-profit status were substantially lower in the DRG era compared to those seen in the control group. The introduction of DRGs induced yardstick competition in the German hospital market, setting strong incentives to increase efficiency and stimulating restructuring efforts across all types of ownership. Our findings thus suggest that it became more challenging for hospitals that were converted to private for-private status in the DRG era to realize further efficiency gains. In the model estimated for hospitals that were converted to private non-profit status, the interaction term between post-privatization performance and the introduction of DRGs was not significant.

The results of our regression analyses for for-profit and non-profit privatization indicate that the efficiency effects of privatization depend on the type of privatization. There are several potential reasons for-profit hospitals generating permanent efficiency gains after privatization while non-profit hospitals do not. Our results show that public hospitals that were converted to private for-profit status realized their substantial efficiency gains by markedly reducing all labor inputs (with the exception of physicians and administrative staff) and expenditure on supplies. In contrast, non-profit privatization only had a significant negative effect on the non-medical categories of personnel and expenditure on supplies. In short, the employment-reducing effect of for-profit privatization, especially in terms of the medical categories of staff (i.e. nursing staff and other clinical staff) was larger than that of non-profit privatization. These findings are similar to those of Picone et al. [26], and Shen [28]. Regarding the incentive structures of private non-profit providers, agency theory and property-rights theory predict that the owners and managers of non-profit organizations frequently diverge from cost- or inefficiency-minimizing behavior and instead maximize quality, quantity, and/or prestige [69, 70]. In other words, private non-profit hospitals may avoid reductions in staff with the intention to avoid reductions in the quality of care. The positive relationship between the staff-to-patient ratio and quality of care has been confirmed previously by a number of studies (e.g., Aiken et al. [71, 72]). Therefore, other measures not considered in our analyses, such as patient satisfaction or other measures of quality of care, might have led to different results.

In line with the evidence found in studies from other countries, especially the U.S., the evidence from Germany suggests that private for-profit ownership is associated with a strong focus on profit-maximization [20, 73, 74]. According to agency theory, the owners of private for-profit hospitals may use profits as their measure of a manager's success and can limit divergences from their interest by making the manager's compensation a positive function of these profits and are thus more likely to achieve greater efficiency [69, 75–77]. The income of physicians in private for-profit hospitals can also be tied to a hospital's financial performance. Within public and private non-profit hospitals, the income of individual decision makers is rarely tied to a hospital's performance, creating little incentive to enforce strong efficient behavior.

Further it should be considered that in the pre-DRG era private for-profit hospitals tended to focus on revenues in order to earn profits and were able to generate significantly higher revenues per case than hospitals with other forms of ownership [73, 74]. As the development of the German DRG-system progresses options to focus on revenues substantially decreased over the last years and thus especially private for-profit hospitals are very likely to increase their focus on efficiency as a kind of compensation. However, the generated profits allowed private for-profit hospitals to substantially invest in their hospital infrastructure that also might have positively affected the efficiency of their service production processes. In addition, private for-profit hospitals started earlier than private non-profit hospitals to specialize on certain diagnoses or procedures in order to realize economies of scale. Finally, these hospitals also tend to form chains and networks with other hospitals realizing better capabilities to negotiate with sickness funds and exploiting economies of scale for example by transferring knowledge or centralizing the purchase of supplies [78].

We tested the robustness of our findings in several ways. First, we employed the average in-hospital mortality rate as an additional output to adjust for variations in the quality of care between hospitals [41]. The results of our quality-adjusted efficiency model show that employing in-hospital mortality as an additional output was not associated with smaller efficiency gains (see Table 9 for the regression results of the quality-adjusted efficiency model). In fact, the regression results for hospitals that were converted to private for-profit status showed that there was even a small increase in coefficients compared to the estimations of the efficiency model. Our findings therefore do not provide any evidence that increases in technical efficiency come at the expense of the quality of care. This may be due to a decrease over the past decade in the asymmetry of information about the quality of care in the German hospital sector following several health care reforms that have aimed to improve quality assurance, such as the introduction of mandatory quality reports. Furthermore, it is important to consider that privatized hospitals are often located in very competitive regions with substantial overcapacities, which may increase the importance of quality of care as a parameter of competition. Indeed, there is evidence that private for-profit hospitals have improved their quality management and hospital outcomes precisely in order to attract patients in such settings [79].

Table 9. Regression results for the quality-adjusted efficiency model

	Public->For-profit		Public->Non-profit	
Post-privatization year	Unmatched	Matched	Unmatched	Matched
1st year after privatization	0.004 (0.008)	0.024** (0.011)	0.028** (0.012)	0.049** (0.021)
2nd year after privatization	0.022*** (0.008)	0.037*** (0.011)	0.015 (0.015)	0.050** (0.024)
3rd year after privatization	0.025*** (0.009)	0.043*** (0.013)	0.019 (0.015)	0.042* (0.024)
4th year after privatization	0.031*** (0.009)	0.055*** (0.013)	0.002 (0.017)	0.022 (0.027)

Second, we re-estimated all second-stage regressions by incorporating firm fixed effects as an additional dimension. To do so, we estimated time and firm fixed effects as a multi-way clustered regression [80]. This resulted in only minor changes in the difference-in-difference coefficients, and our findings remained robust throughout the models. Third, in other economic sectors, Parker and Martin [81] found that pre-privatization gains in efficiency can be even larger than post-privatization gains. Based on this finding, there is reason to assume that local governments make efforts to increase the efficiency of public hospitals prior to privatization to generate higher sales revenue, reducing potential gains in efficiency after privatization. In order to take account of this possibility, we re-ran our models, allowing an alternative pre-privatization period of two years. The direction of the difference-in-difference coefficients did not change throughout the models, and standard errors increased only slightly due to the reduced sample size. Bias due to pre-privatization efficiency gains was thus unlikely. Fourth we re-estimated our DEA models after eliminating those inputs (physicians and other clinical staff) having a strong correlation ($r > 0.90$) to other inputs used in the full DEA model. Thus, we performed 3 alternative DEA models: 1) without physicians, 2) without other clinical staff, 3) without physicians and other clinical staff. All other steps remained unchained. In the re-estimated regression models the coefficients and standard errors hardly changed compared to the full models. The only change occurred in model 3) where standard errors were smaller for non-profit privatization in the 3rd year after privatization. This likely reason for this effect is that variation of both these inputs across hospitals is larger than for most other inputs. Fifth, one could argue that our multi-step procedure to generate results may move the sample too far away from reality. Therefore, we added a further sensitivity analysis to show that results are robust even if we drastically reduce the numbers of steps performed in our analysis. In doing so, we estimated a model with the following specifications: We re-estimated the DEA model without risk-adjusted cases as output. 2) We proceeded without bootstrapping. 3) We estimated the regression based on the unmatched samples i.e. eliminated the matching step. We still see large and significant efficiency gains after for-profit privatizations, coefficients are slightly lower and standard errors tend to be larger. Altogether our study results are very robust to model changes.

Our study has a number of strengths compared to previous investigations of hospital ownership conversions. First, to our knowledge, it is the first quantitative study to examine the effects of privatization on technical efficiency using a panel data approach based on bootstrapped DEA efficiency scores. Second, our study employs a difference-in-difference matching approach to address problems arising both from causal inference and time-invariant differences. Third, our sample of privatized hospitals is large ($n = 132$), providing greater statistical power and more robust estimates than the analyses conducted in previous studies. Finally, our sample is rich, consisting of a large set of environmental and organizational characteristics. This is likely to have yielded more consistent results because it allowed us to control appropriately for determinants of efficiency other than the privatization event.

Our study also has several important limitations. First, additional inputs (e.g., capital) and additional outputs (e.g., hospital outpatient cases) would have improved our model of the hospital production process. Considering the number of hospital outpatient cases in addition to inpatient cases is often recommended in order to measure patient care output [38]. Although we had intended to include a proxy for hospital outpatient activities in our analysis (e.g., outpatient surgery), data inconsistencies and measurement errors prevented us from doing so. Second, including explanatory factors in addition to environmental and organizational characteristics might have provided a better explanation of variation in our estimates, thus potentially affecting our interpretation of the relationship between privatization and organizational efficiency. Third, our study relies on in-hospital mortality data and does not take post-hospital mortality into account, which clearly would have been preferable. This being said, Rosenthal et al. [82] found that (a) in-hospital mortality data were not biased by discharge practices and (b) using in-hospital mortality as a measure of a hospital's quality of care leads to results similar to those obtained with 30 days post-hospital mortality. It should also be considered that mortality represents only one dimension of quality. There are numerous other ways of measuring quality of care, e.g., adherence to guidelines, waiting time, patient satisfaction, which would be worth including in a more comprehensive quality-adjusted DEA model. However, by using the above mentioned data set we are constrained to mortality as a proxy for quality. Thus, our quality-adjusted DEA model is not able to provide a comprehensive picture of the overall quality of care hospitals provide and one should take these limitations into consideration when drawing conclusions based on quality-adjusted efficiency. Moreover, one should generally be careful when interpreting quality-adjusted efficiency in a way that patients may find it acceptable to receive a lower quality of care if efficiency is high [83]. In this study the quality-adjusted efficiency model is only meant to serve as robustness check to show that efficiency gains after privatization do not change completely if mortality as one dimension of quality of care is considered in our models. Fourth, for sensitivity purposes it would have been preferable to use SFA in addition to DEA. When comparing DEA to SFA, however, Linna [84] and Webster et al. [85] found that both methods yielded comparable results when measuring hospital efficiency. Fifth, in DEA model II, we used 1 minus the in-hospital mortality rate per year, which represents an index variable. Syrjänen [39] found that mixing index and volume measures in DEA may lead to biased results for the most commonly used constant returns to scale variant of the Banker and Moorey (BM) model and Charnes, Cooper, and Rhodes (CCR) model. This problem does not apply in our context, however, because we used a variable returns to scale variant of the BCC model [39, 86]. Finally, although we improve over other studies by considering a measure for differences in case-mix among hospitals there are reasons to believe that certain potentially important differences are not captured by this measure. For instance, multimorbidity of patients and the resource use associated with this are often not adequately captured by case-mix measures such as the Elixhauser Index.

5 CONCLUSIONS

In the present study, we investigated the post-acquisition effects of privatization on hospital efficiency in Germany. Our findings show that hospitals converted to private for-profit status showed an increase in efficiency after privatization that was significantly higher than that realized by their non-privatized counterparts over the same period. We defined four alternative post-privatization periods (i.e. first, second, third, and fourth year) and found that the increase in efficiency after conversion to private for-profit status did not appear to be transitory. Our results show, that hospitals that were converted to private for-profit status realized their substantial efficiency gains by markedly reducing all labor inputs (with the exception of physicians and administrative staff) and expenditure on supplies. The results of our study, which remained robust when considering in-hospital mortality as an additional output, do not support frequently voiced concerns that efficiency gains after conversion to private for-profit status are realized at the expense of quality of care. Taking the effect of the introduction of DRG payments into account, it is striking that the efficiency gains of hospitals converted to private for-profit status were significantly lower during the DRG era. We also observed an increase in efficiency one year after hospitals were converted to private non-profit status, but our estimations suggest that this effect is transitory and that hospitals converted to private for-profit status follow a different restructuring strategy than that pursued by their private non-profit counterparts.

Our results indicate that converting hospitals to private for-profit status may be an effective way to ensure better allocation of resources in the hospital sector. Before drawing policy implications, however, a number of issues must be considered. In some cases, public hospitals converted to private non-profit status may not be restructured with the intention of increasing efficiency, but rather with the aim of improving the patient experience, including the quality of care. Although our results remained robust when considering in-hospital mortality for hospitals converted to private non-profit status, other measures not considered in our analysis, such as patient satisfaction, may have led to different results after the privatization event. Moreover, it should also be taken into consideration that the time needed to develop new quality assurance systems in privatized hospitals may be longer than the period we considered in our study. Additional research is needed to investigate the long-term effects of privatization and to examine the decisions behind the approaches taken by private for-profit and private non-profit organizations in their restructuring of public hospitals.

Given the increasing importance of privatization in health systems in Germany and beyond, further studies are needed to investigate the effects of privatization on efficiency and different dimensions of care quality. Outside the hospital sector, privatization activity is also increasing in laboratory diagnostics, nursing care and rehabilitative services. The approach used in our study may be useful in investigating privatization in these other areas of care. In addition, future research should go beyond the standard administrative hospital data base to further explain the wide variation in hospital efficiency after privatization which may be due to hospital decision making, market spillover effects or other reasons.

ACKNOWLEDGMENT

This study was supported by a research grant from the Federal Ministry for Research and Education (BMBF) in Germany (grant number: BMBF 01FL10055). The sponsor had no role in the study design, collection and analysis of data, the writing of the report or the submission of the paper for publication. In addition, the authors would like to thank the Munich Center of Health Sciences (MC-Health) for interesting discussions and helpful comments.

CONFLICT OF INTEREST

The authors have no conflict of interest that is directly related to the content of this study.

Open Access

REFERENCES

1. Burns LR, Shah RJ, Sloan FA, Powell AC (2009) The impact of hospital ownership conversions: review of the literature and results from a comparative field study. In: Savage GT, Fottler MD (eds) Advances in health care management—volume 8. Emerald Group Publishing, Bingley, pp 171–229
2. Megginson WL, Netter JM (2001) From state to market: a survey of empirical studies on privatization. J Econ Lit 39:321–389
3. Federal Statistical Office of Germany (2009) Fachserie 12 Reihe 6.1.1—Grunddaten der Krankenhäuser und Vorsorge—oder Rehabilitationseinrichtungen. http://www.destatis.de/jetspeed/portal/cms/Sites/destatis/Internet/DE/Content/Publikationen/Fachveroeffentlichungen/Gesundheit/Krankenhaeuser/GrunddatenKrankenhaeuser,templateId=renderPrint.psml. Accessed 24 June 2011
4. Busse R, Riesberg A (2004) Health care systems in transition: Germany. European Observatory on Health Systems and Policies, Copenhagen
5. Simar L, Wilson PW (1998) Sensitivity analysis of efficiency scores: how to bootstrap in nonparametric frontier models. Manag Sci 44:49–61
6. Simar L, Wilson PW (2000) A general methodology for bootstrapping in non-parametric frontier models. J Appl Stat 27:779–802
7. Rosenbaum P (2002) Observational studies. Springer, New York

8. Rubin DB (1973) The use of matched sampling and regression adjustment to remove bias in observational studies. Biometrics 29:185–203

9. Rubin DB (2006) Matched sampling for causal effects. Cambridge University Press, New York

10. Simar L, Wilson PW (2007) Estimation and inference in two-stage, semi-parametric models of production processes. J Econ 136:31–64

11. Haskel J, Szymanski S (1993) Privatization, liberalization, wages and employment: theory and evidence for the UK. Economica 60:161–182

12. Shleifer A, Vishny RW (1994) Politicians and firms. Q J Econ 109:995–1025

13. Bös D (1991) Privatization: a theoretical treatment. Oxford University Press, Oxford

14. Boycko M, Shleifer A, Vishny R (1996) A theory of privatisation. Econ J 106:309–319

15. Laffont JJ, Tirole J (1993) Privatization and incentives. In: Laffont JJ, Tirole J (eds) A theory of incentives in procurement and regulation. MIT Press, Cambridge, pp 637–660

16. Sappington D, Stiglitz J (1987) Privatization, information and incentives. J Policy Anal Manage 6:567–582

17. Schmidt K (1996) The cost and benefits of privatization. J Law Econ Organ 12:1–24

18. Vickers J, Yarrow G (1991) Economic perspectives on privatization. J Econ Perspect 5:111–132

19. Villalonga B (2000) Privatization and efficiency: differentiating ownership effects from political, organizational, and dynamic effects. J Econ Behav Organ 42:43–74

20. Shen YC, Eggleston K, Lau J et al (2007) Hospital ownership and financial performance: what explains the different findings in the empirical literature? Inquiry 44:41–68

21. Herr A (2008) Cost and technical efficiency of German hospitals: does ownership matter? Health Econ 17:1057–1071

22. Tiemann O, Schreyögg J (2009) Effects of ownership on hospital efficiency in Germany. Bus Res 2:115–145

23. Megginson WL, Nash RC, van Randenborgh M (1994) The financial and operating performance of newly privatized firms: an international empirical analysis. J Finance 49:403–452

24. Heckman JJ, Ichimura H, Todd PE (1997) Matching as an econometric evaluation estimator: evidence from evaluating a job training programme. Rev Econ Stud 64:605–654

25. Heckman JJ, Hotz VJ (1989) Choosing among alternative nonexperimental methods for estimating the impact of social programs: the case of manpower training. J Am Stat Assoc 84:862–880

26. Picone G, Chou S, Sloan F (2002) Are for-profit hospital conversions harmful to patients and to Medicare? Rand J Econ 33:507–523

27. Shen YC (2002) The effect of hospital ownership choice on patient outcomes after treatment for acute myocardial infarction. J Health Econ 21:901–922

28. Shen YC (2003) Changes in hospital performance after ownership conversions. Inquiry 40:217–234

29. Farsi M (2004) Changes in hospital quality after conversion in ownership status. Int J Health Care Finance Econ 4:211–230

30. Pestieau P (2009) Assessing the performance of the public sector. Ann Publ Cooper Econ 80:133–161

31. Hollingsworth B (2003) Non-parametric and parametric applications measuring efficiency in health care. Health Care Manag Sci 6:203–218

32. Hollingsworth B (2008) The measurement of efficiency and productivity of health care delivery. Health Econ 17:1107–1128

33. Charnes A, Cooper W, Rhodes E (1978) Measuring the efficiency of decision making units. Eur J Oper Res 2:429–444

34. Banker R, Charnes A, Cooper W (1984) Some models for estimating technical and scale inefficiencies in data envelopment analysis. Manag Sci 30:1078–1092

35. Ozcan YA (2008) Health care benchmarking and performance evaluation: an assessment using data envelopment analysis. Springer, New York

36. Coelli T, Rao D, Batteese G (1999) An introduction to efficiency and productivity analysis. Kluwer Academic Publishers, Boston

37. Pilyavsky AI, Aaronson WE, Bernet PM et al (2006) East-west: does it make a difference to hospital efficiencies in Ukraine? Health Econ 15:1173–1186

38. Jacobs R, Smith PC, Street A (2006) Measuring efficiency in health care: analytic techniques and health policy. Cambridge University Press, Cambridge

39. Syrjänen MJ (2004) Non-discretionary and discretionary factors and scale in data envelopment analysis. Eur J Oper Res 158:20–33

40. Burgess J, Wilson P (1998) Variation in inefficiency among US hospitals. INFOR 36:84–102

41. Nayar P, Ozcan Y (2008) Data envelopment analysis: comparison of hospital efficiency and quality. J Med Sys 32:193–199

42. van Walraven C, Austin P, Jennings A et al (2009) A modification of the elixhauser comorbidity measures into a point system for hospital death using administrative data. Med Care 47:626–633

43. Carey K (2000) A multilevel modelling approach to analysis of patient costs under managed care. Health Econ 9:435–446

44. Carey K (2002) Hospital length of stay and cost: a multilevel modeling analysis. Health Serv Outcome Res Meth 3:41–56

45. Dyson R, Allen R, Camanho A et al (2001) Pitfalls and protocols in DEA. Eur J Oper Res 132:245–259

46. Blundell R, Dias MC (2000) Evaluation methods for non-experimental data. Fisc Stud 21:427–468

47. Smith JE, Todd P (2005) Does matching overcome LaLonde's critique of nonexperimental estimators? J Econ 125:305–353

48. Austin PC (2008) A critical appraisal of propensity-score matching in the medical literature between 1996 and 2003. Stat Med 27:2037–2049

49. Rosenbaum P (1989) Optimal matching for observational studies. J Am Stat Assoc 84:1024–1032

50. Schreyögg J, Stargardt T, Tiemann O (2010) Costs and quality of hospitals in different health care systems: a multilevel approach with propensity score matching. Health Econ 20:85–100

51. Austin PC (2009) Some methods of propensity-score matching had superior performance to others: results of an empirical investigation and Monte Carlo simulations. Biom J 51:171–184

52. Imai K, King G, Stuart E (2008) Misunderstandings among experimentalists and observationalists about causal inference. J R Stat Soc 171:481–502

53. Girma S, Görg H (2007) Evaluating the foreign ownership wage premium using a difference-in-differences matching approach. J Int Econ 72:97–112

54. Carey K, James F, Burgess JF Jr (1999) On measuring the hospital cost/quality trade-off. Health Econ 8:509–520

55. Dudley R, Johansen K, Brand R et al (2000) Selective referral to high-volume hospitals: estimating potentially avoidable deaths. JAMA 283:1159–1166

56. Harrison JP, Coppola MN, Wakefield M (2004) Efficiency of federal hospitals in the United States. J Med Syst 28:411–422

57. Chang H, Chang WJ, Das S et al (2004) Health care regulation and the operating efficiency of hospitals: evidence from Taiwan. J Account Publ Pol 23:483–510

58. Rosko MD (1999) Impact of internal and external environmental pressures on hospital inefficiency. Health Care Manag Sci 2:63–74

59. Rosko MD (2001) Cost efficiency of US hospitals: a stochastic frontier approach. Health Econ 10:539–551

60. Rosko MD (2004) Performance of US teaching hospitals: a panel analysis of cost inefficiency. Health Care Manag Sci 7:7–16

61. Rosko MD, Chilingerian JA (1999) Estimating hospital inefficiency: does case mix matter? J Med Syst 23:57–71

62. Garnick D, Luft H, Robinson J et al (1987) Appropriate measures of hospital market areas. Health Serv Res 22:69–89

63. Schreyögg J, Tiemann O, Busse R (2006) Cost accounting to determine prices: how well do prices reflect costs in the German DRG-system? Health Care Manag Sci 9:269–279

64. Research Data Centre of the Statistical Offices of the Länder (2009) Krankenhausstatistik (Teil I: Grunddaten, Teil II: Diagnosen und Teil III: Kostennachweis) 1996–2008, Antrag 1133–2009

65. Sheshinski E, López-Calva L (2003) Privatization and its benefits: theory and evidence. CESifo Econ Stud 49:429–459

66. Biørn E, Hagen TP, Iversen T et al (2003) The effect of activity-based financing on hospital efficiency: a panel data analysis of DEA efficiency scores 1992–2000. Health Care Manag Sci 6:271–283

67. Kjerstad EM (2003) Prospective funding of general hospitals in Norway—incentives for higher production? Int J Health Care Finance Econ 3:231–251

68. Shleifer A (1985) A theory of yardstick competition. Rand J Econ 16:319–327

69. Newhouse JP (1970) Toward a theory of nonprofit Institutions: an economic model of a hospital. Am Econ Rev 60:64–74

70. Weisbrod BA (1988) The nonprofit economy. Harvard University Press, Cambridge

71. Aiken LH, Sloane DM, Lake ET et al (1999) Organization and outcomes of inpatient AIDS care. Med Care 37:760–772

72. Aiken LH, Clarke SP, Sloane DM et al (2002) Hospital nurse staffing and patient mortality, nurse burnout, and job dissatisfaction. JAMA 288:1987–1993

73. Wörz M (2008) Erlöse—Kosten—Qualität: Macht die Krankenhausträgerschaft einen Unterschied? Eine vergleichende Untersuchung von Trägerunterschieden im akutstationären Sektor in Deutschland und den Vereinigten Staaten von Amerika. VS Verlag, Wiesbaden

74. Herr A, Schmitz H, Augurzky B (2011) Profit efficiency and ownership of German hospitals. Health Econ 20:660–674

75. Fama EF, Jensen MC (1983) Separation of ownership and control. J Law Econ 26:301–325

76. Grossman S, Hart O (1983) An analysis of the principal-agent problem. Econometrica 51:7–45

77. Pauly MV, Redisch MS (1973) The not-for-profit hospital as a physician's cooperative. Am Econ Rev 63:87–99

78. Kramer J (2007) Kommunale Krankenhäuser sind zukunftsfähig—Ein Vergleich mit privaten Kliniken. http://www.staedtetag.de/imperia/md/content/schwerpunkte/fachinfos/2007/19.pdf. Accessed 24 June 2011

79. Busse R, Nimptsch U, Mansky T (2009) Measuring, monitoring, and managing quality in Germany's hospitals. Health Aff 28:294–304

80. Cameron AC, Gelbach JB, Miller DL (2006) Robust Inference with Multi-Way Clustering. NBER Technical Working Paper No. 327, University of California, Berkely.

81. Parker D, Martin S (1995) The impact of UK privatization on labor and total factor productivity. Scot J Polit Econ 42:201–220

82. Rosenthal GE, Baker DW, Norris DG et al (2000) Relationships between in-hospital and 30-day standardized hospital mortality: implications for profiling hospitals. Health Serv Res 34:1449–1468

83. Sherman HD, Zhu J (2006) Benchmarking with quality-adjusted DEA (QDEA) to seek lower-cost high-quality service: evidence from a US bank application. Ann Oper Res 145:301–319

84. Linna M (1998) Measuring hospital cost efficiency with panel data models. Health Econ 7:415–427

85. Webster R, Kennedy S, Johnson L (1998) Comparing techniques for measuring efficiency and productivity of Australian private

hospitals. Working Papers in Econometrics and Applied Statistics No. 98/3, Australian Bureau of Statistics Catalogue, Canberra

86. Hollingsworth B, Smith P (2003) Use of ratios in data envelopment analysis. Appl Econ Lett 10:733–735

8

PLANNING AND SCHEDULING OF SEMI-URGENT SURGERIES

Maartje E. Zonderland[1,2], Richard J. Boucherie[2], Nelly Litvak[2], Carmen L. A. M. Vleggeert-Lankamp[3]

[1.]Division ILeiden University Medical CenterLeidenThe Netherlands

[2.]Stochastic Operations ResearchUniversity of TwenteEnschedeThe Netherlands

[3.]Department of NeurosurgeryLeiden University Medical CenterLeidenThe Netherlands

ABSTRACT

This paper investigates the trade-off between cancellations of elective surgeries due to semi-urgent surgeries, and unused operating room (OR) time due to excessive reservation of OR time for semi-urgent surgeries.Semi-urgent surgeries, to be performed soon but not necessarily today, pose an uncertain demand on available hospital resources, and interfere with the planning of elective patients. For a highly utilized OR, reservation of OR time for semi-urgent surgeries avoids excessive cancellations of elective surgeries, but may also result in unused OR time, since arrivals of semi-urgent patients are unpredictable. First, using a queuing theory framework, we evaluate the OR capacity needed to accommodate every incoming semi-urgent surgery. Second, we introduce another queuing model that enables a trade-off between the cancelation rate of elective surgeries and unused OR time. Third, based on Markov decision theory, we develop a decision support tool that assists the scheduling process of elective and semi-urgent surgeries. We demonstrate our results with actual data obtained from a department of neurosurgery.

Keywords: Surgical scheduling, Operating rooms, Emergency patient flow, Queuing theory, Markov decision processes

1 INTRODUCTION

We consider a surgical department where elective, urgent and semi-urgent (synonym: semi-elective) patients are treated. An example of a department with such characteristics is a neurosurgery department. Urgent treatment is, among others, required for ruptured aneurysms, epidural or subdural hematomas, cauda equina syndrome, and (instable) spine fractures compromising the myelum or cauda equina. Semi-urgent pathologies include, among others, intracranial oncology, spine fractures with no or minimal neurological symptoms, drain dysfunctionalities, and disc herniations with unbearable pain or severe neurological deficits. Apart from these pathologies, the majority of neurosurgery patients do not require surgery within one or 2 weeks, and these are regarded as elective.

There is a definite trade-off between two major intertwined issues with respect to available surgical capacity: allocation of capacity to surgical departments and optimization of the surgical schedule within departments. On the one hand, when the target is minimal use of surgical resources, a more efficient surgical schedule may reduce the slack in the schedule, and therefore reduce the required capacity while keeping the societal costs due to patient cancellation and waiting constant. On the other hand, when the target is minimal societal costs due to patient cancellation and waiting, a more efficient surgical schedule may reduce these while keeping the allocated surgical resources constant. The trade-off is thus between societal costs and required surgical capacity. Allocating capacity to a surgical department usually is subject to additional constraints such as the restriction in the total available time, the time allocated to other departments, labor regulations (e.g., opening hours of the operating theater), staff restrictions (e.g., available number of surgeons), and the possibility to handle exceptions (e.g., in over-time).

In this paper we take the capacity allocated to a surgical department as a starting point. We aim for robust patient scheduling schemes. We focus on the setting of a neurosurgery department treating urgent, semi-urgent and elective patients. Urgent patients are usually treated in a separate operating room (OR), but semi-urgent patients need to be fitted in the regular OR schedule. When a semi-urgent patient arrives, an elective patient is canceled to accommodate this (prioritized) patient. The cancellation of a surgery negatively affects the patient [1]. Medical professionals tend to feel sorry for the canceled patient and aim to reschedule the surgery as soon as possible. Thus, a canceled elective patient receives a semi-urgent status, and rescheduling this surgery possibly causes the cancellation of another elective patient. This knock-on effect results in a clear dependency between semi-urgent patient arrivals and cancellation of elective patients in subsequent weeks.

Several strategies are known from literature to cope with non-elective patients. One strategy is to reserve a small amount of time for emergency patients for whom surgery is required on the day of arrival in each elective patient OR [2], instead of dedicating one or several ORs to emergent cases [3]. Another possibility is to determine the elective patient schedule given the expected number of emergencies [4]. In all papers reviewed in [5], acute cases have to be performed at least on the day of arrival, as opposed to the semi-urgent surgeries that are studied in this paper. In both [3] and [6] the authors distinguish between emergency surgeries (which have to be performed *now*) and urgent surgeries (which have to be performed within a day). In [4] and [7] stochastic programming is applied to support the scheduling of add-on cases, but in both papers these cases have to be completed on the day of arrival.

In [8] the authors start from a different viewpoint and determine, using a simulation model, how many elective cases can be performed in a dedicated orthopedic trauma OR. They state that when elective patients are willing to accept that their surgery might be canceled because of an incoming trauma patient, a higher throughput can be achieved. In [9] a trade-off is made between overtime and unused OR time. The paper has an operational viewpoint, by scheduling patients on an individual level. This is similar to the methodology presented in [10], where mathematical algorithms are used to schedule individual cases in available OR blocks.

The problem setting described here shows a similarity with the news vendor problem, where at the start of each decision period for that period the available capacity is matched with the required resources, and unmatched requests are discarded at the end of the period (see e.g. [9, 11–13] for news vendor problems applied to OR problems). The news vendor problem does not incorporate scheduling of discarded requests in subsequent periods, which is precisely the problem when elective surgeries are canceled and re-scheduled in subsequent periods. Modeling this knock-on effect is the natural domain of queuing theory. In this paper, we therefore invoke the powerful theory of queues to analyze the cancellation rate of elective patients given a pre-specified surgical capacity, and the influence of canceling patients on the cancellation rate in the future.

For a surgical department with given capacity handling elective, urgent and semi-urgent patients, this paper investigates reservation schemes of OR time for semi-urgent surgeries. As the arrival pattern of semi-urgent patients is unpredictable, the reserved OR may remain unused since elective patients cannot be scheduled so shortly before their surgery. We study the trade-off between cancellations of elective surgeries due to semi-urgent surgeries, and unused OR time due to excessive reservation of OR time for semi-urgent surgeries.

In the next section we first evaluate, using a queuing theory framework, the long run OR capacity needed to accommodate every incoming semi-urgent surgery. Second, we introduce another queuing model that enables a trade-off between the cancellation rate of elective surgeries and unused OR time. In Section 3 we develop a decision support tool, based on Markov decision theory, that assists the scheduling process of elective and semi-urgent surgeries. We demonstrate our results in Section 4 with actual data obtained from a department of neurosurgery, followed by the discussion and conclusion in Section 5.

2 MODEL AND LONG TERM BEHAVIOR

The goal of the strategic model presented in this section is to provide an estimate for the amount of OR time that should be reserved for all semi-urgent surgeries in the long run. Therefore, we do not distinguish between the 1- and 2-week streams or take overtime into account. These components of the problem are discussed in the tactical model presented in Section 3. Obviously, dynamically adjusting the amount of reserved OR time according to the effectuated inflow of semi-urgent surgeries would result in little unused OR time. However, given hospital policy that dictates that elective patients should be planned weeks in advance, such an adaptive policy would impose canceling the elective patients that were planned in the claimed slots. In order to make the trade-off between cancellation of surgeries and unused OR capacity, a constant amount of OR time is reserved for semi-urgent surgeries.

A summary of the notation used is listed in Table 1.

2.1 Assumptions and model parameters

The time available per OR day is divided into K slots of equal length. Surgeries can have a duration of 1,2,..,K slots ($K < \infty$), and are categorized according to this duration.

When a surgery has an expected duration of more than K slots, it is also included into the category of surgeries with length K slots. The total number of OR slots assigned to the department per week (m) equals the number of OR days per week multiplied by K. In order to accommodate semi-urgent patients, every week a fixed number of slots (s) is reserved ($0 \leq s \leq m$). Given the impact of the surgery on the patient and the undesirability of performing semi-urgent surgeries in overtime, we assume, in line with medical practice (see Section 1), that canceled elective patients become semi-urgent patients the following week. These patients need to undergo surgery within 1 week of their canceled surgery.

Table 1. Notation introduced in Section 2

Symbol	Description
K	Number of slots available per OR day
m	Total number of slots assigned to department
s	Number of slots reserved for semi-urgent surgeries
W_n	Number of semi-urgent slots waiting for surgery at the start of week n
W	Number of semi-urgent slots waiting for surgery at the start of a week in a stationary regime
$\mathbf{q}$	Equilibrium distribution of W
$P_W(z)$	Generating function of W
λ	Arrival rate of semi-urgent surgeries
p_k	$\mathbb{P}$(Surgery is of length k slots), $k = 1, 2, ..K$
R_n	Number of semi-urgent slots that arrive during week n
$P_R(z)$	Generating function of the number of arrivals per week
N_e	Number of unused reserved semi-urgent slots per week
N_c	Number of canceled elective slots per week
C_e	Cost of one unused reserved semi-urgent slot
C_c	Cost of one canceled elective slot
C_t	Total Costs

2.1.1 Progression of the number of semi-urgent slots

We focus on the number of semi-urgent slots waiting at the start of week n (W_n). This equals the amount of semi-urgent slots that arrived during the previous week (R_{n-1}) plus the elective slots that were canceled during the previous week in order to accommodate surplus semi-urgent slots. Elective slots are canceled if the reserved capacity for semi-urgent slots is insufficient. Recall that, in accordance with medical practice, the canceled elective slots from week n become semi-urgent slots in week $n+1$. Therefore, for our analysis of W_n, elective slots are not canceled, but instead the surplus semi-urgent slots from week n are transferred to week $n+1$. An example of the progression in the number of semi-urgent slots waiting at the start of week n is given in Fig. 1.

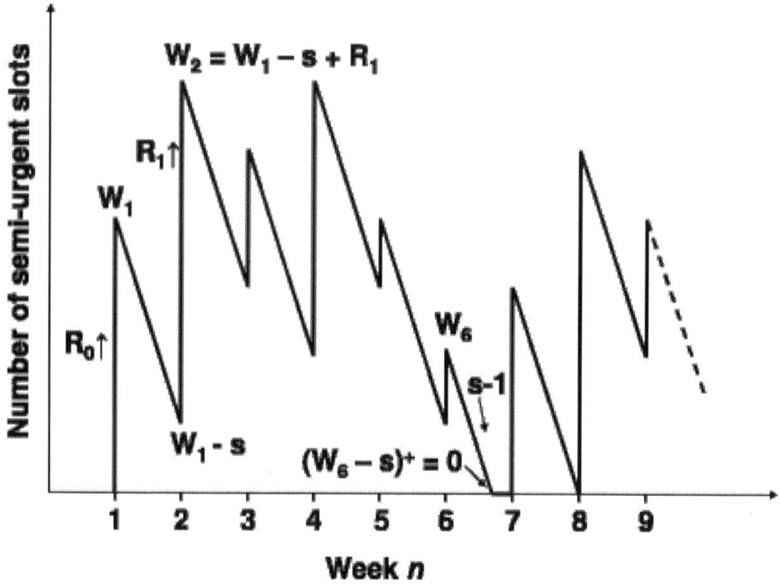

Figure 1. An example of the progression of the number of semi-urgent slots waiting at the start of the week ($s = 3$)

2.1.2 The arrival process

The number of arriving semi-urgent slots per week is equal to the sum of the number of slots per arriving patient. Patients arrive independently according to a Poisson process, furthermore the number of slots per arriving patient is random. Therefore we can model the arrival process with the compound Poisson process [14]. The arrival rate of semi-urgent patients is λ. Let $p_k$denote the probability that an arriving semi-urgent surgery is of size k slots, $k = 1,..,K$. The generating function of the arrival process is [14]:

$$P_R(z) = \sum_{j=0}^{\infty} \mathbb{P}(R = j) z^j = e^{-\lambda(1-\sum_{k=1}^{K} p_k z^k)}, \quad \text{where}$$
$$\sum_{k=1}^{K} p_k = 1, \quad \text{and} \quad |z| \leq 1. \tag{1}$$

2.2 Stability of the system

From the description in Subsection 2.1.1 (see also Fig. 1) it is clear that the number of semi-urgent slots waiting at the start of week $n + 1$ equals the number of semi-urgent slots that arrived during week n plus the number of surplus semi-urgent slots of week n:

$$W_{n+1} = R_n + \{W_n - s\}^+, \quad n = 1, 2, \ldots \quad \text{and} \quad W_1 = R_0,$$

where $\{x\}^+ = 0$ if $x < 0$ and x otherwise. This is the Lindley equation for the sojourn time in a $GI/G/1$ queue [15]. The limit for $n \to \infty$ on W_{n+1} converges in distribution to W if E[R]<sE[R]<s, and therefore we can conclude that as long as the expected weekly amount of semi-urgent slot arrivals, E[R]E[R], is strictly smaller than the number of slots allocated to semi-urgent surgeries, s, the system is stable and the capacity reserved for these slots should be sufficient on average. It follows that there is a minimum amount of capacity (s_{min}) that should be reserved for semi-urgent surgeries: smin=⌈E[R]⌉ where ⌈x⌉ ⌈x⌉ equals x rounded up to the nearest integer.

2.3 Stationary distribution of the number of semi-urgent slots waiting

At the start of every week the state of the system is inspected. We represent the system by a slotted queuing model in discrete time [16]. We can distinguish between two situations: (1) more semi-urgent slots are waiting than can be completed in one week (epochs 2–6 and 9 in Fig. 1), and (2) less (epoch 7 in Fig. 1) or an equal amount of semi-urgent slots are waiting (epoch 8 in Fig. 1) than can bc completed. We obtain the following expressions for the transition probabilities:

$$\mathbb{P}(W_{n+1} = w_{n+1} | W_n = w_n) = \begin{cases} \mathbb{P}(R_n = w_{n+1} - w_n + s) & \text{if} \quad w_n - s > 0 \\ \mathbb{P}(R_n = w_{n+1}) & \text{otherwise.} \end{cases}$$

Define P as the matrix with transition probabilities. Let q=(q0q1⋯) denote the equilibrium distribution of W, the number of semi-urgent slots waiting at the start of a week, where $q_i = \mathbb{P}(W = i)$. The q_i's can be computed as q=qPq=qP. An expression for the generating function of the equilibrium probabilities q_i is [16]:

$$P_W(z) = \frac{P_R(z) \sum_{i=0}^{s-1} q_i (z^s - z^i)}{z^s - P_R(z)}, \quad |z| \leq 1, \tag{2}$$

with $P_R(z)$ as given in (1). To obtain an exact expression for $P_W(z)$ we have to determine the s unknows $q_0, q_1,...,q_{s-1}$. By Rouché's Theorem [17] it can be shown that the denominator of $P_W(z)$ has $s-1$ zeros inside the unit disk [18]. Since $P_W(z)$ is a generating function and therefore bounded for all $|z| \leq 1$, the zeros of the denominator are zeros of the numerator as well [16]. Thus we obtain $s-1$ equations for the s unknowns $q_0, q_1,...,q_{s-1}$. To derive the last equation, we use that $P_W(1) = 1$. In order to find the $s-1$ zeros of the denominator of $P_W(z)$, we start by solving

$$z^s - P_R(z) = 0, \quad \text{which is equivalent to}$$

$$z^s = e^{-\lambda l\left(1-\sum_{k=1}^{K} p_k z^k\right)}.$$

We replace this equation by $s-1$ equations, where each z_j is a solution of the above equation [19]:

$$z_j = F(z_j)e^{2\pi \tilde{\imath} \frac{j}{s}}, \quad \text{with} \quad F(z) = e^{-\frac{\lambda}{s}(1-\sum_{k=1}^{K} p_k z^k)},$$

and $\tilde{\imath} = \sqrt{-1}$. For each value of j ($j = 1,2,...,s-1$), we numerically solve this equation by using fixed point iteration [20]:

$$z_j^{(n+1)} = F\left(z_j^{(n)}\right) e^{2\pi \tilde{\imath} \frac{j}{s}}, \quad n = 0, 1, \ldots \quad \text{and}$$

$$z_j^{(0)} = 0.$$

The z_j's that are found with this procedure are also zeros of the numerator of $P_W(z)$. We thus obtain $s-1$ equations for the unknowns $q_0,..,q_{s-1}$ that with the added equation $P_W(1) = 1$ define $P_W(z)$, $|z| \leq 1$.

2.4 Performance measures

We are particularly interested in the expected number of canceled elective slots per work week (E[Nc]E[Nc]), and the expected number of empty reserved semi-urgent slots per work week (E[Ne]E[Ne]). For the latter it follows from (2) and $P_W(1) = P_R(1) = 1$ that

$$\mathbb{E}[N_e] = \sum_{i=0}^{s-1}(s-i)q_i = s - \mathbb{E}[R].$$

The expected number of elective slots that are canceled per week equals

$$\mathbb{E}[N_c] = \sum_{i=s}^{\infty}(i-s)q_i = \sum_{i=0}^{\infty} iq_i - s + \sum_{i=0}^{s-1}(s-i)q_i$$
$$= P_W'(1) - \mathbb{E}[R].$$

Since

$$P_W'(1) = \mathbb{E}[R] + \frac{\sum_{i=0}^{s-1} q_i(s^2 - i^2 - s + i) - s^2 + s + P_R''(1)}{2(s - \mathbb{E}[R])},$$

$$P_R''(1) = \lambda \sum_{k=1}^{K} k(k-1)p_k + \mathbb{E}^2[R],$$

we see that

$$\mathbb{E}[N_c] = \frac{\sum_{i=0}^{s-1} q_i(s^2 - i^2 - s + i) - s^2 + s + P_R''(1)}{2(s - \mathbb{E}[R])}.$$

2.5 Cost structure

Let C_e and C_c be the costs of one empty semi-urgent slot and one canceled elective slot. The expected total costs then equal

$$\mathbb{E}[C_t] = \mathbb{E}[N_e]C_e + \mathbb{E}[N_c]C_c.$$

The optimal number of slots to reserve for semi-urgent surgeries (s^*) depends on the choice of C_e and C_c, and is the value of s that minimizes E[Ct]E[Ct].

3 OPTIMAL ALLOCATION OF SURGERY SLOTS

Given the stochasticity of the arrival process of semi-urgent patients, there will be weeks when the allocated capacity s^* is not sufficient. In this case the department can choose to perform the surplus semi-urgent patients this week, and cancel elective patients. On the other hand, the department can choose to postpone the semi-urgent surgeries until next week. A major drawback of this operational mode is that new semi-urgent patients arrive, who together with the postponed patients from this week, pose a huge demand on available resources. Furthermore, as mentioned in the introduction, if the number of semi-urgent slots waiting for treatment exceeds the weekly amount of OR slots available, semi-urgent surgeries have to be performed in overtime, which is very undesirable as well. In this section we describe a Markov decision model that provides a scheduling strategy for surplus semi-urgent slots, given the parameters obtained with the queuing model. A summary of the additional notation introduced in this section is given in Table 2.

Table 2. Additional notation introduced in Section 3

Symbol	Description
$W1_n$	Number of 1-week semi-urgent slots waiting for surgery at the start of week n
$W2_n$	Number of 2-week semi-urgent slots waiting for surgery at the start of week n
$w_n = (w1_n, w2_n)$	System state at start of week n
a_n	Action chosen in week n
$R1_n$	Number of 1-week semi-urgent slot arrivals during week n
$R2_n$	Number of 2-week semi-urgent slot arrivals during week n
λ_1	Arrival rate of 1-week semi-urgent surgeries
λ_2	Arrival rate of 2-week semi-urgent surgeries
p_{1k}	$\mathbb{P}$(1-week semi-urgent surgery is of length k slots), $k = 1, 2, .., K$
p_{2k}	$\mathbb{P}$(2-week semi-urgent surgery is of length k slots), $k = 1, 2, .., K$
$N_{e,n}$	Number of unused reserved semi-urgent slots during week n
$N_{c,n}$	Number of canceled elective slots during week n
$N_{o,n}$	Number of slots performed in overtime during week n
C_o	Cost of performing one slot in overtime
$C_{t,n}$	Total costs incurred in week n
α	Discount factor
δ^*	Optimal policy
δ_M	Monotone policy

3.1 Assumptions

In this model we employ a more detailed view of the process, and consider the inflow of the two types of semi-urgent surgeries separately: the first type of semi-urgent surgeries need to be performed within one week, the second type of semi-urgent surgeries need to be performed within two weeks. Given the system status at the beginning of week n, we decide how many 1- and 2-week semi-urgent slots should be performed this week. Since 1-week semi-urgent surgeries have to be performed *this* week, *all* incoming surgeries of this type are scheduled for *this* week. First the reserved slots $(1,2,..,s^*)$ are used, and if additional 1-week semi-urgent demand remains, elective slots are canceled.

One-week semi-urgent demand that is still unaccommodated is performed in overtime. There are several options for scheduling 2-week patients. A logical choice would be to first schedule all 1-week slots, then schedule 2-week slots in the reserved slots of this week that are still available. Subsequently, it has to be decided whether to perform the remaining 2-week slots either this or next week. If the remaining 2-week slots are scheduled for next week, no elective slots have to be canceled this week. On the other hand, postponed 2-week semi-urgent slots have evolved into 1-week semi-urgent slots the next week. The existence of these slots, together with newly arrived 1-week semi-urgent slots, can result in a vast amount of semi-urgent demand that possibly has to be treated in overtime. In this section, a Markov decision model is presented that enables a trade-off between these two factors. For an overview of Markov decision theory, see [21]. In the model, we make the following assumptions:

- All 1-week semi-urgent slots are planned this week.
- Two week semi-urgent slots not planned this week become 1-week semi-urgent slots next week.
- Elective slots canceled this week become 2-week semi-urgent slots next week.

3.2 The Markov decision model

We use a Markov decision model with infinite planning horizon to support the department in deciding how many 2-week slots should be planned in a certain week (action a_n). The system state at the start of week n, $(n = 0,1,\dots,\infty)$, is given by $w_n = (w1_n, w2_n)$, where $w1_n$ and $w2_n$ are the number of 1- and 2-week semi-urgent slots waiting at that moment. The action chosen depends on the number of 2-week slots waiting and on the part of capacity that is already allocated to 1-week slots. Summarizing, the range for action a_n is determined by $(0,1,..,\min(w2n,(m-w1n)+))$.

3.2.1 Transition probabilities

Let the random variables $R1_n$ and $R2_n$ denote the number of 1- and 2-week semi-urgent slot arrivals during week n, where $R1_n + R2_n = R_n$. Similarly to the queuing model presented in Section 2, $R1$ and $R2$ follow a compound Poisson distribution, with arrival rates λ_1 and λ_2, and p_{1k} and p_{2k} the probability that a 1- and 2-week surgery is of length k slots.

Recall that m slots are available each week for both elective and semi-urgent surgeries. Therefore, when the number of 1-week semi-urgent slots waiting exceeds m, or when the sum of 1- and 2-week semi-urgent slots waiting exceeds $2m$, the surplus semi-urgent slots are performed in overtime. Figure 2 shows how the number of slots performed in overtime is calculated. In our model, we take into account the overtime by including (high) costs for each overtime surgery slot. However, the slots performed in overtime do not affect the system state, as they have left the system in the subsequent week. Thus, the state space A of the system is described as follows:

$$A = \{w = (w1, w2) : w1, w2 = 0, 1, \ldots;$$
$$w1 \leq m; w1 + w2 \leq 2m\}.$$

The state space is depicted in Fig. 3. The areas B,C and D and the arrows correspond to the three different cases of handling the overtime slots (see also Fig. 2). For notational purposes, let

$$\begin{aligned}
&\mathbb{P}(w_n|w_{n-1}, a) \\
&= \mathbb{P}(W1_n = w1_n, W2_n = w2_n \big| W1_{n-1} = w1_{n-1}, \\
&\qquad W2_{n-1} = w2_{n-1}, a_{n-1} = a).
\end{aligned}$$

Now we define these transition probabilities for each $w_n \in A$.

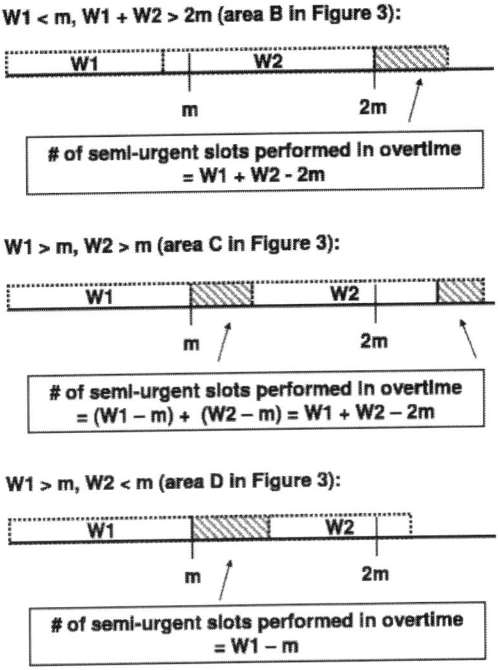

Figure 2. Number of semi-urgent slots performed in overtime: three different cases

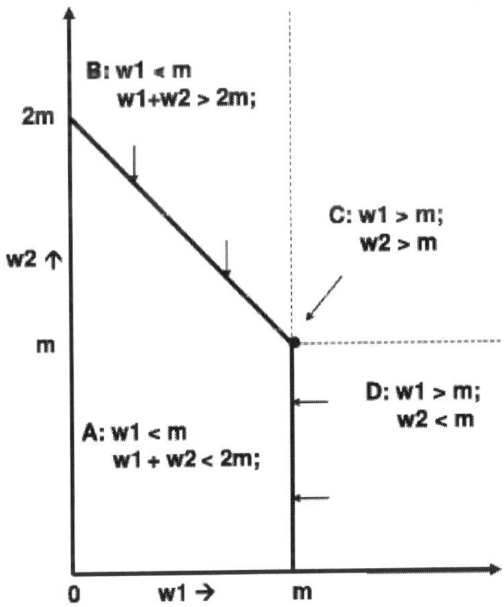

Figure 3. State space of the system

If $w1_n < m$ and $w1_n + w2_n < 2m$ then no slots are performed in overtime in week n and thus we have

$$\begin{aligned}\mathbb{P}(w_n|w_{n-1}, a) = \mathbb{P}(R1_{n-1} &= w1_n - w2_{n-1} + a) \\ &\times \mathbb{P}(R2_{n-1} = w2_n - (w1_{n-1} - s + a)^+), \\ &w1_n < m, w1_n + w2_n < 2m,\end{aligned}$$

and (w1n−1−s+a)+(w1n−1−s+a)+ is the number of canceled elective slots.

Now, assume that at the start of week n we have $w1$ 1-week semi-urgent slots and $w2$ 2-week semi-urgent slots waiting. If $w = (w1,w2) \in B$ then some slots have to be performed in overtime as explained above. Thus, according to the overtime policy depicted in Fig. 2, the next state is given by $w1_n = w1$, $w2_n = 2m - w1_n$, a point on the boundary between A and B, as pointed out with arrows in Fig. 3. Including this into transition probabilities, we derive

$$\begin{aligned}\mathbb{P}(w_n|w_{n-1}, a) = \mathbb{P}(R1_{n-1} &= w1_n - w2_{n-1} + a) \\ &\times \mathbb{P}(R2_{n-1} \geq w2_n - (w1_{n-1} - s + a)^+), \\ w1_n < m, w1_n + w2_n = 2m.&\end{aligned}$$

Analogously, if at the start of week n the number of waiting semi-urgent slots is described by $w \in C$, then the next state is $w_n = (m,m)$, and thus the transition probabilities for this state are given by

$$\begin{aligned}\mathbb{P}(w_n|w_{n-1}, a) = \mathbb{P}(R1_{n-1} &\geq w1_n - w2_{n-1} + a) \\ &\times \mathbb{P}(R2_{n-1} \geq w2_n - (w1_{n-1} - s + a)^+), \\ w_n = (m, m).&\end{aligned}$$

Finally, $w \in D$ will result in the state with $w1_n = m$, and we obtain

$$\begin{aligned}\mathbb{P}(w_n|w_{n-1}, a) = \mathbb{P}(R1_{n-1} &\geq w1_n - w2_{n-1} + a) \\ &\times \mathbb{P}(R2_{n-1} = w2_n - (w1_{n-1} - s + a)^+), \\ w1_n = m, w2_n < m.&\end{aligned}$$

Note that $\mathbb{P}(R1_n \leq x) = \mathbb{P}(R2_n \leq x) = 0$ if $x < 0$.

3.2.2 Performance measures

The performance measures that were introduced for the queuing model are calculated on a weekly basis. Given the state $w_n = (w1_n, w2_n)$ and action a, the number of unused reserved semi-urgent slots and the number of canceled electives can be established as follows:

$$N_{e,n} = (s - w1_n - a)^+, \quad \text{and}$$
$$N_{c,n} = (w1_n - s + a)^+.$$

Besides, we introduce a new performance measure, E[No]E[No] the expected number of semi-urgent slots that have to be performed in overtime next week as a consequence of the chosen action of this week. In week n, this amount depends on the number of slots at the start of week n, as described in Fig. 2. The formula for computing $E[N_{o,n+1}|w_n,a]$ is given in Eq. 3.

$$\begin{aligned}\mathbb{E}[N_{o,n+1}|w_n, a] = & \sum_{\substack{w1<m \\ w1+w2>2m}} (w1 + w2 - 2m) \times \mathbb{P}(R1_n = w1 - w2_n + a) \quad \mathbb{P}(R2_n = w2 - (w1_n - s + a)^+) \\ & + \sum_{\substack{w1>m \\ w1+w2>2m}} (w1 + w2 - 2m) \times \mathbb{P}(R1_n = w1 - w2_n + a) \quad \mathbb{P}(R2_n = w2 - (w1_n - s + a)^+) \\ & + \sum_{\substack{w1>m \\ w2<m}} (w1 - m) \times \mathbb{P}(R1_n = w1 - w2_n + a) \quad \mathbb{P}(R2_{n-1} = w2 - (w1_n - s + a)^+).\end{aligned} \tag{3}$$

3.2.3 Cost structure

The costs incurred for unused semi-urgent slots (C_e) and canceled elective slots (C_c) are equivalent with those introduced in Section 2. An extra cost, C_o, for performing 1- and 2-week slots in overtime is introduced. The expected total costs incurred in week n equal

$$\mathbb{E}[C_{t,n}] = \mathbb{E}[N_{e,n}]C_e + \mathbb{E}[N_{c,n}]C_c + \mathbb{E}[N_{o,n+1}]C_o.$$

3.3 Determination of optimal policy

In the process of coming to an optimal policy δ^* that defines an optimal action for each state w_n, we want to take into account the costs incurred today and in the future. However, we consider the costs experienced today as being more important than those experienced in the future. Therefore we use discount factor α, $\alpha \in (0,1)$, in order to recalculate future costs to the cost level of today. Define $V_\delta(w_0)$ as the expected discounted costs over an infinite horizon, given initial state w_0:

$$V_\delta(w_0) = \mathbb{E}_\delta\left[\sum_{n=0}^{\infty} \alpha^n C_{t,n}\left(W_n, a_n\right) | w_0\right].$$

Let $V(w_0)$ denote the minimal value of $V_\delta(w_0)$:

$$V(w_0) = \min_\delta \quad V_\delta(w_0).$$

For each initial state w_0 and every action a, in an optimal policy it should hold that

$$V(w_0) \leq C_{t,0}\left(w_0, a_0\right) + \alpha \sum_{w_1} \mathbb{P}(w_1 | w_0, a) V(w_1).$$

This gives us the optimality equation

$$V(w_0) = \min_{a \in \delta} \left\{ C_{t,0}\left(w_0, a_0\right) + \alpha \sum_{w_1} \mathbb{P}(w_1 | w_0, a) V(w_1) \right\}.$$

The optimal policy δ^* consists of the values of a that solve the optimality equation for each state. In order to find an optimal policy δ^*, we use the policy iteration algorithm [22]. Since the state and action space are finite, the policy iteration algorithm converges in a finite number of steps.

Note that it is never optimal to perform 2-week slots in overtime, since even if they are postponed and then cannot be treated in regular time, they can be treated in overtime next week as well.

4 CAPACITY PLANNING AND SCHEDULING AT A DEPARTMENT OF NEUROSURGERY

In this section we illustrate our modeling and optimization approach by considering a department of neurosurgery situated in an academic hospital in the Netherlands. Department staff feared that dedicating scarce OR time to the uncertain stream of semi-urgent patients would lead to an excessive amount of unused OR capacity, and therefore decided to plan almost only elective patients in the available OR time. As a consequence, in daily operation, a large portion of elective surgeries was canceled in order to accommodate semi-urgent surgeries. Furthermore, many ad hoc decisions were needed to ensure that all patients would receive the care they needed. Supported by our models, we show possibilities for improvement.

All surgeries performed by the department can be characterized by the estimated OR time as follows: a) one third of an OR day, b) two thirds of an OR day, c) one OR day, and d) more than one OR day. With this in mind the OR day is divided into three slots of equal length ($K = 3$). Type 1 surgeries have an estimated duration of one slot, type 2 of two slots, and type 3 surgeries an estimated duration of three or more slots. Therefore, it is either possible to perform in one OR day i) three type 1 surgeries, ii) one type 1 and one type 2 surgery, or iii) one type 3 surgery. The department is assigned eight OR days each week. With each day consisting of three slots, the department has 24 slots per week at its disposal (i.e. $m = 24$).

4.1 Data

The data needed for the model, semi-urgent patient arrivals, their expected surgery duration and semi-urgent state (i.e. surgery within one or two weeks) were recorded for a consecutive period of ten weeks. The characteristics of the arrival process are in line with the compound Poisson arrival process as outlined in [14]. Furthermore, the variance to mean ratio (vmr), defined as σ2μσ2μ, which equals 1 for the Poisson distribution, shows that modeling the patient arrival process at this department with a Poisson process gives a conservative estimate for the aggregated semi-urgent patient stream (vmr = 0.25, so the variance is lower than would be expected from the Poisson distribution), while it provides a good estimate for the 1-week semi-urgent patient flows (vmr = 1.03) and a slight conservative estimate for the 2-week semi-urgent patient flow (vmr = 0.76). Therefore we feel confident that the compound Poisson process is an appropriate choice for modeling the arrival process of semi-urgent surgeries at this department. Table 3 gives the parameter values derived from the data, used in the queuing model. Since in the Markov decision model a distinction is made between 1- and 2-week semi-urgent surgeries, different parameter values for the compound Poisson process apply (Table 4).

Table 3. Parameter values for queuing model (Section 2)

Parameter	Value
λ	11/2
p_1	29/55
p_2	11/55
p_3	15/55

Table 4. Parameter values for Markov decision model (Section 3)

Parameter	Value
λ_1	31/10
λ_2	12/5
p_{11}	20/31
p_{12}	5/31
p_{13}	6/31
p_{21}	9/24
p_{22}	6/24
p_{23}	9/24

The cost parameters as defined in Sections 2 and 3 should be determined by the department, and depend on the emphasis the department wants to put on either canceling patients or having an empty OR. For example, when $C_e = 10$ and $C_c = 1$, having an empty semi-urgent slot is considered ten times worse than canceling one elective slot. Since the department considers performing semi-urgent slots in overtime as very undesirable, we emphasize on this by fixing $C_o$on 100. We consider three combinations for C_e and C_c (Table 5). For the department under consideration, CC_1 is a reasonable cost configuration. To demonstrate our methodology we also use two other cost configurations.

Table 5. Cost combinations

Name	C_e	C_c	C_o
CC_1	1	1	100
CC_2	10	1	100
CC_3	1	10	100

4.2 Determining the required number of semi-urgent slots

We start by calculating the minimal amount of semi-urgent slots required (s_{min}), which is equal to ⌈E[R]⌉⌈E[R]⌉ (see Section 2.2). Since

$$\mathbb{E}[R] = \lambda \sum_{k=1}^{K} k p_k,$$

we have that smin=[9.6]=10smin=[9.6]=10. The department estimated that approximately 40% of surgeries performed during regular OR days is of the semi-urgent type, which is supported by the data (9.624=409.624=40%). Given that *s* may vary from s_{min} to *m*, we obtain the results from Table 6. The optimal value of E[Ct]E[Ct] for each cost combination is given in bold. Note the vast amount of canceled elective slots for *s* = 10. This shows that focusing on the average behavior of a system can result in unsatisfactory (and maybe unexpected) system outcomes. In Fig. 4 $\mathbb{E}[N_e]$ and $\mathbb{E}[N_c]$]are compared graphically. We see in Table 6 that for CC_1 the optimal value of s^* 13 ($4\frac{1}{3}$ days), for CC_2, s^* equals 11 ($3\frac{2}{3}$), and days), and for CC_3, s^* equals 17 ($5\frac{2}{3}$ days).

Table 6. Queuing model outcomes

s	$\mathbb{E}[N_e]$	$\mathbb{E}[N_c]$	$\mathbb{E}[C_t(CC_1)]$	$\mathbb{E}[C_t(CC_2)]$	$\mathbb{E}[C_t(CC_3)]$
10	0.40	23.81	24.21	27.81	238.54
11	1.40	5.42	6.82	**19.42**	55.64
12	2.40	2.50	4.90	26.50	27.36
13	3.40	1.37	**4.77**	35.37	17.14
14	4.40	0.82	5.22	44.82	12.58
15	5.40	0.51	5.91	54.51	10.47
16	6.40	0.32	6.72	64.32	9.61
17	7.40	0.21	7.61	74.21	**9.45**
18	8.40	0.13	8.53	84.13	9.72
19	9.40	0.08	9.48	94.08	10.25
20	10.40	0.05	10.45	104.05	10.94
21	11.40	0.03	11.43	114.03	11.74
22	12.40	0.02	12.42	124.02	12.62
23	13.40	0.01	13.41	134.01	13.54
24	14.40	0.01	14.41	144.01	14.48

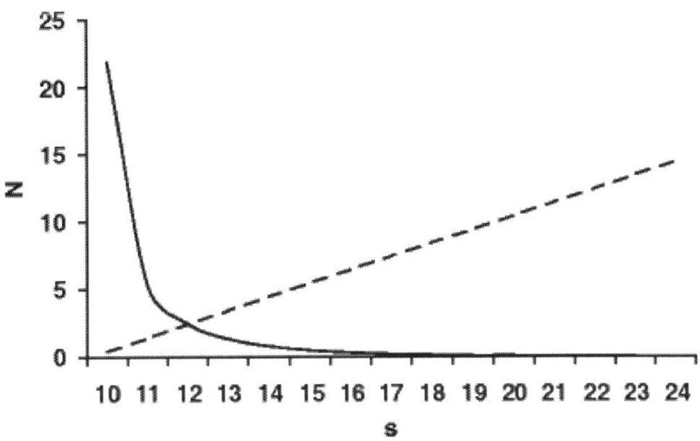

Figure 4. $\mathbb{E}[N_e]$ (interrupted line) and $\mathbb{E}[N_c]$ for $s = (\lceil s_{min} \rceil, .., m)$

4.3 Allocation of 2-week semi-urgent slots

We now use the Markov decision model to schedule the 1- and 2-week semi-urgent slots. Our goal is to find an optimal policy that prescribes the number of 2-week semi-urgent slots to plan, given any possible system state.

4.3.1 Monotone policy

It is possible that in the optimal policy action a is not monotone increasing in $w2_n$. Although this form of the optimal policy is not uncommon in literature [23], it may be hard for medical professionals to implement. Therefore we proceed as follows. We determine an optimal policy δ^*, as described in Section 3.3. We then check whether a is monotone increasing in $w2_n$. If this is the case, we maintain this optimal policy. Otherwise, we create a monotone policy, δ_M, based on the optimal policy, where the number of 2-week slots to plan (the chosen action) is not allowed to decrease. Such a monotone policy is not necessarily optimal, even in the class of monotone policies.

4.3.2 Obtained policies

The cost combinations CC_1, CC_2, and CC_3 are used to obtain three policies from the Markov decision model. For cost combinations CC_1 and CC_3 we find monotone increasing optimal policies, given in Figs. 5 and 6. For cost combination CC_2 a monotone policy was created, given in Fig. 7. A discount factor of $\alpha = 0.95$ is used in all cases. We find that $\mathbb{E}[C_t] = 4.0093$ for CC_1, $\mathbb{E}[C_t] = 20.2070$ for CC_2, and $\mathbb{E}[C_t] = 7.4810$ for CC_3. The horizontal axes in the figures show the possible values of w_1 and w_2. When these are combined the system state is obtained. On the vertical axis the action that is chosen for each state is given. The set of actions for all possible states forms the policy δ. Recall that the action chosen consists only of the number of 2-week semi-urgent slots to plan this week, since 1-week semi-urgent slots are completed this week.

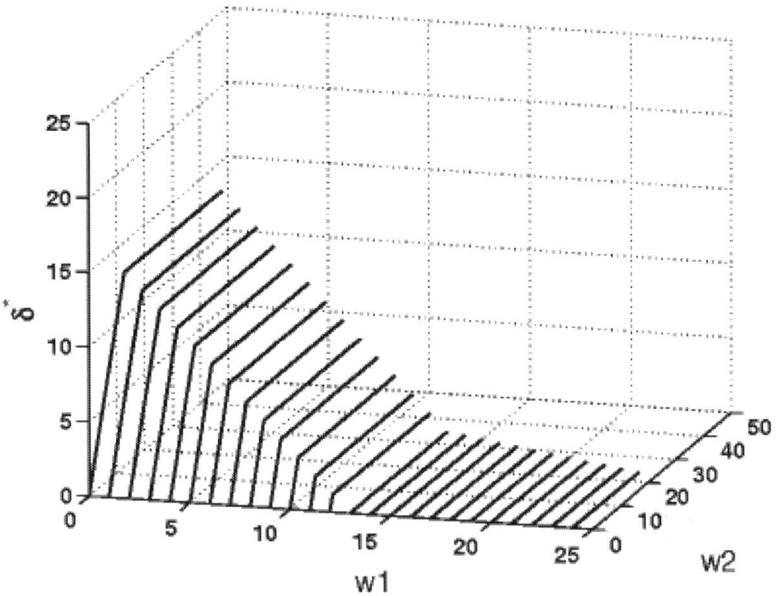

Figure 5. δ^* for CC_1 ($s^* = 13$)

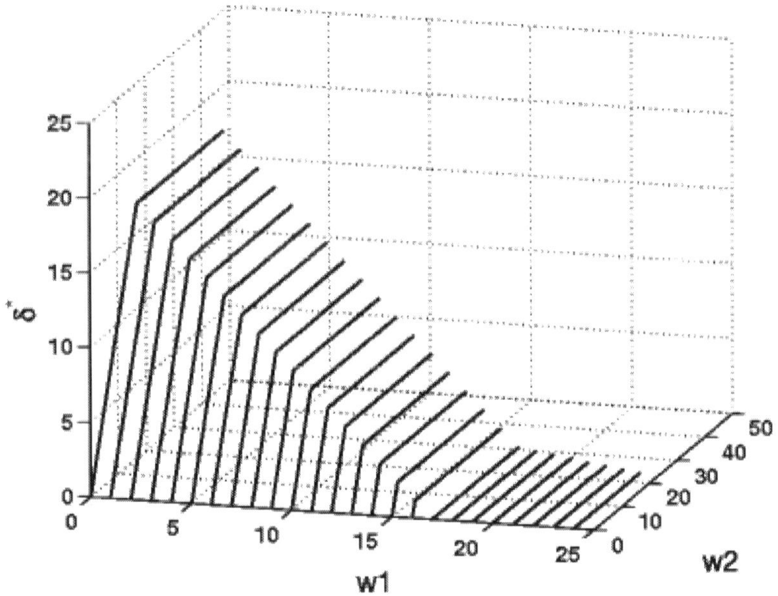

Figure 6. δ_M for CC_2 ($s^* = 11$)

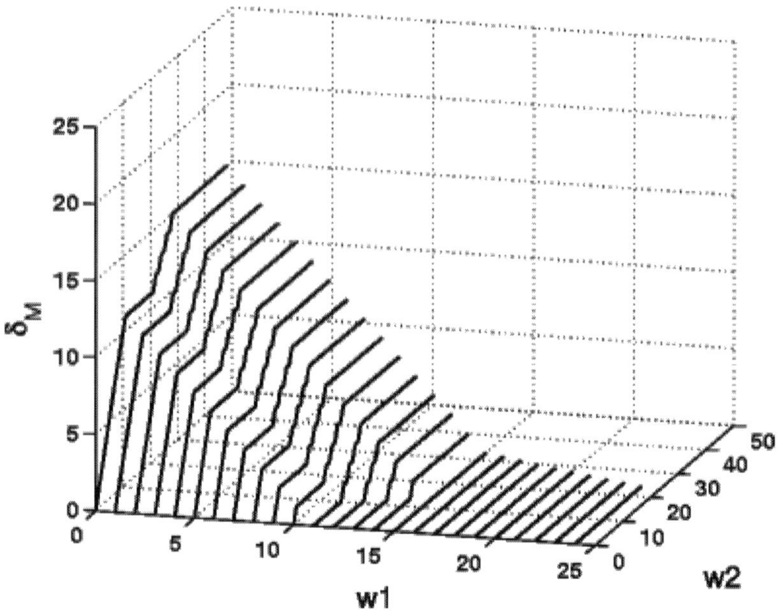

Figure 7. δ^* for CC_3 ($s^* = 17$)

While δ^* for CC_1 and CC_3 is straightforward—plan 2-week slots up to s^* and postpone the remaining 2-week slots until next week, the policy obtained for CC_2 is quite different. In several states it occurs that even when the number of 1-week slots exceeds s^*, elective slots are canceled in order to accommodate 2-week slots. This action is chosen to avoid overtime, a result of s^*being close to s_{min}. Similar to the queuing model outcomes, this shows that maintaining a cost structure similar to CC_2, which results in choosing an s^* which is close to $E[R]$, leads to the cancellation of elective slots.

5 DISCUSSION AND CONCLUSION

In this paper we have developed a methodology to handle the semi-urgent patient flow at a surgical department. On a strategic level, we have determined the OR capacity needed to accommodate all semi-urgent patients on the long run, and we have described a queuing model that allows for a trade-off between the number of elective patients canceled and the amount of unused OR time. Given the amount of slots dedicated to semi-urgent patients, the distribution of the number of elective slots canceled, and the distribution of the number of unused semi-urgent slots can be derived with the queuing model, as is shown in Section 4. An insight that follows from these results is that focusing on only the average behavior of a system can result in undesired system outcomes, in this case the cancellation of many elective patients. Since semi-urgent patient arrivals and elective cancellations are dependent, even over consecutive periods, a natural modeling approach lies in the area of queuing theory.

On a tactical level, we have outlined a Markov decision model that supports the allocation of 1- and 2-week semi-urgent surgeries. This model provides a guideline for the weekly scheduling of semi-urgent patients. The policies obtained with the model can be transferred to a spreadsheet program and with little effort developed into a tool that is easy to use. The added value of the Markov decision model is that it simplifies the scheduling task substantially. Note that all models can be used for arbitrary parameter values.

In the methodology presented, both models involve the planning and scheduling of individual slots. It is not taken into account that when a surgery takes more than one slot, all slots must be scheduled adjacently in the same OR on the same day. To quantify this effect, we calculated the expected number of semi-urgent slots treated for the example in the case study where $s^* = 13$. When considering all possible states, consisting of the number of one-, two- and three-slot semi-urgent surgeries waiting, this expectation equals 8.86 when taking into account the adjacency requirement (i.e. in the situation where we have four full OR days of three slots and a single slot on another OR day). Note that in these calculations we assumed that a rational planner would aim to maximize the number of semi-urgent slots treated in the available time. Given that we consider an instance of the problem where s^* is relatively small, so there is little freedom to fill the OR days, the deviation of 7.7% from the value of 9.60 slots (calculated with the queuing model) will be smaller in most other (larger) instances of the problem. However, the adjency requirement results in a slightly higher demand for semi-urgent slots.

A topic for further research would be to extend the presented methodology with an operational model that schedules individual surgeries. We consider the total OR time allocated to a surgical department by OR management as given. Of course, it is possible to establish the optimal amount of allocated OR time, and doing so first could result in a better performance. One of our other aims is to carry out an extensive data analysis to support an implementation of our methodology at the neurosurgery department discussed in Section 4.

Open Access

REFERENCES

1. Schofield WN, Rubin GL, Piza M, Yin Lai Y, Sindhusake D, Fearnside MR, Klineberg PL (2005) Cancellation of operations on the day of intended surgery at a major Australian referral hospital. MJA 182(12):612–615
2. Wullink G, van Houdenhoven M, Hans EW, van Oostrum JM, van der Lans M, Kazemier G (2007) Closing emergency rooms improves efficiency. J Med Syst 31(6):543–546
3. Bhattacharyya T, Vrahas MS, Morrison SM, Kim E, Wiklund RA, Smith RM, Rubash HE (2006) The value of the dedicated orthopaedic trauma operating room. J Trauma Injury Infect Crit Care 60(6):1336–1341
4. Gerchak, Y, Gupta D, Henig M (1996) Reservation planning for elective surgery under uncertain demand for emergency surgery. Manag Sci 42(3):321–334
5. Cardoen B, Demeulenmeester E, Beliën J (2008) Operating room planning and scheduling: a literature review. Internal report, K.U. Leuven, Belgium. Available at https://lirias.kuleuven.be/handle/123456789/165923
6. Pham DN, Klinkert A (2008) Surgical case scheduling as a generalized job shop scheduling problem. Eur J Oper Res 185(3):1011–1025
7. Lamiri M, Xie X, Dolgui A, Grimaud F (2008) A stochastic model for operating room planning with elective and emergency demand for surgery. Eur J Oper Res 185(3):1026–1037
8. Bowers J, Mould G (2004) Managing uncertainty in orthopaedic trauma theatres. Eur J Oper Res 154(3):599–608
9. Dexter F, Macario A, O'Neill L (2000) Scheduling surgical cases into overflow block time—computer simulation of the effects of scheduling strategies on operating room labor costs. Anesth Analg 90(4):980–988
10. van Houdenhoven M, van Oostrum JM, Hans EW, Wullink G, Kazemier G (2007) Improving operating room efficiency by applying bin-packing and portfolio techniques to surgical case scheduling. Anesth Analg 105(3):707–714
11. 11.
12. Strum DP, Vargas LG, May JH, Bashein G (1997) Surgical suite utilization and capacity planning: a minimal cost analysis model. J Med Syst 21(5):309–322

13. McIntosh C, Dexter F, Epstein RH (2006) The impact of service-specific staffing, case scheduling, turnovers, and first-case starts on anesthesia group and operating room productivity: a tutorial using data from an Australian hospital. Anesth Analg 103(6):1499–1516

14. Pandit JJ, Dexter F (2009) Lack of sensitivity of staffing for 8-hour sessions to standard deviation in daily actual hours of operating room time used for surgeons with long queues. Anesth Analg 108(6):1910–1915

15. Tijms HC (2003) A first course in stochastic models. Wiley, London

16. Wolff RW (1988) Stochastic modeling and the theory of queues. Prentice Hall, Englewood Cliffs, p 474

17. Bruneel H, Wuyts I (1994) Analysis of discrete-time multiserver queueing models with constant service times. Oper Res Lett 15(5):231–236

18. Kleinrock L (1975) Queueing systems, vol I: Theory. Wiley, London

19. Adan IJBF, van Leeuwaarden JSH, Winands EMM (2006) On the application of Rouché's theorem in queueing theory. Oper Res Lett 34(3):355–360

20. Bruneel H, Kim BG (1993) Discrete-time models for communication systems including ATM. Kluwer Academic, Norwell, pp 142–143

21. Atkinson KE (1978) An introduction to numerical analysis, 2nd edn. Wiley, New York

22. Puterman ML (1994) Markov decision processes: Discrete stochastic dynamic programming. Wiley, New York

23. Ross SM (1982) Introduction to stochastic dynamic programming. Academic, New York

24. Koole G (1997) Assigning a single server to inhomogeneous queues with switching costs. Theor Comp Sci 182(1–2):203–216

9

DECISION SUPPORT SYSTEM FOR THE OPERATING ROOM RESCHEDULING PROBLEM

J. Theresia van Essen[1], Johann L. Hurink[1], Woutske Hartholt[12], Bernd J. van den Akker[2]

1.Center of Healthcare Operations Improvement and Research (CHOIR)University of Twente, EnschedeEnschedeThe Netherlands

2.Isala ClinicsZwolleThe Netherlands

ABSTRACT

Due to surgery duration variability and arrivals of emergency surgeries, the planned Operating Room (OR) schedule is disrupted throughout the day which may lead to a change in the start time of the elective surgeries. These changes may result in undesirable situations for patients, wards or other involved departments, and therefore, the OR schedule has to be adjusted. In this paper, we develop a decision support system (DSS) which assists the OR manager in this decision by providing the three best adjusted OR schedules. The system considers the preferences of all involved stakeholders and only evaluates the OR schedules that satisfy the imposed resource constraints. The decision rules used for this system are based on a thorough analysis of the OR rescheduling problem. We model this problem as an Integer Linear Program (ILP) which objective is to minimize the deviation from the preferences of the considered stakeholders. By applying this ILP to instances from practice, we determined that the given preferences mainly lead to (i) shifting a surgery and (ii) scheduling a break between two surgeries. By using these changes in the DSS, the performed simulation study shows that less surgeries are canceled and patients and wards are more satisfied, but also that the perceived workload of several departments increases to compensate this. The system can also be used to judge the acceptability of a proposed initial OR schedule.

Keywords: Operating rooms, Rescheduling, Integer programming, Decision support system

1 INTRODUCTION

The Operating Room (OR) department is one of the most expensive resources of a hospital. However, managing the OR department is hard due to conflicting priorities and preferences of stakeholders. Therefore, planning and scheduling methods are needed to increase the efficiency in OR departments. See Cardoen et al. [3] and Hulshof et al. [12] for an overview on OR planning and scheduling.

In this paper, we focus on the rescheduling of surgeries, or more precisely, on the rescheduling of surgeries throughout the day. On the one hand, emergency patients who need surgery arrive throughout the day. In many hospitals, these surgeries are scheduled in one of the elective ORs which disrupts the OR schedule. On the other hand, a change in the surgery duration of elective surgeries may also disrupt the OR schedule. Therefore, the initial OR schedule may have to be adjusted throughout the day to ensure that it is still possible to execute the schedule. The new OR schedule must fulfil quite a number of restrictions, and in addition, there are several stakeholders whose preferences and priorities must be met. Since it is hard for an OR manager to consider all these restrictions and preferences simultaneously, we develop a decision support system (DSS) which supports the OR manager with rescheduling the ORs. The approach proposed in this paper is general, but the realization and used preferences are based on data from a hospital in the Netherlands.

Most existing literature focuses on operational off-line scheduling, which is done one or several days before surgery, instead of operational on-line scheduling, which is done on the day of surgery. The papers concerning operational off-line scheduling mainly focus on two methods. The first method is reserving time for emergency surgeries to minimize overtime and maximize OR utilization (see e.g. [2, 10, 13]). The second method is sequencing the elective surgeries such that the overtime caused by surgeries with a longer duration than expected is minimized (see e.g. [4, 14, 16]). In addition, some papers concerning operational off-line scheduling include the preferences of stakeholders. For example, Marcon and Dexter [17] consider the preferences of the holding and recovery departments and Marjamaa et al. [18] consider the preferences of the anesthetists.

One of the papers concerning operational on-line scheduling is the paper by Dexter [5] who examined whether moving the last surgery of the day to another OR could decrease overtime labour costs. The developed statistical strategy was based on historical data. However, in practice, often one surgeon operates in an OR on a day or part of the day and therefore, it is not allowed to move a surgery to another OR.

Dexter et al. [8] introduce four ordered priorities on which an OR management decision for changing the OR schedule can be based. The first and most important priority is patient's safety. The second priority states that a surgery can only be canceled if the patient safety is not endangered. The third priority is to minimize overtime, and the fourth and last priority is to reduce patient waiting times. These priorities, however, put minimizing overtime above the patients timing preferences. For patients it is not preferred to schedule their surgery earlier and certainly not later in the day. In addition, no priority considers the workload level on other departments like wards, the holding department, and the recovery department.

Another paper of Dexter et al. [7] considers the sequencing of urgent surgical cases. They proposed a sequencing which is based on the following three objectives: (i) minimize the average waiting time of surgeons and patients, (ii) sequence the surgeries in order of appearance, and (iii) schedule the surgeries in order of medical urgency. However, none of these objectives consider the preferences of the elective patients and other departments.

It seems that none of the existing papers on OR rescheduling considers the preferences and priorities of all the stakeholders simultaneously. This paper tries to fill this gap. Based on a given case in a Dutch hospital, we mainly focus on personal preferences and less on economical preferences, because patient and personnel satisfaction is highly important in the Netherlands due to shortage of personnel and competition between hospitals. In Section 2, we discuss the stakeholders and their restrictions and preferences which are based on a survey performed at the Isala Clinics, which is the above mentioned hospital in the Netherlands. Although these restrictions and preferences may differ between hospitals, the principle ideas of the method developed in this paper should be applicable for other hospitals too. Because we want to develop a DSS that generates adjusted OR schedules within a short amount of time, we first analyze the problem to determine which changes are preferred based on the preferences of the stakeholders. Therefore, we incorporate the restrictions and preferences in an Integer Linear Program (ILP), which has as goal to minimize the deviation from the preferences of the stakeholders. Although we prove that the problem is strongly NP-hard for two or more ORs, we are able to solve this ILP due to the moderate size of the instance. The solutions to the ILP are used to determine the changes made in the optimal OR schedule for instances of the Isala Clinics. These changes are incorporated as decision rules in the DSS which is described in Section 4. As we incorporate the preferences of all stakeholders and as these preferences are given by the stakeholders themselves, we do not expect that the resulting changes are subject to psychological bias as mentioned in other papers (see e.g. [6, 15]). The developed DSS is tested by means of a simulation study to determine what improvements can be made to the OR-schedule when the developed DSS is used in practice. The computational results of this simulation study are given in Section 5. Section 6 draws conclusions and gives recommendations for further research.

2 PROBLEM FORMULATION

In this section, we give an introduction to the OR rescheduling problem and we introduce an ILP model which can be used to determine a new OR schedule throughout the day. The ILP includes all relevant constraints that are imposed on the OR schedule; e.g. the availability of a patient, as well as the availability of an OR with OR assistants, a surgeon and an anesthetist. In addition, the capacity of the holding and recovery department are considered. A detailed description of the constraints is given in the following subsections.

The objective of the ILP is to minimize the deviation of the preferences for the involved stakeholders. When the OR schedule deviates from these preferences some penalty costs are incurred and the weighted sum of these penalty costs is minimized. There can be, for example, penalty costs for deviating from the scheduled start time of a surgery or for the amount of resulting overtime. In addition, we minimize the number of canceled patients, as this is not preferred by any of the stakeholders. The developed ILP can also be used to determine whether a proposed OR schedule is feasible or not, and in case it is feasible, to calculate the deviation from the preferences of the stakeholders.

Before we introduce the model, we first give a short description of the process a patient follows on the day of surgery in the Isala Clinics (see Fig. 1). On or before the day of surgery, the patient is admitted on a ward where he/she is prepared for surgery. Some time before surgery, the patient is transported to the holding department where the patient is further prepared for surgery. Then, the patient is transported to the operating room where the anesthetist administers anesthesia. After this, the surgeon performs the surgical procedure. When the surgical procedure is finished, the anesthetist reverses the anesthesia, and then, the patient is transported to the recovery department where he/she recovers from the effects of the anesthesia. At the time these effects have completely worn off and the patient's condition is considered stable, he/she is transported back to the ward. Emergency patients are not first admitted on one of the wards, but are directly transported to the holding department or, in some very urgent cases, to the emergency room in which the surgery will take place. After surgery, these emergency patients follow the same path as the elective patients.

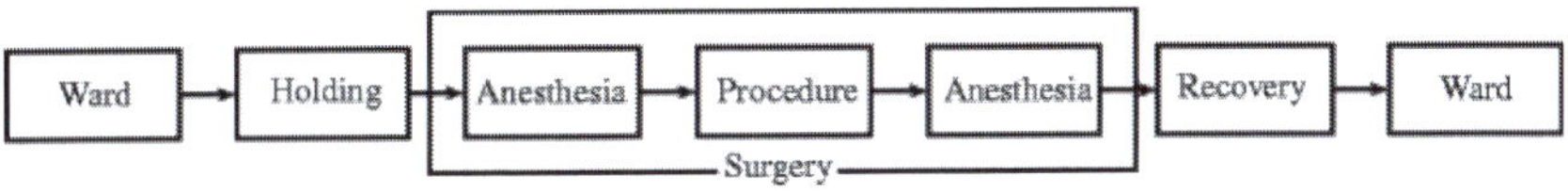

Figure 1. Patient process

For the modeling, we discretize an OR-day into T time periods which have a length of δ minutes. The length of one OR-day is therefore δT minutes. We denote by time $t \in T$ the period $((t-1)\delta, t\delta]$. The set of ORs is given by set J and consists of M ORs. The start time of OR $j \in J$ is denoted by S_j and the end time by F_j. The set of surgeries is given by set I and consists of N surgeries. The subset Ij⊆IIj⊆I denotes the surgeries that are scheduled in OR $j \in J$ and $O_i \in J$ denotes the assigned OR for surgery $i \in I$.

The initial OR schedule, which is given at the beginning of the day and which has already been determined one or several days before, is defined by the assignment of the elective surgeries to an OR and the initially planned start times P_i of the elective surgeries. Each surgery has an expected duration E_i which includes the time for administering and reversing anesthesia, however, in practice, the duration of a surgery generally deviates from this duration and takes longer or shorter than expected. When a surgery takes less time than expected, and the next surgery starts at its assigned time P_i, the initial OR schedule is not disrupted. However, it may be beneficial for the OR and other departments to schedule this next surgery earlier. When a surgery takes longer than expected, the next surgery may have to start later. This results in a shift of the not yet started surgeries in this OR. Because of this, some resource constraints may be violated. In addition to these deviations of the durations of the elective surgeries, emergency surgeries may arrive which also disrupt the initial OR schedule. Therefore, throughout the day, a new OR schedule may have to be created for all not started elective and emergency surgeries. In the following, we denote by set I the set of all these elective and emergency surgeries. The rescheduling is done by assigning a new start time to each surgery $i \in I$. Formally, this is expressed by binary variables s_{it}, which are one when surgery $i \in I$ starts at time $t \in T$, and zero otherwise. It is important to note that we do not allow the elective surgeries to be assigned to another OR, because each surgery has to be performed by the surgeon operating in the OR assigned to the surgery in the initial OR schedule. Thus, all elective surgeries have to be scheduled in the same OR as in the initial schedule. Because we only reschedule the not yet started surgeries, the start time of OR $j \in J$ for the rescheduling problem is either given by the start time of the OR in the morning or the expected end time of the last started surgery in this OR.

Within the rescheduling, it may be necessary to cancel an elective surgery, for example because of an arriving emergency surgery. The decision variable u_i denotes whether elective surgery $i \in I$ is canceled or not, i.e., the variable is one when the surgery is canceled and zero otherwise. When u_i is zero, the surgery is not canceled and therefore a new start time must be assigned, i.e., $\sum_{t \in T} s_{it}$ must be one in this case. When a surgery is canceled, the opposite holds, i.e., if $u_i = 1$ we must have $\sum_{t \in T} s_{it} = 0$. This is ensured by the following constraint.

$$\sum_{t \in T} s_{it} = 1 - u_i, \qquad \forall i \in I \tag{1}$$

Note that we do not consider the rescheduling of a canceled surgery, because we only focus on rescheduling within the day and not from day to day.

The new start time of surgery $i \in I$ should fulfil a number of constraints. It should be greater than or equal to (i) the ready time of the patient which is given by Y_i, (ii) the start time of the assigned surgeon C_i which is given by DCiDCi, and (iii) the start time of the assigned OR O_i. The following constraint ensures this.

$$s_{it} = 0, \qquad \forall i \in I, t < \max\left(S_{O_i}, Y_i, D_{C_i}\right) \tag{2}$$

The subset $I_{MD} \subset I$ denotes the set of surgeries that should start before a certain time because of medical reasons. This medical deadline of surgery $i \in I$ is given by L_i. Furthermore, it is not allowed to cancel these surgeries, i.e., we must have $u_i = 0$ and the surgery has to start before L_i.

$$\begin{aligned} \sum_{t=0}^{L_i} s_{it} &= 1, \qquad \forall i \in I_{MD} \\ u_i &= 0, \qquad \forall i \in I_{MD} \end{aligned} \tag{3}$$

The decision variable s_{it} and u_i completely determine the new OR schedule. However, to model the other restrictions and preferences some extra variables have to be defined which are introduced at the places where they are needed.

In each OR, only one surgery can be performed at a time. To model this, we need to determine if a surgery is ongoing at time $t \in T$. For this, we introduce the binary variables b_{it} which are one when surgery $i \in I$ is performed on time $t \in T$ and zero otherwise. A surgery is ongoing on time $t \in T$ when the start time of surgery $i \in I$ is between time t and time $t - E_i$. This is shown in Fig. 2and expressed by the following constraint.

$$b_{it} = \sum_{\hat{t}=t-E_i+1}^{t} s_{i\hat{t}}, \qquad \forall i \in I, t \in T \tag{4}$$

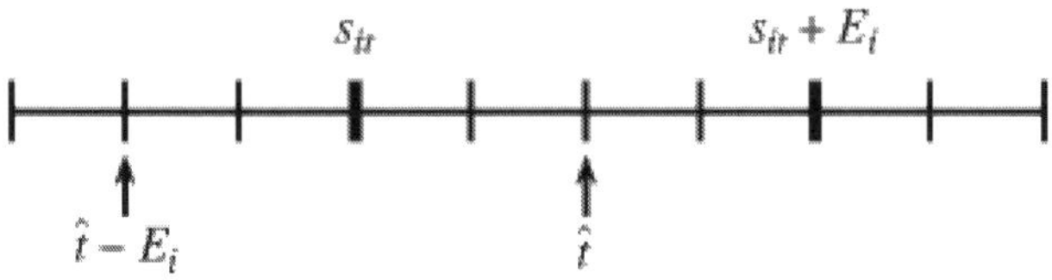

Figure 2. Determine b_{it}

The following constraint ensures that for each OR only one surgery can be performed at a time.

$$\sum_{i \in I_j} b_{it} \leq 1, \qquad \forall j \in J, t \in T \tag{5}$$

The above constraints describe some of the hard constraints for the rescheduling process resulting from the situation in the OR. In the following subsections, we describe and model the involved stakeholders. For each stakeholder, we describe the tasks the stakeholder has to perform during the day, the restrictions they impose on the OR schedule, the impact a change in the OR schedule has on the stakeholder and the preferences of the stakeholder. The impacts are modeled by linear constraints, and penalty costs for deviating from the preferences are incorporated in the objective function. The chosen functions and corresponding parameters used to describe the preferences of the stakeholders and the penalty costs for deviating from these preferences are determined based on a survey at the Isala Clinics (see Appendix A). Applying the model to a different hospital asks for an analysis of the preferences of the stakeholders in this hospital and may lead to other penalty cost functions. However, the principle structure of the proposed approach does not have to be adapted.

2.1 Patient

The key stakeholder is the patient. For patients it is important that the surgery takes place at the scheduled time. Penalty costs are incurred when the new start time deviates from this preference. In order to determine the total penalty costs, we need to know the new start time of the surgery in the OR schedule. This time is denoted by the variable w_i, and in case surgery $i \in I$ is canceled, we define w_i to be equal to the start time of surgery $i \in I$ in the initial OR schedule.

$$w_i = \sum_t ts_{it} + u_i P_i, \qquad \forall i \in I \tag{6}$$

If we now denote by y_i the difference of the initial and new start time of surgery $i \in I$,

$$y_i = w_i - P_i, \qquad \forall i \in I \tag{7}$$

this variable y_i is zero when surgery $i \in I$ is canceled or when the start time of surgery $i \in I$ has not changed. For emergency surgeries, we take as initial planned start time P_i the time the patient arrived at the hospital. This ensures that emergency surgeries are scheduled as soon as possible. The variable y_i is negative when surgery $i \in I$ starts earlier in the new OR schedule and when y_i is positive, surgery $i \in I$ starts later. As patients judge earliness and tardiness different, we split the variable y_i in two cases by introducing variables ylateriyilater and yearlieriyiearlier. The variable ylateriyilatertakes value y_i when y_i is positive, and variable yearlieriyiearlier takes value $-y_i$ when y_i is negative, which is ensured by the following constraints and the fact that the objective tries to minimize these variables.

$$\begin{aligned} y_i^{\text{earlier}} &\geq P_i - w_i, && \forall i \in I \\ y_i^{\text{earlier}} &\geq 0, && \forall i \in I \\ y_i^{\text{later}} &\geq w_i - P_i, && \forall i \in I \\ y_i^{\text{later}} &\geq 0, && \forall i \in I \end{aligned} \tag{8}$$

Note that constraints (8) replace constraint (7) in the ILP.

Based on the survey in the hospital, we concluded that patients assign different penalty costs to different values of y_i. To model this, a function $f_{PT}(y_i)$, denoting the penalty costs when surgery $i \in I$ is shifted y_i time periods, is introduced. This function is also split into two parts,
namely fearlierPT(yearlieri)fPTearlier(yiearlier) and flaterPT(ylateri)fPTlater(yilater).

Based on the patient survey, the penalty cost functions can be modeled best by step functions which are combinations of linear functions, see Fig. 3. The specific value of the steps are also given by the questionnaire. To determine the correct value of the function fearlierPTfPTearlier for a specific value of yearlieriyiearlier, we introduce two parameters. The first is f_k, which denotes the function value in interval k, and the second is γ_k, which denotes the right endpoint of interval k.

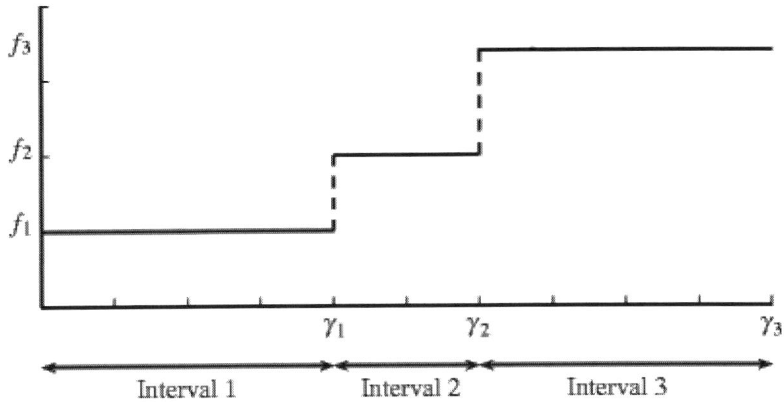

Figure 3. Step function

To be able to incorporate these step functions in an ILP model, we introduce binary variables λ_{ik} which are one when yearlieriyiearlier is in interval k and zero otherwise. This is ensured by the following two constraints.

$$\begin{aligned} \sum_k \lambda_{ik}\gamma_k \geq y_i^{\text{earlier}}, \qquad & \forall i \in I \\ \sum_k \lambda_{ik} = 1, \qquad & \forall i \in I \end{aligned} \tag{9}$$

The value of the penalty function is now determined by:

$$f_{PT}^{\text{earlier}}\left(y_i^{\text{earlier}}\right) = \sum_k \lambda_{ik} f_k, \qquad \forall i \in I. \tag{10}$$

The total penalty costs of the patient group is given by p_{PT}, and is defined as the sum of the penalty costs of each patient.

$$p_{PT} = \sum_{i \in I} \left(f_{PT}^{\text{earlier}}\left(y_i^{\text{earlier}}\right) + f_{PT}^{\text{later}}\left(y_i^{\text{later}}\right)\right) \tag{11}$$

Note that the two penalty functions fearlierPTfPTearlier and flaterPTfPTlater in general have different parameters. Because we minimize the total penalty costs, this method is only applicable for non-decreasing step functions.

2.2 Ward

Prior to surgery, the patient is admitted to a ward. On this ward, the patient is prepared for surgery. The survey showed that when a surgery starts earlier than scheduled, the workload on the ward increases if the patient is not ready yet. When a surgery starts later than scheduled, the workload can also increase. Therefore, penalty costs are incurred when there is a change in the start time of a surgery. The total penalty costs are calculated in the same way as for the patient. Based on the outcome of the survey a step function $f_W(y_i)$ is defined, which denotes the penalty costs for the wards if the start time of a surgery is shifted for y_i time periods. Note, that we do not distinguish between a surgery being scheduled earlier or later. The total penalty costs for wards is then given by $p_W = \sum_{i\in I} f_W(y_i)$.

2.3 Holding department

After the preparation on the ward, the patient is transported to the holding department where he/she is prepared further. The length of stay of patients on the holding department is given by V which can be longer than the preparation time needed. The holding department has a limited number of beds O_1 which provides a maximum for the number of patients treated at this department at the same time. Another limit on the number of patients who can be treated simultaneously is given by the available number of nurses at time $t \in T$ which is denoted by X_t. A nurse needs ρ minutes to prepare a patient, implying that X_t nurses can prepare at most δρXtδρXtpatients in time period t. Concluding, we define the capacity of the holding at time t by min($\left(O_1, \frac{\delta}{\rho} X_t\right)$). The number of patients present on the holding on time $t \in T$ is denoted by l_t and is given by:

$$l_t = \sum_{i\in I} \sum_{\hat{t}=t+1}^{t+V} s_{i\hat{t}}, \qquad \forall t \in T \tag{12}$$

This number should be smaller than or equal to the capacity of the holding which is ensured by the following constraint.

$$l_t \leq \min\left(O_1, \frac{\delta}{\rho} X_t\right), \qquad \forall t \in T \tag{13}$$

Note that when δρXt≤O1δρXt≤O1 for some $t \in T$, constraint (13) may exclude some feasible solutions (for an example, see Fig. 4). If we want to prohibit this, we also need to schedule the preparation time of the patients. However, this increases the complexity of our problem. Note that this issue does not occur when the length of stay V equals δ which is the case for the instances used.

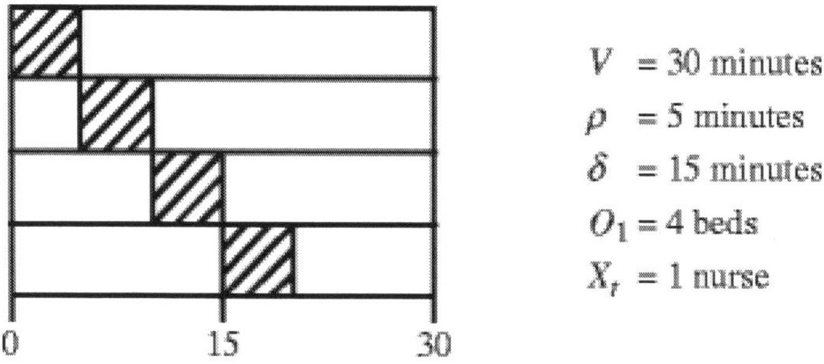

Figure 4. Excluded feasible solution

The survey at the Isala Clinics showed that the holding department prefers a levelled amount of patients that are present at each point of time. Therefore, penalty costs given by the step function $f_{HD}(l_t)$, are incurred when the number of patients l_t exceeds a certain threshold. The penalty costs for different values of l_t are specified by the manager of the holding department. As at the beginning of the day (until a prespecified time ψ), personnel from the recovery department assist on the holding department (no patients are present at the recovery department at this time), penalty costs are only incurred from time ψ on. The total penalty costs p_{HD} are given by $\sum_{t=\psi+1}^{T} f_{HD}(l_t)$.

2.4 Anesthetist

The anesthetist is responsible for administering and reversing anesthesia on one or more ORs. Therefore, he/she has to administer and reverse all anesthesias in these ORs. However, during the surgical procedure, the anesthetist does not have to be present in the OR, because the presence of an anesthesia nurse is enough. Therefore, similar to constraints (4) and (5), we include constraints which prohibits that more than one anesthesia is administered or reversed at a time in the ORs to which the anesthetist is assigned. For more details, see [11].

However, there are a few exceptions. When a surgery is complex, for example when the patient is younger than 6 months, the anesthetist must be present during the complete surgery which includes the surgical procedure. This means that during this time no anesthesia can be administered or reversed in one of the other assigned ORs. This is also ensured by constraints similar to constraint (5).

2.5 Surgeon

The surgeon is assigned to one OR and only has to perform the surgical procedure. This means that he/she does not have to be present during administering and reversing anesthesia. The constraints that ensure this are of the same structure as constraints (4) and (5).

2.6 OR assistants

The OR assistants do not impose any restrictions on the OR schedule. Their only preference is that overtime is minimized. Overtime can occur because of arriving emergency surgeries and surgeries whose duration is longer than expected. Therefore, penalty costs are incurred when there is overtime. The amount of overtime in OR $j \in J$ is denoted by variable o_j. The value of this variable o_j is calculated by the following constraint.

$$o_j = \sum_{i \in I_j} \sum_{t=F_j+1}^{T} b_{it}, \qquad \forall j \in J \tag{14}$$

The step function $f_{OS}(o_j)$ provides the penalty costs for OR $j \in J$ when overtime of o_j time periods is incurred. The OR assistants specified the penalty costs for different values of o_j. The total penalty costs for the OR assistants is given by $p_{OS} = \sum_{j \in J} f_{OS}(o_j)$.

2.7 Recovery department

After surgery, the patient is transported to the recovery department. Here, the patient is monitored while he/she recovers from surgery. The length of stay on this department varies with the expected duration of the surgery and is given by max(U,12Ei)max(U,12Ei), where U is the minimum length of stay on this department. The number of patients present at the recovery department at time $t \in T$ is denoted by z_t and can be determined in the same way as for the holding department. The capacity of the recovery department is restricted by the number of beds O_2.

Another restriction is given by the number of patients who can be treated simultaneously, which depends on the number of available nurses R_t at time $t \in T$. Each nurse can monitor φ patients at a time, and therefore, φR_t patients can be treated simultaneously. Combining this with the number of beds O_2, the capacity of the recovery at time $t \in T$ is given by min(O2,φRt)min(O2,φRt). The number of patients present on the recovery department at time $t \in T$ should be less than or equal to this capacity. This is ensured by constraints that are of the same structure as constraints (12) and (13).

Like the holding department, the recovery department also prefers a levelled amount of patients that are present at each point of time. Therefore, penalty costs are incurred when the number of patients exceeds a certain threshold. This is modeled by the step function $f_{RC}(z_t)$ which provides the penalty costs incurred when z_t patients are present at time $t \in T$. The total penalty costs for the recovery is then given by $p_{RC} = \sum_{t \in T} f_{RC}(z_t)$.

2.8 Radiology department

For some surgeries, an X-ray machine is needed during surgery. These surgeries are given by the set IRL⊆IIRL⊆I. For these surgeries a radiology technician should be present during administering anesthesia and the surgical procedure. This means that he/she does not have to be present during reversing anesthesia. The set of radiology technicians is given by set K and consists of χ radiology technicians. We restrict the number of required radiology technicians $d_t$at time $t \in T$ to be smaller than or equal to the number of available radiology technicians. The constraints that ensure this are similar to constraints (4) and (5).

The survey showed that it is important for the radiology department that their employees at the OR department finish as early as possible such that they can carry out other work at the radiology department. Therefore, penalty costs are incurred when a radiology technician finishes later than needed, i.e., when the time the radiology technicians are present is longer than the time the radiology technicians are needed. In the following, we show how this is incorporated in the ILP.

For all radiology technicians k, we determine when their work is finished at the OR. These finish times are denoted by τ_k and are calculated by determining the latest time period where at least k radiology technicians where needed. First, for each time period $t \in T$, we introduce binary variables d~tkd~tk which are one when k or more radiology technicians are needed in time period t, and zero otherwise. This is ensured by the following constraint.

$$\tilde{d}_{tk} \geq \frac{d_t - k + 1}{\chi}, \qquad \forall t \in T, k \in K \tag{15}$$

The finish time τ_k of radiology technician k is now given by the latest time period that d~tkd~tk is equal to one, i.e.,

$$\tau_k \geq t\tilde{d}_{tk}, \qquad \forall t \in T, k \in K. \tag{16}$$

Using the above constraints and the fact that we minimize the working time of the radiology technicians, τ_k denotes the time the radiology technicians finish. However, these values do not equal the number of time periods they are actually present at the OR. To obtain this value, the start time and break time should be subtracted. The start time of the radiology technicians is given by min $_jS_j$, i.e., the start time of the OR department. For other hospitals, the start times of the radiology technicians may not be fixed. When this is the case, the start times can be determined with constraints similar to (15) and (16). In addition, all radiology technicians have a break of 45 min, i.e., 45δ45δ time periods. The amount of periods the radiology technicians are having a break is thus given by υ=45χδυ=45χδ. Therefore, the amount of time periods the radiology technicians are present at the OR is given by $\sum_k \tau_k - \chi S_j - \upsilon$. This is an underestimation in case one or more radiology technicians finish before their break. However, we expect that this will rarely happen in practice.

The amount of time periods the radiology technicians are actually working at the OR is given by $\sum_{i \in I_{RL}} (E_i - Q_2)$,), where Q_2 is the amount of time it takes to reverse anesthesia and E_i is the duration of surgery $i \in I_{RL}$. Now, the variable x defined by

$$x = 100 \left(\frac{\sum_k \tau_k - \chi S_j - \upsilon}{\sum_{i \in I_{RL}} (E_i - Q_2) + 1} \right) \tag{17}$$

denotes the inverse of the fraction of time the radiology technicians are busy. The step function $f_{RL}(x)$ denotes the penalty costs incurred for a value of x, specified by the radiology department, and gives the total penalty costs p_{RL} incurred.

2.9 Pathology department

During some surgeries, tissue is removed from a patient which needs to be examined by a pathologist. These surgeries are denoted by the set IPA⊆IIPA⊆I. After the surgical procedure, the tissue is transported from the OR to the pathology department. When tissue arrives after closing time, overtime is incurred. Let q_i be an integer variable which denotes the amount of overtime which would be created by a single surgery $i \in I$, i.e., the number of time periods the tissue arrives late plus the examination duration W.

As after closing time only one pathologist is available at the pathology department, the available pathologist has to successively process the tissues that arrive late. In most cases this means that the pathologists has to work $\sum_{i \in I, q_i > 0} 1$ periods in overtime. However, sometimes tissue will arrive so late, that the amount of overtime equals max $_{i\in I}q_i$. Therefore, the amount of overtime q_{total} is estimated as follows:

$$q_{\text{total}} = \max\left(\max_{i\in I} q_i, \sum_{i\in I, q_i>0} W\right) \tag{18}$$

When two sets of tissue arrive really late at approximately the same time, this number is a lowerbound on the amount of overtime. However, this situation is not likely to occur in practice.

Again, a step function $f_{PA}(q_{\text{total}})$ is used to express the penalty costs incurred for a value of $q_{\text{total}}$and represents the total penalty costs p_{PA} incurred for the pathology department.

2.10 **Logistic department**

The logistic department is responsible for preparing materials needed during surgery. The materials are laid out in the order in which the surgeries are scheduled. When two surgeries are interchanged, the logistic assistant incurs penalty costs, because they have to change the order in which the materials are laid out. Two surgeries $i \in I$ and i^∈Ii^∈I can only be interchanged when they are scheduled in the same OR, i.e., when Oi=Oi^Oi=Oi^. These two surgeries are interchanged when (Pi−Pi^)(wi^−wi)>0, where P_i is the start time in the initial OR schedule and w_i is the start time in the new OR schedule. When this holds, we either have that both (Pi−Pi^)(Pi−Pi^) and (wi^−wi)(wi^−wi) are positive or that both are negative. When both are positive, we have that Pi>Pi^Pi>Pi^and wi<wi^wi<wi^. This means that in the initial OR schedule, surgery $i \in I$ was scheduled later than surgery i^∈Ii^∈I and that in the new OR schedule, surgery $i \in I$ was scheduled earlier than surgery i^∈Ii^∈I. When both are negative, we have the opposite case.

We introduce binary variables κii^κii^ which are one when surgery $i \in I$ and i^∈Ii^∈I are interchanged and zero otherwise. This is ensured by constraints (19), where T is the number of time periods per day. When (Pi−Pi^)(wi^−wi)>, the variable κii^κii^ is set to one, however, when (Pi−Pi^)(wi^−wi)≤0 the variable κii^κii^ could be set to either one or zero. But because we want to minimize the number of exchanged surgeries, the variable κii^κii^ gets the value zero.

$$\left(P_i - P_{\hat{i}}\right)\left(w_{\hat{i}} - w_i\right) \leq T^2 \kappa_{i\hat{i}}, \forall \left(i > \hat{i}\right) \in I, O_i = O_{\hat{i}} \tag{19}$$

Let f_{LD} be the penalty cost incurred when two surgeries are interchanged, which value is specified by the logistic department. Then the total amount of penalty cost p_{LD} incurred for the logistic department is given by

$$p_{LD} = \sum_{j \in J} \sum_{(i,\hat{i}) \in I_j, i > \hat{i}} \kappa_{i\hat{i}} f_{LD}. \tag{20}$$

2.11 Objective function

The goal of our model is to minimize the deviation from the preferences of the stakeholders. We denote the set of stakeholders by Π and we consider each stakeholder to be equally important. Since the order of magnitude of the cost functions introduced for the different stakeholders may differ, we have to introduce a weighted sum of the penalty costs p_π to compensate these differences. In this function, the priority β_π assigned to stakeholder $\pi \in \Pi$ is determined such that all stakeholders contribute approximately the same amount to the objective function value. The general concept of the weighted sum of penalties has furthermore the advantage that by varying the priorities, we can develop, for example, also a more patient centred OR schedule.

Next to the penalty costs for deviation from the preferences of stakeholders, we also include penalty costs η for canceling a surgery. These penalty costs are set such that they contribute more than the combined total penalty costs of the stakeholders in case surgeries are canceled. This way, it is clear that canceling a surgery is not preferred, however, if needed it is possible to do it. Note that the resulting changes in the OR schedule are not risk-averse (see [19]), because by given the objective 'minimizing the number of cancellations' a very high weight, the OR utilization is maximized. Summarizing, the objective function is given by

$$\min \sum_{\pi \in \Pi} \beta_\pi p_\pi + \sum_{i \in I} \eta u_i. \tag{21}$$

2.12 Problem complexity

The problem introduced in the previous subsections has been modeled as an ILP. The following theorem justifies this approach, since it shows that efficient exact approaches are unlikely to exist.

Theorem 1

The OR rescheduling problem is strongly NP-hard for two or more operating rooms.

Proof

We prove the theorem by reducing 3-partition to the OR rescheduling problem. The 3-partition problem can be formulated as follows. Given positive integers $a_1,...,a_{3t}$, and b with ∑3tj=1aj=tb∑j=13taj=tb, do there exist t pairwise disjoint subsets Rk⊂{1,...,3t}Rk⊂{1,...,3t} such that ∑j∈Rkaj=b∑j∈Rkaj=b for $k = 1,...,t$? The 3-partition problem is proven to be strongly NP-hard (see Garey and Johnson [9]).

The reduction is based on the following transformation, where we set the priorities for the patient, ward, and the holding, recovery, radiology, pathology and logistic department to zero. Therefore, we only aim to minimize overtime and the number of cancellations. Furthermore, we consider 2 ORs which have their own anesthetist and $6t - 2$ surgeries with the following processing times and ready times:

$$
\begin{aligned}
&E_i = b, && Y_i = 0 && \forall 1 \leq i \leq t-1,\\
& && && i \in I_1, I_{RL},\\
&E_i = a_{i-t+1}, && Y_i = 0 && \forall t \leq i \leq 4t-1,\\
& && && i \in I_1,\\
&E_i = b, && Y_i = 2b\,(i-4t) && \forall 4t \leq i \leq 5t-1,\\
& && && i \in I_2, I_{RL},\\
&E_i = b, && Y_i = b\,(i-(5t-1)) && \forall 5t \leq i \leq 6t-2,\\
& && && i \in I_2.
\end{aligned}
$$

The end and start times of the 2 ORs are:

$$S_j = 0,\ F_j = (2t-1)b \text{ for } j \in J.$$

The capacities of the holding and recovery departments are assumed to be larger than $6t - 2$, thus we do not have to consider the given constraints for these departments. Furthermore, only one radiology technician is available, and therefore, we have to consider the given constraints for the radiology department. Our goal is to create an OR schedule with objective value less than or equal to zero.

First note that, because of their ready times, the surgeries from {4t,4t+1,...,6t−2} in OR 2 have to be scheduled as in Fig. 5 to achieve an objective value of zero, i.e., no overtime and cancellations may occur. In Fig. 5, the grey blocks denote surgeries that need a radiology technician and the white blocks denote surgeries that do not need a radiology technician. Because the surgeries from {1,2,...t−1} in OR 1 need a radiology technician, they have to be scheduled in the time intervals where the radiology technician is not busy in OR 2, i.e., as in Fig. 5. This leaves us with t blocks of length b in OR 1 which have to be filled with the surgeries from {t,t+1,...,4t−1} } to achieve zero overtime with zero cancellations, and thus, an objective value of zero. Therefore, our problem has a solution with objective value zero if and only if there exists a solution to the 3-partition problem. □

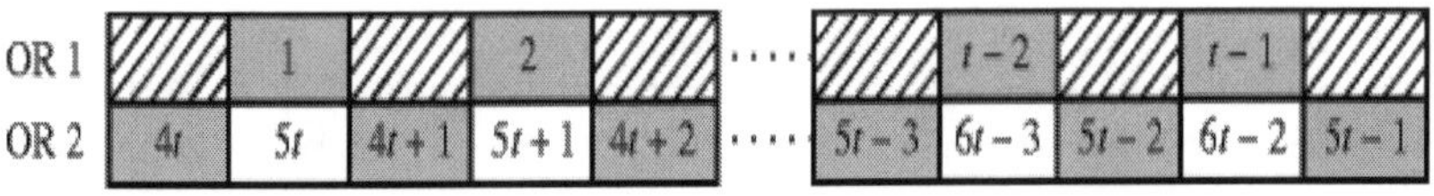

Figure 5. Reduction of 3-partition problem to the OR rescheduling problem

The proof of this theorem shows that already a very restricted version of the OR rescheduling problem is strongly NP-hard.

3 COMPUTATIONAL RESULTS ILP

We tested our ILP on data from the Isala Clinics, a hospital in the Netherlands. The data consists of 1168 surgeries scheduled over 27 days. The surgeries consist of 354 emergency surgeries, 193 surgeries who need X-ray, 79 surgeries during which tissue is removed, and 7 complex surgeries. The average expected duration of the surgeries is 103 min, and the average realized duration of the surgeries is 91 min. Because rescheduling is only performed during working hours, we removed the emergency surgeries that start before 07:30 and after 18:00. We implemented our model in AIMMS 3.10 and solved it with CPLEX 12.1 on an AMD Ahtlon X2 Dual Core L310 1.2 GHz processor with 4 GB RAM.

In the first two subsections, we discuss the parameter settings for the ILP model and the achieved results which are used to derive the decision rules for the DSS. In the last subsection, we determine the penalty costs for the initial OR schedule used at the Isala Clinics and the OR schedule realized at the end of the day. In addition, we optimize both the initial and realized OR schedule to show what improvements potentially can be realized when the developed method is used.

3.1 Parameter settings

In this subsection, we discuss the parameter settings for the time periods and the priorities for each stakeholder.

To determine the appropriate length δ of the time periods, we solved the model for time periods of 5, 10, 15 and 20 min. We interrupted the ILP solver after 10 min of computation time. If after this time no optimal solution was found, we took the best solution found as our final solution. In Fig. 6, the runtime for each combination of day and δ is given.

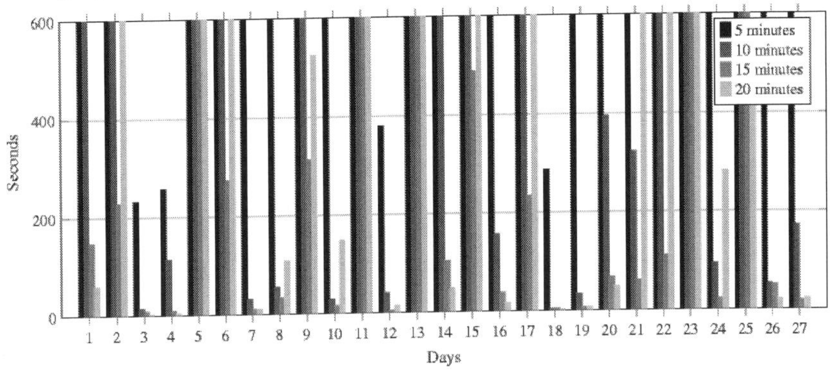

Figure 6. Runtime for different values of δ

We would expect that a smaller value of δ would increase the runtime of our model. For most days in our instance this holds, however, in some cases, the runtime for our model with δ equal to 15 min is shorter than the runtime for our model with δ equal to 20 min. Figure 7 shows that for δ equal to 5 min, an optimal solution was only found for 4 of the 27 days. For δ equal to 10 and 20 min, this number increased to 14 and 17 days, respectively. The model with δ equal to 15 min performs the best, because an optimal solution was found for 22 of the 27 days. This result seems to be the consequence of the input data, since most of the data is given in multiples of 15 min, for example, the expected surgery duration and the length of stay on the holding department.

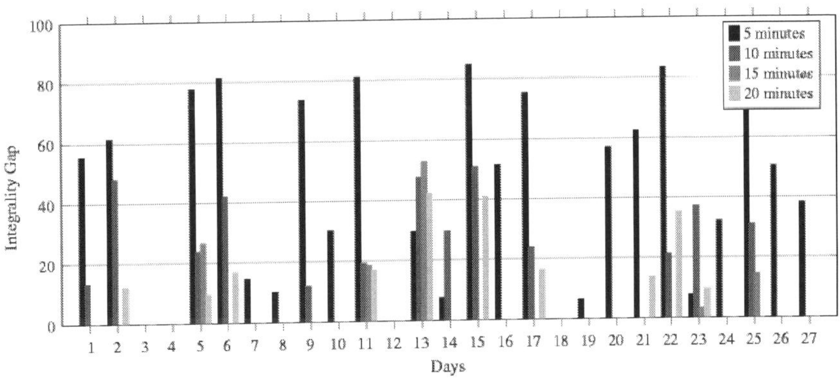

Figure 7. Integrality gap for different values of δ

In Fig. 8, we give the objective function value for each combination of δ and day. If solved to optimality, the objective value should increase when δ increases, because there is more flexibility in the OR schedule when δ is lower, i.e., the model with $\delta = 5$, should be able to provide the same or even a better solution than the model with δ set to 10, 15 or 20 min. However, Fig. 8 shows that the worst objective values are achieved when δ equals 5. This is because for most days no optimal solution was found within 10 min. From Fig. 8, we can conclude that our model with δ set to 15 min results in the lowest objective function value. Combining the results for the runtime and objective function, we choose to set δ to 15 min for further tests.

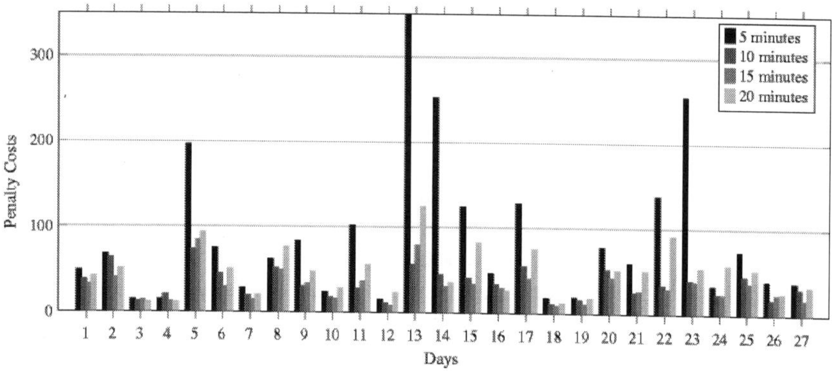

Figure 8. Objective function value for different values of δ

For each of the stakeholders, we have to determine its priority in the objective function. In the objective function, the total penalty costs of each stakeholder is multiplied by this priority. Our goal is that each stakeholder has approximately the same contribution in the objective function. In the following, we describe how we have determined the priority of each of the stakeholders.

First, we solve our model where all stakeholders have priority one. Next, we adjust the priorities in such a way that the weighted cost of each of the stakeholders for the achieved solution is approximately the same. This is done by setting the priority of the stakeholder with the lowest total penalty costs to one and the priorities of the other stakeholders such that their weighted costs equals the lowest total penalty costs. Table 1 shows the results if this method is applied to our data, where the total penalty costs are the average total penalty costs incurred per day.

Table 1. Total penalty costs and priorities

	Patient	Ward	Holding	OR assistants	Recovery	Radiology	Pathology	Logistics
Total penalty costs	7.45	5.26	0.00	1.11	1.91	1.00	0.56	0.91
Priority	0.08	0.11	1.00	0.50	0.29	0.56	1.00	0.62
Weighted costs	0.56	0.56	0.00	0.56	0.56	0.56	0.56	0.56

Note, that the holding department does not incur any penalty costs, because penalty costs are only incurred when four patients are treated simultaneously. The constraints imposed, however, limit the number of patients present on the holding department to three. This means that the holding department is not a bottleneck in the current situation.

We conducted some further tests where we varied these priorities slightly. The results from these tests show that patients, wards, and OR assistants have opposite interests compared to the recovery, radiology, pathology, and logistic department.

3.2 Deriving decision rules

The main goal of applying the ILP model is to determine which adjustments to the initial OR schedule are allowed and preferred based on the given preferences of the stakeholders. To determine this, we use our ILP model to create at three points $t \in T$ a new OR schedule which minimizes the deviation from the preferences of the stakeholders. For each of these three scenario's, the initial OR schedule is given as input as well as the realization of the duration of the surgeries that started before time t. These realized durations may change the initial OR schedule, because this schedule was based on the expected durations. Since we cannot change the OR schedule for the already started surgeries, we start rescheduling at the new start time S_j of OR j, which we define as the end time of the last started surgery before time t. In addition, we schedule not yet started emergency surgeries that arrived before time t. We assign a new start time s_{it} to each elective and emergency surgery that has not started at time t or, when allowed, cancel this surgery such that the resource constraints are fulfilled and the deviation from the preferences is minimized. The three scenario's are summarized below.

1. Scenario 1

After 10 a.m.: In this scenario, the realized durations of the surgery that started before 10 a.m. are known. An emergency surgery is only included if it arrived before 10 a.m..

2. Scenario 2

After 12 p.m.: In this scenario, the realized durations of the surgery that started before 12 p.m. are known. An emergency surgery is only included if it arrived before 12 p.m..

3. Scenario 3

After 2 p.m.: In this scenario, the realized durations of the surgery that started before 2 p.m. are known. An emergency surgery is only included if it arrived before 2 p.m..

These three scenario's are used to determine what adjustments our model makes to the OR schedule. For each of the scenario's, we determine how often one of the following adjustments occurred: (i) shifting a surgery, (ii) exchanging the sequence of two surgeries, and (iii) canceling a surgery. In addition, we determine how often a break of a certain length was scheduled between two surgeries. The results are shown in Table 2.

Table 2. Results scenario 1, 2, and 3

	10 a.m.	12 p.m.	2 p.m.
Rescheduled surgeries	566	416	213
Shifted surgeries	375	297	176
Exchanged surgeries	1	0	0
Canceled surgeries	0	0	1
No break	264	183	71
Break 15 min	166	112	66
Break 30 min	62	33	21
Break 45 min	22	19	11
Break > 45 min	38	37	13
Mean break	15.84	18.71	19.78

Table 2 shows that shifting a surgery is the most frequent adjustment used, and often we see that a break is scheduled between two surgeries. The average length of a break is 15–20 min. When we only consider OR utilization, this may not seem to be optimal, however, these breaks can improve the perceived workload of other departments or may be necessary to fulfil the resource constraints. From the results we conclude that only two types of adjustments are preferred to be used. A surgery can be shifted or a break can be scheduled between two surgeries. This means that the order of surgeries stays the same during the day. So when we only allow these two adjustments, the number of feasible solutions decreases significantly, because we only have to consider one sequence of the surgeries instead of all possible sequences. Based on this, it is possible to develop a simple heuristic to determine a good OR schedule. A further benefit of this is that we do not need an expensive ILP solver to implement our approach.

Following the above considerations, we have incorporated this simple heuristic in a DSS which is described in Section 4.

3.3 Potential improvements

To determine what improvements the DSS could potentially make compared to the OR schedules used at the Isala Clinics, we calculated, using the ILP model, the optimal initial OR schedule based on the expected surgery durations. Note, that for this optimization the assignment of the surgeries to an OR is given as in the given initial OR schedule. Thus, we only change the sequences of the surgeries in each OR. None of the surgeries can be canceled, and because it is an initial OR schedule, the change in the start time of the surgeries is not incorporated in the ILP model. This implies that the penalty costs for the patients, wards and logistic department are zero. Also, there are no emergency surgeries to be scheduled, because they have not arrived yet. This resulting fourth scenario is summarized below.

1 Scenario 4

Initial OR schedule: In this scenario, we compare the initial OR schedule used at the Isala Clinics with a new OR schedule determined by the ILP model, where we rescheduled all elective surgeries. Therefore, there are no emergency surgeries to be scheduled, and only the expected duration of each surgery is given.

In addition, we want to determine what improvements the DSS could make to the realized OR schedule. Filling in the actual surgery durations in the initial OR schedule will most likely result in an infeasible solution and because we do not know the exact decisions the OR manager will make, we can only guess what improvements can be achieved. To provide an upperbound on these improvements, and thus a lowerbound on the penalty costs, we optimized the realized OR schedule and compared it to the realized OR schedule provided by the Isala Clinics. The realized OR schedule of the Isala Clinics denotes how the surgeries were actually performed. This means that several changes have been made to the initial OR schedule, and therefore, we can determine the penalty costs achieved for these changes. For the optimal realized OR schedule, we assume that all realized durations of the elective and emergency surgeries are considered to be known in advance, and also the canceled surgeries are taken into account. In practice, this information is not known beforehand, and thus, this optimal realized OR schedule can not be achieved in practice. However, it provides a bound and, therefore, an indication of the room for improvement.

To define the input more precisely, we take all elective surgeries with their realized duration that were planned in the initial OR schedule, and in addition, we include all performed emergency surgeries with their realized duration. For the canceled surgeries, we use the given expected surgery durations. For this scenario, it can happen that surgeries are canceled or that their start time changes, which results in penalty costs for patients, ward, and the logistic department. This fifth scenario is summarized below.

1. Scenario 5

Realization: This scenario consists of all the elective surgeries scheduled in the initial OR schedule and all emergency surgeries that arrived during the day. The realized duration of all surgeries is known.

Table 3 provides the average total penalty costs per day for each of the stakeholders and compares the initial and realized OR schedule of the Isala Clinics to the optimal OR schedules created by our ILP model. In the total costs, the priorities of the stakeholders are included.

Table 3. Results scenario 4 and 5

Total penalty	Initial OR schedule		Realized OR schedule	
costs	Original	Optimal	Original	Optimal
Cancellation	0.00	0.00	66.67	22.22
Patient	0.00	0.00	40.91	36.50
Ward	0.00	0.00	34.40	28.56
Holding	0.00	0.00	0.00	0.00
OR assistants	0.00	0.68	6.43	4.20
Recovery	4.93	0.74	8.85	3.11
Radiology	1.63	0.56	2.41	1.07
Pathology	0.64	0.15	0.70	0.51
Logistics	0.00	0.00	9.26	5.93
Total costs	3.00	1.03	87.03	35.82

Table 3 shows that in Scenario 4, the initial OR schedule, the total penalty costs for the recovery and radiology department decreases. However, this can only be achieved by scheduling some surgeries in overtime. This follows from the slight increase of the total penalty costs for the OR assistants. For Scenario 5, the realization, the results show that the objective function value is reduced with approximately 60%. The major decrease is caused by the reduction of the number of cancellations. Also, the total penalty costs for the recovery department decreases significantly. In practice, the penalty costs for the realized OR schedule will lay somewhere between 35.82 en 87.03 when the DSS, discussed in the next section, is used.

Concluding, our model can potentially improve the initial and realized OR schedule significantly.

4 DECISION SUPPORT SYSTEM

To make our method applicable in practice, we have developed a DSS which can be used by the OR manager. We incorporated the two decision rules that are derived from the results in Section 3.2. The first decision rule is that the order of surgeries must be maintained, but that a surgery can be shifted in time. In addition, the second decision rule states that it is allowed to schedule a break of at most one hour between two surgeries. This may help to decrease the perceived workload of several stakeholders and may be necessary to fulfil the resource constraints.

During the day, the OR schedule must be adjusted, because of arriving emergency surgeries and elective surgeries that take shorter or longer than expected. The user can indicate for which OR the schedule should be adjusted. Because we have to consider all preferences and restrictions with respect to the other ORS, adjusting the schedule of the chosen OR is not straightforward. However, since we only have small instances, we evaluate, by means of complete enumeration, all possible solutions for this OR with respect to the two decisions rules. This means that between each two surgeries a break is scheduled with a duration that varies between 0 and 4 time periods. When n surgeries have to be rescheduled, this results in 5^{n-1} possible solutions. In most cases n will be smaller than 5, which gives approximately 100 possible solutions. After all possible solutions are evaluated, the DSS presents the three best options to the user. Only feasible solutions with respect to the constraints described in Section 2 are considered. A screen-shot of the DSS is shown in Fig. 9. The first column of the screen-shot gives the specified priorities of all stakeholders. These values can be changed to create, for example, a patient centred OR schedule. The next column shows the penalty costs and weighted costs of the current OR schedule. The last three columns show the three best OR schedules with their penalty costs and weighted costs from which the user can choose. In addition, the DSS provides a Gantt chart of the current OR schedule and the three best feasible OR schedules (see Fig. 10).

Stakeholder	Priority	Planning Penalty Costs	Planning Weighted Costs	Option 1 Penalty Costs	Option 1 Weighted Costs	Option 2 Penalty Costs	Option 2 Weighted Costs	Option 3 Penalty Costs	Option 3 Weighted Costs
Patient	0.05	26.20	1.31	25.90	1.26	26.20	1.31	26.20	1.31
Ward	0.08	26.60	2.13	25.20	2.07	26.60	2.13	26.60	2.13
Holding	1.00	0.00	0.00	0.00	0.00	0.00	0.00	0.00	0.00
OR assistants	0.54	0.00	0.00	0.00	0.00	0.00	0.00	0.60	0.32
Recovery	0.16	13.00	2.08	11.00	1.76	13.00	2.08	13.00	2.08
Radiology	0.20	2.00	0.40	2.00	0.40	2.00	0.40	2.00	0.40
Pathology	0.10	0.70	0.07	0.70	0.07	0.70	0.07	0.70	0.07
Logistics	0.43	0.00	0.00	0.00	0.00	0.00	0.00	0.00	0.00
Total costs			5.99		5.56		5.99		6.31

Figure 9. Decision support system - penalty costs

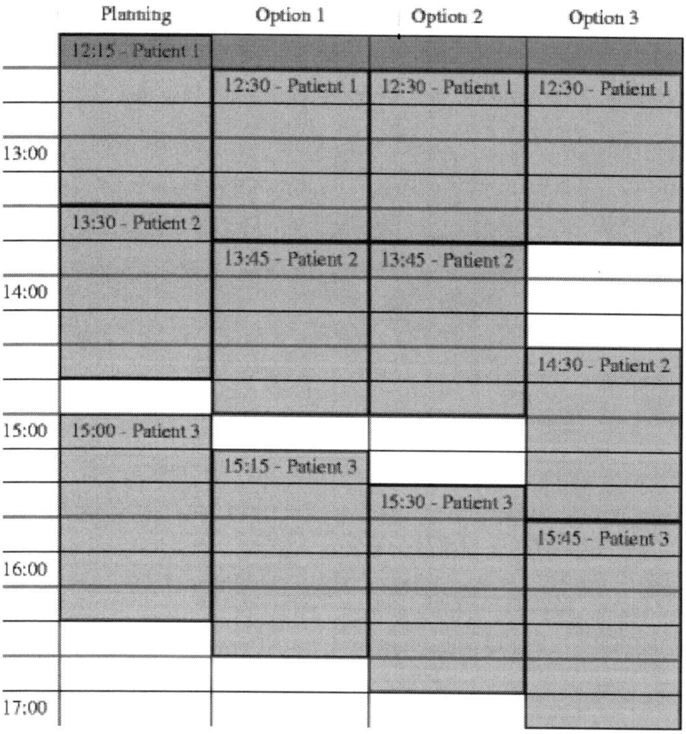

Figure 10. Decision support system - Gantt chart

The DSS gives insight in how other departments are influenced by a change in the OR schedule by denoting the penalty costs and weighted costs incurred for each stakeholder. This can convince surgeons that it can be useful to schedule a break between two surgeries. In addition, the DSS can determine whether the initial OR schedule is feasible or not by checking all constraints given in Section 2. The system denotes for each constraint how many times it is violated in the proposed OR schedule. It furthermore can be used to adjust the schedule such that it is feasible. Also, the penalty costs for the proposed OR schedule are calculated which gives an indication of how good the schedule is. The last advantage of the DSS is that the realized OR schedule can be evaluated. This way, the OR manager can learn from his decisions made in the past.

5 SIMULATION STUDY DSS

To determine the effect of using the DSS in practice, we tested the developed DSS on the instance given in Section 3 by means of a simulation study. In this study, we simulate the use of the DSS by rescheduling an OR immediately when it is disturbed. We choose to evaluate this rescheduling strategy, because we believe that this strategy will provide the best results.

At the beginning of each of the days in the considered instance, only the information that at that time is also known in practice is given. More specific, only the initial OR schedule is known, which is defined by the assignment of the elective surgeries to an OR and the initially planned start times P_i of the elective surgeries together which their expected duration E_i. This means that the emergency surgeries are not known in advance in contrast to the considered Scenario 5.

For each point in time during the simulation, we insert the arrived emergency surgeries to the OR schedule and we update the surgery duration for each of the ongoing surgeries. For each arrived emergency surgery, we set the planned start time equal to their time of arrival and set their duration equal to the expected surgery duration. In addition, each emergency surgery has to be performed in the same OR as it was performed in the realized OR schedule of the Isala Clinics.

For the ongoing surgeries, we update the duration according to the following rules. When the realized duration of a surgery is less than the expected duration, we set the duration equal to the expected duration until the surgery is finished. At the moment in time the surgery is finished, we set the duration equal to the realized duration. When the realized duration of a surgery is larger than the expected duration, we set the duration equal to the maximum of the expected duration and the already executed duration thus far. When the already executed duration equals the realized duration, the surgery is finished and thus, the duration is set to the realized duration. In the next step of our simulation, we determine for each OR whether it becomes empty or whether an elective surgery which is scheduled to start at this point in time cannot be started. When an OR becomes empty, a new surgery may be started which could potentially improve the OR schedule for one or more of the stakeholders.

In case an elective surgery which is scheduled to start cannot be started, we have the situation that an already started surgery assigned to the same OR takes longer than its expected duration. When one of these two cases occur, we reschedule this OR to decrease the penalty costs or to make the OR schedule feasible again. We reschedule this OR with respect to the fixed schedule in the other ORs as described in Section 4.

The results of the simulation study in Table 4 show that the DSS provides a much better solution than the original realized OR schedule of the Isala Clinics. However, as expected, the penalty costs for the DSS are higher than the penalty costs for the optimal realized OR schedule. When compared to the original realized OR schedule, the total penalty costs are reduced by approximately 50% for the DSS and by approximately 60% for the optimal realized OR schedule. In addition, the results show that the penalty costs for the patients and wards decrease when compared to the realized OR schedule of the Isala Clinics and the optimal realized OR schedule, however, the penalty costs for the OR assistants and the recovery, radiology and pathology departments increase. The penalty costs for the mentioned stakeholders increase because surgeries cannot be canceled or exchanged and thus, more surgeries have to be done in overtime. Concluding, the use of the DSS provides a better trade-off between the preferences of the involved stakeholders and by this reduces the incurred penalty costs significantly.

Table 4. Results simulation study DSS

Total penalty costs	Realized OR schedule		
	Original	Optimal	DSS
Cancellation	66.67	22.22	0.00
Patient	40.91	36.50	29.50
Ward	34.40	28.56	21.44
Holding	0.00	0.00	0.00
OR assistants	6.43	4.20	12.21
Recovery	8.85	3.11	14.70
Radiology	2.41	1.07	2.78
Pathology	0.70	0.51	1.14
Logistics	9.26	5.93	0.00
Total costs	87.03	35.82	45.13

6 CONCLUSIONS

In this paper, we considered the problem of rescheduling surgeries on the day of execution. We formulated an ILP which determines the best adjusted OR schedule at a given point in time. The results show that patients, wards, and OR assistants have opposite interests compared to the recovery, radiology, pathology, and logistic department. Furthermore, the achieved results show that, without a few exceptions, the only used adjustments are (i) shifting surgeries, and (ii) scheduling breaks between two surgeries. These two decision rules are incorporated in a developed DSS. This system determines the best adjusted schedule for one OR with respect to the given constraints and gives insight in how the workload of stakeholders is influenced by adjusting the OR schedule throughout the day. The simulation study shows that by using this DSS, less surgeries are canceled and patients and wards are more satisfied, but also that the workload of several departments increases to compensate this.

A drawback of the developed DSS is that the decision rules may not be applicable when the priorities of the stakeholders change. A change in these priorities for the ILP can result in, for example, more exchanges or cancellations of surgeries. However, this is not expected in hospitals that have a similar group of stakeholders as the Isala Clinics, because these two adjustments are less preferred than shifting a surgery.

Another aspect of the DSS, which may be seen as a drawback, is that it only improves the OR schedule for one OR at a time. The idea for such a type of approach comes from the Shifting Bottleneck heuristic [1], where in each step the schedule of the bottleneck resource is optimized with respect to the schedule for the other resources. As for the Shifting Bottleneck procedure, our approach is only a heuristic approach and thus will not result in optimal solutions. However, the results of the simulation study show that the DSS performs relatively good when compared to the optimal OR schedule. In addition, the Isala Clinics do not prefer to reschedule multiple ORs at once, because then the process of optimization may be unclear to the user and the necessary changes to the OR-schedule at one point in time may be quite large resulting in a decrease of the acceptance of the achieved results.

Further research could focus on including the Central Sterile Supply Department (CSSD) into the model. This department prepares the instrument sets needed for a surgery. When a surgery is added to the OR schedule during the day, this may influence the workload on the CSSD. In addition, the CSSD may impose some extra constraints on the OR schedule.

There are several ways in which the developed DSS can be used, for example, reschedule an OR immediately when it is disturbed or reschedule all ORs at some moments in time. The last example also raises the question in what order the ORs should be rescheduled. Therefore, it would be interesting to investigate the best way to use the DSS.

ACKNOWLEDGEMENTS

This research is supported by the Dutch Technology Foundation STW, applied science division of NWO and the Technology Program of the Ministry of Economic Affairs. We would like to thank the anonymous referees for their useful comments which helped to improve the paper.

Open Access

REFERENCES

1. Adams J, Balas E, Zawack D (1988) The shifting bottleneck procedure for job shop scheduling. Manage Sci 34(3):91–401
2. Bowers J, Mould G (2004) Managing uncertainty in orthopaedic trauma theatres. Eur J Oper Res 154(3):599–608
3. Cardoen B, Demeulemeester E, Beliën J (2010) Operating room planning and scheduling: a literature review. Eur J Oper Res 201(3):921–932
4. Denton B, Viapiano J, Vogl A (2007) Optimization of surgery sequencing and scheduling decisions under uncertainty. Health Care Manage Sci 10(1):13–24
5. Dexter F (2000) A strategy to decide whether to move the last case of the day in an operating room to another empty operating room to decrease overtime labor costs. Anesth Analg 91(4):925–928
6. Dexter F, Lee JD, Dow AJ, Lubarsky DA (2007) A psychological basis for anesthesiologists' operating room managerial decision-making on the day of surgery. Anesth Analg 105(2):430–434
7. Dexter F, Macario A, Traub RD (1999) Optimal sequencing of urgent surgical cases. J Clin Monit Comput 15(3):153–162
8. Dexter F, Willemsen-Dunlap A, Lee JD (2007) Operating room managerial decision-making on the day of surgery with and

without computer cecommendations and status displays. Anesth Analg 105(2):419–429

9. Garey MR, Johnson DS (1979) Computers and intractability: a guide to the theory of NP-completeness. W. H. Freeman & Co Ltd
10. Hans E, Wullink G, van Houdenhoven M, Kazemier G (2008) Robust surgery loading. Eur J Oper Res 185(3):1038–1050
11. Hartholt W (2010) Beslissingsondersteuning voor het aanpassen van de online OK-planning. Master's thesis, Universiteit Twente
12. Hulshof PJH, Boucherie RJ, van Essen JT, Hans EW, Hurink JL, Kortbeek N, Litvak N, Vanberkel PT, van der Veen E, Veltman B, Vliegen IMH, Zonderland ME (2011) ORchestra: an online reference database of OR/MS literature in health care. Health Care Manage Sci 14(4):383–384
13. Lamiri M, Xie X, Dolgui A, Grimaud F (2008) A stochastic model for operating room planning with elective and emergency demand for surgery. Eur J Oper Res 185(3):1026–1037
14. Lebowitz P (2003) Schedule the short procedure first to improve OR efficiency. AORN 78(4):651–659
15. Ledolter J, Dexter F, Wachtel RE (2010) Control chart monitoring of the numbers of cases waiting when anesthesiologists do not bring in members of call team. Anesth Analg 111(1):196–203
16. Marcon E, Dexter F (2006) Impact of surgical sequencing on post anesthesia care unit staffing. Health Care Manage Sci 9(1):87–98
17. Marcon E, Dexter F (2007) An observational study of surgeons' sequencing of cases and its impact on postanesthesia care unit and holding area staffing requirements at hospitals. Anesth Analg 105(1):119–126
18. Marjamaa RA, Torkki PM, Hirvensalo EJ, Kirvelä OA (2009) What is the best workflow for an operating room? A simulation study of five scenarios. Health Care Manage Sci 12(2):142–146
19. Stepaniak PS, Mannaerts GHH, de Quelerij M, de Vries G (2009) The effect of the operating room coordinator's risk appreciation on operating room efficiency. Anesth Analg 108(4):1249–1256

10

A THEORY-BASED APPROACH FOR DEVELOPING INTERVENTIONS TO CHANGE PATIENT BEHAVIOURS: A MEDICATION ADHERENCE EXAMPLE FROM PAEDIATRIC SECONDARY CARE

Gemma Heath [1], Richard Cooke [1] and Elaine Cameron [2]

[1]Department of Psychology, School of Life and Health Sciences, Aston University, Birmingham B4 7ET, UK

[2]Manchester Centre for Health Psychology, University of Manchester, Coupland 1 Building, Coupland Street, Manchester M13 9PL, UK

ABSTRACT

In this article we introduce a Health Psychology approach to changing patient behaviour, in order to demonstrate the value of Health Psychology professional practice as applied within healthcare settings. Health Psychologists are experts in understanding, predicting and changing health-related behaviours at the individual, group and population level. They combine psychological theory, research evidence and service-user views to design interventions to solve clinically relevant behavioural problems and improve health outcomes. We provide a pragmatic overview of a theory and evidence-based Intervention Mapping approach for developing, implementing and evaluating interventions to change health-related behaviour. An example of a real behaviour change intervention designed to improve medication adherence in an adolescent patient with poorly controlled asthma is described to illustrate the main stages of the intervention development process.

Keywords: intervention; paediatrics; adherence; behaviour change; self-management

1. INTRODUCTION

Patient behaviours are central to the success of any treatment programme, and consequently to health outcomes. It is no surprise, therefore, that health professional training programmes increasingly teach student practitioners to understand the cultural, psychological and social factors affecting patients' behaviours [1]. However, there is far less training in the methods needed to turn this understanding into action to help patients change detrimental behaviours. A commonly recommended approach is to offer patient education or advice. However, this is often insufficient for generating and maintaining behaviour change as patients' health decisions are typically driven by multiple influencing factors, not merely lack of knowledge. Dissemination of alternative methods is therefore required to help health professionals to support patient behaviour change.

Health Psychologists are experts in understanding and changing health behaviours in individuals, groups and populations. They combine psychological theory, research evidence and service-user views to design interventions to solve clinically relevant behavioural problems and improve health outcomes [2]. Health Psychologists are distinct from Clinical Psychologists in that Health Psychologists use their knowledge of psychology to understand the predictors, causes, and consequences of *physical* illness and health, and to influence health outcomes as well as healthcare systems and policies [3]. Health Psychology practitioner posts are not yet widely funded in the UK National Health Service (NHS), meaning that the majority of health professionals cannot access Health Psychology services or Health Psychologist-led training. Yet, the need to support patients in changing their behaviour remains. This article aims to provide a practical guide for practitioners and researchers looking to develop behaviour change programmes within healthcare settings.

1.1. An Introduction to Behaviour Change Interventions

The term "intervention" simply refers to any combination of strategies designed to produce desirable behavioural or health outcomes at the individual, group or population level. In the development and evaluation of complex (*i.e.*, multi-component) interventions, emphasis is placed on the use of theory [4] as evidence suggests that theoretically-informed interventions lead to better outcomes [5]. Theories help us to make sense of complex phenomena by providing tentative explanations for why and under what circumstances behaviours occur. Interventions can then target these factors. Using behaviour change theory to develop interventions also provides a way of understanding an intervention's effectiveness, or lack thereof [6].

Within the context of behavioural research, interventions have often been based on whole individual theories such as the Health Belief Model [7] so that the theory can be tested and a contribution made to the theoretical evidence-base. However, in healthcare settings there is a need for interventions that address clinical problems to improve health outcomes, without needing to adhere to rigid theoretical frameworks. Consequently, new methods have been developed which take the behavioural problem as a starting point and use insights from different theories to assess, solve or prevent that problem [8].

One such method, Intervention Mapping (IM) [9], is a "problem-driven" approach which combines one or multiple theories, empirical evidence and new research to develop behaviour change interventions. This approach aligns with Medical Research Council guidance for the development and evaluation of complex interventions [4] and helps to solve the problem of identifying, selecting and applying suitable theories. The following example was developed using an approach guided by Intervention Mapping.

1.2. An Introduction to the Illustrative Example

The behaviour change intervention described here was developed, implemented and evaluated as part of a service improvement consultancy conducted by author EC [10]. Although informed consent was obtained from the patient and their parent, the work was not conducted as research and ethical approval was not sought. Consequently the focus of this article will be on the intervention development process, rather than the effectiveness of the intervention. However, descriptions of intervention mechanisms and outcomes will be provided where helpful.

The Health Psychologist in Training (EC) was contracted by a paediatric respiratory service to design an intervention to address medication non-adherence in adolescent patients with poorly controlled asthma. Many of these patients exhibited problems adhering to their prescribed preventive medication regimens. It was anticipated that improved adherence would prevent escalation of treatment to stronger and more costly medications, and reduce the risk of exacerbations and hospitalisation [11].

The intervention was developed for one individual patient with the intention that it would be refined and adapted for use with other patients following evaluation. This ensured that the intervention content could be tailored to each individual, and fit with the existing one-to-one service model. In other contexts group interventions may be feasible. Regardless of mode of delivery, the underlying principles of intervention design are the same, but an individualised approach allows greater tailoring of intervention content, while a group approach is less resource intensive.

2. THE PROCESS OF INTERVENTION DEVELOPMENT

An overview of the intervention development process is presented in Table 1. Each of the stages is discussed in detail below.

Table 1. Overview of the intervention development process.

Stages of Intervention Development	Brief Description of Each Stage
Conducting a needs assessment	Develop understanding of why and how the target population needs to change. Specify the health problem and it associated consequences and the target problem behaviour(s).
Identifying determinants of the target behaviour	Develop an understanding of what is influencing or causing the problematic behaviour. Try to identify factors leading to or inhibiting that behaviour.
Setting intervention objectives	Set goals for your intervention in terms of changing the target behaviour, behavioural determinants and associated health outcomes.
Selecting behaviour change techniques (BCTs)	Choose behaviour change techniques that can be used in your intervention programme to help achieve your intervention goals.
Developing practical plans	Select methods for delivering your intervention that will be acceptable and engaging for the target population. Consider how you will assess intervention effectiveness.
Reporting intervention outcomes	Communicate the effects of your intervention to relevant others (e.g., health practitioners, researchers, commissioners, patients).

2.1. Stage One: Conducting a Needs Assessment

The first stage involves justifying the need for an intervention by assessing why and how target recipients need to change. This means specifying three components: (1) who the intervention is intended to target; (2) the health problem; and (3) the problematic behaviour.

Whether the intervention is intended for an individual or group, the recipients can be defined in terms of a "target population", for example adolescents with asthma or adults with diabetes. The target population should be specified as explicitly as possible, as the population characteristics will influence the design, scope and feasibility of the intervention. In the clinical example the target population was defined as follows:

Adolescent patients (aged 12 to 16 years) receiving secondary outpatient care for asthma, who experience frequent symptoms despite being prescribed appropriate medications, who are not suspected to have refractory asthma, who are suspected or known to have poor adherence to medicines (e.g., taking inhalers infrequently or at the wrong dosage level), and who have no contraindications for receiving the intervention, such as social, psychological or communication issues.

This specification encompasses age range, clinical context, diagnosis, symptoms, and suspected behavioural issues. Other characteristics might include gender, ethnicity, time since diagnosis, prescribed medications and so on, depending on the objectives of the intervention. Specifying the target population can be achieved through discussion with clinicians and/or those who intend to deliver, use or commission the intervention. It is also important to consider individuals for whom a behaviour change intervention may not be helpful.

Next, an understanding of the health problem (e.g., poorly controlled asthma) must be elucidated in terms of the prevalence (e.g., percentage of target population experiencing the problem), patterns (e.g., differences related to sex, ethnicity, age) and consequences of the problem (e.g., hospital admissions), which justify the need for an intervention. A range of specific health outcomes should also be identified, which will inform the selection of intervention outcome measures later in the process. Both of these aspects can be generated through reviewing research literature and clinical guidelines, and by accessing clinical expertise. In the example, the following health outcomes were identified from the British Thoracic Society guidelines [12]:

"Control of asthmatic condition indicated by presence of daily symptoms (including coughing, wheezing, chest tightness and breathlessness), sleep disturbance, frequency of exacerbations, use of rescue medication, and the extent to which activities are limited".

Other health outcomes might include health service utilisation, physiological functioning, body mass index, or quality of life. While accessing the literature and clinical expertise, it is also advisable to note how each of the health outcomes might be measured. The identified asthma outcomes were measured using self-report questionnaires, but other means such as patient self-report diaries, direct observation, dosage metering devices, and prescription refill records would all have been appropriate.

Finally, the problematic behaviour which will be the main target of the intervention must be assessed and fully described. This involves reviewing literature on the prevalence of the behaviour within the target population, and consequences of the behaviour for health and other outcomes. The target behaviour should be broken down into behavioural components where possible. For instance, in the asthma example rather than describing the behaviour of interest merely as "taking asthma medications as prescribed", specific elements of the behaviour were identified:

Taking medications as prescribed, including "preventer" inhalers, "rescue" inhalers, and any given tablets or other medicines; taking these at the prescribed dosage using the correct inhalation technique or consumption method; taking them at the required intervals and at the required times without missing any doses; and refilling prescriptions when necessary to ensure no doses are missed.

At the end of the needs assessment there should be a thorough documented understanding of the problem to be addressed, including a specification for whom the intervention is intended (target population), and overviews of the health issue (including prevalence, consequences, health outcomes, possible measures) and the target problem behaviour (including prevalence, consequences, behavioural components, and possible measures).

In cases where the intervention is intended for a known patient or group, a personalised assessment can also be conducted through discussion with them and their key health professionals, and through checking health records. Discussion with the adolescent patient and asthma nurses in the clinical example revealed that frequency of symptoms and the need for reliever inhaler medication were particularly salient outcomes for them. Although the overall problem behaviour was "non-adherence to medication", the behavioural component most relevant to this patient was missing doses of one particular tablet.

2.2. Stage Two: Identifying Determinants of the Target Behaviour

Having specified the problem behaviour, the next task is to identify factors that influence that behaviour. These behavioural 'determinants' will be targeted directly by intervention strategies as it is presumed that changing the influencing factors will consequently change behaviour. Identifying influencing factors will also inform which behaviour change techniques (BCTs) are likely to work and why.

2.2.1. Determinants in the Target Population

To assess behavioural determinants in the target population a literature review can be conducted or an existing review identified. Where there is little existing evidence, new research can be carried out. Relevant literature includes studies exploring patients' motives for the behaviour or their perceptions of factors influencing the behaviour; studies examining predictors of the behaviour; theory-testing studies; and existing intervention studies that describe associations between manipulated factors and behavioural outcomes. Data can also be collected on the effectiveness and acceptability of different intervention modalities (e.g., face-to-face, telephone support). For the asthma intervention a narrative review of research literature and clinical guidelines was conducted to establish factors influencing non-adherence in adolescent asthmatic patients. The review identified 28 determinants, which were grouped into nine categories (see Table 2).

The results of a literature review may include findings regarding social, environmental, cultural and other factors in addition to psychological variables (e.g., beliefs about illness/treatment). All identified factors should be recorded as these may inform intervention development and interpretation of outcomes. However the main factors required for developing a behaviour change intervention are the psychological variables, as these are amenable to change.

2.2.2. Individual Determinants

Behavioural determinants can be evaluated through clinical assessment with the individual patient or by conducting focus groups or surveys with groups. Questions should relate to the patient's experience of performing the behaviour, their views about the health condition to which the behaviour relates, perceived barriers and facilitators of the behaviour, and their attitudes and beliefs about the behaviour, associated healthcare services, and health outcomes (see Table 3 for questions asked in the clinical example). Supplementary discussions with family members and healthcare providers may elucidate additional factors. Knowledge and skills related to the behaviour should also be assessed. As aforementioned, targeting knowledge and skills may be insufficient to change behaviour, but they are nonetheless prerequisites for successful behavioural performance.

A clinical assessment with the patient could also include questionnaire measures of factors identified from the literature review. For example, during the needs assessment stage the adolescent asthma patient completed questionnaires measuring beliefs about medicines [13], beliefs about asthma [14], beliefs about the consequences of taking the medication [15], and confidence in managing the condition [16]. Questionnaires were selected based on evidence that beliefs about asthma, medications, and self-efficacy were important determinants of adolescents' adherence to asthma medicines. They highlighted several sub-optimal patient responses which were then selected for targeting within the intervention.

Table 2. Determinants of adolescent asthma medication adherence identified in the literature.

1. Beliefs and Attitudes
Beliefs about asthma (e.g., cause, severity, controllability)
Beliefs about medicines
Attitude towards clinic visits
Attitude towards non-adherence (e.g., anticipated regret)
2. Experiences
Perceived impact of asthma and medicines on daily life
Experience of symptoms
Previous experience of adherence and management
Prior experience of consequences (e.g., hospitalization)
3. Knowledge
Knowledge and understanding of asthma and medicines
Knowledge of appropriate response in acute attacks
Recognising danger signals and symptoms
4. Social Influences
Peer group influences (e.g., feeling normal, embarrassed, perceived support)
Family factors (e.g., parent involvement in medicine-taking)
Relationships with healthcare professionals
5. Motivations and Intention
Motivation to manage asthma
Tolerance of current illness state
Prioritising asthma and treatment
Intention to take medications
Preference for alternative therapies
6. Capability
Skills to use the medication devices
Organisational and scheduling abilities
Self-efficacy (e.g., perceived ability, confidence)
Practical barriers (e.g., lost medicines)
7. Self-Perceptions
Self-identity
Perceived autonomy in taking medications
Feelings of responsibility for health
8. Emotions and Psychological Wellbeing (e.g., fear of asthma exacerbations)
9. Forgetting and Confusion

Table 3. Example qualitative questions asked of the adolescent asthma patient to elicit personal determinants of non-adherence behaviour.

Example Qualitative Questions
- What is it like for you having asthma?
- How do you feel about having asthma?
- What bothers you most about having asthma?
- Tell me about the medicines you have to take for your asthma?
- How often do you miss a dose of your medicine?
- Why is it that you miss some doses?
- When are you most likely to miss a dose?
- What do you do if you miss a dose?
- What makes it difficult to take your medicine regularly?
- Do you ever miss a dose on purpose?
- What would make it easier for you to take your medicine regularly?

At the end of this stage a list of behavioural determinants should have been identified from the literature and any clinical assessments which are hypothesised to influence the behaviour (including psychological variables that are amenable to change).

2.2.3. Organising Framework

When gathering information on behavioural determinants it can be helpful to organise identified factors using a theoretical framework. Useful behaviour change frameworks include the Capability, Opportunity, Motivation model of Behaviour (COM-B) [17] and the Theoretical Domains Framework (TDF) [18,19]. The COM-B model hypothesises that interaction between three core components causes the performance or non-performance of behaviour: physical and/or psychological capability; physical and/or social opportunity; and reflective and/or automatic motivation. For example, a patient could be highly motivated to take their medications, but due to chronic stress does not have the psychological capability to consistently remember to take them, or is only able to take them during break-times meaning they have limited opportunity to take them. The TDF expands on the COM-B model, synthesising 128 behavioural determinants taken from different theories into 14 overall domains including: knowledge; skills; identity; beliefs about capabilities; optimism; beliefs about consequences; reinforcement; intentions; goals; memory, attention and decision processes; environmental context and resources; social influences; emotions; and behavioural regulation [19].

2.3. Stage Three: Setting Behaviour Change Intervention Objectives

The first two stages in the intervention development process provide a thorough knowledge base on which to establish the intervention. In this third stage the aim is to describe the objectives of the intervention in terms of changes in health outcomes, behavioural changes, and changes in psychological factors (the targeted behavioural determinants).

2.3.1. Health and Behaviour Change Objectives

From the work conducted in the needs assessment, appropriate health and behaviour outcome objectives can be selected. These outcomes will be measured before and after the intervention is delivered to assess its effectiveness. They must therefore be measurable, achievable and relevant for the patient. Working in collaboration with the patient and their healthcare provider can help to achieve this. Objectives should also be specific in their description, including the direction and magnitude of the intended change. In the clinical example, health and behaviour objectives were:

-Health objective: To achieve a decrease in general asthma symptoms (coughing, wheezing, chest tightness, breathlessness) from 1 to 2 days per week to no days per week.

-Behavioural objective: To achieve a decrease in the frequency of missed doses of (named medication) from once per week to no times per week.

2.3.2. Behavioural Determinant Change Objectives

Next, from the identified behavioural determinants the intervention developers must select and justify those to target within the intervention. Which ones and how many are a matter for consideration. For some there will be greater evidence of a stronger connection with the behaviour; some will be more clearly relevant to the patient; some will be more feasible to change; and some will have clearer existing links with BCTs. It may be impractical to target all identified determinants, and also ill-advised as the resulting intervention might be difficult to evaluate. In some cases there may be one obvious determinant that is clearly and strongly causally linked to the behaviour, meaning the selection of a single determinant to target in the intervention is appropriate. However, generally interventions containing more than one strategy offer greater opportunity for inducing change [20].

2.3.3. Mapping Determinants to Theory

This stage also involves mapping the identified empirical determinants to theoretical constructs. This means translating the determinants into components of behavioural theories or into stand-alone theoretical concepts that can be measured and tested for their ability to predict or explain behaviour. One benefit of doing this is that theoretical constructs are more "testable" than descriptive determinants, as they often have specific definitions and existing validated measures. The intervention outcomes can also be more easily applied in other contexts if well-defined constructs are used. Furthermore, the selection of BCTs in the next stage may be easier in relation to theoretical constructs, as some theories explicitly recommend certain techniques.

This translational process is one part of the intervention development process that requires the most psychological expertise, as methods for interpreting empirical determinants as theoretical constructs rely on the intervention developers' knowledge of behavioural theories. However, mapping determinants to the Theoretical Domains Framework [19] is also possible. An example of this in relation to non-adherence might be translating the empirical determinant, "belief that medicine causes weight gain" into the theoretical construct "physical outcome expectation" from Social Cognitive Theory [21] or "outcome expectancies" in the domain "beliefs about consequences" from the TDF [19]. In cases where a behavioural determinant cannot be translated into a theoretical construct (e.g., knowledge), it should still be included, but as an empirical rather than theoretical factor.

In the clinical example, two theories were identified as potentially useful for measuring and changing behavioural determinants. First, the extended Common-Sense Self-Regulation Model [22,23], which encompasses beliefs about the illness and medications. Second, Social Cognitive Theory [21], which encompasses self-efficacy (confidence in one's own ability to perform the behaviour) and outcome expectations. Other determinants remained as stand-alone constructs, such as knowledge about asthma.

The selected theoretical constructs can then be used as the basis for a simple explanatory model describing the mechanisms by which behaviour and health outcomes are influenced by the determinants. A simplified section of the explanatory model generated in the clinical example is shown in Figure 1. Note that in accordance with behavioural theories, determinants may influence behaviours directly or via the patient's *intention* to perform the behaviour.

The final list of behavioural determinants, in the form of theoretical constructs and untranslated empirical constructs, should then be stated explicitly as "change objectives" [9]. For instance:

Determinant change objective: The patient will demonstrate an increase in perceived necessity of (named medication) for maintaining health and reducing symptoms (measured by the Beliefs about Medicines Questionnaire).

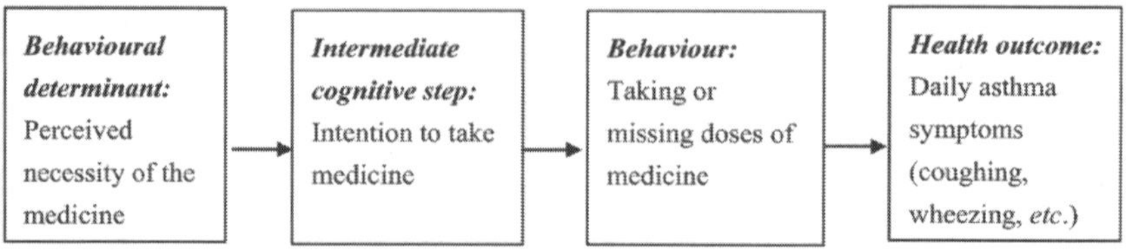

Figure 1. Explanatory model of adherence behavior.

2.4. Stage Four: Selecting Behaviour Change Techniques

Having developed a model of determinants of the behaviour and specified change objectives for the intervention, the next phase involves linking behavioural determinants to a set of BCTs thought to be effective for eliciting/changing the target behaviours. That is, techniques that will bring about change to behavioural determinants and achieve the change objectives [24]. A BCT can be defined as an "active ingredient" of an intervention, or "an observable, replicable, and irreducible component of an intervention designed to alter or redirect causal processes that regulate behaviour" [25].

The components of some theories (e.g., self-efficacy from Social Cognitive Theory) already recommend specific techniques for changing behaviour, such as modelling and verbal persuasion [26]. For the remainder, Michie *et al.* (2013) have devised a categorised list of 93 BCTs which have been mapped to theoretical constructs using a consensus method [25,27,28]. These resources were used in the asthma example to select BCTs. The technique "information about health consequences" from the 93-item BCT taxonomy (Michie *et al.*, 2013) [25] (BCT 5.1) was selected to target the patient's perceived necessity of their medicine, while another technique "prompts/cues" (BCT 7.1) was used to target the patient's remembering to take the medicine. Every determinant to be targeted should be addressed by at least one BCT, and all BCTs should be intended to influence at least one determinant. There should be no unmatched determinants or BCTs.

2.5. Stage Five: Developing Practical Plans

Having identified potentially useful BCTs (e.g., goal setting, coping skills), these need to be translated into a practical intervention programme, outlining the timelines, measures, methods, materials and personnel to be used to deliver and evaluate the intervention. Interventions can be implemented in a variety of ways, for example, face-to-face, via telephone, using text messaging or mobile phone apps or paper-based methods, on a one-to-one basis or as group sessions. They can also be delivered by a range of health professionals (e.g., nurses, physiotherapists, psychologists) or trained "lay" facilitators. It is recommended that the intervention delivery information is compiled in a comprehensive manual that can be used by subsequent intervention deliverers. When it comes to delivering the intervention, practical plans should be implemented as closely as possible to those documented in the intervention manual. Any deviations should be recorded and taken into account when evaluating the intervention outcomes.

Components of the clinical example intervention were developed into practical plans with input from the asthma nursing team. These plans took into account the time and resource demands of usual healthcare practice. The intervention was therefore planned as three sessions, delivered with the patient over a four week period; one session each for the baseline assessment, delivery of BCTs, and evaluation. Sessions were designed to be one hour long, delivered one-to-one at either the patient's home or in the hospital outpatient department. To deliver the BCTs the following methods were used: workbooks providing information, diagrams and links to online videos about asthma and the effects of medications, (BCT 5.1 "Information about health consequences"); and worksheets to facilitate the patient devising their own prompts for remembering the behaviour (BCT 7.1 "Prompts/cues").

Planning an Evaluation

Evaluation involves employing methods to discover whether the intervention worked, how well it worked and how it worked. Methods of evaluation should be considered at the intervention development stage [6] and should include measures of process, effect and acceptability.

Intervention effectiveness and outcomes can be measured by assessing changes to the behaviour and health outcomes using validated measures wherever possible. It is also important to measure the proposed mechanisms of action, that is, the psychological constructs that were targeted in the intervention (e.g., self-efficacy, illness perceptions) as this reveals which factors mediated the intervention effects. In other words, how the intervention worked and why it worked (or didn't work). This is important as it forms the basis for future interventions [29]. Where existing questionnaires are not available, measures can be developed or adapted specifically for the intervention. For example, questions about knowledge of the condition may be developed using patient information leaflets.

In the asthma example, intervention effectiveness was evaluated using questionnaire measures and qualitative questioning conducted at baseline and in the final evaluation session. Measures were also taken at the end of the BCT delivery session, so that changes could be tracked across the whole programme. Measures included a questionnaire on current asthma symptoms to assess health outcomes (adapted from Asthma UK symptom diaries, 2012), the Medication Adherence Report Scale to assess behavioural outcomes [30], the Brief Illness Perception Questionnaire [14], the Beliefs about Medicines Questionnaire [13], the Child Self-Efficacy Asthma Self-Management Scale [16], and outcome expectancy scales developed according to guidance by Luszczynska and Schwarzer [15] to assess changes in determinants. The intervention was also evaluated using patient and parent feedback via programme evaluation forms, asking questions regarding how useful, enjoyable, and difficult they found the intervention.

2.6. Stage Six: Reporting the Intervention

A clear and thorough description of the intervention should be provided to enable replication by other clinicians or researchers, and to facilitate synthesis of findings in any evidence reviews [25,31]. Under-reporting of intervention content and using variable terminology to describe BCTs has been highlighted as a weakness of previous intervention studies [4]. However the development and introduction of tools such as the Behaviour Change Technique taxonomy [25,31] provide a common language for describing the "active ingredients" of interventions in sufficient detail. Guidelines for reporting behavioural interventions have also been developed, including a Template for Intervention Description and Replication (TIDieR) [32] and Standards for Quality Improvement Reporting Excellence (SQUIRE) [33].

When reporting the outcomes of interventions developed for research purposes, the aim may be to comment on statistically significant changes in determinants, behaviours and health outcomes, and the generalisability of the findings to the wider patient population, in which case appropriate statistical methods should be used. However, for interventions developed in clinical practice, outcomes could be usefully reported in patient notes. In such circumstances, changes in responses to the qualitative questions and questionnaire measures should be carefully considered and reported in terms of both direction and magnitude of change.

3. DISCUSSION AND CONCLUSIONS

In this article we describe an approach to developing behaviour change interventions, with a clinical example designed to improve adherence to treatment in adolescents with poorly controlled asthma, which was guided by Intervention Mapping [9]. This systematic framework offers a transparent, problem-solving approach to address health needs, using theory, research evidence and service-user perspectives to tailor the intervention to the target behaviour and population.

From the early stages of intervention development, we were able to identify psychological factors amenable to change in the target population that were linked with the target behaviour (adherence to treatment). Eliciting information directly from the patient enabled the selection of intervention objectives that directly addressed the patient's individual needs. A mapping process was then used to interpret empirical determinants as theoretical constructs, from which appropriate BCTs were selected and implemented. The intervention was evaluated in terms of process and effect using qualitative and quantitative methods.

There are several characteristics of this approach that should be considered by would-be intervention developers. The first is the explicit involvement of patients and healthcare providers in selecting behavioural targets, psychological determinants and BCTs. Developing a shared understanding of the behavioural problem with the patient, prioritising patient-identified behaviours and beliefs and agreeing on intervention objectives builds confidence, skills and motivation to implement and maintain behavioural changes, and so increases the likelihood of intervention effectiveness. However, this may comprise a limitation if engagement of these parties is low. Consequently, intervention developers may need to devise strategies for increasing service-user and health professional involvement.

A second consideration is the time and resources required to plan, implement and evaluate the intervention. The flexibility of this approach means that it is suitable for both resource-rich and resource-poor environments. In resource-rich environments, full literature reviews and comprehensive individual assessments can be conducted. In resource-poor environments however, the method can be adapted. Greater reliance can be placed on clinical expertise to inform understanding of the health and behavioural issues; determinants may be identified from existing reviews and clinical guidelines, supplemented by patient reports; and determinants can be directly mapped to an overarching theoretical framework rather than individual theories.

This case study demonstrates the feasibility of developing evidence and theory-based interventions to change patient behaviour within healthcare settings. The empirical and theoretical basis of this approach means that interventions have a greater chance of being effective, and the reasons for these effects can be deduced. Consequently, interventions can be refined and adapted iteratively to meet the needs of subsequent patients. The principles and processes of a Health Psychology approach to intervention design are comprehensively described so that lessons can be drawn by health professionals working to address behavioural challenges in various clinical populations.

ACKNOWLEDGMENTS

Gemma Heath and Elaine Cameron were funded by the National Institute for Health Research (NIHR) through the Collaboration for Leadership in Applied Health Research and Care for Birmingham and Black Country (CLAHRC-BBC) programme. The views expressed are those of the authors and not necessarily those of the NHS, the NIHR or the Department of Health.

AUTHOR CONTRIBUTIONS

All authors were involved in the development of the concept of the article and drafting the manuscript. Gemma Heath and Elaine Cameron wrote the first draft of the manuscript. Elaine Cameron provided the illustrative example; Richard Cooke supervised the illustrative example and contributed to drafts of the manuscript. All authors read and approved the final manuscript.

CONFLICTS OF INTEREST

The authors declare no conflict of interest.

REFERENCES

1. General Medical Council. Tomorrow's Doctors: Outcomes and Standards for Undergraduate Medical Education; General Medical Council: Manchester, UK, 2009.
2. Bartholomew, L.K.; Mullen, P.D. Five roles for using theory and evidence in the design and testing of behavior change interventions. J. Public Health Dent. 2011, 71, S20–S33.
3. British Psychological Society. Careers: Your Journey into Psychology. Available online: http://careers.bps.org.uk/ (accessed on 8 October 2015).
4. Craig, P.; Dieppe, P.; Macintyre, S.; Michie, S.; Nazareth, I.; Petticrew, M. Developing and evaluating complex interventions: The new Medical Research Council guidance. BMJ 2008.

5. Michie, S.; Prestwich, A. Are interventions theory-based? Development of a theory coding scheme. Health Psychol.2010, 29, 1–8. [PubMed]

6. National Institute for Health and Care Excellence. Behaviour Change: Individual Approaches, in NICE Public Health Guidance. Available online: https://www.nice.org.uk/guidance/ph49 (accessed on 8 October 2015).

7. Becker, M.H. The health belief model and personal health behavior. Health Educ. Behav. 1974, 2, 354–386.

8. Brug, J.; Oenema, A.; Ferreira, I. Theory, evidence and Intervention Mapping to improve behavior nutrition and physical activity interventions. Int. J. Behav. Nutr. Phys. Act. 2005, 2, 2–8.

9. Bartholomew, L.K.; Parcel, G.S.; Kok, G.; Gottlieb, N.H. Planning Health Promotion Programmes: An Intervention Mapping Approach, 3rd ed.; John Wiley & Sons: San Francisco, CA, USA, 2011.

10. Cameron, E. Behaviour change intervention competence, stage two qualification in health psychology. Unpublished report. 2014.

11. Horne, R. Compliance, adherence, and concordance: Implications for asthma treatment. CHEST J. 2006, 130, 65S–72S.

12. British Thoracic Society Scottish Intercollegiate Guidelines Network. British Guideline on the Management of Asthma: A National Clinical Guideline. Available online: https://www.brit-thoracic.org.uk/document-library/clinical-information/asthma/btssign-guideline-on-the-management-of-asthma/ (accessed on 8 October 2015).

13. Horne, R.; Weinman, J.; Hankins, M. The beliefs about medicines questionnaire: The development and evaluation of a new method for asscssing the cognitive representation of medication. Psychol. Hcalth 1999, 14, 1–24.

14. Broadbent, E.; Petrie, K.J.; Main, J.; Weinman, J. The brief illness perception questionnaire. J. Psychosom. Res. 2006, 60, 631–637.

15. Luszczynska, A.; Schwarzer, R. Social cognitive theory. In Predicting Health Behaviour; Connor, M., Norman, P., Eds.; Open University Press: Berkshire, UK, 2005.

16. Bursch, B.; Schwankovsky, L.; Gilbert, J.; Zeiger, R. Construction and validation of four childhood asthma self-management scales: Parent barriers, child and parent self-efficacy, and parent belief in treatment efficacy. J. Asthma1999, 36, 115–128.

17. Michie, S.; van Stralen, M.M.; West, R. The behaviour change wheel: A new method for characterising and designing behaviour change interventions. Implement. Sci. 2011, 6, 631–637.

18. Michie, S.; Johnston, M.; Abraham, C.; Lawton, R.; Parker, D.; Walker, A. Making psychological theory useful for implementing evidence based practice: A consensus approach. Qual. Saf. Health Care 2005, 14, 26–33.

19. Cane, J.; O'Connor, D.; Michie, S. Validation of the theoretical domains framework for use in behaviour change and implementation research. Implement. Sci. 2012.

20. Webb, T.; Joseph, J.; Yardley, L.; Michie, S. Using the internet to promote health behavior change: A systematic review and meta-analysis of the impact of theoretical basis, use of behavior change techniques, and mode of delivery on efficacy. J. Med. Internet Res. 2010.

21. Bandura, A. Social Foundations of Thought and Action: A Social Cognitive Theory; Prentice-Hall, Inc.: Englewood, NJ, USA, 1986.

22. Leventhal, H.; Leventhal, E.; Contrada, R.J. Self-regulation, health, and behaviour: A perceptual-cognitive approach. Psychol. Health 1998, 13, 717–733.

23. Horne, R.; Weinman, J. Self-regulation and self-management in asthma: Exploring the role of illness perceptions and treatment beliefs in explaining non-adherence to preventer medication. Psychol. Health 2002, 17, 17–32.

24. Abraham, C. Interventions to change health-related behaviour patterns. In Health Psychology; French, D., Vedhara, K., Kaptein, A.A., Weinma, J., Eds.; BPS Blackwell: Oxford, UK, 2010; pp. 99–110.

25. Michie, S.; Richardson, M.; Johnston, M.; Abraham, C.; Francis, J.; Hardeman, W.; Eccles, M.P.; Cane, J.; Wood, C.E. The behavior change technique taxonomy (v1) of 93 hierarchically clustered techniques: Building an international consensus for the reporting of behavior change interventions. Ann. Behav. Med. 2013, 46, 81–95.

26. Bandura, A. Self Efficacy: The Exercise of Control; W.H. Freeman and Company: New York, NY, USA, 1997.

27. Michie, S.; Johnston, M.; Francis, J.; Hardeman, W.; Eccles, M. From theory to intervention: Mapping theoretically derived behavioural determinants to behaviour change techniques. Appl. Psychol. 2008, 57, 660–680.

28. Michie, S.; Atkins, L.; West, R. The Behaviour Change Wheel: A Guide to Designing Interventions; University College London Press: London, UK, 2014.

29. Michie, S.; Johnston, M. Theories and techniques of behaviour change: Developing a cumulative science of behaviour change. Health Psychol. Rev. 2012, 6, 1–6.

30. Rand, C.S.; Wise, R.A. Measuring adherence to asthma medication regimens. Am. J. Respir. Crit. Care Med. 1994, 149, S69–S76.

31. Abraham, C.; Michie, S. A taxonomy of behaviour change techniques used in interventions. Health Psychol. 2008, 27, 379–387.

32. Hoffmann, T.C.; Glasziou, P.P.; Boutron, I.; Milne, R.; Perera, R.; Moher, D.; Barbour, V.; Macdonald, H.; Johnston, M.; Lamb, S.E.; et al. Better reporting of interventions: Template for intervention description and replication (TIDieR) checklist and guide. BMJ 2014.

33. Davidoff, F.; Batalden, P.; Stevens, D.; Ogrinc, G.; Mooney, S. Publication guidelines for quality improvement in health care: Evolution of the SQUIRE project. Qual. Saf. Health Care 2008, 17, i3–i9.

11

ESTIMATING THE WAITING TIME OF MULTI-PRIORITY EMERGENCY PATIENTS WITH DOWNSTREAM BLOCKING

Di Lin[1], Jonathan Patrick[2], Fabrice Labeau[1]

1. Department of Electrical and Computer EngineeringMcGill UniversityMontrealCanada

2. Telfer School of Management University of Ottawa Ottawa Canada

ABSTRACT

To characterize the coupling effect between patient flow to access the emergency department (ED) and that to access the inpatient unit (IU), we develop a model with two connected queues: one upstream queue for the patient flow to access the ED and one downstream queue for the patient flow to access the IU. Building on this patient flow model, we employ queueing theory to estimate the average waiting time across patients. Using priority specific wait time targets, we further estimate the necessary number of ED and IU resources. Finally, we investigate how an alternative way of accessing ED (Fast Track) impacts the average waiting time of patients as well as the necessary number of ED/IU resources. This model as well as the analysis on patient flow can help the designer or manager of a hospital make decisions on the allocation of ED/IU resources in a hospital.

Keywords: Emergency department, Waiting time, Queueing theory, Hospital management

1 INTRODUCTION

Overcrowding in the emergency department (ED) is a worldwide problem [1–3] impairing the ability of hospitals to offer emergency care within a reasonable time frame [4]. By observing more than 20 million patient visits to emergency departments over five years, Guttmann et al. in [5] determined that the risk of death and hospital readmission increases with the degree of crowding in the emergency department, and estimated that about 150 fewer patients would die in Ontario each year if the average waiting time to access the emergency department was less than an hour.

The issue of what constitutes timely access to emergency care is obviously dependent on the acuity of the patient. Without an accurate triage and acuity scale, patients who need immediate emergency care will experience a delay in treatment that may aggravate their condition. The Canadian government published its own acuity guidelines in 1998, and subsequently revised them in 2004 and in 2008. In these guidelines, the severity of patients is classified into five levels: resuscitation, emergent, urgent, less urgent and non urgent [6]. This classification is based on a patient's presenting complaints, vital signs (including the hemodynamic stability, hypertension, temperature, level of consciousness, respiratory distress, etc.), pain severity, and injury level. For patients in each severity level, their target waiting time to see a physician is detailed in Table 1.

Table 1. Triage levels for emergency department [9]

Triage level	Expected waiting time to see a physician
I: Resuscitation	Immediate
II: Emergent	<15 min
III: Urgent	<30 min
IV: Less urgent	<60 min
V: Non urgent	<120 min

However, strict adherence to the priority system may mean that a low priority patient may wait a long time to receive a relatively simple procedure that would tie up ED resources for very little time whereas the higher acuity patients have complex needs that require significant resources. As a means of addressing this issue, many hospitals have introduced a fast-track system for the lower (less urgent and non-urgent) priority patients on the premise that they can be served quickly and easily without tying up too many resources. This policy essentially means that a single queue is broken into two and the ones who inevitably suffer from such a policy are the patients at the end of the first queue (priority III patients). Thus, though the impact of the fast-track system is to reduce over-crowding by serving low acuity patients quickly, it is our contention that, unless resources are increased, this is accomplished at the cost of increasing the wait times for priority III patients. This contention has been partially confirmed. Cooke et al. in [7] and Miquel et al. in [8] show that the fast track can reduce the waiting time for patients who are qualified to access the fast track but will slightly lengthen the waiting time of the other patients. In this paper, we therefore concentrate on a standard priority system without a fast-track but also provide some results for a system with a fast track.

Even with a good acuity scale in place, insufficient resources can still cause overcrowding. As shown in Fig. 1, the resources available in the ED and in the inpatient unit (IU) will influence patient flow potentially leading to long wait times to access the ED. While the lack of ED resources can block patients in the waiting room, an insufficient number of IU resources may block transfers to the IU further delaying other patients in the waiting room from accessing the ED. Limited budgets however mean that it is inefficient to carry too many resources either in the ED or the IU. Thus, it is imperative that a methodology be developed that correctly estimates the necessary resource capacity in a hospital in order to provide timely access to the ED both to avoid overcrowding and idle time. In this paper, we concentrate on bed capacity in the ED and the IUs. Clearly there are other resources that play a role in determining the service time in the ED such as lab capacity and testing equipment. The assumption here is that other resources are not the rate limiting step to meeting the targets set out in Table 1.

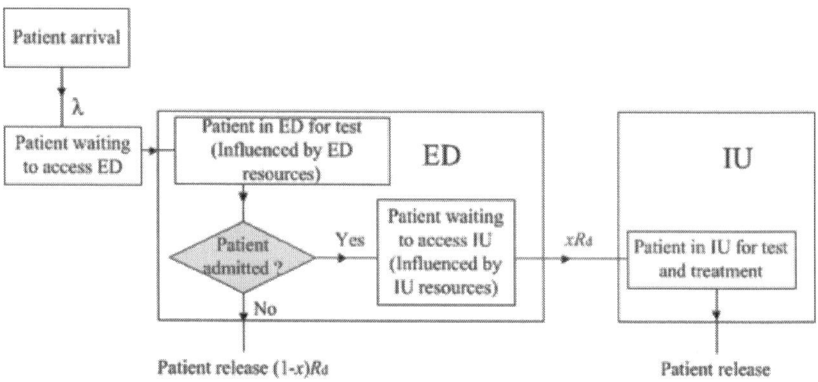

Figure 1. Patient flow to access and depart ED [1]

In this paper, we develop a queueing model to estimate the waiting time of patients to access the ED as well as the necessary amount of resources to achieve the wait time targets for each priority class. This queueing model is composed of two queues: the first one is a $M/G/c1/\infty M/G/c1/\infty$with five priorities. In the above notation, the M refers to the assumption that the arrival of demand follows a Poisson distribution, the G means that the service rate can follow a general distribution and the $c1c1$ refers to the number of available resources in the ED. This queue characterizes the patient flow from accessing the ED to departing the ED. The five priorities represent five severity levels classified by Table 1. The second queue is a $G/GI/c2/c2G/GI/c2/c2$ (general arrival distribution, general but independent service times with $c2c2$ servers and $c2c2$ capacity in IU) without priority and no buffer, and it characterizes the patient flow from accessing the IU to discharge.

Additionally, in order to represent the coupling effect that occurs when patients are blocked from entering the IU, we estimate the probability of all servers being busy in the second queue and the probability of patients in the ED waiting for transfer to the IU being blocked. Building on this queueing model, we attempt to estimate the necessary number of ED and IU resources to achieve the performance targets of Canadian Triage And Acuity Scale (CTAS), shown in Table 1.

2 RELATED WORK

Studies relevant to the estimation of the necessary amount of ED resources can be classified into two stages: (1) Rough estimation stage and (2) further adjustment stage. First, the ED manager needs to estimate the average resource requirements over an extended period of time. Studies in this stream usually estimate the number of resources by the steady state of their estimation models providing a long run average estimation of the resource requirements. This would constitute the first stage. Afterwards, the ED manager may need to adjust the resource assignment to meet the daily fluctuations in demand that are characteristic of ED departments [10–12].

From the perspective of methodologies, while the studies of the first type often utilize queueing [2, 10–12] and Markov chain models [3] to estimate the necessary amount of ED resources in the steady state, the studies of the second type usually utilize an autoregressive integrated moving average model (ARIMA) [13–15], Monte-Carlo simulation [1, 17], or Markov decision process (MDP) [16, 19, 20] to dynamically analyze the necessary amount of resource as a function of time. From the perspective of the length of the planning horizon, the adjustment stage studies can further be classified into short-term estimation and long-term estimation.

For short-term estimation (the length of the planning horizon is at most one day) the variation of arrival rate is measured at the hourly level [13–16]. For long-term estimation (the length of observation ranges from more than one day to a few months), the daily variation or even seasonal variation is factored into the planning decisions [19, 20].

Our study is of the first type, namely, estimating the steady state resource requirements in a hospital in order to provide timely access to the ED. To our knowledge no paper has dealt with both the coupling effect between two resources (such as the ED and IU) as well as the presence of multiple priority classes in the demand stream. Patrick et al. in [19, 20] present how to estimate the required capacity for a diagnostic imaging department dealing with multiple priority classes but deal with only a single resource. Kolb et al. in [1, 17] take into account the coupling effect between the ED and the IU but do not consider the different triage levels of patients. Similarly, Koizumi et al. in [21] present a model that deals with a series of resources with potential blocking but with no acuity scale differentiating patients. For the purposes of estimating resource requirements in the ED to achieve priority-specific performance targets, it is important to propose a model that takes into account both factors. The model proposed in the next sections achieves that goal.

3 MODELS OF PATIENT FLOW

In this section, we present the arrival process of emergency patients as well as the model to describe this process. Building on this model, we estimate the average waiting time of an emergency patient accessing the ED.

Patients arrive at the ED either as walk-in patients or ambulatory patients. After entering the main entrance, the patient moves from the greeter desk to triage to registration before waiting for a physician consult. In our model these steps are combined under the heading 'Patients waiting to access the ED' (see Fig. 1). Once a patient accesses the ED, they are assigned a bed by a nurse. After a pre-examination by the ED nurse, the patient will see a physician for further examination, tests and treatments. If the physician determines the patient can be discharged after examination, an ED nurse facilitates the process of releasing the patient who then departs the ED. If the physician decides to transfer the patient to the inpatient units (IUs), a consulting physician from the IU will arrange the admission. Depending on the availability of IU beds, the patient is either transferred immediately or has to wait in the ED till an IU bed becomes available. These steps in our model are combined under the heading 'Patients staying in the ED'. A patient in the IU will receive tests and treatments until he/she is deemed ready for discharge. After a final examination by a physician, the patient will depart the IU. These steps in our model are combined under the heading 'Patients staying in the IU'.

3.1 Arrival process of demand accessing the ED and the IU

Demand for ED service fluctuates significantly throughout the day. In consequence, Koizumi et al. in [21] divide the whole day into several segments such that the arrival rate in each segment can be assumed to be constant. They demonstrate that the arrival process of emergency patients in most time segments can be modeled as a Poisson process with varying rates.

As mentioned in the previous section, our model looks to provide the steady state resource requirements over a longer period than a day and thus we do not take into account the within day variations. Given the results from our model, a further model (perhaps using a Markov Decision Process approach) could be used to allocate the available resources in order to take into account the within-day fluctuations in demand.

The data presented in Table 2 was provided by a local hospital and represents the average arrival rate of patients entering the ED per hour (broken down by CTAS) and the average arrival of patients entering the IU per hour (broken down by point of entry) for fiscal year 2011/2012.

Table 2. Patient flow into the ED and the IU

Destination	CTAS/Point of Entry	Arrival Rates
ED	I	0.075
	II	0.662
	III	3.749
	IV	2.86
	V	0.226
	All	7.572
IU	From ED	0.479
	Direct	0.267
	All	0.746

3.2 Queueing models to estimate the waiting time

Building on the flowchart of patients accessing and departing the ED (shown in Fig. 1), we use queueing theory to estimate the waiting time of a patient to access the ED with the waiting time of a patient referring to the time between arriving at the waiting room until treatment. To estimate the waiting time, we need to model two patient flows. (1) The patient flow from arriving at the waiting room until departing the ED can be viewed as a M/GI/c1/∞M/GI/c1/∞ queue to model the patient flow arriving at and departing from waiting rooms or ambulances since the size of the waiting room is rarely the limiting factor. A M/GI/c1/∞M/GI/c1/∞ queue has a Poisson arrival process, independent and identically distributed service times with a general distribution, c1c1 ED beds and infinite buffer capacity. (2) The patient flow into the IU through to discharge can be viewed as a G/GI/c2/c2 queue, which has a general arrival process, independent and identically distributed service times with a general distribution, c2c2 IU beds and no buffer capacity.

Model for patient flow in the ED

Let λ represent the arrival rate of emergency patients and μ1μ1 represent the average service rate in the ED without taking into account the coupling effect. Due to the potential for patients being blocked from leaving the ED, we can adjust the average service time in the ED, 1/μ, (represented by a M/G/c1/∞ queue) as

$$1/\mu = 1/\mu_1 + P_b \times mean(\min_i T_i) \qquad (1)$$

where Ti (i=1,2···c2) is the waiting time until *i*th inpatient is discharged and PbPb is the blocking probability to access the IUs. The rate of patients transferring to the IU is xR_d, where $R_d = min\{\lambda, c_1\mu\}$ and x and *x* is the proportion of patients transferred into the IU.

Thus, this modified average service time represents the actual service in the ED plus the time spent waiting in the ED for an IU bed. The time waiting to access the IU equals the average length of waiting until the next inpatient departure, denoted as miniTiminiTi.

To incorporate the priority classification system of emergency patients, we use the theory for a preemptive resume multi-priority M/G/c1/∞ queue to calculate the length of waiting time to access the ED. The rationale for using preemptive resume queue models is that high priority (Level I or level II) patients must receive immediate service. If no physician is available when such a patient arrives, a physician treating a lower priority patient (or stabilized higher priority one) must leave his/her current patient and resume only after they offer the emergency treatment to the high priority patient. The detailed calculation on the length of the waiting time is presented in Section 4.

Model for patient flow in the IU

The flow of patients accessing and departing the IUs can be modeled as a G/GI/c2/c2 queue [22]. In this queueing model, we focus on the blocking probability PbPb, that is, the probability that there are no available beds in the IUs. This can be determined by

$$P_b = \frac{\alpha\beta e^{-k\beta/v}}{(1 - e^{-k\beta/v})\rho_d\sqrt{c_2}} \tag{2}$$

where c2c2 is the number of beds available in the IUs, λdλd is the arrival rate of patients directly accessing the IUs and μμ is the service rate. Other parameters in Eq. 2 can be calculated as:

$$\rho_d = \frac{xR_d + \lambda_d}{c_2\mu}, \qquad \beta = \sqrt{c_2}(1 - \rho_d),$$

$$k = \sqrt{c_2}, \qquad v = \frac{1 + C_a^2}{2},$$

$$\alpha = \left[1 + \beta\Phi(\beta)/\varphi(\beta)\right]^{-1},$$

where C2a is the squared coefficient of variation (SCV) of the service time at inpatient units and Φ(·) and φ(·) are the cumulative distribution function (CDF) and probability density function (PDF) of a standard normal distribution.

3.3 Steady state conditions of queuing models

In this paper, we employ queueing models to represent the steady state of a queueing system to access the ED. As shown in Fig. 1, the patient flow for accessing and departing the ED is represented by two coupled queueing models. In the following, we will explore the conditions for both queueing models to reach the steady state.

Given the arrival rate λλ, the necessary and sufficient steady state condition for the first queue is λ≤c1μ and that for the second queue is xRd+λd≤c2μI. Given the parameters of these two queues, we can decide whether these queues can reach steady state if we know the exact μμ, which determines both the service rate in the first queue and the arrival rate of the second queue. Unfortunately μμ is interdependent with another unknown parameter PbPb (shown in Eqs. 1 and 2), and neither of them can be shown in a closed form. Thus, the key to attaining the necessary and sufficient steady state conditions for both queues is to calculate μμ. In the following, relaxing the constraints, we first present a sufficient (not necessary) condition as well as a necessary (not sufficient) condition without requiring the exact μμ. Second, we develop an iterative algorithm to numerically compute μμ from which a necessary and sufficient steady state condition can be approximated.

Sufficient (but not necessary) and necessary (but not sufficient) conditions

As the blocking probability satisfies 0≤Pb≤10≤Pb≤1, we can obtain constraints on μμ as μmin≤μ≤μmaxμmin≤μ≤μmax, where

$$\mu_{min} = 1 \Big/ (1/\mu_1 + mean(\min_i T_i)) \text{ and} \tag{3}$$

$$\mu_{max} = \mu_1, \tag{4}$$

where μminμmin is the value of μμ (refer to Eq. 1) when Pb=1Pb=1 (the worst case in which an ED patient transferring into IU is always blocked), and μmaxμmax is the value of μμ when Pb=0Pb=0 (the best case in which an ED patient transferring into IU is never blocked). Thus, the sufficient steady state condition of the first queue is λ≤c1μminλ≤c1μmin, and its necessary steady state condition is λ≤c1μmaxλ≤c1μmax. Correspondingly, the sufficient steady state condition of the second queue is xmin{λ,c1μmin}+λd≤c2μI, and its necessary steady state condition is xmin $\{\lambda, c_1\mu_{\max}\} + \lambda_d \leq c_2\mu_I.$

Necessary and sufficient condition

In the following, we will discuss the necessary and sufficient steady state conditon. First of all, we represent Eq. 1 as

$$y_1(\mu) + y_2(\mu) - 1/\mu = y_0 \tag{5}$$

where y1(μ)=1/μy1(μ)=1/μ, y2(μ)=1/μ−Pb×mean(miniTi), and y0=1/μ1y. In the following, we show that there is at least one feasible solution to Eq. 5, and this solution μ^∈[μmin,μmax]

Proof We will prove it by contradiction. Let y(μ)=y1(μ)+y2(μ)−1/μ. From Eq. 2, we know y2(μ)≤y(μ)≤y1(μ). Assume that there is no feasible solution to Eq. 5, then y0=y2(μ)<y(μ) at μ= otherwise μminμmin will be the feasible solution. Because of the continuity of y(μ) and our assumption of no feasible solution in [μmin,μmax]], we can deduce that y(μ)>y0 for μ∈[μmin,μmax]]. At μ=μmax, we can conclude that $y(\mu)>y0=y1(\mu)$, which is contradicted by the fact $y(\mu)\leq y1(\mu)$ from Eq. 2. □

Beyond the proof, we can also demonstrate that at least one solution exists intuitively from Fig. 2. Certainly a feasible solution exists (shown in circle), because of the constraints: $y2(\mu)\leq y(\mu)\leq y1(\mu)$, $y2(\mu min)=y0$, and $y1(\mu max)=y0$

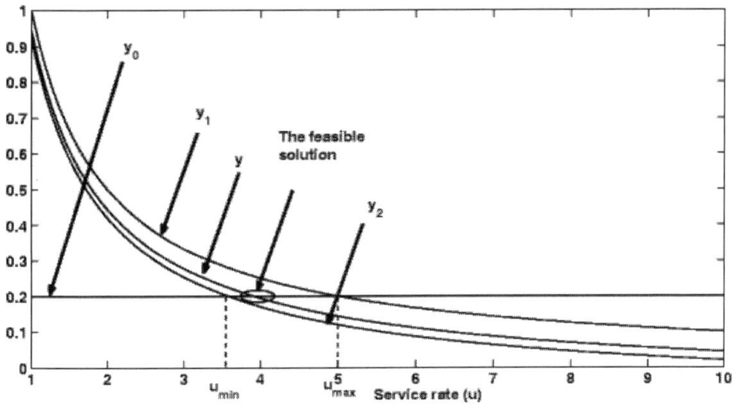

Figure 2 Intuitively understanding the proof

If there is only a single solution μ^, then it is easy to show the necessary and sufficient steady state condition as $\lambda\leq c1\mu$^ for the first queue and $x min\{\lambda,c1\mu$^$\}+\lambda d\leq c2\mu Ix min$ for the second queue.If there are multiple solutions, then no necessary and sufficient steady state condition exists. In the latter case, we can at least find a tighter sufficient condition and a tighter necessary condition by replacing μminμmin and μmaxμmax by μ^min and μ^maxμ^max, respectively. Please note that μ^min and μ^max are the minimal and maximal feasible solutions. The detailed process of searching for the minimal and maximal feasible solutions is shown in Algorithm 1.

Algorithm 1 Numerical estimation of μ

Input: Equation (5)
Output: Return the minimal and maximal feasible solutions

1 Search the minimal feasible solution $\hat{\mu}_{min}$ by starting with μ_{min};
2 Search the maximal feasible solution $\hat{\mu}_{max}$ by starting with μ_{max};
3 If $\hat{\mu}_{max} = \hat{\mu}_{min}$, output 'A single solution' and $\hat{\mu}_{max}$;
4 If $\hat{\mu}_{max} \neq \hat{\mu}_{min}$, output 'Multiple solutions' and $\hat{\mu}_{max}$ as well as $\hat{\mu}_{min}$;

If μ^minμ^min and μ^maxμ^max[1] are the same, the sufficient and necessary condition exists and this condition is: λ≤c1μ^ for the first queue and xmin{λ,c1μ^}+λd≤c2μIxmin I for the second queue. Otherwise, there is no sufficient and necessary condition, and we can use the tightest sufficient condition: λ≤c1μ^min for the first queue and xmin{λ,c1μ^min}+λd≤c2μIxmin for the second queue to guarantee the stability of the queue.

4 ESTIMATION OF THE WAITING TIME USING THE QUEUEING MODELS

In this section, we present the estimation of the waiting time in the ED. As shown in Eq. 1, this waiting time is dependent on mean(miniTi)mean(mini⁡Ti), namely, the average waiting time to be transferred to the IUs. In the following, we first estimate mean(miniTi)mean(mini⁡Ti) and then estimate the waiting time in the ED. Also we take into account two cases: patient flow with a fast track and without a fast track. Specifically, we present the estimation of waiting time in the case of no fast track in IV. B., and the case with a fast track in IV. C.

4.1 Estimation of the waiting time to be transferred into the IUs

In this section, we discuss how to calculate the average waiting time to access the IUs, namely, mean(miniTi)mean(mini⁡Ti). Given Fi(z) as the cumulative distribution function (CDF) of Ti (i=1,⋯,c2), which is estimated as a triangular distribution in [17], the CDF of miniTi (denoted as Fmin(z)) can be expressed as [18]

$$F_{\min}(z) = 1 - \prod_{i=1}^{c_2} [1 - F_i(z)] \tag{6}$$

Building on Eq. 6, we can calculate the mean of miniTimini⁡Ti as

$$mean(\min_i T_i) = \int z dF_{\min}(z) \tag{7}$$

By substituting Eqs. 6 and 7 into Eq. 1, we can attain the expression of the modified average service time 1/μ.

4.2 Estimation of the waiting time in the ED

As presented in Table 2, emergency care patients can be classified into 5 categories. Patients with severity level I and II are provided priority over ambulatory patients waiting for admittance to the ER. The prioritizing frequently includes pre-empting or suspending service for patients fitting the profile of categories IV and V so that appropriate care can be provided in life threatening situations [29]. From the perspective of queuing models, a pre-empting multiple-priority queue is appropriate for this scenario [28–30].

As presented in III.B.(1), we will use a M/G/c/∞ queue to characterize the patient flow. Few studies provide the exact closed-form expression of waiting time in a M/G/c/∞ queue. The exact waiting time is difficult to calculate because such a queue does not possess an embedded Markov chain [24]. Instead, most studies focus on an approximation of a M/G/c/∞ queue. Hokstad in [25] and Miyazawa in [26] both suggest using a probability generating function (PGF) to generate an approximation of M/G/c/∞M/G/c/∞ queues. Tijms et al. in [27] propose a regenerative approach to simulate a M/G/c/∞ queue. The aforementioned approximation methods are reliable but all require knowledge of the exact distribution of the service time, which is not applicable in our scenario because the distribution of our modified service time is unknown (shown in Eq. 1).

By using heuristics, Bondi et al. in [31] present the estimation of the waiting time in a preemptive resume multi-priority M/G/c1/∞ queue. Given the number of priorities *K*, the mean waiting time of patients with priority k (k=1,⋯,K), Wkc1, can be estimated as [31]

$$W_{c_1}^k \approx \frac{W_{c_1}^F W_1^k}{W_1^F} \tag{8}$$

where W_1^k. represents the mean waiting time of patients with priority *k* in a preemptive resume multi-priority M/G/1/∞ queue, W_1^k. represents the waiting time of a FCFS M/G/1/∞ queue and WFc1 represents the waiting time of a First-come, first-served (FCFS) M/G/c1/∞ queue. Here we note that the priority increases with *k* such that priority *k* represents the triage level K+1−k, shown in Table 1. In the following, we focus on computing W1F, Wc1F, as well as Wk.

Estimation of WF1

The waiting time in a FCFS M/G/1/∞M/G/1/∞ queue can be easily computed following [32]

$$W_1^F = \frac{\lambda S^2}{2(1-\rho)} \tag{9}$$

where ρ=λS, λ represents the arrival rate of patients across all priorities, *S* represents the mean service time for patients across all priorities and S2S2 represents the second moment of the service time of patients across all priorities.

Estimation of WFc1Wc1F

The waiting time in a FCFS M/G/c1/∞M/G/c1/∞ queue has been estimated in [33] as

$$W_{c_1}^F \approx \left[S + \frac{SP_Q}{c_1 - \lambda S}\right]\frac{1+C^2}{2} \tag{10}$$

where C2 represents the SCV of the service time for patients across all priorities, λλ represents the arrival rate of patients across all priorities and *S* represents the mean service time for patients across all priorities. PQ represents the probability given in [33] as

$$P_Q = \frac{(c_1\rho)^{c_1}}{c_1!(1-\rho)}\left[\sum\nolimits_{t=1}^{c_1-1}\frac{(c_1\rho)^t}{t!} + \sum\nolimits_{t=c_1}^{\infty}\frac{(c_1\rho)^t}{c_1!c_i^{t-c_1}}\right]^{-1} \tag{11}$$

where ρ=λS/c1.

Estimation of W_1^k.

The waiting time in a preemptive resume multi-priority M/G/1/∞ queue has been well studied. Specifically, given the number of priorities *K*, for each priority k=1,⋯,K, the mean waiting time is expressed in [32] as

$$W_1^k = \begin{cases} \frac{(1-\rho_1)S_1+R_1}{1-\rho_1}, & \text{for } k=1 \\ \frac{(1-\rho_1-\cdots-\rho_k)S_k+R_k}{(1-\rho_1-\cdots-\rho_{k-1})(1-\rho_1-\cdots-\rho_k)}, & \text{for } k>1 \end{cases} \tag{12}$$

where $\rho_k = \lambda_k \overline{S}_{(k)}, \lambda_k$ represents the arrival rate of patients with priority $k, \overline{S}_{(k)}$ represents the mean service time for patients with priority k (after taking into account the coupling effects), $R_k = \frac{1}{2}\sum_{i=1}^{k} \lambda_i \overline{S}^2_{(k)}$, and $\overline{S}^2_{(k)}$ is the second moment of the service time of kth-priority patients.

Estimating the mean and second moment of service time in the ED

Building on Eqs. 10, 11 and 12, the estimation of W_1^F, $W_{c_1}^F$, and W_1^k are determined by the mean and second moment of service time for patients in each priority as well as the average across various priorities. Building on Eq. 1, we can attain the mean and second moment for kth-priority patients as in Eq. 13 below.

$$\overline{S}_{(k)} = S_{(k)} + P_b[mean(\min_i T_i)] \tag{13}$$

and

$$\overline{S}^2_{(k)} = S^2_{(k)} + 2S_{(k)} P_b \times mean(\min_i T_i) + P_b^2[mean(\min_i T_i)]^2$$

where S(k) represents the emergency service time in the ED, and $S^2_{(k)}$ represents the second moment of emergency service time in the ED.

The average service time of the first queue across various priorities, μμ, equals the average of the mean service time of each priority. Namely, $\mu = 1 \Big/ \sum_k q_k \overline{S}_{(k)}$, where $q_k =$,

where qk= $\lambda_k / \sum_k \lambda_k$. Substituting this into Eq. 2, we can denote PbPb as a function of $\sum_k \overline{S}_{(k)}$.

To compute the mean and the second moment of service time for patients in each priority, we develop a numerical algorithm, shown in Algorithm 2. The Algorithm 2 iteratively calculates S(k) $S^2_{(k)}$, PbPb, and μμ until the estimation of S(k) and $S^2_{(k)}$ in two consecutive iterations has a difference below a threshold. If the output is not 'No solution', then, this output can be viewed as an estimation of the exact mean and second moment of the service time within an acceptable difference. Building on this algorithm as well as Eqs. 10, 11 and 12, we can attain the estimation of the waiting time of patients to access the ED, $W_{c_1}^k$.

Algorithm 2 Numerical estimation of the mean and second moment of service time in the ED taking into account the coupling effects and the multiple priority classes

Input: The mean emergency service time for the kth-priority patients in the ED $S_{(k)}$, the second moment of emergency service time for the kth-priority patients in ED $S_{(k)}^2$, as well as the thresholds to terminate this algorithm ε_1 and ε_2

Output: The estimation of $\overline{S}_{(k)}$ and $\overline{S}_{(k)}^2$

1 Initialize $t = 1$; $\varepsilon_1 = \varepsilon_1^*$; $\varepsilon_2 = \varepsilon_2^*$; $\overline{S}_{(k)}^{(0)} = S_{(k)}$; $\overline{S}_{(k)}^{2(0)} = S_{(k)}^2$; $\mu^{(0)} = K \Big/ \sum_k \overline{S}_{(k)}^{(0)}$; $P_b^{(0)} = P_b(\mu^{(0)})$; $\overline{S}_{(k)}^{(1)} = \overline{S}_{(k)}(P_b^{(0)})$; $\overline{S}_{(k)}^{2(1)} = \overline{S}_{(k)}^2(P_b^{(0)})$; $\mu^{(1)} = K \Big/ \sum_k \overline{S}_{(k)}^{(1)}$; go to step 2

2 If $\left|\overline{S}_{(k)}^{(t)} - \overline{S}_{(k)}^{(t-1)}\right| \le \varepsilon_1$ and $\left|\overline{S}_{(k)}^{2(t)} - \overline{S}_{(k)}^{2(t-1)}\right| \le \varepsilon_2$, then, $\overline{S}_{(k)} = \overline{S}_{(k)}^{(t)}$, $\overline{S}_{(k)}^2 = \overline{S}_{(k)}^{2(t)}$, $\mu = \mu^{(t)}$, $P_b = P_b^{(t)}$; go to step 5; Otherwise, go to step 3

3 If $\lambda \le c_1\mu^{(t)}$, then, $R_d = \lambda$; Otherwise, $R_d = c_1\mu^{(t)}$; go to step 4

4 Calculate $P_b^{(t)} = P_b(\mu^{(t)})$ by Eq. 1, $\overline{S}_{(k)}^{(t+1)} = \overline{S}_{(k)}(P_b^{(t)})$ by Eq. 13, and $\overline{S}_{(k)}^{2(1)} = \overline{S}_{(k)}^2(P_b^{(0)})$ by Eq. 13; $t = t + 1$; go to step 2

5 If $0 \le P_b \le 1$, output $S_{(k)}$ and $S_{(k)}^2$; Otherwise, output 'No solution'.

4.3 Estimation of waiting time for an ED with a fast track

While the previous sections investigated the case of ED without a fast track, we now turn our attention to the case with a fast track. A fast track is designed for patients with less serious illnesses and injuries to shorten both waiting and treatment times for these patients. More specifically, after evaluation by a triage nurse, patients with less emergent issues (triage level IV and V) are placed in the fast track [34].

In our model, a system with a fast track places paitents at triage level IV and V on an express line, and the other patients will be put on the regular line. Also c1c1 beds in ED will be split into two parts: one part for Fast Track (the number of beds is denoted as cI1cI1) and one part for regular line (the number of beds is denoted as cII1cII1). According to Eqs. (1) and (2), the averge service time (denoted as 1/μI1/μI) in the Fast Track and the average service time (denoted as 1/μII1/μII) in the regular line are shown as Eq. 14.

$$\begin{aligned} 1/\mu^{I} &= 1/\mu_1^{I} + P_b \times mean(\min_i T_i) \\ 1/\mu^{II} &= 1/\mu_1^{II} + P_b \times mean(\min_i T_i) \\ \mu_1^{I} + \mu_1^{II} &= \mu_1 \end{aligned} \tag{14}$$

where PbPb is shown in Eq. 2.

The average service time (denoted as 1/μF1/μF) across all triage levels is shown in Eq. 15

$$\begin{aligned} 1/\mu^{F} &= \frac{1}{P_r^{I}\mu^{I} + P_r^{II}\mu^{II}} \\ P_r^{I} + P_r^{II} &= 1 \end{aligned} \tag{15}$$

where PIrPrI is the probability of a patient whose triage level is at level I-III, while PIIrPrII is the probability of a patient whose triage level is at level IV–V.

By substituting Eq. 15 into Eq. 8, we can estimate the average waiting time of Fast Track by setting the number of beds in ED as cI1cI1, while estimating the average waiting time in the regular line (acute side) by setting the number of beds in ED as cII1cII1. Definitely, both of these waiting times are dependent on the proportion of patients who are switched over to the fast track, namely, the probability of a patient whose triage level is at level I–III PIrPrI.

5 RESULT AND DISCUSSION

In the following we investigate the necessary capacity of ED and IU in various scenarios to meet the waiting time targets from arrival to first physician assessment in the ED (shown in Table 1). For triage level I, we replace 'immediate' by '<<3 min'. The other parameters in our model include the arrival rate $\lambda\lambda$ as the average arrival rate of emergency patients throughout the day (shown in Table 2) and the arrival rate $\lambda'\lambda'$ as the average arrival rate of patients that directly access the inpatient units throughout the day (shown in Table 2). In addition, the distribution of the service time in the ED is triangular with a lower limit of 0.1 hour, upper limit of 1 hour, and mode of 0.5 hour (see Section 4.1). The distribution of the service time in the IU is triangular with a lower limit of 1 day, upper limit of 7 days; and mode of 4 days. Building on Eq. 8, we can estimate the waiting time to access the ED without a fast track as well as with a fast track, and compare the results in both scenarios in Section 5.4. The other parameters in Eqs. 1–10 can be calculated from the aforementioned parameters.

5.1 Relationship between ED and IU resource requirements

Given a set of priority specific wait time targets, the model presented here can be used to estimate the necessary capacity both in the ED and the IU in order to meet the performance targets. Figure 3 shows the impact of changes in the available IU capacity on the necessary ED capacity. In our queueing model, the average of length of stay in the IU is 4 days, the arrival rate to access the ED is 7.572 patients per hour, and we assume here that there is no fast track. Also our analytical results are verified by Monte-Carlo simulations, in which we mimic two individual queues which link with each other and calculate the necessary capacity of ED resources by repeating the simulation 50000 times.

Unsurprisingly, the necessary ED capacity increases as the size of the IU decreases. However, the impact of additional IU capacity on ED resource requirements decreases significantly as the IU increases suggesting that there is a threshold size of the IU beyond which additional increases cease to be advisable. However, attempting to reduce the size of the IU below that threshold leads to a steep increase in the required ED capacity in order to meet the same targets and therefore is likely not cost-effective.

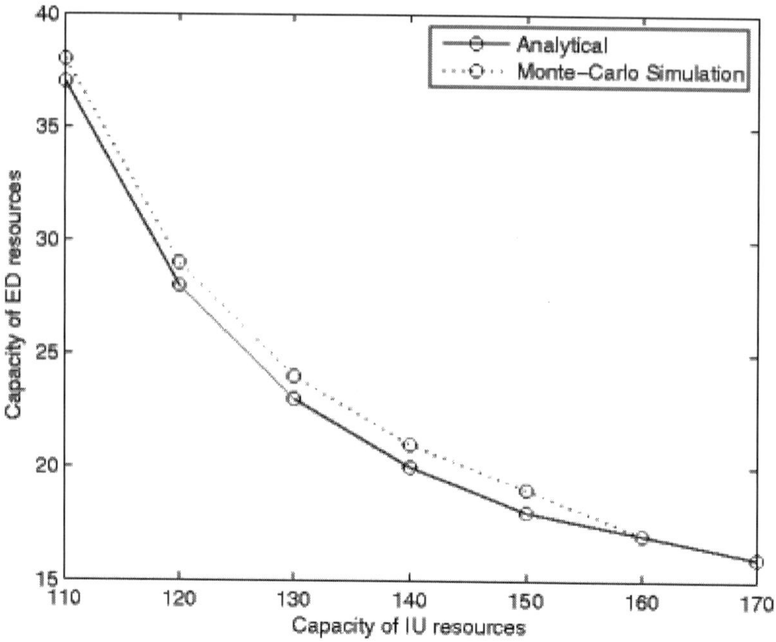

Figure 3. Capacity of ED resources vs. capacity of IU resources

5.2 Capacity of resources and length of stay in the IU

Clearly, the probability of congestion in the IU leading to backlogs in the ED is dependent on the rate of turnover in the IU which is regulated by the length of stay of patients. Thus, it is of interest to analyze changes in the necessary capacity of the IU/ED resources as the length of stay in the IU is varied. In the queueing model, we first vary the average length of stay in IU through 110–150 hours. Given a number of ED resources, we can determine the necessary IU resources as the length of stay in the IU is varied. Secondly, by varying the number of ED resources through 10–20, we can obtain the 3-dimensional plot which determines how the necessary ED/IU resources change as the length of stay in the IU varies (shown in Fig. 4). In both cases, we fix the arrival rate to the ED at 7.572 patients per hour and assume that there is no fast track.

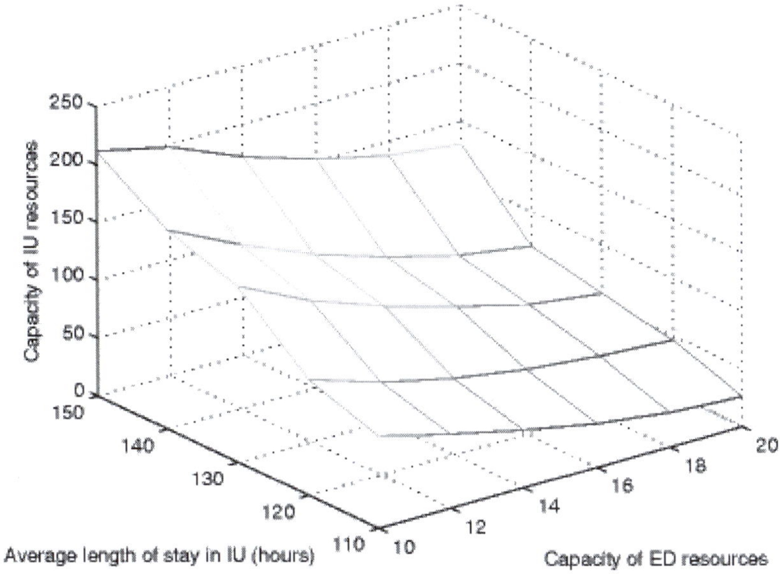

Figure 4. Capacity of ED/IU resources vs. average length of stay in IU

With the increase in the length of stay in the IU, the capacity of both IU resources and ED resources will, of course, increase. However, the rate of increase in the necessary IU resources as the length of stay is increased is significantly higher than for the ED (shown in Fig. 4). In other words, an increase in the length of stay in the IU causes a larger increase in the necessary IU resources. Thus, in the face of greater uncertainty in the length of stay of patients, it is preferable to carry additional or "excess" IU capacity rather than hoping to manage this problem by using the ED as a holding bay for the IU; a reality that is surprisingly common in practice.

5.3 Capacity of resources and arrival rate of ED patients

Obviously, the necessary ED and IU resources to guarantee an acceptable waiting time to see a physician are dependent on the arrival rate to the ED, so it is of interest to investigate the impact on ED and IU resource requirements of increases in this arrival rate. We focus on how much additional ED/IU capacity should be anticipated as necessary given a forecast of increasing demand. In the queueing model, we first fix the number of IU resources at 125 and determine the necessary ED resources as the arrival rate to the ED is varied. Secondly, we fix the number of ED resources at 20 and determine how the necessary IU resources change as the arrival rate to the ED is varied. In both cases, we fix the length of stay in IU at 150 hours and assume that there is no fast track.

With the increase in the arrival rate to the ED, the required capacity of ED and IU resources will, of course, increase. However, the rate of increase in the necessary IU resources as the arrival rate is increased is significantly higher than for the ED (shown in Fig. 5). In other words, an increase in the arrival rate to the ED causes a larger increase in the necessary IU resources. Thus, again in the face of greater uncertainty in the arrival rate of ED patients, it is preferable to carry additional or "excess" IU capacity rather than hoping to manage this problem by using the ED as a holding bay for the IU.

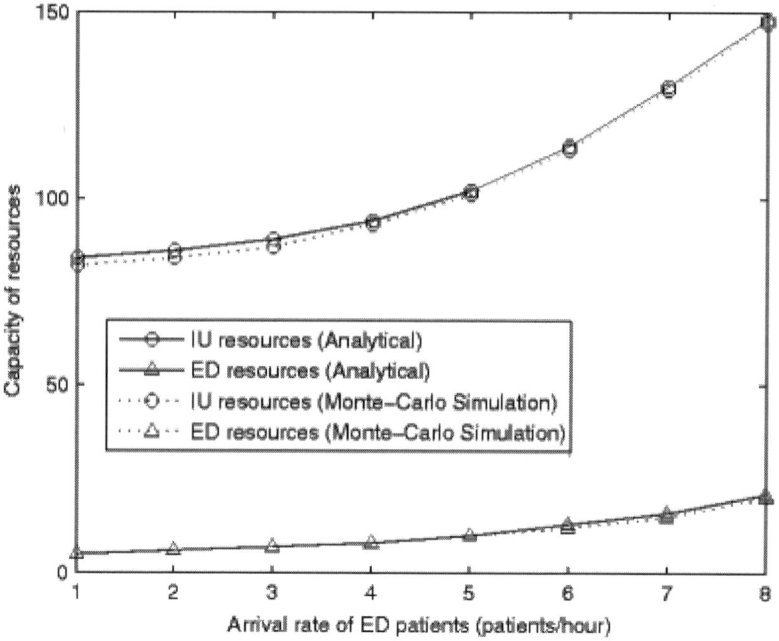

Figure 5. Capacity of ED/IU resources vs. arrival rate of ED patients

5.4 Average waiting time to access the ED with and without a fast track

The aforementioned discussion assumes that a hospital does not implement a fast track for patients at triage level IV and V. In the following, we focus on the influence of a fast track on the average waiting time to access the ED. In this scenario, the average length of stay in the IU is 4 days, and the number of IU resources is 125. In the scenario with a fast track, we allocated 20 % of ED capacity to the fast track.

As shown in Fig. 6, a fast track reduces the average waiting time across all patients to access the ED by approximately 0.3–1 hour. The explanation is as follows. The fast track provides for the prompt treatment of patients with non-life-threatening injuries. In a non-fast track system, these patients are forced to queue behind patients whose complexity requires long service times. The fast track provides short wait times for a cohort of patients who otherwise would have the longest wait, thus reducing the average wait time.

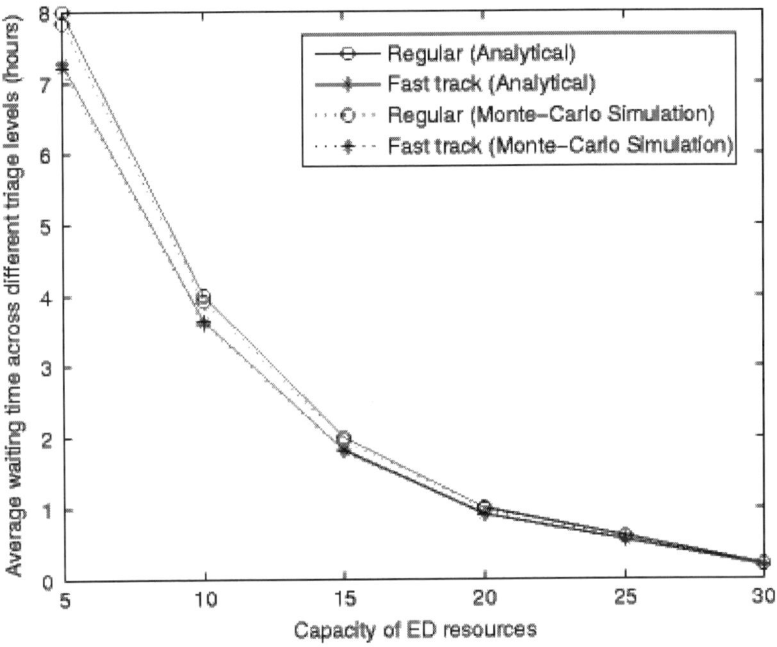

Figurc 6. Avcragc waiting time across various triage levels vs. capacly of ED resources

However, the reduction in the average waiting time across all patients comes at the cost of increasing the waiting time of patients who do not qualify for the fast track. As shown in Figs. 7and 8, the average waiting time of patients at triage level III increases by around 0.1–0.5 hours in a system that implements a fast track. In this scenario, the number of ED resources is 25.

5.5 Limitations of our patient flow model

The patient flow model in our paper has the following limitations: firstly, we assume that the inpatient unit can accommodate all types of patients, but in reality, a few specialized units can only accommodate a specific type of patient. For example, an injured patient cannot stay in a cardiovascular disease unit. Secondly, in our model, we assume that one resource can only be offered to one patient, so c patients will consume c resources in the ED. However, in real scenarios, EDs with c beds can accommodate more than c patients by using hall beds and internal waiting rooms [35]. Thirdly, our model employs steady-state and average arrival rates, which do not take into account that the arrival rate is non-stationary. Finally, our model does not cover the real-life cost implications of Length of Stay (LOS) reductions.

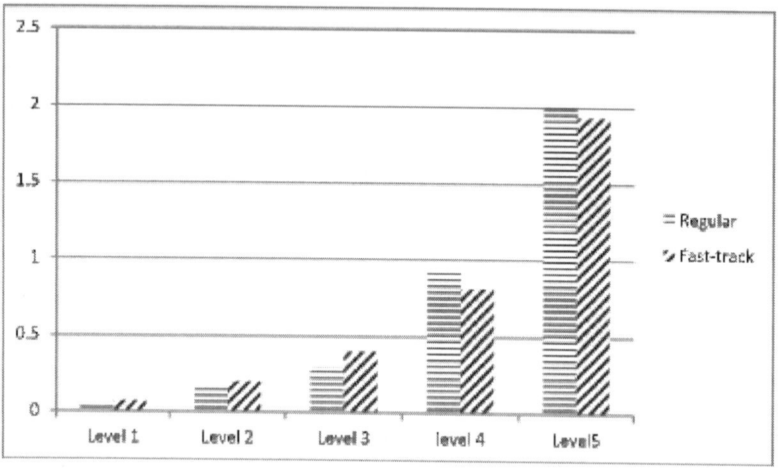

Figure 7. Waiting time to see a doctor across various triage levels [hours]

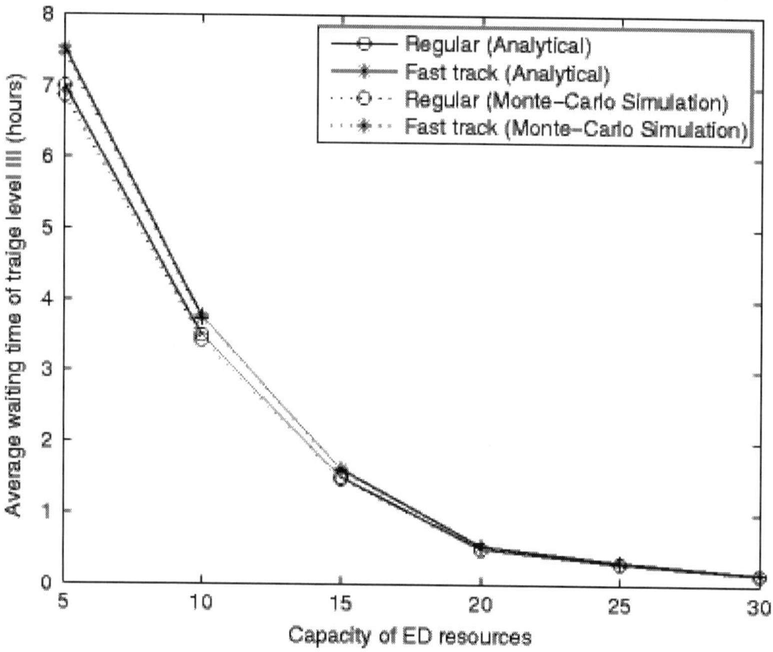

Figure 8. Average waiting time of triage level III vs. capaciy of ED resources

6 CONCLUSIONS

In this paper, we develop a two-stream model to characterize the coupling effect between patient flow to access the ED and that to access the IU. Building on this patient flow model, we employ queueing theory methods to estimate the average waiting time across patients as well as the necessary ED and IU resources in order to meet target waiting times for patients at each triage level. In addition, we investigate the influence of a fast track stream on the average waiting time of patients. Our model improves on previous research by taking into account both the reality of multiple priority classes competing for ED resources and the strong potential for downstream congestion impacting on the timely access of patients to the ED.

In addition to providing hospital management with a means of determining the necessary capacity in the ED and the IU in order to meet priority specific wait time targets for timely access to the ED, this paper also provides the following insights. (1) There is a threshold size for the IU such that reductions in the IU below that threshold lead to steep increases in the necessary ED capacity in order to meet the same targets. Thus, there exists a "optimal" IU capacity such that either increasing or decreasing IU resources will lead to higher costs associated with the same performance. (2) Uncertainty in the LOS in the IU or in the arrival rate to the ED is best accommodated by carrying extra IU capacity rather than by increasing the size of the ED. (3) While a fast track can reduce the average waiting time across patients from all the triage levels, it is accomplished by a large reduction in the wait times of patients from triage levels IV and V that offset a concurrent increase in the wait times of patients from triage level III. In other words, a fast track actually worsens the ability of an ED to provide timely access to patients whose conditions could potentially progress to a more serious problem requiring emergency intervention, such as asthma, vaginal bleeding, moderate trauma, Gastrointestinal (GI) bleeding, and acute pain. These three insights are partially verified by relevant research literature [7, 8, 36]. Erik et al. in [36] explain that increasing IU resources instead of ED resources with the aid of "IU buffers" can solve the problem of overcrowding and shows the "best buffering capacity" in IU, but this paper does not take into account the triage levels of patients. Also Cooke et al. in [7] and Miquel et al. in [8] show that the fast track can reduce the waiting time for patients who are qualified to access ED but will slightly lengthen the waiting time of the other patients. However, these two papers do not consider the coupling effects between the ED and IU.

We would like to extend our results by varying the proportion of ED resources allocated to the fast track, and develop a general rule to determine the optimal allocation depending on the proportion of demand that is eligible for the fast track and the relative resource consumption of the two groups. We would like to explore whether there exists an optimal proportion of ED resources to allocate to the fast track in order to minimize the demand of IU resources and satisfy all CTAS time requirements.

FOOTNOTES

1 Searching for the closest solution from the starting point can be done by any standard method. We use the Matlab function 'fsolve' to carry out the search, and its default internal algorithm is the trust-region dogleg algorithm [23].

ACKNOWLEDGMENTS

Thanks to Prof. Wojtek Michalowski who worked with us and offered us quite a few fantastic ideas to finish this draft. This work was partially supported by the Natural Sciences and Engineering Research Council (NSERC) and industrial and government partners, through the Healthcare Support through Information Technology Enhancements (hSITE) Strategic Research Network, and was partially supported by Quebec MDEIE PSR-SiiRi program.

REFERENCES

1. Kolb EMW, Peck J et al (2008) Reducing emergency department overcrowding - five patient buffer concepts in comparison. Simulation conference, 2008. WSC 2008. Winter
2. Akcali E, Cote MJ et al (2006) A network flow approach to optimizing hospital bed capacity decisions. Health Care Manag Sci 9(4):391–404
3. Haifeng X, Chaussalet TJ et al (2006) A model-based approach to the analysis of patterns of length of stay in institutional long-term care. IEEE Trans Inf Technol Biomed 10(3):512–518
4. Rowe BH, Bondm K, Ospina MB, Blitz S, Friesen C, Schull M, Innes G, Afilalo M, Bullard M, Campbell SG, Curry G, Holroyd B, Yoon P, Sinclair D (2006) Emergency department overcrowding in Canada: what are the issues and what can be done? [Technology overview no 21]. Ottawa, Canadian Agency for Drugs and Technologies in Health

5. Guttmann A, Schull MJ, Vermeulen MJ, Stukel TA (2011) Association between waiting times and short term mortality and hospital admission after departure from emergency department: population based cohort study from Ontario, Canada. British Medical Journal. Retrieved from http://www.bmj.com/content/342/bmj.d2983.

6. Murray MJ, Bullard M, Grafstein E (2004) Revisions to the Canadian emergency department triage and acuity scale implementation guidelines. Can J Emerg Med 6:421–427

7. Cooke MW, Wilson S, Pearson S (2002) The effect of a separate stream for minor injuries on accident and emergency department waiting times. Emerg Med J 19(1):28–30.

8. Sanchez M, Smally AJ, Grant RJ, Jacobs LM (2006) Effects of a fast-track area on emergency department performance. J Emerg Med 31(1):117–120. ISSN 0736-4679,

9. Beveridge R, Clarke B, Janes L et al (1998) Emplementation guidelines for the Canadian emergency department triage and acuity scale (CTAS). Canadian association of emergency physicians

10. Green LV, Soares J, Giglio JF, Green RA (2006) Using queuing theory to increase the effectiveness of emergency department provider staffing. Acad Emerg Med J 13(1):61–68

11. Hall RW (2006) Patient flow: the new queuing theory for healthcare, OR/MS Today

12. Au-Yeung SWM, Harrison PG, Knottenbelt WJ (2006) A queuing network model of patient flow in an accident and emergency department. Department of Computing, Imperial College of London

13. Abraham G, Byrnes GB et al (2009) Short-term forecasting of emergency inpatient flow. IEEE Trans Inf Technol Biomed 13(3):380–388

14. Lin WT (1989) Modeling and forecasting hospital patient movements: Univariate and multiple time series approaches. Int J Forecast 5(2):195–208

15. Arul E, Mark IC, Donald NG, Leo YS (2005) Using autoregressive integrated moving average (ARIMA) models to predict and monitor the number of beds occupied during a SARS outbreak in a tertiary hospital in Singapore. BMC Health Serv Res 5(36):1–8

16. Thompson S, Nunez M, Garfinkel R, Dean MD (2009) OR practice—efficient short-term allocation and reallocation of patients to floors of a hospital during demand surges. Oper Res 57(2):261–273.

17. Kolb EMW, Taesik L et al (2007) Effect of coupling between emergency department and IU on the overcrowding in emergency department. Simulation Conference, 2007 Winter

18. Rice JA (1994) Mathematical statistics and data analysis. Duxbury Resource Center

19. Patrick J, Puterman ML, Queyranne M (2008) Dynamic multi-priority patient scheduling for a diagnostic resource. Oper Res 56(6):1507–1525

20. Patrick J, Puterman ML (2008) Reducing wait times through operations research: optimizing the use of surge capacity. Health Policy 3(3):75–88

21. Koizumi N, Kuno E, Smith T (2005) Modeling patients flows using a queuing network with blocking. Health Care Manag Sci 8(1):49–60

22. Whitt W (2004) A diffusion approximation for the G/GI/n/m queue. Oper Res 52(6):922–941

23. Celis M, Dennis JE, Tapia RA (1985) A trust region strategy for nonlinear equality constrained optimization. Numerical Optimization, Philadelphia: SIAM, pp 71–82

24. Gross D, Shortle JF, Thompson JM, Harris CM (2008) Fundamentals of queueing theory. Wiley, Hoboken

25. Hokstad P (1978) Approximations for the M/G/m queue. Oper Res 26:510–523

26. Miyazawa M (1986) Approximation of the queue-length distribution of an MIGI/s queue by the basic equations. J Appl Probab 23(2):443–458

27. Tijms HC, van Hoorn MH (1982) Computational methods for single-server and multi-server queues with Markovian input and general service times. Appl Probab Comput Sci 3:71–102

28. Shimshak DG, Gropp Damico D, Burden HD (1981) A priority queuing model of a hospital pharmacy unit. Eur J Oper Res 7:350–354

29. Siddharthan K, Jones WJ, Johnson JA (1996) A priority queuing model to reduce waiting times in emergency care. Int J Health Care Qual Assur 9(5):10–16

30. Fiems D, Koole G, Nain P (2007) Waiting times of scheduled patients in the presence of emergency requests. http://www.math.vu.nl/koole/articles/report05a/art.pdf

31. Bondi A, Buzen J (1984) The response times of priority classes under preemptive resume in M/G/m queues. In ACM Sigmetrics, pp 195–201

32. Gross D, Harris CM (1985) Fundamentals of queuing theory. Wiley, New York

33. Lee AM, Longton PA (1959) Queueing process associated with airline passenger check-in. Oper Res Q 10:56–71

34. Chan TC, Killeen JP, Kelly D et al (2005) Impact of rapid entry and accelerated care at triage on reducing emergency department wait times, length of stay, and rate of left without being seen. Ann Emerg Med 46:491–497

35. Jeffery KC, Kevin TR (2009) A multi-class queuing network analysis methodology for improving hospital emergency department performance. Comput Oper Res 36(5):1497–1512

36. Kolb EMW, Schoening S, Peck J, Lee T (2008) Reducing emergency department overcrowding: five patient buffer concepts in comparison. In: Mason S, Hill R, Mnch L, Rose O (eds) Proceedings of the 40th conference on winter simulation (WSC '08). Winter Simulation Conference, pp 1516–1525

12

ESTIMATION OF THE EFFICIENCY OF JAPANESE HOSPITALS USING A DYNAMIC AND NETWORK DATA ENVELOPMENT ANALYSIS MODEL

Hiroyuki Kawaguchi[1], Kaoru Tone[2],Miki Tsutsui[3]

[1.]Economics FacultySeijo UniversityTokyoJapan

[2.]National Graduate Institute for Policy StudiesTokyoJapan

[3.]Central Research Institute of Electric Power IndustryTokyoJapan

ABSTRACT

The purpose of this study was to perform an interim evaluation of the policy effect of the current reform of Japan's municipal hospitals. We focused on efficiency improvements both within hospitals and within two separate internal hospital organizations. Hospitals have two heterogeneous internal organizations: the medical examination division and administration division. The administration division carries out business management and the medical-examination division provides medical care services. We employed a dynamic-network data envelopment analysis model (DN model) to perform the evaluation. The model makes it possible to simultaneously estimate both the efficiencies of separate organizations and the dynamic changes of the efficiencies. This study is the first empirical application of the DN model in the healthcare field. Results showed that the average overall efficiency obtained with the DN model was 0.854 for 2007. The dynamic change in efficiency scores from 2007 to 2009 was slightly lower. The average efficiency score was 0.862 for 2007 and 0.860 for 2009. The average estimated efficiency of the administration division decreased from 0.867 for 2007 to 0.8508 for 2009. In contrast, the average efficiency of the medical-examination division increased from 0.858 for 2007 to 0.870 for 2009. We were unable to find any significant improvement in efficiency despite the reform policy. Thus, there are no positive policy effects despite the increased financial support from the central government.

Keywords: Dynamic and network data envelopment analysis model, Municipal hospital, Efficiency, Production function

1 INTRODUCTION

Japanese municipal hospitals have experienced financial crises throughout the last few decades. In 2007, the Japanese government established a set of guidelines for municipal governments for reform and facilitated a restructure of hospital operations. There are 9,000 hospitals in Japan, half of which are owned by private not-for-profit organizations, and the remainder is run by public organizations. One thousand public hospitals are owned and operated by municipal governments, most of which have been losing money for some time. As Japanese local governments have huge cumulative deficits, it is important that municipal hospitals have sound financial foundations.

The master plan for the reform of Japan's municipal hospitals includes five steps from fiscal year 2007 to fiscal year 2014 as described below. First, the central government designed guidelines regarding proposed reforms and a timeframe for those reforms in 2007. The government ordered the reform of all municipals hospitals according to the guidelines. Therefore, all reforms were to start in fiscal year 2007.

Second, the central government ordered individual municipal hospitals to formulate a reform plan, including performance indicators for the evaluation of the reform within fiscal year 2008. The contents of the reform plan had some range of autonomy and municipal hospitals could freely select countermeasures.

Third, municipal hospitals are required to annually report the results of the reform plan to central government. The first report was submitted in fiscal year 2009 (being the first evaluation of the reform).

Fourth, municipal hospitals were required to submit intermediate reports on the results of efficiency promotion from fiscal year 2007 to fiscal year 2010 at the end of fiscal year 2011.

Fifth, municipal hospitals are required to submit a final report on the results of the individual reform plan at the end of fiscal year 2014. The fiscal year 2014 is the deadline for the reform. If the reform has not been effective, then central government will request that the municipal hospital shut down or sell the operation of the hospital.

As explained above, the guidelines of the reform mainly target hospital administration because the main objective is to reduce deficit and to reduce the amount of subsidies received from local government. The central government is more interested in the financial situation of the hospital than the quality of medical services.

The guidelines illustrate several countermeasures for the reform of municipal hospitals. Such countermeasures can be grouped into four categories. The first is the introduction of private business management systems. For example, the guidelines recommend outsourcing to private companies and the adoption of a "Private Finance Initiative". The second category is the restructuring and consolidation of the hospital organization. For example, the guidelines recommend the merging of several hospitals and the conversion of hospitals into long-term care facilities. The third category refers to a reduction in hospitals' operating costs. For example, the guidelines propose a revision of wage systems and reductions in the purchase prices of medical materials. The fourth category is an increase in revenue. For example, the guidelines recommend increasing occupancy rates and unit values per inpatient (nearly equal to "unit revenue per inpatient per day").

Municipal hospitals can choose the countermeasures from the examples in the guidelines and can include their own reform countermeasures. Individual reform plans propose the recruitment of highly skilled professionals, further education for healthcare professionals and a revision of the range of medical services. Thus, each hospital formulates its own reform plan and then self evaluates the results.

Harris [1] pointed out that a hospital can be considered as two separate firms. There are two heterogeneous internal organizations: a medical-examination division and an administration division. The administration division carries out business management activities to contain medical expenses within medical revenue. The medical-examination division provides various medical care services directly. These two organizations can be described as internal mutual exchange services. The administration division provides medical beds to the medical-examination division, and the medical-examination division repays the revenue through the use of medical beds for inpatient services.

Japanese hospitals have acute beds and long-term care beds in various ratios. The larger hospitals tend to concentrate on acute care services. In addition, physicians and surgeons are hired and paid by hospitals as in the case of National Health Service hospitals in the United Kingdom. These physicians provide services not only to inpatients but also to outpatients at the same hospitals.

For local residents, many of the problems with municipal hospitals arise through the curtailment of certain medical services. Thus, such residents are no longer able to receive specialized care at those hospitals. The chief medical officer in charge of the medical-examination division is typically the target of criticism from the stakeholders of the hospital. The administration division tends to operate from behind closed doors and avoids blame for any failures. However, previous research has not compared efficiency improvements between the two divisions.

The purpose of this study is to evaluate policy effects of the reform for municipal hospitals in Japan. We estimated efficiency scores from 2007 to 2009 not only for the hospital as a whole but also for two divisions. In addition, we consider further policy implications to address the financial problems of Japanese municipal hospitals.

The structure of this paper is as follows. The background and purpose of our study has been discussed in this first section. The methods and data analyses are discussed in the second section. The results of the analyses are presented in the third section. After the estimation of efficiency, we report the efficiency scores. The last section includes a discussion of the results and future challenges.

2 METHOD AND DATA

2.1 Dynamic–network data envelopment analysis (DEA)

2.1.1 Concept of dynamic-network DEA

DEA is a nonparametric method used in operations research to evaluate the efficiency performance of decision-making units (DMUs). The traditional DEA model is often considered a "black-box" model (BB model), because it does not take account of the internal structure of DMUs. DEA is a popular method with which to estimate the efficiency of hospitals [2]. Several previous studies have evaluated the efficiency of Japanese hospitals using the method [3–6]. These studies used cross-sectional data from Japanese public hospitals and adopted largely traditional DEA approaches. Average efficiency scores ranged from 0.8869 to 0.9456 in terms of revenue efficiency [3, 4]; for technical efficiency, they ranged from 0.8585 to 0.90008 [5, 6].

As an extension of the above BB model, the "network DEA model" accounts for divisional efficiencies as well as overall efficiency in a unified framework. Through the network DEA model, we can observe not only efficiency of DMUs but also divisional efficiencies as its components. Network DEA models were first introduced by Färe and Grosskopf [7–9]. Their models have been extended by several authors. The network DEA model proposed by Lewis and Sexton [10] presents a multi-stage structure as an extension of the two-stage DEA model proposed in Sexton and Lewis [11]. That study solves the DEA model for each node independently. Prieto and Zofio [12] applied a network efficiency analysis within an input–output model as initiated by Koopmans [13]. Löthgren and Tambour [14] applied a network DEA model to a sample of Swedish pharmacies with organizational objectives that necessitated the monitoring of efficiency, productivity and customer satisfaction. They compared the results of the network DEA models with those of traditional DEA models. Tone and Tsutsui [15] developed this model using a slacks-based measure called the network slacks-based measure (NSBM) approach. The NSBM is a non-radial method and is suitable for measuring efficiencies when inputs and outputs may change non-proportionally.

In contrast, the dynamic DEA model can measure the efficiency score obtained from long-term optimization using carry-over variables. The traditional DEA model only focuses on a single period, therefore, the measurement of inter-temporal efficiency change has long been a subject of concern in DEA. The window analysis by Klopp [16] was the first approach to account for inter-temporal efficiency change. Based on Malmquist [17], Färe et al. [9] developed the Malmquist index in the DEA framework. The dynamic DEA model proposed by Färe and Grosskopf [8] is the first innovative scheme to formally deal with these inter-connecting activities. Tone and Tsutsui [15] extended their model within the slacks-based measurement framework proposed by Tone [18] and Pastor et al. [19]. Hence, the model is non-radial and can deal with inputs/outputs individually, which enables us to obtain non-uniform input/output factor efficiencies. This is contrary to radial approaches, which assume proportional changes in inputs/outputs and provide only uniform input/output factor efficiency.

The dynamic–network DEA model (DN model) takes into account the internal heterogeneous organizations of DMUs, where divisions are mutually connected by link variables and trade internal products with each other. This DN model with can evaluate (1) the overall efficiency over the entire observed term, (2) dynamic change in the period efficiency and (3) dynamic change in the divisional efficiency. In addition, each DMU has carry-over variables that take into account a positive or negative factor in the previous period.

We employed a dynamic DEA model involving the network structure proposed by Tone and Tsutsui [20]. This model has the huge advantage of being able to evaluate the policy effect on the individual divisions of each

DMU. Tone and Tsutsui [20] provides detailed information about the notation of the DN model.

2.1.2 Formulas for efficiency in the dynamic-network DEA

Notation of inputs, outputs, links, and carry-overs

We are dealing with n DMUs ($j = 1,\ldots, n$), which consist of K divisions ($k = 1,\ldots, K$) over T time periods ($t = 1,\ldots,T$). Let m_k and r_k be, respectively, the numbers of inputs and outputs to division k. We denote the link leading from division k to division h by $(k, h)_l$ and the set of links by L_{kh}. The observed data are as follows:

$x_{ijk}^t \in R_+ \ (i = 1, \ldots, m_k; j = 1, \ldots, n; k = 1, \ldots, K; t = 1, \ldots, T)$

is the input resource i to DMU$_j$ for division k in period t, and

$y_{rjk}^t \in R_+ (r = 1, \ldots, r_k; j = 1, \ldots, n; k = 1, \ldots, K; t = 1, \ldots, T)$

is the output product r from DMU$_j$, division k in period t.

If some outputs are undesirable, we treat them as inputs to division k.

$z^t_{j(kh)_l} \in R_+ (j = 1, \ldots, n; l = 1, \ldots, L_{kh}; t = 1, \ldots, T)$ represents the linking intermediate products of DMUj from division k to division h in period t, where L_{kh} is the number of items in the links from k to h.

$z_{jk_l}^{(t,\ t+1)} \in R_+ (j = 1, \ldots, n; l = 1, \ldots, L_k; k = 1, \ldots, K, t = 1, \ldots, T-1)$

is the carry-over of DMUj, at division k from period t to period $t + 1$, where L_k is the number of items in the carry-over from division k.

Expression for DMU$_o$

DMU$_o$ ($o = 1,\ldots,n$)$\in P^t$ can be expressed as follows. The input and output constraints are

$$\begin{aligned} \mathbf{x}_{ok}^t &= \mathbf{X}_k^t \boldsymbol{\lambda}_k^t + \mathbf{s}_{ko}^{t-} \quad (\forall k, \forall t) \\ \mathbf{y}_{ok}^t &= \mathbf{Y}_k^t \boldsymbol{\lambda}_k^t - \mathbf{s}_{ko}^{t+} \quad (\forall k, \forall t) \\ \mathbf{e}\ \boldsymbol{\lambda}_k^t &= 1 \quad (\forall k, \forall t) \\ \boldsymbol{\lambda}_k^t \geq \mathbf{0}&, \ \mathbf{s}_{ko}^{t-} \geq \mathbf{0}, \ \mathbf{s}_{ko}^{t+} \geq \mathbf{0}, \quad (\forall k, \forall t) \end{aligned} \tag{1}$$

where $\mathbf{X}_k^t = (\mathbf{x}_{1k}^t, \ldots, \mathbf{x}_{nk}^t) \in R^{m_k \times n}$ and $\mathbf{Y}_k^t = (\mathbf{y}_{1k}^t, \ldots, \mathbf{y}_{nk}^t) \in R^{r_k \times n}$ signify the input and output matrices and $\mathbf{s}_{ko}{}^{t-}$ and $\mathbf{s}_{ko}{}^{t+}$ are, respectively, the input and output slacks.

With regard to the linking constraints, there are several options, for which we present four possible cases. There are, for example, "as input" and "as output" link value cases.

In the "as input" link value case, the linking activities are treated as an input to the succeeding division, and excesses are accounted for in the input inefficiency:

$$\mathbf{z}^{t}_{o(kh)in} = \mathbf{Z}^{t}_{(kh)in}\boldsymbol{\lambda}^{t}_{k} + \mathbf{s}^{t}_{o(kh)in} \quad ((kh)in = 1, \ldots, linkin_{k}) \tag{2}$$

where sto(kh)in∈RL(kh)inso(kh)int∈RL(kh)in represents slacks and is non-negative, and $linkin_k$ is the number of "as input" links from division *k*.

In the "as output" link value case, the linking activities are treated as an output from the preceding division, and shortages are accounted for in the output inefficiency:

$$\mathbf{z}^{t}_{o(kh)out} = \mathbf{Z}^{t}_{(kh)out}\boldsymbol{\lambda}^{t}_{k} - \mathbf{s}^{t}_{o(kh)out} \quad ((kh)out = 1, \ldots, linkout_{k}) \tag{3}$$

where $\mathbf{s}^{t}_{o(kh)out} \in R^{L_{(kh)out}}$ represents slacks and is non-negative and $linkout_k$ is the number of "as output" links from division *k*.

We classify carry-over activities into four categories as follows. Corresponding to each category of carry-over, we derive the following equations:

$$\begin{aligned}
z^{(t,\ t+1)}_{ok_l good} &= \sum_{j=1}^{n} z^{(t,\ t+1)}_{jk_l good}\lambda^{t}_{jk} - s^{(t,\ t+1)}_{ok_l good} \quad (k_l = 1, \ldots, ngood_k; \forall k;\ \forall t) \\
z^{(t,\ t+1)}_{ok_l bad} &= \sum_{j=1}^{n} z^{(t,\ t+1)}_{jk_l bad}\lambda^{t}_{jk} + s^{(t,\ t+1)}_{ok_l bad} \quad (k_l = 1, \ldots, nbad_k; \forall k;\ \forall t) \\
z^{(t,\ t+1)}_{ok_l free} &= \sum_{j=1}^{n} z^{(t,\ t+1)}_{jk_l free}\lambda^{t}_{jk} + s^{(t,\ t+1)}_{ok_l free} \quad (k_l = 1, \ldots, nfree_k;\ \forall k;\ \forall t) \\
z^{(t,\ t+1)}_{ok_l fix} &= \sum_{j=1}^{n} z^{(t,\ t+1)}_{jk_l fix}\lambda^{t}_{jk} \quad (k_l = 1, \ldots, nfix_k;\ \forall k;\ \forall t) \\
s^{(t,\ t+1)}_{ok_l good} &\geq 0,\ s^{(t,\ t+1)}_{ok_l bad} \geq 0 \text{ and } s^{(t,\ t+1)}_{ok_l free} : free \quad (\forall k_l; \forall t)
\end{aligned} \tag{4}$$

where $s^{(t,\ t+1)}_{ok_l good}$, $s^{(t,\ t+1)}_{ok_l bad}$ and $s^{(t,\ t+1)}_{ok_l free}$ represent slacks denoting, respectively, carry-over shortfall, carry-over excess, and carry-over deviation; and $ngood_k$, $nbad_k$, and $nfree_k$ indicate, respectively, the number of desirable (good), undesirable (bad), and free carry-overs for each division *k*. The notation for data and variables is summarized in Table 1.

Table 1. Notation of data and variables in DN model

Data		
Input	x^t_{ijk}	Input resource *i* to DMU*j* for division *k* at period *t*
Output	y^t_{rjk}	Output product *r* from DMU*j* for division *k* at period *t*
Link	$z^t_{j(kh)_l}$	Linking intermediate product of DMU_j from division *k* to division *h* at period *t*
Carry-over	$z^{(t,\ t+1)}_{jk_l}$	Carry-over of DMU_j at division *k* from period *t* to period *t*+1
Variable		
Input slack	s^{t-}_{iok}	Slack of input *i* of DMU_o for division *k* at period *t*.
Output slack	s^{t+}_{rok}	Slack of output *r* of DMU_o for division *k* at period *t*.
Link slack	$s^t_{o(kh)_l\alpha}$	Slack of link $(kh)_l$ of DMU_o at period *t*. α stands for *free*, *as-input*, and *asoutput*.
Carry-over slack	$s^{(t,t+1)}_{ok_l\alpha}$	Slack of carry-over k_l from period *t* to period *t*+1. α stands for *free*, *good* and *bad*.
Intensity	λ^t_{jk}	Intensity of DMU_j corresponding to division *k* at period *t*

Objective function for overall efficiency, period efficiency, and divisional efficiency

Overall efficiency is evaluated by the following program:

$$\theta^*_o = \min \frac{\sum_{t=1}^{T} W^t \left[\sum_{k=1}^{K} w^k \left[1 - \frac{1}{m_k + linkin_k + nbad_k}\left(\sum_{i=1}^{m_k} \frac{s^{t-}_{iok}}{x^t_{iok}} + \sum_{(kh)_l=1}^{linkin_k} \frac{s^t_{o(kh)_l in}}{z^t_{o(kh)_l in}} + \sum_{k_l=1}^{nbad_k} \frac{s^{(t,t+1)}_{ok_l bad}}{z^{(t,t+1)}_{ok_l bad}}\right)\right]\right]}{\sum_{t=1}^{T} W^t \left[\sum_{k=1}^{K} w^k \left[1 + \frac{1}{r_k + linkout_k + ngood_k}\left(\sum_{r=1}^{r_k} \frac{s^{t+}_{rok}}{y^t_{rok}} + \sum_{(kh)_l=1}^{linkout_k} \frac{s^t_{o(kh)_l out}}{z^t_{o(kh)_l out}} + \sum_{k_l=1}^{ngood_k} \frac{s^{(t,t+1)}_{ok_l good}}{z^{(t,t+1)}_{ok_l good}}\right)\right]\right]} \quad (5)$$

subject to (1) to (4), where $W^t(\forall t)$ is the weight to period *t* and $w^k(\forall k)$ is the weight to division *k*. These weights satisfy the condition $\sum_{t=1}^{T} W^t = 1,\ \sum_{k=1}^{K} w^k = 1,\ W^t \geq 0(\forall t),\ w^k \geq 0\ (\forall k)$. They are supplied exogenously. The numerator includes terms associated with relative slacks of inputs ("as-input" links and bad carry-overs), whereas the denominator includes relative slacks of output ("as-output" links and good carry-overs). They are weighted by the divisional weight w_k and further by the period weight W^t, and they result in the overall efficiency θ_o*. This objective function is a generalization of the slacks-based measure developed by Tone [18]. The divisional weights indicate the importance of the division, e.g., cost and manpower, whereas the period weights reflect, for example, discount rate by period. $\theta_o^* \leq 1$ and $\theta_o^* = 1$ hold if and only if all slacks are zero. The input-/output-oriented model can be defined by dealing with the numerator/denominator of the above objective function. Utilizing the optimal slacks obtained by solving program (5), we define the period and divisional efficiencies as follows. Period efficiency is defined by

$$\tau_o^{t*} = \frac{\sum_{k=1}^{K} w^k \left[1 - \frac{1}{m_k + linkin_k + nbad_k}\left(\sum_{i=1}^{m_k} \frac{s_{iok}^{t-}}{x_{iok}^{t}} + \sum_{(kh)_l=1}^{linkin_k} \frac{s_{o(kh)_l in}^{t}}{z_{o(kh)_l in}^{t}} + \sum_{k_l=1}^{nbad_k} \frac{s_{ok_l bad}^{(t,t+1)}}{z_{ok_l bad}^{(t,t+1)}}\right)\right]}{\sum_{k=1}^{K} w^k \left[1 + \frac{1}{r_k + linkout_k + ngood_k}\left(\sum_{r=1}^{r_k} \frac{s_{rok}^{t+}}{y_{rok}^{t}} + \sum_{(kh)_l=1}^{linkout_k} \frac{s_{o(kh)_l out}^{t}}{z_{o(kh)_l out}^{t}} + \sum_{k_l=1}^{ngood_k} \frac{s_{ok_l good}^{(t,t+1)}}{z_{ok_l good}^{(t,t+1)}}\right)\right]} \quad (\forall t) \tag{6}$$

where variables on the right-hand side indicate optimal values for the overall efficiency θ_o*.

Divisional efficiency is defined by

$$\delta_{ok}^{*} = \frac{\sum_{t=1}^{T} W^t \left[1 - \frac{1}{m_k + linkin_k + nbad_k}\left(\sum_{i=1}^{m_k} \frac{s_{iok}^{t-}}{x_{iok}^{t}} + \sum_{(kh)_l=1}^{linkin_k} \frac{s_{o(kh)_l in}^{t}}{z_{o(kh)_l in}^{t}} + \sum_{k_l=1}^{nbad_k} \frac{s_{ok_l bad}^{(t,t+1)}}{z_{ok_l bad}^{(t,t+1)}}\right)\right]}{\sum_{t=1}^{T} W^t \left[1 + \frac{1}{r_k + linkout_k + ngood_k}\left(\sum_{r=1}^{r_k} \frac{s_{rok}^{t+}}{y_{rok}^{t}} + \sum_{(kh)_l=1}^{linkout_k} \frac{s_{o(kh)_l out}^{t}}{z_{o(kh)_l out}^{t}} + \sum_{k_l=1}^{ngood_k} \frac{s_{ok_l good}^{(t,t+1)}}{z_{ok_l good}^{(t,t+1)}}\right)\right]} \quad (\forall k) \tag{7}$$

Finally, period-divisional efficiency is defined by

$$\rho_{ok}^{t*} = \frac{1 - \frac{1}{m_k + linkin_k + nbad_k}\left(\sum_{i=1}^{m_k} \frac{s_{iok}^{t-}}{x_{iok}^{t}} + \sum_{(kh)_l=1}^{linkin_k} \frac{s_{o(kh)_l in}^{t}}{z_{o(kh)_l in}^{t}} + \sum_{k_l=1}^{nbad_k} \frac{s_{ok_l bad}^{(t,t+1)}}{z_{ok_l bad}^{(t,t+1)}}\right)}{1 + \frac{1}{r_k + linkout_k + ngood_k}\left(\sum_{r=1}^{r_k} \frac{s_{rok}^{t+}}{y_{rok}^{t}} + \sum_{(kh)_l=1}^{linkout_k} \frac{s_{o(kh)_l out}^{t}}{z_{o(kh)_l out}^{t}} + \sum_{k_l=1}^{ngood_k} \frac{s_{ok_l good}^{(t,t+1)}}{z_{ok_l good}^{(t,t+1)}}\right)} \quad (\forall k; \forall t) \tag{8}$$

In the input-/output-oriented model, the numerator/denominator of the above formulas is applied.

2.1.3 Adopted variables of dynamic-network DEA

The DN model makes it possible to have a two-stage production structure in one hospital, that is, both the administration division and medical-examination division. The administration division raises funds for and maintains medical beds. The medical-examination division uses the medical beds and provides medical services. Furthermore, the medical-examination division earns medical revenue in return for medical services and the administration division collects the revenue from the medical-examination division and manages financial matters. Previous literature that adopted BB models in the study of Japanese hospitals did not consider intermediate products in a hospital. In case of the DN model, we can use link variables as intermediate products for both divisions. This benefit of the DN model (compared with the BB model) is that it makes it possible to reflect on the actual situation. We adopted two link variables in our model.

In addition, if we add variables related to the administration division in the BB model, we would suffer from inadequate correspondence between inputs and outputs. For example, the administration staff does not directly engage in the production of medical services. In the case of the BB model, this input may correspond with the number of inpatients as an output. However, the relationship between the administration staff and the number of inpatients would cause an undesirable bias in the efficiency estimation. Therefore, the DN model conceptually reduces bias (compared with the BB model) in the estimation of efficiency by both considering the multiple-step production structure and by excluding inadequate interactions between inputs and outputs. However, we do not consider more detailed divisions in this study. For example, we did not consider pharmaceutical or clinical laboratory divisions.

2.2 Empirical data

The data used in this empirical investigation concerns 112 municipal hospitals from 2007 to 2009 in a balanced panel. There are approximately 1,000 municipal hospitals in Japan and there is large heterogeneity among them. We selected municipal hospitals with more than 300 beds. Therefore, this sample may represent larger acute hospitals owned by Japanese municipals. The data were collected from the *Annual Databook of Local Public Enterprise* published by the Ministry of Internal Affairs and Communications. It is a legal requirement that the local chief executive of municipal governments submit audited financial statements to the ministry. Therefore, the data should be accurate. Accuracy is required for DEA because it cannot take into account measurement errors in the data. DEA also implicitly assumes the correct model specification and the correct specification of inputs, outputs and other variables.

The objective function of the administration division is to realize a sound financial situation through labor inputs and capital inputs. The objective function of the medical-examination division is to provide a certain amount of medical services using hospital beds that are maintained by the administration division at the same hospital.

Many previous studies that have adopted BB models to examine Japanese hospitals have focused on the activities of the medical-examination division. These studies typically adopt the number of doctors and nurses as inputs and the number of inpatients and outpatients as outputs. Therefore, such studies do not contain the activities of the administration division, by way of either input variable or output variable. However, the DN model enables us to consider activities in both divisions. We can observe the activities of the administration division separately from the medical-examination division.

The inputs, outputs, links and carry-overs of the DN model are described below. For Division 1 (administration division), we adopted two labor inputs and three capital inputs. The administration division does not directly provide a medical service to patients. The division is in charge of providing medical beds to the medical-examination division and maintains a sound financial situation for the hospital. Therefore, administration staffs should manage the financial situation of the hospital. They also receive subsidies from the municipal government and manage the reimbursement of issued hospital bonds. Maintenance staffs maintain all the hospital buildings for hospital activities. As labor inputs, we used both the number of administration officers and the number of maintenance officers. All labor inputs are full-time equivalents (FTEs). However, we did not consider staff differences in productivity and wage levels. As capital inputs, we used the interest cost for financial arrangements and municipal subsidies to cover deficits.

For the output of Division 1, we intended to adopt the "balance ratio of medical incomes to medical expenses"; the break-even point has a value of 1 and a surplus has a value exceeding 1. However, using a ratio as an input or output makes the convexity issue of DEA problematic [21]. Emrouznejad and Amin [22] recommended not using constant returns to scale when there is a ratio in the input/output variables. Therefore, we decomposed the ratio to medical income and medical expenses: the numerator was used as output for Division 1 and the denominator as input for Division 1.

For Division 2 (the medical-examination division), we adopted four labor inputs: the number of doctors, number of nurses, number of assistant nurses and number of medical technologists. All labor inputs are FTEs. For the outputs of Division 2, we adopted the number of inpatients per operation day, the number of outpatients per operation day and the number of beds in emergency units. In Japan, there is no gate-keeping system involving general practitioners. Therefore, hospitals accept a large number of outpatients to attract potential inpatients. In this study the number of beds in emergency units was used as a surrogate variable for emergency care service because we could not distinguish between emergency care patients and ordinary patients from the data source.

Previous studies regarding efficiency estimations on Japanese hospitals did not include emergency medical services. A core function of public hospitals in Japan is to ensure a quick response for emergency patients. However, some municipal hospitals have closed their emergency units to reduce costs despite the increasing need for emergency medical services. Although we consider that the evaluation of efficiency of municipal hospitals should include the number of emergency patients, we were not able to obtain numbers from the available data. Therefore, we adopted the number of emergency beds as a proxy for the number of emergency patients. This proxy variable has limitations because it did not control for the difference in severity of emergency patients, the quality of emergency medical service and the occupancy rate of the emergency beds.

The existence of a link variable is one of the key differences between the DN model and the BB model. The link variable is an intermediate product that acts simultaneously as an output for Division 1 and an input to Division 2. Using an intermediate product, we can evaluate multiple production steps among divisions in one DMU. Tone and Tsutsui [20] present four possible scenarios. For example, the "fixed link value case" means that the linking activities are unchanged.

We set the "number of beds" as a link variable from Division 1 to Division 2. We assumed that Division 1 is in charge of the funding and maintenance of medical beds. Division 1 supplies these beds to Division 2. Division 2 uses the medical beds and delivers medical care services to patients. We adopted a non-discretionary "fixed" link, where the linking activity remains the same. The reason for this is that it would be unusual for the medical-examination division to negotiate with the administration division to change the number of beds. The administration division also has an incentive to generate sufficient medical revenue (to offset the medical expenses) and to use all available beds.

We used "average revenue per inpatient per day" as a link variable from Division 2 to Division 1. We assumed that the average revenue is the consideration to be paid to Division 1 for the beds from Division 2. The average revenue per inpatient may represent the density of medical care services. We adopted the "as-output" link, where the linking activity is treated as an output from Division 1. The reason for this is that this matter is not negotiable between the two divisions. Division 1 should be efficient enough to provide higher density medical services under the given resource concentrations (Fig. 1).

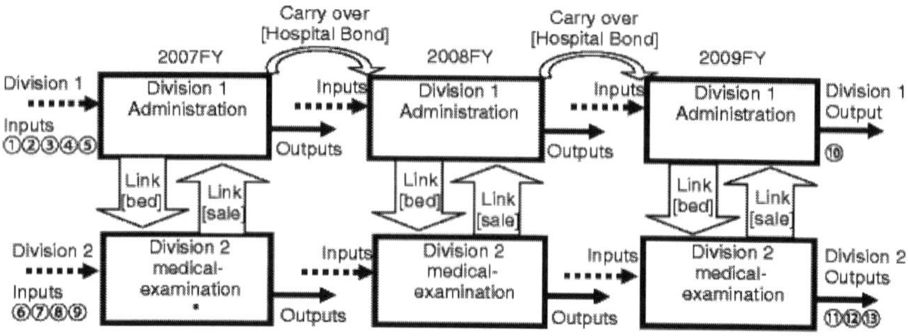

Figure 1. Structure of the dynamic and network data envelopment analysis model. We estimated the efficiency of Japanese municipal hospitals in two parts. The first division is the administration division, which is responsible for financial management. The second division is the medical-examination division, which directly provides a medical service. There are two links between the divisions. The number of beds is a link from Division 1 to Division 2. The average revenue per inpatient per day is a link from Division 2 to Division 1. The dynamic-network data envelopment analysis model also indicates the relationship between the two divisions in terms of efficiency improvement from 1 year to the next. The carry-over variable is used to represent the inter-temporal relationship

The carry-over variable is one of the benefits of using a DN model compared with a BB model. A DMU ordinarily continues activities over several terms. Furthermore, some inter-temporal factors can affect its efficiencies. The carry-over variable makes it possible to account for the effect from connecting activities between continuing terms. The carry-over variable has four characteristics in Tone and Tsutsui [20]. For example, "desirable (good) carry-over" variables are treated as outputs and a comparative shortage of carry-overs is seen as inefficiency.

We set the "balance account of the public enterprise bond (hospital bond)" as an undesirable (bad) carry-over. The hospital bond was chosen as the carry-over because municipal hospitals issue these bonds to raise funds for capital investment in terms of hospital beds. The municipal hospital gradually redeems the issued bond from any revenue surplus. We adopted the "undesirable (bad)" carry-over; thus, the connecting activity from Period 1 to Period 2 is treated as an input. The reason for this is that newly built hospitals are more attractive to patients but represent a heavier fiscal burden in terms of repaying the principal. Therefore, to treat the public enterprise bond as a carry-over reflects accurately the competitive condition of the market in which patients can freely access any hospital. However, we did not consider both the average life and interest rate of the hospital bonds.

According to the first principle that a public hospital is expected to accomplish a policy goal with a minimum budget, we selected an input-oriented model. We adopted both constant returns to scale (CRS) and variable returns to scale (VRS) models in the analysis. Descriptive statistics of all variables in the analysis are provided in Table 2.

Table 2. Basic description of variables

		Variable names	Average	S.D.	Max	Min	Units
Division1	Input	① Number of administration officers	29.35	13.14	89.00	9.00	Person
		② Number of maintenance officers	17.96	15.54	83.00	0.00	Person
		③ Interest cost per year	510.15	394.23	1,666.92	0.80	Milion Yen
		④ Subsidy from municipal	23.68	17.59	89.70	2.80	Milion Yen
		⑤ Medical expense	9,531	5,232	28,286	2,048	Milion Yen
	Output	⑩ Medical income	8,355	4,853	24,769	1,314	Milion Yen
Link(Div1→Div2)		Number of beds	482	180	1334	300	Unite
Division2	Input	⑥ Number of doctors	62.17	35.89	166.00	6.00	Person
		⑦ Number of nurses	314.41	152.76	800.00	79.00	Person
		⑧ Number of assistant nurses	5.33	6.45	46.00	0.00	Person
		⑨ Number of medical technologist	65.77	32.61	171.00	8.00	Person
	Output	⑪ Number of inpatients per an operation day	378.14	156.79	964.00	73.00	Person
		⑫ Number of outpatients per an operation day	742.14	425.64	2224.00	19.00	Person
		⑬ Number of beds for emergency unites	14.09	14.73	66.00	0.00	Unite
Link(Div2→Div1)		Average revenue per inpatient per day	16,822	6,629	31,841	3,661	Yen
Carry over		Balance account of the public enterprise bond	752,228	1,109,846	9,612,400	0	Thousand Yen

Figure 2 shows the structure of the BB model. The inputs and outputs of the BB model are exactly the same as those of the DN model. The inputs are denoted as Input 1 to Input 9. The outputs are denoted as Output 10 to Output 13 as in Table 2. The variables for links and carry-overs do not apply in the case of the BB model.

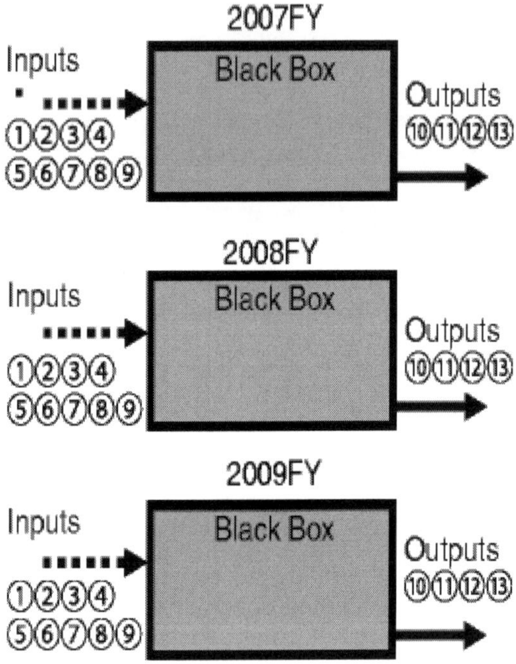

Figure 2. Structure of the black box (BB model). The inputs and outputs of the BB model are exactly the same as those of the dynamic-network (DN model). The inputs are denoted Input ① to Input ⑨. The outputs are denoted Output ⑩ to Output ⑬. The variables for links and carry-over do not apply in the case of the BB model

3 RESULTS

The right side of Table 3 presents the key statistics of the estimated efficiency scores obtained by the DN model and those of the BB model are shown on the left. The average efficiency score estimated by the BB model is 0.988 in 2007 and is higher than the average efficiency estimated in previous studies on Japanese municipal hospitals. We suspect that the reason for this is the higher number of variables used in the model.

Table 3. Efficiency scores obtained from the DN model and BB model

Black box DEA model					Dynamic-network DEA model					
Model	Year	2007	2008	2009	Division	Model	Year	2007	2008	2009
CRS-I	Average	0.9742	0.9725	0.9736	Overall	CRS-I	Average	0.7633	0.7714	0.7824
	SD	0.0634	0.0610	0.0578			SD	0.1663	0.1618	0.1669
	Maximum	1	1	1			Maximum	1	1	1
	Minimum	0.6447	0.6807	0.6487			Minimum	0.3339	0.3175	0.4249
VRS-I	Average	0.9876	0.9869	0.9881		VRS-I	Average	0.8624	0.8612	0.8600
	SD	0.0402	0.0361	0.0359			SD	0.1422	0.1463	0.1476
	Maximum	1	1	1			Maximum	1	1	1
	Minimum	0.7980	0.8140	0.7955			Minimum	0.4868	0.4879	0.4992
					Division1 (admin)	CRS-I	Average	0.7705	0.7742	0.7810
							SD	0.2079	0.2025	0.2088
							Maximum	1	1	1
							Minimum	0.2706	0.2268	0.2664
						VRS-I	Average	0.8667	0.8533	0.8508
							SD	0.1650	0.1837	0.1813
							Maximum	1	1	1
							Minimum	0.3965	0.4061	0.4284
					Division 2 (medical)	CRS-I	Average	0.7560	0.7686	0.7838
							SD	0.1726	0.1696	0.1723
							Maximum	1	1	1
							Minimum	0.3669	0.4082	0.4122
						VRS-I	Average	0.8581	0.8691	0.8693
							SD	0.1530	0.1487	0.1516
							Maximum	1	1	1
							Minimum	0.4835	0.5172	0.4795

On the right of Table 3, the first row shows the efficiency scores of the overall hospital organization as determined by the DN model. The second row shows the efficiency scores of the administration divisions of the sample hospitals. The third row shows the efficiency scores of the medical-examination divisions of the sample hospitals. From the results of DN model, we obtained four key findings.

First, the average overall efficiency obtained with the DN model was 0.854 (VRS model) for 2007. The average efficiency score estimated by the DN model was smaller than the average efficiency estimated in previous studies on Japanese municipal hospitals [3–6]. In the same year, the ratio of efficient DMUs was 39.0 %.

Second, the dynamic change in efficiency scores from 2007 to 2009 is slightly less. The average efficiency score was 0.862 for 2007 and 0.860 for 2009 (VRS model).

Third, because of the advantage of the network structure in the DN model, we can observe the efficiency change separately for different internal organizations. The average level of estimated period-divisional efficiency of the administration division decreased from 0.867 in 2007 to 0.8508 in 2009 (VRS model). In contrast, the average period-divisional efficiency of the medical-examination division increased from 0.858 in 2007 to 0.870

in 2009 (VRS model). On average, there was no significant efficiency change in both divisions for the 3-year period.

The Pearson's product–moment correlation coefficient of period-divisional efficiency scores on 2009 between the two divisions was 0.569 (statistically significant at $p < 0.01$). The value of the Spearman's rank-correlation coefficient was 0.597 (statistically significant at $p < 0.01$). Thus, there was only a weak correlation between the period-divisional efficiencies in each division (Fig. 3).

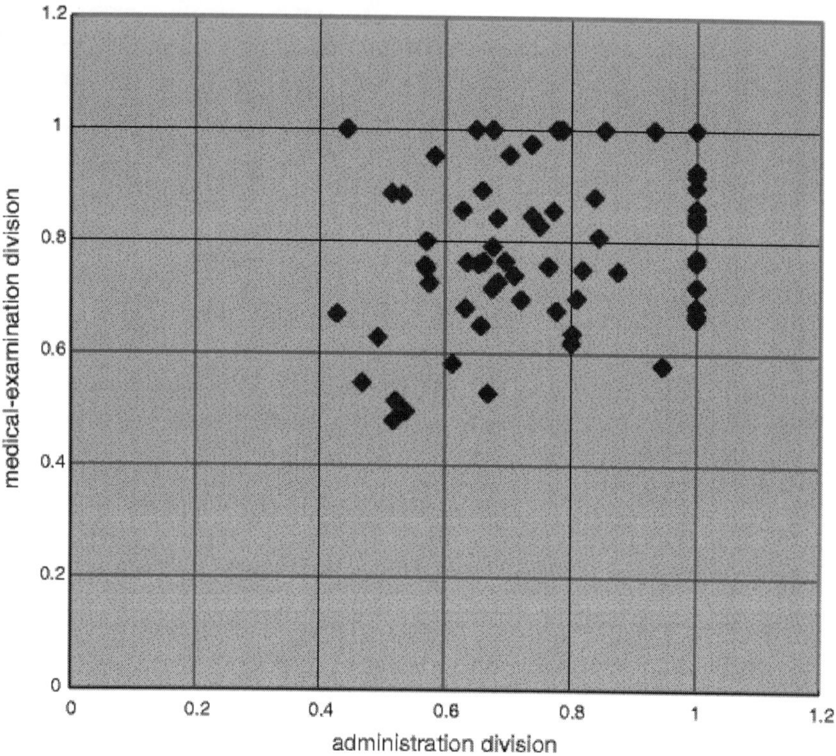

Figure 3. The scatter plot shows the estimated efficiency scores for the two divisions obtained with the dynamic and network data envelopment analysis model (DN model). The *horizontal axis* represents the average efficiency score of Division 1 (administration division). The *vertical axis* indicates the individual efficiency score of Division 2 (medical-examination division). These two efficiency scores appear to be weakly correlated

In addition, we investigated individual hospitals in terms of the relationship between the dynamic changes of period-divisional efficiencies of two divisions between 2007 and 2009. We separated all sample hospitals into four areas. Area 1 is low efficiency improvement (less than or equal to 0) in Division 1 and high efficiency improvement (more than 0) in Division 2. The number of hospitals located in Area 1 was 19 (16.96 % of sample hospitals).

Area 2 is high efficiency improvement in Division 1 and high efficiency improvement in Division 2. The number of hospitals located in Area 2 was 18 (16.07 % of sample hospitals). Area 3 is low efficiency improvement in Division 1 and low efficiency improvement in Division 2. The number of hospitals located in Area 3 was 66 (58.92 % of sample hospitals). Area 4 is high efficiency improvement in Division 1 and low efficiency improvement in Division 2. The number of hospitals located in Area 4 was 9 (8.03 % of sample hospitals). These results indicated that more than half of the sample hospitals had no improvement in efficiency scores in both divisions (Fig. 4).

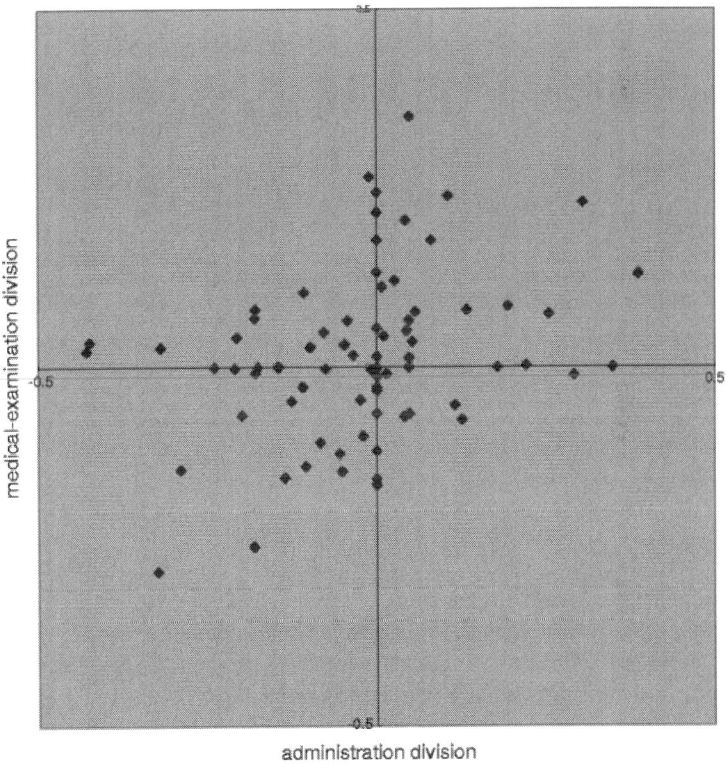

Figure 4. The scatter plot shows the dynamic change in efficiency scores from 2007 to 2009. The *horizontal axis* represents the dynamic change in the efficiency score of Division 1 (administration division). The *vertical axis* indicates the dynamic change of the efficiency score in Division 2 (medical-examination division). The dynamic changes in the efficiency scores of the two divisions tend to be separated into four areas

We also examined the difference in characteristics of the above four areas by comparing the average values of variables used to estimate the efficiency scores. We conducted Tukey's honestly significant difference test on those values. The results showed a statistical difference only for "the number of medical technologists" between Area 3 and Area 4. Otherwise, we found no particular differences in the characteristics among the four areas (Table 4).

Table 4. Average values of variables in the four areas

	Area1	Area2	Area3	Area4
Number of administration officers	30.26	31.56	28.47	35.78
Number of maintenance officers	12.84	20.33	15.64	22.89
Interest cost per year	390.32	448.35	483.82	511.72
Subsidy from municipal	27.33	27.31	22.94	16.7
Medical expense	10,096,832	9,304,397	9,603,294	12,629,624
Medical income	8,538,576	8,348,293	8,655,323	11,401,202
Number of beds	474	439.17	480.09	559.11
Number of doctors	64.21	61.67	62.26	84.78
Number of nurses	313.95	323.33	311.68	424.56
Number of assistant nurses	2.63	5.28	4.85	3
Number of medical technologist	69.11	68.78	61.95*	93.78*
Number of inpatients per an operation day	346.79	355.5	371.26	445
Number of outpatients per an operation day	680.79	677.22	721.39	1015.89
Number of beds for emergency unites	9.53	10.5	15.58	22.67
Average revenue per inpatient per day	17,387	18,289	16,759	20,194
Balance account of the public enterprise	938,937	253,166	699,074	357,156

4 DISCUSSION

There are two heterogeneous internal organizations in Japanese municipal hospitals. The first is the administration division, which is responsible for financial management. The second is the medical-examination division, which provides medical services. The purpose of this study was to separately assess the changes in the dynamic efficiency of the two internal organizations. In this study, we estimated the dynamic change of efficiency scores of Japanese municipal hospitals in terms of these two divisions (Division 1: administration division; Division 2: medical-examination division).

We employed the DN model as presented by Tone and Tsutsui [20]. Based on our results, we obtained three policy implications. First, the dynamic change in period-divisional efficiency scores from 2007 to 2009 was quite small in both divisions. Therefore, on average, we could not find a positive policy effect on Japanese municipal hospitals.

Second, when we looked at individual hospitals, a DMU with an efficient medical-examination division sometimes had an inefficient administration division, and vice versa. We could not show strong correlation between the efficiency scores of the administration division and medical-examination division. The Pearson's product–moment correlation coefficient of the efficiency scores between the two divisions for 2009 was 0.569 (statistically significant at $p < 0.01$). The value of the Spearman's rank-correlation coefficient was 0.597 (statistically significant at $p < 0.01$).

Third, we also focused on the efficiency improvements of the two divisions in terms of individual hospitals. The ratio of sample hospitals where both divisions improved their efficiency score was 16.96 %. In contrast, the ratio of sample hospitals where both divisions maintained or had reduced efficiency scores was 58.92 %. The ratio of sample hospitals where the direction of change differed for the two divisions was 24.12 %. Among these hospitals, the hospitals' worsening efficiency scores in the administration division was twice that of hospitals' worsening efficiency score in the medical-examination division. It would be misleading to use the change in average efficiency scores to evaluate policy effects.

From these results, we note that we did not find any significant improvement in efficiency despite the implemented policy for reform. Thus, we found that there are no positive policy effects on average despite the financial support from central government. In terms of further reform, appropriate countermeasures for different internal organizations should be implemented, taking into account the efficiency improvement to-date of each division.

The Ministry of Internal Affairs and Communication (2011) established the following two points in a sample survey of annual reports from fiscal 2009 of municipal hospitals [23]. First, almost all such hospitals did not achieve the targets that had been set for that year. Second, as an interim evaluation, the ministry concluded that reformation of municipal hospitals should be considered and effective measures implemented.

This study is the first empirical application of the DN model, and thus there are limitations that need to be addressed. For example, we were unable to use variables regarding the "quality" of medical services and the "severity" of patient condition. Therefore, we assumed that the sample hospitals would be homogeneous in terms of quality of service and severity of patient condition. We could, however, narrow the range of samples according to the number of hospital beds to ensure the homogeneity of the sample hospitals on some level. We should also examine omitted variables, e.g., the presence of large and costly medical devices such as magnetic resonance imagers. However, it is difficult to introduce criteria for determining which device should be included in the input or output of the production function. We used the number of beds in emergency units as an output and used total number of medical beds as the link variable. This double counting of medical beds could affect the results in some way.

There are other limitations regarding the control of several factors, which would influence to the estimated efficiencies. For example, the price of medical services, which is insured by public health insurance, changes every 2 years in Japan. The price increased on average by 2 % in fiscal year 2008. Many Japanese acute hospitals decided to voluntarily change their reimbursement system from "fee for service" to "per diem based on diagnosis groups". This study did not fully consider these external environmental changes in the Japanese hospital market.

Regarding policy implications, we did not consider both the relative costs of the two divisions and the relative costs to improve efficiency in each division. For example, one division may be less efficient on average, but the other may be more costly so that a given efficiency improvement is more beneficial. When playing an active role in policy implementation, we need to consider relative costs in addition to the efficiency scores.

Future study will require a larger sample set and a more complex model.

ACKNOWLEDGMENTS

We would like to thank the attendees of the DEA Symposium 2012 for their helpful comments on our earlier study. We also appreciate the valuable comments from the reviewers. This study was supported by a Grant-in-Aid for Scientific Research (KAKENHI; grant number: 22320092).

CONFLICT OF INTEREST

The authors declare that they have no conflict of interest in connection with this paper.

REFERENCES

1. Harris JE (1977) The internal organization of hospitals: some economic implications. Bell J Econ 8:467–482
2. Hollingsworth B (2008) The measurement of efficiency and productivity of health care delivery. Health Econ 17:1107–1128

3. Num S, Ishikawa K (1994) An application of DEA for labor efficiency of Japanese hospitals. Oper Res Soc Jpn 39:292–296

4. Num S, Gunji A (1994) A study on managerial efficiency in medical facilities: evaluating human resource efficiency in municipal hospitals using data envelopment analysis. J Jpn Soc Healthc Adm 131:33–39

5. Nakayama N (2003) A comparison of parametric and non-parametric distance functions: a case study of Japanese public hospitals. Iryo to Shakai 13:83–95

6. Nakayama N (2004) Technical efficiency and subsidies in Japanese public hospitals. Iryo to Shakai 14:69–79

7. Färe R, Grosskopf S (2000) Network DEA. Socio Econ Plan Sci 34:35–49

8. Färe R, Grosskopf S (1996) Intertemporal production frontiers: with dynamic DEA. Kluwer, Norwell

9. Färe R, Grosskopf S, Norris S, Zhang Z (1994) Productivity growth, technical progress, and efficiency change in industrialized countries. Am Econ Rev 84(1):66–83

10. Lewis HF, Sexton TR (2004) Network DEA: efficiency analysis of organisations with complex internal structure. Comput Oper Res 31:1365–1410

11. Sexton TR, Lewis HF (2003) Two-stage DEA: an application to major league baseball. J Prod Anal 19:227–249

12. Prieto AM, Zofio JL (2007) Network DEA efficiency in input–output models: with an application to OECD countries. Eur J Oper Res 178:292–304

13. Koopmans T (1951) An analysis of production as an efficient combination of activities. In: Koopmans T (ed) Activity analysis of production and allocation, Cowles Commission for Research in Economics, Monograph, vol 13. John Wiley and Sons, New York

14. Löthgren M, Tambour M (1999) Productivity and customer satisfaction in Swedish pharmacies: a DEA network model. Eur J Oper Res 115:449–458

15. Tone K, Tsutsui M (2009) Network DEA: a slacks based measurement approach. Eur J Oper Res 197:243–252

16. Klopp GA (1985) The analysis of the efficiency of production system with multiple inputs and outputs, Ph.D. dissertation. University of Illinois at Chicago, Industrial and System Engineering College

17. Malmquist S (1953) Index numbers and indifference surfaces. Trabajos de Estadistica 4(2):209–242

18. Tone K (1999) A slacks-based measure of efficiency in data envelopment analysis. Eur J Oper Res 130(3):498–509

19. Pastor JT, Ruiz JL, Sirvent I (1999) An enhanced DEA Russell graph efficiency measure. Eur J Oper Res 115(3):596–607

20. Tone K, Tsutsui M (2014) Dynamic DEA with network structure: a slacks-based measure approach. Omega 42(1):124–131

21. Hollingsworth B, Smith PC (2003) The use of ratios in data envelopment analysis. Appl Econ Lett 10:733–735

22. Emrouznejad A, Amin GR (2009) DEA models for ratio data: convexity consideration. Appl Math Model 33(1):486–498

23. Ministry of Internal Affairs and Communication (2011) Results from a survey of implementation of the reformation plans of municipal hospitals

INDEX